Entangled Lives

In this book the authors engage with three questions about the past: How can we rethink human histories by including animals and plants? How can we overcome nationally territorialised narratives? And how can we balance academic history-writing and indigenous understandings of history? They make a tentative foray into the connections between these questions. Each has, in recent years, been subject to wide-ranging scholarly debate, but rarely in combination – and never for the region that they focus on.

Entangled Lives explores these questions for a large region that historians seldom choose as their unit of enquiry: the Eastern Himalayan Triangle. Five countries administer the Triangle: India, Myanmar/Burma, Bangladesh, Bhutan and China. For most historians it has very low visibility, so they marginalise or ignore it in their accounts of the past. As a result, it appears as a remote expanse without historical dynamism or relevance to wider processes. But grant it a central role and we learn about dynamic connections and mobile actors that force us to reassess its significance vis-à-vis the processes, territorial units and personalities that historians habitually foreground.

The Triangle's nonhuman actors are important because they have always co-designed human societies, just as humans have co-designed nonhuman lives. This book looks at these interactions over a wide span of time, from 'deep history' to the present. It is a case study in environmental history, multispecies history, more-than-human history, posthumanism and environmental humanities. It aims to advance histories of humans and nonhumans together and show the enduring intimacy of all sentient beings.

Joy L. K. Pachuau is a professor at the Centre for Historical Studies, Jawaharlal Nehru University, New Delhi. Besides the socio-cultural history of Northeast India, her research interests include European expansion in the sixteenth and seventeenth centuries including the history of Christianity in Asia. Her publications include *Being Mizo: Identity and Belonging in Northeast India* (2014). She also published the co-edited volume (with Neeladri Bhattacharya) *Landscape, Culture, and Belonging: Writing the History of Northeast India* with the Press in 2019.

Willem van Schendel (University of Amsterdam and International Institute of Social History, the Netherlands) works in the fields of history, sociology and anthropology of Asia. His books include *A History of Bangladesh* (2020), *Embedding Agricultural Commodities: Using Historical Evidence, 1840s–1940s* (2017, ed.) and *The Bengal Borderland: Beyond State and Nation in South Asia* (2005). His publications can be found at uva.academia.edu/WillemVanSchendel/.

Both of them jointly published the monograph *The Camera as Witness: A Social History of Mizoram, Northeast India* with the Press in 2015.

Entangled Lives

Human–Animal–Plant Histories of the Eastern Himalayan Triangle

Joy L. K. Pachuau
Willem van Schendel

CAMBRIDGE
UNIVERSITY PRESS

University Printing House, Cambridge CB2 8BS, United Kingdom

One Liberty Plaza, 20th Floor, New York, NY 10006, USA

477 Williamstown Road, Port Melbourne, vic 3207, Australia

314 to 321, 3rd Floor, Plot No.3, Splendor Forum, Jasola District Centre, New Delhi 110025, India

103 Penang Road, #05–06/07, Visioncrest Commercial, Singapore 238467

Cambridge University Press is part of the University of Cambridge.

It furthers the University's mission by disseminating knowledge in the pursuit of education, learning and research at the highest international levels of excellence.

www.cambridge.org
Information on this title: www.cambridge.org/9781009215473

© Joy L. K. Pachuau and Willem van Schendel 2022

This publication is in copyright. Subject to statutory exception and to the provisions of relevant collective licensing agreements, no reproduction of any part may take place without the written permission of Cambridge University Press.

First published 2022

Printed in India by Avantika Printers Pvt. Ltd.

A catalogue record for this publication is available from the British Library

ISBN 978-1-009-21547-3 Hardback

Cambridge University Press has no responsibility for the persistence or accuracy of URLs for external or third-party internet websites referred to in this publication, and does not guarantee that any content on such websites is, or will remain, accurate or appropriate.

Every effort has been made to trace copyright holders and to obtain their permission for the use of copyright material. The publisher apologises for any errors or omissions and would be grateful if notified of any corrections that should be incorporated in future reprints or editions of this book.

Contents

List of Maps and Plates	vii
Acknowledgements	xiii
Introduction	1

Part I   The Deep Past

1.	An Epic Crash	21
2.	Human Beginnings	31
3.	Changing the Environment	38
4.	Livelihoods	52

Part II   Cosmologies

5.	Stories of Human Origins	63
6.	Human–Animal Histories	91
7.	Human–Plant Histories	127

Part III   More-Than-Human Histories

8.	Cultural Geographies	153
9.	Exploiting Natural Resources	188
10.	Dealing with Environmental Decay	211
11.	The Elephant Strikes Back	242

Conclusion	258

Copyrights and Sources	264
Bibliography	269
Index	348

Maps and Plates

Maps

I.1	Location of the Triangle	2
1.1	The eastern Himalayas and the Indo-Burma Arc	22
1.2	The Eastern Himalayan Triangle	24
1.3	The Eastern Himalayan Triangle	24
1.4	Three global biodiversity hotspots	27
5.1	Cultural groups mentioned in this book	67
8.1	Traditional areas of milking and non-milking	158
8.2	Habitat of the mithun	174

Plates

1.1	Early morning in Mizoram	21
1.2	Snow leopard	29
1.3	Asian black bear	29
3.1	Archaeological excavation in progress	39
3.2	Fragments of corded pottery	40
3.3	Some varieties of bamboo	46
3.4	A gaur	50
3.5	A free-ranging mithun	50
4.1	Female yak with calf	53
4.2	Shifting cultivation in the Indo-Burma Arc	55

4.3	A terraced field in Arunachal Pradesh	57
4.4	Using a traditional wooden scoop	58
4.5	A human-controlled landscape	59
5.1	Representations of the moon in Angami art	74
5.2	The stars of Orion's belt	75
5.3	The Donyipolo flag	77
5.4	Migration history in stone	84
6.1	Eighteenth-century manuscript painting of elephants	93
6.2	Composition on a bamboo case	96
6.3	The Manipur royal emblem	99
6.4	A Konyak Naga diviner	100
6.5	An 'ill-omened' animal	101
6.6	Elephant hunt	104
6.7	A Mising hunter with bow	105
6.8	Killing the tiger	107
6.9	Children holding up a giant flying squirrel	109
6.10	Boys proudly carrying a hunter's guns	110
6.11	Skulls of gaur, wild buffalo	113
6.12	Men wearing hats adorned with fur	113
6.13	A woman with her pigs	114
6.14	Pig feed being cooked	115
6.15	Travelling dog traders	116
6.16	Goats about to be sacrificed	121
6.17	Buffalo skull on the Ugrotara temple	122
6.18	Sacrificial camels on the road	124
6.19	A mithun to be ceremonially killed	125
7.1	Crops of worship, sociability or vice?	131
7.2	Women sowing a freshly burned field	139
7.3	A man with a dibble planting rice and cotton	140

Maps and Plates ix

7.4	'Our memorial to collective weeding'	142
7.5	Bamboo and rattan bridge	143
7.6	Bamboo and other plants used in egg-topped altars	144
7.7	A 'phallic joker' with his bamboo pole	145
7.8	Bamboo art	149
8.1	A photo of people in the Chin Hills	155
8.2	Drinking home-made alcohol in the Chin Hills	160
8.3	Victims of a bamboo–rodent–human encounter	163
8.4	A Bawm-Zo weaver at her loom	164
8.5	Two men wearing cowries-encrusted aprons	168
8.6	A hornbill beak tops the ceremonial hat	170
8.7	A man wearing ceremonial headgear	171
8.8	A visitor eyeing a poster at the Hornbill Festival	172
8.9	Logo of the annual Pakke Paga Hornbill Festival	173
8.10	Villagers holding a spear for mithun sacrifices	176
8.11	A precolonial memorial stone	177
8.12	Two contemporary megaliths in a Manipur village	178
8.13	The official seal of the state of Nagaland	179
8.14	A signboard linking animal and human identities	180
8.15	Men at a village gathering	180
8.16	Zomi National Day, Manipur	181
8.17	Entrance gate to an urban neighbourhood	181
8.18	Konyak bachelors' dormitory	182
8.19	A mule caravan crossing a road	185
8.20	Ox labour in Guwahati, Assam	185
8.21	Horse carts being loaded in Bangladesh	186
8.22	Polo players and their ponies	187
9.1	Next to a fast-flowing river, women are cleaning bamboo shoots	190
9.2	Fishing with a poisonous creeper in Assam	192

9.3	Enormous rafts of bamboo from state forests	193
9.4	Horsemen with dogs hunting deer	194
9.5	A party of hunters returning to their village	194
9.6	Hunter with tiger and shotgun	195
9.7	Hunter and friends proudly posing with a wild gaur	196
9.8	Women engaged in a daily chore	199
9.9	Jagannath Dighi, one of several huge ponds	200
9.10	The Kaptai hydroelectric project	201
9.11	Women repairing a mud hut in Bangladesh	202
9.12	Removing sand and clay from the Brahmaputra	203
9.13	Mining amber in northern Myanmar	207
9.14	Coal tubs leaving the Tipong colliery	208
9.15	Working the Makum coalfield	209
10.1	A tea plantation in Assam	214
10.2	A rubber plantation in Meghalaya	215
10.3	A greater adjutant in Assam	219
10.4	A man holding a grey peacock pheasant	220
10.5	A baby leaf muntjac	222
10.6	The high-altitude Arunachal macaque	223
10.7	The black (or Myanmar) snub-nosed monkey	223
10.8	This orchid was discovered in Bhutan	224
10.9	A new snakehead fish	224
10.10	A new species of bush frog	225
10.11	Humans, elephants and bullocks felling timber for tea boxes	227
10.12	Hunting map of the northern Triangle	231
10.13	'Result of a fortnight's sport'	232
10.14	Tourists on elephants, armed forest guards and a rhinoceros	234
10.15	A notice cautions locals in Ziro	237

11.1	Sacrificing a mithun	244
11.2	Forest guard trying to tranquilise a wild leopard	248
11.3	A wild elephant causing panic	249
11.4	An evicted woman is trying to stop armed police	249
11.5	Killed by a train, an elephant lies on railway tracks	250
11.6	Grazing domestic cattle encounter a rhinoceros	253
11.7	Meat of a protected river dolphin for sale	254

Acknowledgements

We would like to thank the many people who generously shared their images with us and who gave us permission to reproduce these in this volume. We are especially grateful to Romila Thapar, David Vumlallian Zou and two anonymous reviewers for reading the entire manuscript and offering us their critical assessments, detailed comments and probing questions. In addition, we wish to express our gratitude to many colleagues and friends who helped us with information about specifics and in our search for hard-to-find materials.

Introduction

This book considers three questions about understanding the past. How can we rethink human histories by including animals and plants? How can we overcome nationally territorialised narratives? And how can we balance academic history-writing and indigenous understandings of history? This is a tentative foray into the connections between these questions. Each has, in recent years, been subject to wide-ranging scholarly debate, but rarely in combination – and never for the region that we focus on.

We explore these questions for an area that historians seldom choose as their unit of enquiry. For most it has very low visibility, so they marginalise or ignore it in their accounts about the past. As a result, it appears as a remote expanse without historical dynamism or relevance to wider processes – a space where only trivial, local and derivative events and interactions occur. But grant it a central role and we learn about key moments, dynamic connections and mobile actors that force us to reinterpret and reassess the significance of processes, territorial units and personalities that historians habitually foreground.

The area we are concerned with does not even have an established name. For brevity's sake, we decided to refer to it as the Triangle (short for Eastern Himalayan Triangle). In Chapter 1 we explain its dimensions and our reasons for treating it as a unit – but suffice it here to say that it is a roughly triangular region that is dominated by two mountain ranges, the eastern Himalayas and the Indo-Burma Arc, and the basins formed by the rivers that flow from them. It forms a corridor between the two most populous societies on earth, China and India. At its heart is Northeast India, so another way to describe it is to speak of Northeast India and its surrounding areas. We are especially interested in the uplands of the region, not least because historians have been 'less fond of mountaineering' than other researchers.[1] Today five states administer the Triangle: India, Myanmar or Burma, Bangladesh, Bhutan and China (Map I.1).

---

[1] 'The highlands of Asia still attract little attention from historians, compared to the major kingdoms and empires that surround them.... Perhaps historians are less fond of mountaineering [than those adept at field enquiries].' Michaud, 'Editorial – Zomia and Beyond', 188–9.

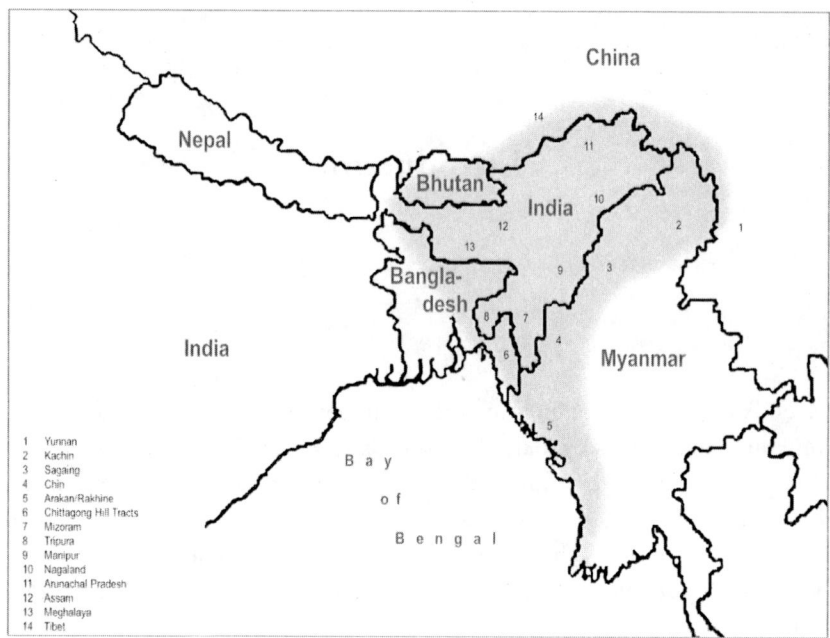

Map I.1 Location of the Triangle

Source: Authors.

More-than-human histories

We live in a period in which the social sciences are being vigorously reconstructed in response to our rapidly growing awareness of planetary changes. These range from climate change to a massive loss of biodiversity. This scholarly rethinking has been spurred on by new ideas, notably the hypothesis of the 'Anthropocene', which holds that we are living in a new epoch of geological history that is marked by the emergence of humankind as a dominant factor shaping the evolution of our planet.[2] This idea challenges long-held convictions about humans being proudly detached from other-than-human organisms, or 'nature'. The social sciences are beginning to shed extreme forms of 'anthropocentrism', 'human exceptionalism' and 'speciesism' that blinker us and force us into unhelpfully narrow narratives about ourselves.[3]

---

[2] 'The hypothesis of the Anthropocene has called for a revision and surpassing of various deeply rooted distinctions in historical epistemology, such as, for instance, between natural history and human history, written history and deep history, human history and multispecies history, national history and planetary history.' Tamm, 'Introduction: A Framework', 7. See also Neckel, 'Scholastic Fallacies'.

[3] For introductions, see Ingold (ed.), *What Is an Animal*; Boddice (ed.), *Anthropocentrism*; Van Dooren, Kirksey and Münster, 'Multispecies Studies'; Harris and Cipolla, 'Multispecies Archaeology'; Kopnina et al., 'Anthropocentrism'; Hopster, 'The Speciesism Debate'.

Introduction

Following this major paradigm shift, historians are now engaged in debates about 'more-than-human', 'multispecies', 'environmental', 'posthumanist' and 'human–non-human' histories. Among historians, this has been a relatively cautious process compared with developments in some other disciplines within the emerging field of 'environmental humanities'.[4] Many historians have, of course, reflected on the clarion call for change, especially since a subgroup began to style themselves environmental historians half a century ago. But how do we translate 'the collapse of the age-old humanist distinction between natural history and human history' into new historical narratives?[5] This is far more easily said than done.

Non-human animals and plants have always figured in historians' narratives – usually with the scholarly eye fixed steadily on human protagonists and their agency. Today, this approach is being abandoned for a more nuanced one.[6] It downplays human agency and suggests that the course of history is steered by 'agential entanglements' between humans and their environment.[7] We are becoming more aware of communication between different species of living beings. It is not only the case that humans communicate with one another and with non-human animals, or that animals communicate with other animals, but also that rapid advances in plant science show convincingly that plants have biochemical ways of communicating with other plants as well as with animals.[8] Humans, animals and plants are participants in a never-ending three-cornered conversation.

---

[4] Tamm and Simon, 'More-than-Human History'. See also Van Dooren, Kirksey and Münster, 'Multispecies Studies'; Emmett and Nye, *The Environmental Humanities*; Heise, Christensen and Niemann (eds.), *The Routledge Companion*. Anthropologists have been particularly active (Haraway, *When Species Meet*; Viveiros de Castro, *Cosmological Perspectivism*; Kohn, *How Forests Think*). In the Triangle, 'environmental humanities' are only just taking off, and they are primarily concerned with contemporary anthropogenic impacts on the environment – historical studies are rare. See Smyer Yü, 'Situating Environmental Humanities'.

[5] Chakrabarty, 'The Climate of History', 201. For an overview, see O'Gorman and Gaynor, 'More-Than-Human Histories'; Holmes, Gaynor and Morgan, 'Doing Environmental History'.

[6] See Nash, 'The Agency of Nature', 69:

> It is worth considering how our stories might be different if human beings appeared not as the motor of history but as partners in a conversation with a larger world, both animate and inanimate, about the possibilities of existence. If that is one of our goals, then social history is not our model, and longstanding assumptions about 'structure' and 'agency' will not suffice.

[7] Saha, 'Colonizing Elephants', 171. Scholars promoting actor–network theory (ANT) have influentially conceptualised such entanglements. For introductions, see Jones, 'Nature–Culture'; Farías, Blok and Roberts, 'Actor–Network Theory'.

[8] Kimmerer, *Braiding Sweetgrass*, 16–21; Gagliano, Ryan and Vieira (eds.), *The Language of Plants*; Núñez-Farfán and Valverde (eds.), *Evolutionary Ecology*.

So how can historians deal with these insights? A new 'animal history' is emerging, but it 'has remained little studied and elusive, a hybrid creature roaming the disciplinary deep forest, nibbling at the edges of conferences and journals, straying into unexpected territories, and prone both to local extirpations and bursts of fecundity'.[9]

Fortunately, historians of the Triangle are beginning to coax animal – or more broadly, multispecies – history out of this 'deep forest'. They assert that plants and animals do have histories of their own, which constantly interweave with human histories in material, symbolic and emotional ways.[10] Think of how the lives and deaths of humans, animals and plants are entangled: humans may 'harvest nature' by means of hunting, fishing, foraging and agriculture, just as pathogens and predators may 'harvest humans'.[11] In the following chapters we will explore how humans in the Triangle hunted, protected and revered certain animals (such as tigers or hornbills), gathered wild plants (such as bamboo and herbs), cultivated plants (such as rice and cotton) and coped with pathogens (such as viruses and parasites). We will also consider how some other-than-human organisms (such as rodents and dogs) adapted to humans, moving closer and becoming companions; how others (such as bears and leopards) confronted humans; and how yet others (such as elephants) could take both these roles.[12] By behaving in a variety of ways, the Triangle's non-humans have always co-designed human societies, just as humans have co-designed 'nature'.[13]

---

[9] Swart, 'Animals in African History'.

[10] Karlsson ('Introduction', 9–10) makes this point in his call for attention to 'the agency of plants and animals' in studies of the region.

[11] See Walker, 'Animals and the Intimacy', 45:

> Animals permeate our history and we theirs.... The debate regarding whether humans are anomalous and outside nature or separate from other animals is complicated when the stomach enzymes from an animal, whether wolf or crocodile, digest a human being.... My contention is that our reluctance to join the rest of the animal kingdom on its terms, on more natural terms, exposes a lingering devotion to human 'exceptionalism', one that is inherent in the humanities and social sciences.

[12] For a description of the multiple dimensions of 'human–elephant companionship' and 'multispecies conviviality' in another Asian location, see Lorimer, 'Elephants as Companion Species'. See also Lainé, 'Les éléphants sous la cour ahom'; Lainé, 'Conduct and Collaboration'; Lainé, 'Travail Interespèces et conservation'; Lainé, '*Phi Muangs*'; Lainé, *Living and Working with Giants*; Trautmann, *Elephants and Kings*; Saha, 'Colonizing Elephants'.

[13] As O'Gorman and Gaynor ('More-Than-Human Histories', 716) put it: 'Relational views of the world converging in more-than-human and multispecies approaches, see the past and the present as dynamically co-constituted by multiple organisms, including plants, animals, and fungi, as well as by elements and forces, from water to minerals.'

We will use the term 'more-than-human histories' as shorthand for several overlapping approaches that go by different names and represent slightly different scholarly entry points: environmental history, multispecies history, environmental humanities and so on. They all aim at developing conjoined histories of humans and non-humans by showing the enduring intimacy of all sentient beings.[14] This requires pooling insights from many different disciplines – geology, genetics, archaeology, geography, linguistics, biology, environmental studies and anthropology – because conventional historical sources, such as written records, are simply not up to the job. On the contrary,

> many of the questions asked by environmental historians cry out for reliable proxy records ... that may reflect, for example, deforestation, erosion, salinization, or changes in species compositions.... While these disparate sources of data do not always combine as easily as we might like, the various material 'proxy' records are an essential part of researching environmental history, even in very recent periods.[15]

In the following pages we attempt to construct more-than-human histories of the Triangle over a very long time span. We will touch on the deep history of the region, the arrival of modern humans and the millennia that followed, up to the present. Inevitably, it can only be an introductory, exploratory and highly selective survey – merely a first attempt to connect some of the dots and sketch an outline. We hope that this will prompt others to look at this region as a whole in much more detail and amend and revise the very rough draft that we present here.

Nationally territorialised narratives

In addition to trying to rethink human histories by including animals and plants, we also aim at questioning historians' spatial practices. Most historians produce nationally territorialised narratives. As a result, a number of excellent studies cover parts of the Triangle, but they stop at the borders of (post)colonial administrative units and are embedded in national narratives. Thus, more-than-human histories of India or Myanmar naturally deal only with the part of the Triangle that is

---

[14] They all aim at understanding 'human beings as they have lived, worked, and thought in relationship to the rest of nature through the changes brought by time.... The changes humans have made in the environment have in turn affected our societies and our histories'. Hughes, *What Is Environmental History*, 2.

[15] Morrison, 'Conceiving Ecology', 42. For suggestions on how to develop methodologies for more-than-human history, see O'Gorman and Gaynor, 'More-Than-Human Histories', 726–8.

today administered by those states.[16] In the same vein, we have wonderful studies of administrative subregions, but here, too, some readers may be left with the impression that beyond their borders another history is playing out.[17] However, an important change is currently noticeable: a small but growing number of historians have become invested in developing cross-border narratives of the Triangle.[18]

In this book, we seek to go beyond the practice of viewing state territories as isolating containers. We try to be more like ornithologists – who follow the birds they study across state borders[19] – or geologists or climate experts – who think in units that have little to do with current political borders and state territories.[20] This is fairly difficult for historians because most of us were trained to nationalise space and rely heavily on source material produced by states. It is important to reflect specifically on the fact that official and semi-official records created by the British colonial state (which used to administer most of the region) have had an inordinate effect on how we make sense of Triangle histories. For studies on purely human subjects, such as political history, the state context may be highly relevant, but for studies looking at more-than-human (or multispecies) histories this is not necessarily the case. We often need a broader scope – to help us understand many plant, animal and human connections that cross borders – or a narrower scope – to help us grasp how multispecies histories are anchored in particular landscapes and ecological zones.[21]

Like state territories, however, the Triangle is a spatial construct that is not rooted in local perceptions of space. Over time, and across the region, humans have imagined countless spiritual, social and political spaces that were relevant to them.[22] There are no indications that they ever imagined the Triangle as a meaningful unit. Thus, the non-indigenous quality of the space that we refer to as 'the Triangle' in this book puts significant limits on its use. Its main value lies, we

---

[16] See, for example, Rangarajan and Sivaramakrishnan (eds.), *Shifting Ground*; Fisher, *An Environmental History of India*; Bryant, *The Political Ecology*.

[17] For example, Saikia, *Forests and Ecological History*; Jhala, *An Endangered History*.

[18] To name some of them: Mandy Sadan, David Vumlallian Zou, Gunnel Cederlöf, Jianxiong Ma, Pum Khan Pau, Dan Smyer Yü, Bérénice Guyot-Réchard, Arupjyoti Saikia, Iftekhar Iqbal, Jayati Bhattacharya, David Ludden and Kyaw Minn Htin.

[19] An example is Renner ('Bird Species-Richness'), who covers a cross-border region comprising parts of Tibet, Northeast India and Myanmar in his survey of species richness.

[20] Mountain ranges or biodiversity hotspots figure in studies like these: Searle, *Colliding Continents*; Morley et al., 'Structural and Tectonic Development'; Sharma et al., *Climate Change Impacts*; Kano et al., 'Impacts of Dams'.

[21] Aisher and Damodaran, 'Introduction'.

[22] For example, Zou, 'Production of Place'.

think, in its heuristic potential. It can act as a provisional springboard to challenge both nationally territorialised and highly localised narratives – and thereby offer us an opening to alternative spatial perspectives.[23]

What holds true for spatial limitations also holds true for temporal ones. Rethinking more-than-human histories has enabled historians to apply alternative ideas of time. The first issue is periodisation, which we deal with here, and the second is the plural construction of time, which we will discuss in the next section. Organising historical narratives in chunks of time, or periods, is unavoidable and necessary – and therefore it makes sense to reflect on the best way of doing so. In considering more-than-human histories of the Triangle there is little mileage in following the common practice of adopting state-oriented chunks of time – or 'nationalised periods'. Periods of dynastic rule or colonial occupation are of little help because, across the Triangle, these explain very little. Considerable parts of the region were beyond state control until the late nineteenth century; the five states that now control the Triangle have experienced different periods of rule; and local ideas of time have rarely been in tune with state time. In writing more-than-human histories, we also need to take into account non-human time, whether in terms of geological eras, the evolution of nature, the mobility of animals and plants, or the life span of different organisms. We have to feel our way forward to the most effective approach to combining such disparate measures of time.

In this book we experiment, moving from deep history to archaeological time to historical time to the present. The first two take us back way beyond the domain of conventional historiography. It makes sense to broaden our historical horizon, however, if we are to trace the earliest human–non-human interactions. It is important to be aware that 'of the entire past history of humankind, conventional historiography covers only a trifling part – just a few seconds, if we were to liken the history of humanity to a clock with twenty-four-hour display'.[24] Therefore, 'the definition of history should not be based on the invention of writing, but upon the evolution of anatomically modern humans'.[25] This is especially relevant in the Triangle, where humans appeared at least 40,000 years ago. And even if we consider the practice of writing, there are huge differences. In some parts of the region, writing has been used for two millennia, but in others it was introduced a mere century ago. Moreover, many inhabitants of the region continue to be illiterate today.

---

[23] See Smyer Yü, 'Perpendicular Geospatiality', for an overview and assessment of other spatial constructs regarding this region.

[24] Tamm, 'Introduction', 4.

[25] Ibid., 5.

Studying the Triangle in this way creates numerous practical challenges regarding historical traces and sources of information. Historical material is often scanty, uneven, contradictory, in multiple languages, full of gaps and difficult to access. Comparing fragmented information produced by different institutions, each covering only a part of the region, is a huge challenge. Archaeological and historical studies of human–non-human relations are still thin on the ground. Therefore, as authors, we must resort to 'proxy' sources of information that we have little or no expertise on, starting with human and animal bones, plant seeds and stone tools. But if we are to 'offer new responses to old questions about time and its structures, perceptions, and meanings, [we need] to open up dialogues across disciplines and methods' and should not shy away from wider vistas.[26] Following this line of thought, throughout the book we lean heavily on research by others, notably geologists, palaeo-anthropologists, archaeo-botanists, archaeologists, biologists, anthropologists, linguists and environmentalists. We are aware that sketching the history of the Triangle in this way is a precarious undertaking. And yet, we hope that it may help us develop new lines of enquiry and encourage new communities of historians working together across boundaries, periods and disciplines.

Academic history-writing and indigenous understandings of the past

The third question that animates this book – in addition to how we can rethink human histories to include animals and plants, and how we can overcome nationally territorialised narratives – is the issue of how we can balance academic history-writing and indigenous understandings of history. Historians use specific procedures to construct and organise their narratives about the past. These include notions of what constitutes relevant evidence, who can be considered an actor in the making of history and which causal explanations are acceptable. In this way, academically trained historians produce regimented, selective stories about our past.

It is especially important to reflect on the conventional way in which historians think about time. In the previous section we looked at periodisation but here we consider a more fundamental issue. In the nineteenth century, religious chronology in Europe (a time frame interpreted from the Bible) was jolted by the discovery of bones of unfamiliar, extinct animals together with human bones. Around the same time, a grand theory of natural evolution was formulated. Suddenly, a much longer human past opened up than the few thousand years that

---

[26] Champion, 'A Fuller History', 256.

people had inferred from Bible texts. As a result, historians became concerned with exorcising religious, mythical time frames from their discipline. They felt the urge to join the move towards a scientific explanation of the world that was becoming dominant in Western thought. They did this by clinging to the linearity of 'chronometric time', which is carefully measured in years, days and hours. And they created periods ('Antiquity', 'the Middle Ages', 'the Early Modern Era' and so on), separated by turning points.[27] From now on, their scholarly claim to truth would be grounded in coherent, connected narratives of accurately datable events. This linear, developmental understanding of time became the hallmark of historical research.[28]

But this sequential time is hardly the only way to construct time. Nineteenth-century scholars who were interested in other concepts of time branched off from the new history-writing to become anthropologists. Many of them studied alternative ways to narrate the past, especially beyond Europe. They found historical narratives, legends, myths and spiritual stories that were concerned not with the historian's standard chronology but with connecting to the past in other ways. Like historians, anthropologists also developed specific procedures about what constitutes relevant and reliable evidence and how to validate explanations – but their purpose was not to anchor the sequences of events, as told in these stories, in chronometric time. Rather, they sought to understand how these sequences expressed a shared sense of the past and how they offered maps to navigate the present and the future.

In essence, of course, this is exactly the task that historians had also set themselves: to study the past to offer maps to navigate the present and the future. But the two scholarly practices began to diverge. Historians suggested that their linear understanding of time was 'modern', whereas the constructions of time explored and explained by anthropologists were 'pre-modern', 'traditional' or 'tribal'. Hence, historical accounts were 'true' in a modern way. According to this logic, historians created coherent, authoritative and impartial narratives based on causality and explanation, validated by carefully dated archival documents – and in this way gave presence to a forgotten past.[29] Anthropologists, they suggested, depended on observations and analysis of the narratives of 'traditional' storytellers to interpret a sense of 'onceness' that underlay the events being told.[30]

---

[27] Luttikhuis and Van der Meer, 'New Turning Points'.
[28] Hughes, 'Introduction'.
[29] Hanss, 'The Fetish of Accuracy'.
[30] 'Such narratives might displace the problem of time by invoking mythic tenses of primacy or onceness, but the problem remained in the sequential ordering of events within the narrative itself.' Hughes, 'Introduction', 1.

What was lost in this divergence between the two disciplines was their basic unity: history-writing and anthropology both depend on the interpretation of recorded memories to construct coherent stories about the past.

It took more than a century for this divergence to collapse. Today historians have become far more aware of the importance of 'other pasts' because, for many of the people whose lives they study, chronometric time was just one dimension of a much more complex universe of memories and time – as it is for many of us today.[31] This is not just an academic issue. It is widely recognised that writing history is a political practice and that the decisions we make about what to study, who to focus on, what to omit and what to forget have political repercussions, today and in the future.[32] And this includes the issue of time.

Historians have come to realise that time is not a neutral concept and that their research is never detached: they choose a particular construction of time to make their narrative cohere. If, in the past, they often did not show an interest in previous or local understandings of time, this is now changing.[33] Historians working with non-European source material – such as can be found in abundance in the Triangle – have long argued that they find a range of temporal structures (or 'timescapes') unknown in European texts, and that these necessitate a thorough shake-up of historical theory to make it 'globally inclusive'.[34] They have joined a chorus of scholars from other disciplines who speak of 'temporalities' to highlight that time 'cannot be considered as an object separate from human configurations [and] perceptions'.[35]

Historians are now discussing their 'chronopolitics', the temporal assumptions and habits that have shaped their field.[36] They are re-examining their previous assumptions about how time was experienced in the past (as presumably slow, static or circular), as well as about their belief in an accelerating 'arrow of modernity' puncturing the stagnant, circular temporality of the past.[37] Present-day predictions of ecological collapse have undermined convictions of future purpose and development – and, as a result, that 'arrow of modernity' now seems to have been following a wobbly course.

---

[31] For example, Saikia, *Fragmented Memories*.

[32] Ray, 'Boundaries Blurred'.

[33] 'Viewpoints: Temporalities'. For overviews, see West-Pavlov, *Temporalities*; Grange, 'Time, Space and Islands'.

[34] Sastrawan, 'Temporalities in Southeast Asian', 226.

[35] Champion, 'The History of Temporalities', 247.

[36] Hanss, 'The Fetish of Accuracy', 282. See also Zhang, 'The Matter of Time'.

[37] Champion, 'The History of Temporalities', 250. See also Nandy, 'History's Forgotten Doubles'.

All this is relevant when we consider the more-than-human histories of the Triangle. If time is not a neutral ground but a relational dimension of every society, its complexities will vary and change over time. For example, at least fourteen different calendrical systems are available in parts of the Triangle administered by Bangladesh, with three dominant ones ('Bengali Time', 'Islamic Time' and 'English Time') vying for symbolic supremacy in a passionate identity politics.[38] In this time-rich, multi-temporal society, simply referring to a date may be construed as an openly political act.[39]

We can also see that time is not a neutral concept by considering official time in the Triangle. It is deliberately nationalised, and the Triangle is a veritable hotchpotch of state time regimes. The sections that are administered by Bhutan and Bangladesh stick to the international time-zone system: they are six hours ahead of Greenwich Mean Time (GMT). But the Indian section is five and a half hours ahead, the Myanmar one six and a half hours and the Chinese one eight hours.

Such time politics revolve around competing styles of chronometric time, but the history of temporalities goes well beyond that. Studying it offers historians a chance to learn about the ways in which other disciplines debate and study time.[40] The rhythms of human–non-human interaction in the Triangle produce temporalities that have attracted the attention of a broad array of researchers, ranging from natural scientists and linguists to geneticists and folklorists. We will come across their insights throughout this book.

As we shall see, people in the Triangle have expressed their relationships with the past in the form of multiple understandings of time. Historians must take these local temporalities seriously. This is a region in which human lives have always been dominated by the time scales of natural cycles, not least because the region remained overwhelmingly rural until the very end of the twentieth century. It is unified by a pronounced monsoon climate, and millennia of agricultural production have fashioned annual cycles of manipulation of plants and soil that persist today.

---

[38] A popular local almanac opened with the statement that it was the almanac for the Bengali year 1405, which corresponded to 1998–99 CE (or AD), 1418–19 Hijri, 1920–21 Saka, 2055–56 Sangbat, 1405–06 Fasali and Amali, 13560–61 Magi, 1406 Bagri, 1408 Tripuri, 513–14 Chaitanya, 268–69 Loknath, 187–88 Hari, 549–50 Kamrupi Sankara, and 2541–42 Buddhist Era. However, this list does not take into account the local temporalities of non-Bengali groups such as Marma and Khasi. Van Schendel, 'Modern Times in Bangladesh', 39. For several other styles of reckoning time in the Triangle, see Terwiel, 'Myths Associated with Belief', 121–66; Bareigts, *Les Lautu*, 137–9; Gurdon, *The Khasis*, 190–1; Yin and Liu, 'Traditional Continuation', 93–4.

[39] See also Debbarma, 'Celebrating a New "New Year"'.

[40] Hoskins, *The Play of Time*.

The year may be divided into up to six seasons, each with their own names and related human activities. These are based on well-defined moments for preparing the land (burning or ploughing), planting, manuring, weeding and harvesting. Hunting and fishing practices followed the patterns of animal procreation and migration. Life was also adapted to much longer natural processes, such as the slow growth of fruit trees, the need to leave fields fallow to regenerate for a decade or more, the 22-month gestation period of elephants, the gradual silting up of meandering rivers, the pace of contagion by infectious diseases and the 50-year cycle of bamboo famines. Floods and cyclones happened frequently, and very severe ones struck roughly once a decade, just as earthquakes often hit the region, and major ones occurred at irregular intervals.

These logics of existence have shaped human temporalities, human cultures and human imaginations of the future in countless ways.[41] Rhythms of nature have inspired cosmologies all over the world, so Triangle cosmologies were not unique in their focus on symbols of human–non-human unity. But they were specific in how they reflected the ways in which people in this region had come to experience time through enduring entanglements with animals and plants. An example of such entanglements is how human life cycle events involved non-humans. Human births and deaths could require animal sacrifices.[42] The first feeding of boiled rice to an infant, a major ritual, was a celebration of the life-bond between humans and their major food crop.[43] And weddings could entail a bride-price paid in pigs, fowls, bovines, grain or an exchange of betel nuts and rice liquor.[44]

These deep-rooted temporalities have not disappeared. Some actually turned into powerful markers of modernity. The revival of precolonial ceremonies is a point in case. In Mizoram (India) most people have been Christians for four or five generations. They are powerfully organised in church associations that disapprove of pre-Christian traditions, such as alcohol consumption and animal sacrifice. And yet, in recent times, popular pressure has resulted in the resurrection, in contemporary urban settings, of old rural rituals such as the Spring Festival (Chapchâr Kût) and the Maize Festival (Mîm Kût).[45] Imbued with novel

---

[41] Das, 'From Millet to Rice'.

[42] Parry, *The Lakhers*, 378–90; Mills, *The Lhota Nagas*, 157.

[43] Marak, 'Rice from *A·ba*', 1.

[44] Hutton, *The Angami Nagas*, 168, 220; Carey and Tuck, *The Chin Hills*, 1:189, 146; Shakespear, *The Lushei Kuki Clans*, 154–5, 199, 218–20; Gurdon, *The Khasis*, 129; Head, *Hand Book*; Bareigts, *Les Lautu*, 244–6; Jimo, 'Text, Knowledge'.

[45] See De Maaker, 'Performing the Garo Nation', for the revival of the Wangala festival among urban Christian Garo. See also Sitlhou, 'Land and Identity', 130–1. For the somewhat similar case of urban hunting practices, see Kikon and McDuie-Ra, *Ceasefire City*, chap. 4.

meanings, these pre-Christian celebrations of plant temporality became 'primary markers of modern Mizo authenticity'.[46] They are elements in Mizo modernity, which simultaneously embraces the temporalities of academic history-writing, the Biblical past and ancient stories of the Mizo people originally having sprung from a covered cave.[47] Thus, the modern Mizo 'timescape' is both complex and distinct, and its evolution is a vital topic for historians.

Sophisticated multi-temporal sensibilities like these can be found across the Triangle. None excludes other temporal configurations – they are intertwined, vary from place to place, persist and are dynamically reworked. This is hardly surprising because most of them are – or have been until very recently – transmitted by word of mouth.

> We know that oral tradition is never static, that performance and improvisation generate variation. It is dynamic in another sense, too: transmitted over time, oral tradition is inherently temporal. Oral stories are not necessarily historically accurate, but history does influence their content … events of the past two hundred years have left their mark on Apatani stories, especially in their articulation of local identity.[48]

The richness and variation of oral transmission in the Triangle underscores the point that it matters how time is told, who tells it and to what purpose. By restricting 'historical time' to the invention of writing and the 'fetish of accuracy', many historians have arguably crippled their understanding of the past.[49] Shedding conventional 'epistemic incuriosity' and being open to proxy sources and the temporalities offered by oral stories is especially helpful if we are to construct long-term histories of human–non-human interaction.[50] These stories are rich in references to historical connections between humans and other animals, as well as plants.[51] They neatly connect the region's deep history with ideas about the history of humankind and contemporary life. But they do not allow for historical accuracy – and balancing them with scholarly history-writing about the Triangle is a real challenge.[52]

---

[46] Pachau and Van Schendel, *The Camera as Witness*, 276. See also Sitlhou, 'The Shifting "Stages" of Performance'; Kikon and McDuie-Ra, *Ceasefire City*, chap. 4.

[47] Shakespear, *The Lushei Kuki Clans*, 94, 150, 177; Pachau, *Being Mizo*, 111–20; Chakraborty, 'Identity and Virtual Spaces'.

[48] Blackburn, *Himalayan Tribal Tales*, 6.

[49] Tamm, 'Introduction', 5; Hanss, 'The Fetish of Accuracy'.

[50] Lewis, 'Releasing a Tradition', 31; Morrison, 'Conceiving Ecology', 42.

[51] Nongbri, 'Culture and Biodiversity'; Gros, 'Nature De-naturalised'.

[52] Such balancing acts are now undertaken in many scholarly fields. For a plant scientist's endeavour, see Kimmerer, *Braiding Sweetgrass*.

Ultimately, historians have the heavy responsibility to decide whose account of the past is heard – and whose is silenced. In this book we explore some examples of non-chronometric temporal sensibilities. These should not be dismissed as being 'pre-modern', 'traditional' or 'tribal' because such terms explain nothing. They coexist with technologies of modernity, which they modify to suit emergent identities and practical uses. Triangle ideas about time need to be part of Triangle histories because, as we shall see, they motivate contemporary human behaviour towards non-humans, from conservation practices to food habits to medical procedures.

Triangle ideas about time are but one aspect of the intricacy of Triangle lifeworlds. We argue that historians need to pay very close attention to these lifeworlds because the most relevant historical narratives are bound to emerge from collaborations between scholars and local tellers of the past. Scholars have too often ignored, misunderstood or derided such local thinkers, preferring to base their narratives on what outsiders and rulers said or wrote about local pasts. The more co-produced historical narratives are, however, the more meaningful they will be.

Terminology

Anyone writing about the long-term history of the Triangle is faced with a terminological minefield. Names for areas, communities and languages in the region have changed over time, reflecting dynamic political and cultural processes. Names that were perfectly acceptable a century ago have become obsolete or contested. Others have been invented. An example is the term Assam. It refers to a region named after a precolonial dynasty (the Ahom) that became a colonial administrative unit. In our account, Assam is an unstable category because, since the mid-twentieth century, it has shrunk considerably: parts broke away to become Meghalaya, Nagaland and Mizoram within India, or join a newly invented state, Pakistan, that later morphed into Bangladesh.

The names of many communities and languages have also changed or are contested. This is partly a result of emancipation – communities demanding to be referred to by their self-appellation (endonym) rather than the names that others know them by (exonym). Examples are Marma (instead of Magh), Adi (instead of Abor) and Pnar (instead of Jaintia). Such changes also result from newly emerging community identities or nation-building projects that required an umbrella term, such as Kachin, Zo, Naga or Jumma. Some embraced these terms, but others contested them.[53]

---

[53] For example, see Uddin, 'In Search of Self'; Pelletier, 'Identity Formation'; Pau and Mung, 'Fragmented Tribes'.

In addition, both scholars and representatives of various groups in the Triangle are deeply invested in labelling communities. Researchers and activists alike have had little time for processes of spatial mobility, ethnic border crossing or the creation of new ethnic identities. And yet, this is what has been going on for as long as we know. People continually crossed ethnic borders and took on new identities.[54]

As a result, the Triangle is a hotbed of cultural innovation. In a process sometimes described as creolisation, new cultural forms are forever being created. This is most notable in the emergence of creole languages (Nefamese, Nagamese, Assam Sadri), but also in how people constantly adopt, refashion and recombine selected cultural elements from the many cultures they encounter. The current compartmentalised way of portraying the region's inhabitants understates this fluidity and mobility, and it frames them largely in terms of fixed, administratively recognised ethnic labels. Because we must depend on available insights and knowledge production, we, too, will not be able to get away from labelling Triangle groups. There is, however, a real need to push beyond present ethnic container concepts and accentuate commonalities across the Triangle.

Finally, there is the issue of landscape features having multiple local names. The Triangle's mightiest river is known as Yarlung Tsangpo in Tibet, Brahmaputra in India and Jamuna in Bangladesh. In addition, there are many other appellations for this river in different regional languages. The highest peak in Bangladesh, on the border with Myanmar, is variously known as Saka Haphong, Mowdok Taung and Tlang Moy. The capital of Arakan (or Rakhine) is known as Akyab, Saittwe or Sittwe. All over the Triangle, this multiplicity of regional names has been further complicated by a layer of colonial names. Thus, we have locations that Europeans renamed (Chin Hills, Black Mountains) or overlaid with references to themselves, for example, the towns of Cox's Bazar (after a British officer), Margherita (after an Italian queen) and Lorrainville (after Christian missionaries).

There is no simple, consistent way of dealing with these issues without cluttering the text with explanatory footnotes. Therefore, we have tried to steer a middle course. We use terms sparingly, and we use terms that we hope are readily understood by most readers, sometimes adding an alternative term in brackets.

---

[54] Such group changing was known as *saphun* in Mizoram (Pachuau, *Being Mizo*). Ramirez ('Ethnic Conversions; *People of the Margins*; 'Conversions, Population Movements') discusses ethnic flexibilities in terms of 'floating ethnonyms' and 'ethnic conversions', and Vanderhelsken and Karlsson ('Fluid Attachments') speak of 'fluid attachments'. See also Stack and Lyall, *The Mikirs*, 23; Shaw, *Notes on the Thadou Kukis*, 12; Zou, 'A Historical Study'; Sadan, *Being and Becoming Kachin*; McDuie-Ra, 'Adjacent Identities'; Pau, 'Transborder People'; Piang, 'Contestation of Etic Categorizations'.

Finally, we have tried to resolve another issue. Historically, names have been spelled in different ways, and this may cause confusion. Thus, we have Munnipore or Manipur, Garrow or Garo, Sema or Sümi, Bootan or Bhutan, Khyen or Chin, Tipperah or Tripura, Cosseah or Khasi, and so on. In these cases, we have opted for the contemporary version.

A three-part book

The Triangle has been home to a bewildering variety of human societies and cultural traditions. In this book we will encounter many, but certainly not all. We seek to introduce shared more-than-human histories in the region, so our focus is on general patterns and processes of human–non-human interaction, not on ethnic idiosyncrasies, racialised categories or class distinctions among humans, or on human-to-human interactions. By cutting across cultural and class boundaries and simply speaking of 'humans', we do not follow the historiographical and anthropological conventions of the region, which put great emphasis on the distinctive separateness of ethnic groups and cultures. We could not have done without these scholarly traditions, however. Throughout the book we sample their rich record of published and unpublished material, and we acknowledge and identify the ethnic groups concerned. We cast our net widely, but we do not aim to be encyclopaedic. Instead, we step back from human cultural differentiation, and this means, unfortunately, that quite a few cultural communities make no appearance at all, or only a very fleeting one. The argument we make is about commonalities, not particularities, in how humans and non-humans have co-created life in the Triangle.

In the same vein, we present many examples of human relationships with animals and plants, but we can do no more than scratch the surface. There are untold thousands of these relationships. Certain ones – such as with rice, bamboo, mithuns (gayals) and tigers – receive some attention, but many other interspecies relationships are hardly covered, or not at all. Given the introductory format of the book, this is inevitable. We have taken care to provide footnotes that act as windows to a far fuller range of interspecies relationships.

The book is divided into three parts. Each has a different time scale. We move from the vastness of geological time to the timescape of humankind and to changes in the past 150 years. As we move from the past to the present, we will be able to base our account on increasingly detailed information. 'The Deep Past' (Chapters 1–4) explains the geological background of the Triangle, the arrival of the first humans and the beginnings of human–non-human interactions. This is followed by 'Cosmologies' (Chapters 5–7), which focuses on what the stories being told in the Triangle reveal about human origins and how human relationships with animals, plants and inanimate nature developed. The third part, 'More-Than-Human Histories' (Chapters 8–11), is concerned with how these relationships changed in the past century and a half, as humans intensified their exploitation of the Triangle's natural resources, leading to ecological devastation, attempts at conservation and new forms of human–non-human conflict. The book concludes with a consideration of the Triangle's long-term transformation because of the ever-increasing footprint of *Homo sapiens*.

Part I
The Deep Past

1

An Epic Crash

Is there anything more peaceful than the timeless panorama of a mountain landscape? Well, appearances can be misleading. The mountains and cloud-filled valleys of Plate 1.1 hide a sinister story. Far from being a scene of ageless serenity, they are evidence of a ferocious, ongoing collision.

Plate 1.1 Early morning in Mizoram (India)
Source: Photo by Willem van Schendel.

We are not immediately aware of the landscape's dynamism because the calamitous clash that it represents is played out in very, very slow motion. It began some 50 million years ago, but its impact on everyday life continues to this day.

It is the story of a large land mass (the Indian tectonic plate) moving north through what is now the Indian Ocean and crashing into the Eurasian plate. This gigantic collision never stopped. The Indian plate continues to push north, sliding underneath the Eurasian plate. The violence of the crash is clearly visible in how the earth's crust formed huge creases, wrinkles and folds, and it is noticeable in how the contact zone is shaken by frequent earthquakes. The most spectacular crease is the Himalayas, the highest (and youngest) mountain range on earth,

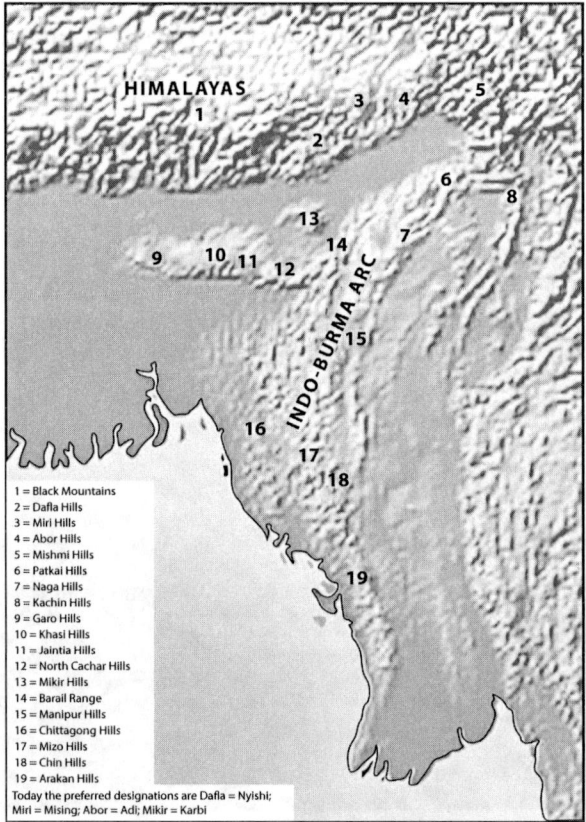

Map 1.1 The eastern Himalayas and the Indo-Burma Arc, with local names for segments

Source: Authors.

Note: The designation 'hills' is something of a misnomer for these mountain segments that are far too high to fit the conventional definition of being under 300 metres above sea level.

which is still being pushed up by the movement of the Indian plate. Connected to the eastern Himalayas is another crumple zone with folded mountain ranges that run from north to south for some 1,200 kilometres. Geologists call it 'the Indo-Burma Arc'.[1] This term is not used locally: various sections of this 'rugged knot of hills and mountain ranges' – or the extended eastern Himalayas – are known by other names (Map 1.1).[2] The mountains of the Indo-Burma Arc are lower than the Himalayas, but they are steep, with some reaching over 3,000 metres above sea level.

An experimental space: The Triangle

This book is about the effects of this calamitous collision on climate, ecosystems and human histories in a roughly triangular region formed by the mountain knot of the eastern Himalayas and the Indo-Burma Arc, and the rivers flowing from these mountains.[3] It is a region without sharp boundaries or administrative unity, it often drops off conventional maps and it has no ready-made name. For lack of a better designation, we call it 'the Eastern Himalayan Triangle' or simply 'the Triangle'.[4] Today it is divided between five countries: India, Myanmar/Burma, Bangladesh, Bhutan and China. It also crosses the boundaries between uplands (also theorised as 'Highland Asia'[5]) and lowlands.

---

[1] For introductions to the geological literature on the Indo-Burma Arc, see Brunnschweiler, 'On the Geology of the Indoburman Ranges'; Acharyya, 'Indo-Burma Range'; Westerweel et al., 'Burma Terrane Part of the Trans-Tethyan Arc'; and Morley et al., 'Structural and Tectonic Development'. For a map demonstrating that much of the Triangle was still geological *terra incognita* a century ago, see *Imperial Gazetteer*, plate 3.

[2] Fisher, *An Environmental History of India*, 15. See Guyot-Réchard, 'Tangled Lands', 2–3. In ancient Chinese documents, the Indo-Burma Arc is called the Black Mountains. Pelliot, 'Deux itinéraires de Chine en Inde à la fin du VIIIe siècle', 177, 371.

[3] Rippa, Murton and Rest describe a 'mountain knot' as comprising 'a number of specific threads that, when pulled apart, help to highlight particular processes and, as such, also justify its utility as an analytical concept'. Rippa, Murton and Rest, 'Building Highland Asia in the Twenty-First Century', 88. For another experimental map of these areas, see Bhattacharya, 'Old Routes, New Dreams', 311.

[4] By coincidence, there is also a much smaller area within what we call 'the Eastern Himalayan Triangle' that colonial administrators sometimes happened to refer to as 'the Triangle'. This was the lightly administered wedge of land in Kachin State (Myanmar) between two rivers – the Mali Hka and the Nmai Hka – to the north of Myitsone, where these rivers met and continued southwards as the Ayeyarwadi (Irrawaddy). We reserve 'the Triangle' for the larger area discussed in this chapter.

[5] Wouters and Heneise, 'Introduction to Highland Asia'.

The Triangle's northeastern landmark is the 7,700-metre-high Namcha Barwa in Tibet, the highest mountain peak in the eastern Himalayas. It is here that the mighty Brahmaputra River makes a sharp turn on its way to Assam. From Namcha Barwa, the Triangle's boundary runs west to Thimphu (the capital of Bhutan) and then south to coastal Sandoway (in Rakhine State of Myanmar) (see Maps 1.2 and 1.3). Setting limits to this region is complicated and debatable. We use an indicative measure: it is loosely bounded by the catchment areas of two major rivers, the Brahmaputra in the west and the Chindwin in the east.

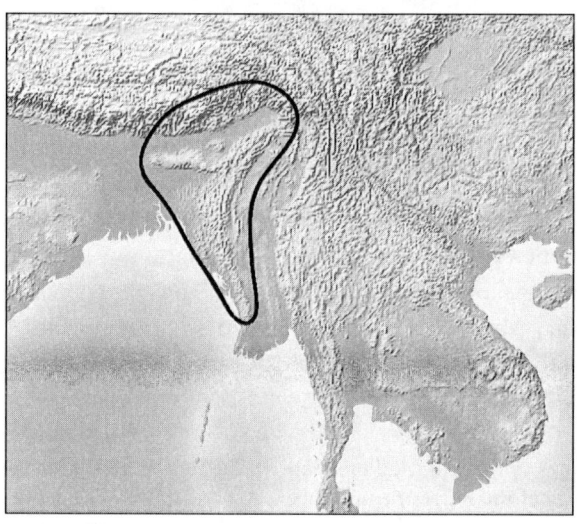

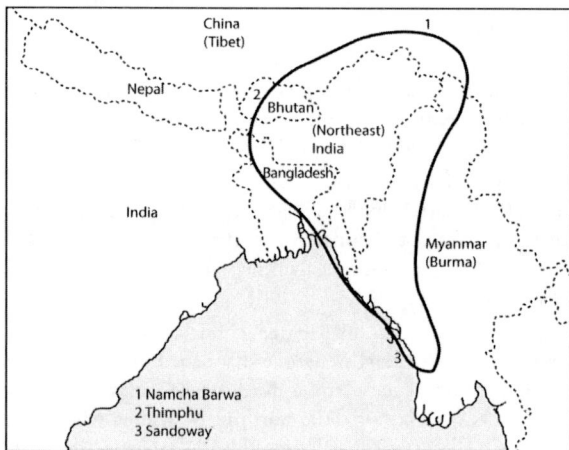

Maps 1.2 and 1.3 The Eastern Himalayan Triangle

Source: Authors.

One way of thinking about the Triangle is to consider it not so much a fixed area as an experimental space. What can we learn from spotlighting a space that consists not only of adjoining portions of five national territories but also of adjoining portions of uplands and lowlands – a space where geology is destiny? It is marked by stark differences in altitude from sea level to the high Himalayas. The Triangle's geology is of far more than regional importance. It has recently added a term to the international geological lexicon. Since 2019 geologists around the world have started using the term 'Meghalayan' to refer to the current stage of the world's history, which began with a new global climate regime around 2200 BCE. Evidence for this was found in a stalagmite in Mawmluh Cave in the Khasi Hills (see Map 1.1), today located in the Indian state of Meghalaya.[6]

Millions of years earlier, however, the rise of the Himalayas and the Tibetan Plateau had already had enormous consequences for the global climate. Climate historians think that it created the South Asia monsoon. The mountains began to act as a wall that blocked the moisture-laden clouds that would seasonally drift north from the warm Indian Ocean.[7] The clouds were forced upwards, their temperature dropped and they released rain and snow. As a result, the Himalayan foreland became drenched, whereas the Tibetan Plateau to the north received very little rain. The intense seasonality of the South Asia monsoon – very wet and hot from June to October, and mostly dry and cooler from October to June[8] – has dominated the pace of life ever since. And the Eastern Himalayan Triangle stood out because it acted as a funnel, trapping more rain than other parts of South Asia. With more than 11 metres of rain a year, the Khasi Hills (Map 1.1) claim to be the wettest place on earth. Current predictions on global climate change indicate that in the decades to come the Triangle will experience both heavier monsoon precipitation and higher temperatures.[9]

Intense rainfall led to further unification of the Triangle: it fed numerous rivers that connected the uplands with the lowlands. Vertical landscapes come

---

[6] Walker et al., 'Subdividing the Holocene Series/Epoch'.

[7] There is intense debate about the origins of the South Asia monsoon. For an introduction to the debate, see Spicer, 'Tibet, the Himalaya, Asian Monsoons and Biodiversity'. The monsoon is also thought to have varied in intensity since it commenced. For an overview, see Blinkhorn and Petraglia, 'Environments and Cultural Change in the Indian Subcontinent', S467; Dutt et al., 'Indian Summer Monsoon Variability in Northeastern India'.

[8] Within this overarching pattern, there are smaller variations, for example, thunderstorms, which may occur in March and April, and are known as 'nor'westers' in Bangladesh and 'borodoisila' in Assam.

[9] IPCC, *Climate Change 2021*.

with pronounced connectivity. The major watercourse, the Brahmaputra,[10] originated in Tibet and curled around Namcha Barwa, the easternmost major peak of the Himalayas, before breaking through the mountain range and plunging down to lower heights in Assam. Joining other Himalayan rivers, flowing west and then south, this enormous stream slowed down and created a vast delta in Bangladesh, before releasing its water and silt into the Bay of Bengal.[11] Today the Brahmaputra links up with the Ganges in the central Bengal delta but, geologically speaking, this is a recent development.[12] For long periods of history, the two majestic rivers had separate deltas: the Ganges in the western part of Bengal and the Brahmaputra in the east.[13] The Brahmaputra shared its delta with rivers originating on the western side of the Indo-Burma Arc, notably the Barak–Surma–Meghna.[14] The eastern Indo-Burma Arc drained into the Chindwin and other rivers. These joined the Ayeyarwadi (Irrawaddy) in central Myanmar.

These physical attributes of the Triangle – its deep geological association, its monsoon climate and its ancient river connections[15] – have made it a hotspot for geologists. These same attributes also make the case for treating it as a unit of deep historical analysis, even though this is hardly ever done. As we have seen, historical studies tend to be hidebound. By and large they stay within contemporary national (or former colonial) boundaries and are less inquisitive about processes that comprise neighbouring areas. By contrast, this book seeks to include such processes. How are what we currently call 'Northeast India' and its surrounding areas historically connected? How can we cast them in a new light by exploring these connections? How should we think about history and time in this region? But before we start dealing with human histories, there is another layer of connectedness that we need to lay bare.

---

[10] Saikia, *The Unquiet River*.
[11] Curray, 'The Bengal Depositional System'.
[12] Uddin and Lundberg, 'A Paleo-Brahmaputra?'; Coleman, 'Brahmaputra River'; Jahan, 'Archaeology of Wari-Bateshwar'.
[13] This is the reason why we will not refer much to Sikkim, or the Tista River, which runs down from the Sikkim mountains, even though today the Tista is a tributary of the Brahmaputra (as is the Ganges). Before the late eighteenth century, the Tista was part of the Ganges Delta. It was only after an earthquake and floods forced both the Brahmaputra and the Tista to change their course that the Tista began to discharge into the new channel of the Brahmaputra, as did, downstream, the Ganges. Richards, Brammer and Saunders, 'The Historical Avulsion of the Tista River'.
[14] Chapman et al., 'Chemical Fluxes'; Ludden, 'India's Spatial History'.
[15] Iqbal, 'From Zomia to Holon'.

Ecologies

The Triangle's tortuous beginnings created 'perhaps the most complex topography on Earth'.[16] Its subterranean dynamics set the stage for a long chain of events that ultimately led to the present. It was the starting shot for what geologists call 'surface processes'. As we have seen, these included epochal changes in climate, river courses and delta formation, all of which continue today. And these in turn shaped dynamic landscapes, some of them extremely changeable, for example, the fluid, seeping, fertile delta landscapes that the flood-prone, meandering rivers create.[17] Countless life forms could flourish in these dynamic landscapes, shaping a plethora of ecological niches. The Triangle never was a closed-off entity. Its many ecological options invited the passage and settlement of new plants and animals, resulting in extraordinary diversity. By the time humans wandered into the Triangle, very late in the day, the Triangle was a biologically rich environment where several of the world's most biodiverse regions met and overlapped. Today three of these are designated 'global biodiversity hotspots' and known internationally as 'Himalaya', 'Indo-Burma' and 'Mountains of Southwest China' (Map 1.4).[18]

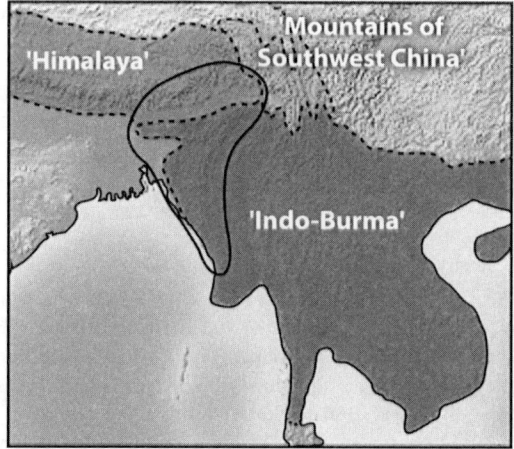

Map 1.4 Three global biodiversity hotspots
Source: Authors.

---

[16] Qu et al., 'Lineage Diversification and Historical Demography', 2. See also Dumbacher et al., 'Avifauna of the Gaoligong Shan Mountains'.

[17] Cederlöf, 'Fixed Boundaries, Fluid Landscapes'; Crémin, 'Between Land Erosion and Land Eviction'; Cons, 'Seepage'; Saikia, *The Unquiet River*.

[18] Marchese, 'Biodiversity Hotspots'.

Biodiversity scholars have recently begun to refer to the meeting point of these hotspots as the 'Far-Eastern Himalayas'.[19]

A hotspot is characterised by a high number of plants and animals that are found nowhere else ('endemic') – a result of its geography, soils and climate. Each hotspot is made up of many local ecoregions, some of which are home to locally endemic species.[20] The term 'hotspot' refers to contemporary threats to their survival.

Because of its distinct monsoon climate and variation in elevation, the Triangle boasted tropical and subtropical rainforests, cloud forests, coniferous forests, alpine shrublands and coastal swamps. These hosted thousands of species and created numerous local ecosystems or microbiomes. A dazzling range of plants – from alpine rhododendron and pine to tropical bamboo, orchid, wild rice, teak, sal, palm and mangrove – had colonised the well-watered land. Local species of insects, invertebrates, amphibians, reptiles, mammals and birds made their home in these forests, feeding on plants and dispersing their seeds, and eating other animals. Likewise, many species of fish inhabited the lakes, rivers and coastal waters. The Triangle was a welcoming place for migratory species. Falcons from northeastern Siberia would rest here before flying to their winter habitats in southern Africa. Geese from Mongolia would soar to amazing heights over the Himalayas to winter in the Triangle.

Very little is known about the Triangle's oldest fauna. The earliest finds are of dinosaur bones and small animals caught in amber, dated to some 70–99 million years ago.[21] Other finds include fossilised remains of more recently extinct species

---

[19] Basnet et al., 'Biodiversity Research Trends'.

[20] For example, a plant known as Mishmi teeta (*Coptis teeta*), whose rhizomes have long been sought after for medicinal use in both China and India. Its habitat is restricted to the far northeastern corner of the Triangle. Rowlatt, 'Report of an Expedition', 485, 489; Mills, 'The Mishmis of the Lohit Valley', 5; Kingdon-Ward, 'Report on the Forests', 319–20; Pandit and Babu, 'Biology and Conservation of *Coptis teeta*'; Huang and Long, '*Coptis teeta*–based Agroforestry System'. On various species of orchid that are locally endemic in different states of Northeast India, see De et al., *Commercial Orchids*, 20–1. See also Renner et al., *Avifauna of the Southeastern Himalayan Mountains Country*; Suarez-Rubio et al., 'Hkakabo Razi Landscape'. A recently rediscovered agarwood tree in Meghalaya is described in Mir, Roy and Upadhaya, 'Taxonomy, Recollection and Conservation Implications'. And the critically endangered white-bellied heron (*Ardea insignis*) – with no more than some dozens of individuals currently thought to be in existence – is found only in the northern Triangle. Menzies, Rao and Naniwadekar, 'Assessing the Status of the Critically Endangered White-bellied Heron'.

[21] Ross, 'The Remarkable Palaeodiversity in Burmese Amber'; Ross, *Burmese (Myanmar) amber taxa*; Mishra and Sen, 'Dinosaur Bones from Meghalaya'.

An Epic Crash

Plate 1.2 Snow leopard
Source: Photo by Willem van Schendel.

Plate 1.3 Asian black bear
Source: Photo by Willem van Schendel.

of mollusc, insect, fish, elephant, deer and whale.[22] During the last 200,000 years or so, the abundance of this damp, warm, mostly tropical area is thought to have remained largely stable during climate changes. Thus, the major Ice Ages may have turned southern Asia into a refugium for animals that could not survive elsewhere. The rate of animal extinction may have been quite low here.[23]

The region sustained large numbers of the biggest herbivores: elephant, three species of rhinoceros, wild water buffalo, gaur, wild yak, takin, tapir and serow. It was also home to an array of top predators: tiger, snow leopard (Plate 1.2), wolf, hyena, wild dog, clouded leopard, black bear (Plate 1.3), marsh crocodile and river dolphin. There were many different types of monkeys (macaque, langur) and loris, and there was one ape: the hoolock gibbon. This was what the Triangle was like – until another ape made its appearance.

---

[22] For a helpful database, see Ross, *Burmese (Myanmar) amber taxa*. See also Mishra and Sen, 'Dinosaur Bones from Meghalaya'; Lokho, Singh and Bhandari, 'A Synoptic Review of Eocene-Miocene Faunal'.

[23] Roberts et al., 'Continuity of Mammalian Fauna'.

2

Human Beginnings

Over 40,000 years ago, a new species drifted into the Triangle, and it would change life here forever. This invasive species was an intelligent ape. It calls itself *Homo sapiens*, or (modern) human being. It was not the first member of the *Homo* family in Asia: a pre-modern cousin (*Homo erectus*) had arrived long before. Evidence of its presence has been found relatively close to the Triangle – in Yuanmou (southwestern China) and in the Kyaw and Upper Ayeyarwadi valleys (Myanmar)[1] – but not yet in the Triangle itself.

We know little about the beginnings of modern human life in the Triangle because early *Homo sapiens* left few traces, and remarkably little scholarly research has been done into their whereabouts and lifestyles in this region.[2] Generally speaking, the 'archaeology of northeastern India, the Indo-Burmese borderlands, Burma and the northern Bay of Bengal littoral is virtually unresearched'.[3] This means that archaeological assumptions about the region are rarely backed up by evidence – and yet it is, of course, important to be aware that 'the absence of evidence does not constitute the evidence of absence'.[4]

---

[1] The Yuanmou finds are currently dated to more than 1.5 million years ago. The finds in Myanmar (referred to as Anyathian – *an-ya-tha* = Upper Burman) have also been dated to the Pleistocene. Luo et al., 'The First Radiometric Age by Isochron'; Terra et al., 'Research on Early Man in Burma'. For debates about the origins and dispersal of *Homo erectus*, see Norton and Braun, *Asian Paleoanthropology*. See also Chauhan, 'General Observations on the Northeast Indian Zone', 33.

[2] Currently, the oldest dated finds are from the adjacent area of western Bengal. Basak and Srivastava, 'Earliest Dates of Microlithic Industries (42–25 ka)'.

[3] Van Driem, 'The Domestications and the Domesticators of Asian Rice', 190. See also Blench, 'The Contribution of Linguistics'; the subtitle of Hazarika, *Prehistory and Archaeology of Northeast India*; Penjore, 'Digging the Past'; and Rahman et al., 'Agricultural Systems in Bangladesh'.

[4] Van Driem, 'The Domestications and the Domesticators of Asian Rice', 191. See also Jamir, 'Piecing Together from Fragments', 63.

Luckily, striking advances in fossil, climate and genetic studies are beginning to give us more clues about the distribution and migrations of these earliest modern humans. New findings lend support to the 'sub-Himalayan route' thesis. This is the idea that the peopling of Southeast and East Asia (and ultimately the Americas and Australia[5]) owes much to eastward overland migration out of Africa. According to this theory, modern humans dispersed in the regions south of the Himalayas, perhaps as early as 100,000 years ago, and gradually gravitated further east.[6] On the way, they may have interbred to some extent with other branches of the *Homo* family, now extinct, just as in westerly parts of Eurasia modern humans interbred with Neanderthals. Eventually, groups of modern humans entered the relatively narrow corridor between the Himalayas and the Bay of Bengal – in other words, the Triangle. Some settled there and others pushed on across the Indo-Burma Arc into what we now call Southeast Asia and East Asia.

This sub-Himalayan thesis qualifies two earlier assumptions about the earliest dispersal of *Homo sapiens* in Asia. The first is that East Asians descend from groups of humans that moved from Africa to central Asia and crossed the steppes north of the Tibetan Plateau. The second posits that early migrants took sea routes along the coasts and so reached Southeast Asia.

The evidence for the sub-Himalayan route is still limited but this has not stopped scholars from using the available genetic and linguistic material to build their case.[7] The thesis points to the Triangle as an absolutely crucial passageway for the peopling of Asia. However, with archaeological research in the region only just starting to explore human beginnings systematically, it is hard to support the thesis with local findings. Scholars are aware that there is a world to be won here but for the time being they must rely largely on advances in palaeogenetics, which analyses DNA to reconstruct the earliest dispersals of human beings. Unfortunately, this rapidly expanding field of research produces results that are, as yet, contradictory and far from conclusive. Some scholars disagree with the sub-Himalayan thesis and interpret currently available DNA data as possibly suggesting that modern humans

---

[5] Reich, *Who We Are and How We Got Here*, 197.

[6] The date of the earliest dispersal of modern humans in South Asia is subject to intense debate. For an intervention that suggests c. 55,000 years ago, see Mellars et al., 'Genetic and Archaeological Perspectives'. For earlier dates, see Bae, Douka and Petraglia, 'On the Origin of Modern Humans'.

[7] Reddy et al., 'Austro-Asiatic Tribes of Northeast India'; Van Driem, 'The Eastern Himalayan Corridor in Prehistory'; Van Driem, 'From the Dhaulagiri to Lappland'; Bae, Douka and Petraglia, 'Human Colonization of Asia in the Late Pleistocene', S375; Reyes-Centeno et al., 'Testing Modern Human Out-of-Africa Dispersal Models'; McColl et al., 'The Prehistoric Peopling of Southeast Asia'.

first took the northern route to East Asia, from where a cooling climate forced them southwards to Southeast Asia, down the Brahmaputra valley, and into South Asia.[8]

What is becoming clear, however, is that we should not think of the first modern humans in the Triangle as arriving in a single wave from a single direction. In a long-term genetic sense, nobody can claim to be 'indigenous' here. It is more likely that there were several groups that reached the region at different times. Major ones may have come via the sub-Himalayan route – following the southern contours of the Himalayas – and via the coastal route – reaching the Brahmaputra delta as they travelled up the eastern coast of India.

What is also clear is that the initial arrival of modern humans was followed by numerous later migrations from all directions – the Triangle became a busy passageway for people on the move. Some scholars think that the Himalayas and the Indo-Burma Arc were formidable barriers to human dispersal, but others maintain that these ranges were quite permeable and allowed for cross-mountain migrations.[9] Today's inhabitants of the Triangle are unlikely to be able to trace their origins simply to the first arrivals. If they are related at all, their genetic material is the result of admixtures with many later immigrants. Climate change also played a role. There are indications that various groups arrived from Southeast Asia and southern China during the last Ice Age, about 20,000 years ago, and merged with descendants of initial settlers.[10] Around the same time groups moved from the Triangle to the east, into Myanmar, ending up in the Andaman Islands via an Ice Age land bridge.[11]

Although it is hazardous to link genetics and language use, recent advances in research on human DNA and linguistics have resulted in a bold new theory that puts

---

[8] Marrero et al., 'Carriers of Human Mitochondrial DNA'; Gnecchi Ruscone, 'Unraveling the Combined Effects of Demography'; Arciero et al., 'Demographic History and Genetic Adaptation'.

[9] A seventh-century source asserted that it took two months to travel the breadth of the Triangle, from Assam to southwest China. 'But the mountains and rivers present obstacles, and the pestilential air, the poisonous vapours, the fatal snakes, the destructive vegetation, all these causes of death prevail.' Beal (ed.), *Si-Yu-Ki: Buddhist Records of the Western World*, 2:198–9. At least three major trade and travel routes are known to have connected Yunnan and Pundravardhana (now Mahasthangarh, Bogra district, Bangladesh) from very early times. One route ran via the Hukawng valley in northern Myanmar, another via Nagaland and the Barail range and a third via Manipur. Pelliot ('Deux itinéraires de Chine en Inde', 179) and Luce and Oey (*Man Shu*, map 117); Luce, *Phases of Pre-Pagán Burma*, 77–9; Yang, 'Horses, Silver, and Cowries'; Jamir and Vasa, 'Archaeological Evidence of Beads from Naga Ancestral Sites'.

[10] Chandrasekar et al., 'Updating Phylogeny of Mitochondrial DNA', 9; Gnecchi Ruscone, 'Unraveling the Combined Effects of Demography'.

[11] Wang et al., 'Mitochondrial DNA Evidence'.

the Triangle squarely in the spotlight. It argues that the vast majority of languages spoken today in East and Southeast Asia, as well as in Siberia, originated in the eastern Himalayas. The region 'furnished the ultimate cradle for the ethnogenesis of the various Uralo-Siberian and East Asian language families'.[12] Focusing on the Sino-Tibetan languages, scholars posit that 'in its earliest phase Sino-Tibetan was a congeries of [languages of] diverse foragers in the Eastern Himalayan region', some 8,000 years ago.[13] Around 5,000 years ago, forms of vegeculture (taro, plantains) and livestock management developed here, and the spread of languages eastwards towards China occurred some 1,000 years later.[14] This theory presents a radical approach to the Sino-Tibetan language family because it states that the Sinitic branch (to which the Chinese language belongs) 'is not a primary branch, but simply the language of one of many migratory groups' that left the Triangle'.[15] It is for this reason that scholars point out that it makes sense to speak of the 'Trans-Himalayan language family' and drop the conventional designations 'Sino-Tibetan' and 'Tibeto-Burman'.[16]

Others suggest, however, that the Trans-Himalayan language family arrived in the Triangle with groups from Southeast Asia and southern China.[17] Similarly, scholars cannot agree on the Austroasiatic languages – today represented in the Triangle mainly by Khasi (with neighbouring languages) and Santali. Did they emerge in the littoral of the northern Bay of Bengal and then move east across the Triangle into Southeast Asia, or did they migrate the other way around?[18]

---

[12] Van Driem, 'From the Dhaulagiri to Lappland, the Americas and Oceania', 67.

[13] Blench and Post, 'Rethinking Sino-Tibetan Phylogeny', 89. See also Blench, 'Contribution of Linguistics'.

[14] Blench and Post, 'Rethinking Sino-Tibetan', 89.

[15] Ibid., 90, and see their map on 91.

[16] Owen-Smith and Hill (eds.), *Trans-Himalayan Linguistics*; Van Driem, 'Trans-Himalayan'; Van Driem, 'The Eastern Himalaya and the Mongoloid Myth'; Van Driem, 'From the Dhaulagiri to Lappland, the Americas and Oceania'.

[17] Wang et al. suggest that the ancestors of Tibeto-Burman (or Sino-Tibetan)–speaking groups now living in the Indo-Burma Arc region followed another route than those now living in the eastern Himalaya region, the former passing through Yunnan (southwestern China) and the latter through Tibet. Wang et al., 'Reconstruction of Y-Chromosome Phylogeny'. See also Reich, *Who We Are and How We Got Here*, 197.

[18] For the argument in favour of a northern Bay of Bengal homeland, see Van Driem, 'The Domestications and the Domesticators of Asian Rice', 195–202. Reddy et al., 'Austro-Asiatic Tribes of Northeast India', also suggest a West–East dispersal, as do Borkar et al., 'Paleolithic Spread of Y-chromosomal Lineage'. For counterarguments, see Riccio et al., 'The Austroasiatic Munda Population from India and Its Enigmatic Origin'; Zhang et al., 'Y-Chromosome Diversity Suggests Southern Origin'; Van Driem, 'From the Dhaulagiri to Lappland, the Americas and Oceania'.

The dazzling complexity of the Triangle's human history is indicated by the fact that today more than 250 languages are spoken in the region. Many have hardly been studied. Some may be isolates (not related to any other known language).[19] In recent times human flows across the region have continued, as they do today, contributing to a highly complex demographic history, a unique linguistic contact zone and a genetic puzzle that is still largely unmapped, let alone resolved.[20]

Most genetic differences are not visible: for example, a DNA adaptation to life at high altitude in some upland groups.[21] But others are observable because they produce bodily differences, such as height or skin colour. These may take on social meaning, as the recent history of the region demonstrates.[22] We do not know what the earliest humans looked like, or to what extent they resembled modern inhabitants, but it is clear that they acted in ways that have shaped the environment of the region ever since.

Niches

Students of ecology have long recognised that living organisms do not just inhabit their environment but actively change it. Microorganisms, plants and animals alike are 'ecological engineers' that compete for nutrients, sunlight and space. In an unrelenting struggle, they 'control the availability of resources to other organisms by causing physical state changes in biotic or abiotic materials' – they actively modify, maintain or create habitats.[23] If successful, they construct 'niches' that provide a species with the conditions to survive in its habitat. Thus, both fungi and rhinoceroses can be considered 'landscape architects'.[24] Niche construction is an ongoing evolutionary process. Once created, a niche may outlive its ecological engineers and become vacant or get occupied by new organisms. In other words, living organisms inherit their genetic code from their genetic ancestors and their ecological niche from their environmental predecessors.[25]

---

[19] Post, 'Morphosyntactic Reconstruction in an Areal-Historical Context'.

[20] Some suggest that, in modern human history, the region may have become less of an open corridor than it had been in the early millennia of human presence here. Cordaux et al., 'The Northeast Indian Passageway'.

[21] Huerta-Sánchez and Casey, 'Archaic Inheritance'; Arciero et al., 'Demographic History and Genetic Adaptation'; Reich, *Who We Are and How We Got Here*, 65.

[22] Wouters and Subba, 'The "Indian Face"'; McDuie-Ra, *Debating Race in Contemporary India*.

[23] Jones, Lawton and Shachak, 'Positive and Negative Effects of Organisms', 1947.

[24] Bose, 'From Eminence to Near Extinction'.

[25] Odling-Smee, Laland and Feldman, *Niche Construction*.

Niche construction by one species can be beneficial or harmful to other species, and each new species needs to create its own niche to survive. Importantly, however, niche construction is never merely competitive; it is also interdependent. Organisms creating the best living conditions for themselves can only be successful if they form webs of co-creation that we think of as ecosystems. The vibrancy of these ecosystems relies on the open-ended balancing of myriads of evolving and symbiotic niches.

This approach can clarify the environmental impact of early modern humans. The human species has been described as 'the ultimate ecosystem engineer or niche constructor'.[26] Like other organisms, humans altered their environment to create suitable habitats, but three qualities set them apart. First is their genetic advantage. Humans had developed an unrivalled ability to work together, to share, to appraise others' mental states and to connect by means of language. Second, they had mastered fire, which made it possible for them to purposely alter their environment as no other organism could. And third, they developed highly adaptable cultures that could transfer accumulated knowledge from one generation to the next. These three qualities made them superior ecosystem engineers and kick-started a process of incessant habitat upgrading.

We know little about how the earliest humans in the Triangle applied their engineering skills to alter the landscape and create nurturing habitats for themselves. We can surmise that, at first, they made use of existing niches (for example, following elephant trails through the rainforest, collecting birds' eggs from nests or digging up roots) and created new ones (for example, burning vegetation to promote the growth of useful plants, using fire to keep predators at bay or constructing enclosures to ambush herds of deer). At present, however, there is no surviving evidence for the period predating the fifth millennium Before the Common Era (BCE), and hence we cannot say anything definitive about human life during earlier periods.

The Triangle in history

We have seen how the Triangle was shaped by geological and ecological processes long before humans made their appearance. However, their arrival turned it into an arena of human history as well. As we are interested in exploring human–non-human relations, it is important to understand that in this sense a 'region' is necessarily dynamic. The spatial limits of the Triangle varied over time as humans were mobile and altered its material and social features. We think of the Triangle as a spatial unit that is forever in flux. Social and natural processes impinge on it;

---

[26] Arroyo-Kalin et al., 'Civilisation and Human Niche Construction', 106.

political boundaries come and go; technologies and cultural expressions are always changing;[27] and humans, animals and plants adapt to history's inexorable dynamism.

It is true that geology has provided the unifying framework over millennia and that our human timescales rarely accommodate geological change. But a new concept connects the two. A growing awareness of global climate change, diminishing biodiversity and the role of humankind in shaping our planet's evolution has produced the idea that we are witnessing a new epoch of human-dominated geological history, the Anthropocene. This makes detailed historical study of the interactions between humans and other-than-humans in locations all over the world an urgent assignment. The geological formation of the Triangle provides an excellent starting point for such located historical enquiries.

---

[27] Blinkhorn and Petraglia, 'Environments and Cultural Change in the Indian Subcontinent'.

3

Changing the Environment

The record of human life in the Triangle becomes clearer when the first surviving signs of human habitation appear.¹ All over the region, and in areas surrounding it, stone tools are important guides. Archaeologists think that these tools were used in many ways: for cutting, cleaving, drilling, digging, smashing bones, scraping, sewing, hewing wood, carving bamboo and perhaps making stone-tipped spears or harpoons.

The oldest dated traces of human habitation have so far been found in the Indo-Burma Arc. Here a large cave has yielded stone and bone tools, ash and many bones of small game animals, as well as a partial human skeleton.² The people who used the cave are thought to have been hunter-gatherers who lived here in the fifth millennium BCE (Plate 3.1).

It has proven extremely difficult to date archaeological finds in this region, partly because, until recently, sophisticated fieldwork was rare. Dating is becoming easier because problem-oriented, methodologically rigorous and multidisciplinary archaeological studies are now emerging.³ According to archaeologist Manjil Hazarika, there are specific local obstacles. In the flooded river valleys, annual deposits of sediments cover older deposits, and thick vegetation in the mountains makes it difficult to prospect for surface objects.⁴ Extreme monsoon rainfall hampers fieldwork, and so do various regional insurgencies.

---

¹ For an overview of artefact-yielding sites in Northeast India, see Hazarika, 'Lithic Industries with Palaeolithic Elements'. See also Jamir and Hazarika (eds.), *50 Years after Daojali-Hading*; Taylor et al., 'Soil Micromorphological Analysis of Sediments'. For a list of artefact-yielding sites in eastern Bangladesh, see Singh Roy and Ahsan, 'Raw Material and Technology'; and for Myanmar, see Aung, 'Raw Material Utilization, Technology, and Typology'.

² Jamir, Tetso and Venuh, 'Recent Archaeological Investigation'; Pokharia et al., 'Late First Millennium BC to Second Millennium AD Agriculture in Nagaland', 1352.

³ Sarma and Hazarika, 'Situating Northeast Indian Archaeology', 42–4.

⁴ See also Van Driem, 'Domestications and the Domesticators', 190; Chauhan, 'General Observations'.

Changing the Environment

Plate 3.1 Archaeological excavation in progress, Ranyak Khen, Nagaland, Northeast India

Source: Photo by Tiatoshi Jamir.

Mountain cultivation disturbs the topsoil and likely destroys archaeological contexts. Finally, high groundwater levels make it difficult to establish stratigraphic sequences, and the year-round humid climate leads to rapid decomposition of

Plate 3.2 Fragments of corded pottery from Pynthorlangtein, Meghalaya, Northeast India

Source: Shankar (ed.), *Indian Archaeology 1992–93*, plate XXIIIB (Archaeological Survey of India); Hazarika, 'Cord-impressed Pottery in Neolithic-Chalcolithic Context', 94.

materials other than stone.⁵ It is likely that humans made tools from all kinds of material, notably wood, bamboo, bone and plant fibre (for example, to make animal snares). In river valleys and deltas stone was rare; but for this early period, only stone, fossil wood and bone tools have survived – or, at least, have so far been recovered.⁶ Material remains from these early times point towards affinities with Southeast Asia rather than with the Indian peninsula.

This era is usually referred to as the Palaeolithic (or Old Stone Age) and the next, when crop cultivation develops, as the Neolithic – but these terms are problematic. They are derived from European archaeological narratives and should be treated with circumspection because they may not be directly applicable to local conditions. Here early stages of human development may have unfolded differently. Current understandings are that here 'Palaeolithic' groups co-occurred with 'Neolithic' groups for a very long time, probably millennia.⁷

The range of human artefacts expands considerably in the second millennium BCE.⁸ In this period, humans polished their stone tools and were able to make pottery. Some tools were made of jade, which is mined on the eastern edge of the Triangle.⁹ Current techniques make it possible to date excavated potsherds to around 1000 BCE.¹⁰ Many are marked by cord impressions, suggesting that basketry was practised as well (Plate 3.2).

Domestication

What marks this period more than anything, however, is that human niche construction entered a totally different phase. Humans stepped up their ecological engineering. Now they not only hunted animals and gathered plants, but they also began to change them. By doing so, they disturbed the niches of other organisms as never before, at the same time creating new niches for certain plants and animals to evolve into.¹¹ As their behaviour began to broaden, humans added new elements to the foraging techniques that had helped them survive for so long.

---

⁵ Hazarika, 'Archaeological Research in North-East India', 2–4.
⁶ Hazarika et al., 'Geo-archaeological Explorations in Tripura'.
⁷ For archaeologists' various attempts to clarify the regional chronology, see Jamir, 'Piecing Together from Fragments'; Sarma and Hazarika, 'Situating Northeast Indian Archaeology', 44–7.
⁸ Dikshit and Hazarika, 'The Neolithic Cultures of Northeast India'.
⁹ Steel, 'Report on Jade Celts'.
¹⁰ Sharma and Singh, 'Luminescence Dating'; see also Hazarika, 'Neolithic Pottery of Eastern Himalaya'. For much earlier dated pottery, from nearby northern Myanmar, see Hudson and Lwin, 'Earthenware from a Firing Site'; and Pryce et al., 'A First Absolute Chronology'.
¹¹ Fuller and Stevens, 'Open for Competition', 117.

Although this is usually described as humans domesticating animals and plants, 'domestication' is a problematic term because it denotes a process that is far from clear-cut or irreversible. There is little agreement about when we should begin speaking of domestication:

> What counts as the Rubicon of domestication? Is it tending wild plants, weeding them, moving them to a new spot, broadcasting a handful of seeds on rich silt, depositing a seed or two in a depression made with a dibble stick, or ploughing? There appears to be no 'aha!' or 'Edison light bulb' moment.[12]

One way of marking the beginning of domestication is to focus not on the use of plants and animals but on their physical alteration. Selective breeding for specific characteristics – larger seeds, tastier fruits, tamer animals – created organisms that began to differ from their 'wild' cousins. In this way, the human-induced divergence of domesticates can be interpreted as the beginning of domestication.

Whatever definition we use, however, four things are important here. First, domestication is not a uniquely human behaviour. We may call any species domesticated 'whenever another species knows how to harvest it'.[13] Take, for example, the symbiotic relationship between certain ants and aphids. The ants tend the aphids and make sure that they are safe and well fed; in return, the ants harvest and consume the aphids' honeydew. Other species of ants cultivate plants and can be described as non-human farmers. In such cases it is hard to decide which species 'domesticates' the other, so biologists speak of interaction, symbiosis or mutualism.[14]

What set humans apart was that they developed ever more sophisticated skills to 'harvest' other organisms systematically by means of both foraging and domestication. There was, and still is, no clear separation between these two forms of subsistence. In this region, as in many parts of the world, hunting and managing semi-wild animals (such as the mithun, a large bovine) and protecting and collecting wild plants (such as bananas, mangoes and yams) have been combined with domestication and alteration of plants and animals for millennia.

Second, the varied terrain of the Triangle produced different forms of domestication of plants and animals, and local styles of agroforestry, cultivation and animal husbandry. As human niche construction expanded all over the region, it diversified and created quite distinct sub-regional trajectories. Thus, the terms 'crop cultivation' and 'animal husbandry' can mean very different things in different sub-regions.

---

[12] Scott, *Against the Grain*, 11.
[13] Terrell et al., 'Domesticated Landscapes', 325.
[14] Stadler and Dixon, 'Ecology and Evolution'; Chomicki et al., 'Tradeoffs in the Evolution'.

Third, as human niches expanded in a long hit-or-miss pattern, it was not just individual organisms but also entire landscapes that became geared towards human subsistence, and hence domesticated. Examples are crop cultivation on permanent fields, or the clearing of the tropical forest for grazing grounds, terraces or orchards. Such domesticated landscapes are thought often to have offered subsistence for larger populations of humans.

And fourth, some organisms proved to be more capable, or willing, than others to interact with humans and to respond to human attempts at managing and changing them. Many species were unresponsive, or they benefited only from human niche creation by invading domesticated spaces. Humans would see them as pests, parasites and weeds.[15] Human–non-human interactions covered the entire range from mutualism to indifference to avoidance.

Exploiting plants

The rich biodiversity of the region meant that humans were surrounded by an abundance of plant species that they could exploit for their roots, fruits, stems, flowers, leaves, wood and so on. Early humans must have had vast knowledge of plant life and may have experimented with ways to harvest them more efficiently. It is impossible to survey the entire process of how humans began to manipulate plants in this region effectively, and much is still uncertain. Here we focus on just two relatively well-studied examples. Both are grasses and both became vitally important to human subsistence in the region, but in very different ways. They are rice and bamboo.

Rice

Various types of wild rice occur naturally in the region.[16] It is unclear when humans here switched from collecting rice seeds for consumption to planting and cultivating rice plants. Currently, the earliest dated discoveries of (charred) rice are from Nagaland (over 2,000 years ago[17]) and the Yunnan–Myanmar borderland (3,400 years ago[18]). But cultivation is not the same as domestication – this rice is 'wild' in the sense that it has not yet developed 'domesticated' characteristics, notably genetic

---

[15] Fuller and Stevens, 'Open for Competition'.

[16] Choudhury, Khan and Dayanandan, 'Genetic Structure and Diversity'.

[17] Pokharia et al., 'Late First Millennium BC to Second Millennium AD'. For information on early rice cultivation in the wider surroundings, see Fuller et al., 'The Contribution of Rice Agriculture and Livestock Pastoralism'; Kingwell-Banham, 'Early Rice Agriculture in South Asia', 42–6.

[18] Notably in Shifodong and Haimenkou. d'Alpoim Guedes and Butler, 'Modeling Constraints on the Spread of Agriculture', 30, 33; He et al., 'Prehistoric Evolution'.

modifications leading to a very reduced shattering of seeds. Some speculate that such non-shattering rice was present in the Triangle by 1200 BCE (although there is evidence for domesticated rice cultivation just east of the Triangle around 2500 BCE).[19] But it did not entirely replace the older forms. In the Brahmaputra valley, 'rice was long cultivated before it was domesticated through selective breeding by humans, and grain shattering cultivars [varieties] are still cultivated to this day'.[20]

The history of rice domestication has been hotly disputed, but today there is a growing consensus that rice was domesticated independently at least three times, in different regions of Asia, creating three major rice varieties, known as (*Oryza sativa*) *indica*, *japonica* and *aus* (or *ahu*[21]).[22] According to some plant biologists, 'the gene center [of *Oryza sativa*] is the area including Assam in India, northern Myanmar, northern Thailand, Laos, and Yunnan'.[23] It has been suggested that humans first domesticated *indica* in the lands below the eastern Himalayas and *aus* in the hills surrounding the Brahmaputra River basin.[24]

Much is still uncertain about the early cultivation of rice, but what is clear is that for millennia the inhabitants were not particularly interested in it. Even though rice cultivation had been developed and practised in surrounding regions (including Southeast Asia, India and China) for thousands of years, human lifestyles in the lush Triangle environment happily stuck to hunting, foraging and fishing. Early communities dependent on foraging have been described as affluent and prosperous, and they could be highly mobile or relatively sedentary.[25] The conventional conviction that the transition to agriculture marked the

---

[19] Silva et al., 'A Tale of Two Rice Varieties'; Dal Martello et al., 'Early Agriculture at the Crossroads of China and Southeast Asia'.

[20] Van Driem, 'Domestications and the Domesticators', 185; see also 193.

[21] Van Driem proposes to use the Assamese word *ahu* instead of *aus*, because 'the Bengali name *āus̄* ... has the tendency to get unrecognisably transmogrified in the mouths of English speakers'. Van Driem, 'Domestications and the Domesticators', 184. See also Saikia, *The Unquiet River*, 48–50.

[22] Londo et al., 'Phylogeography of Asian Wild Rice'; Van Driem, 'Domestications and the Domesticators'. See also Choi et al., 'The Rice Paradox'. For a critique, see Van Driem, 'Domestications and the Domesticators', 190–5. Rahman et al. report domesticated *japonica* rice for central Bangladesh in the first millennium BCE and therefore suggest 'the diffusion of rice into Bangladesh from the east before the fourth century BC'. Rahman et al., 'Agricultural Systems in Bangladesh', 10.

[23] Okoshi et al., 'Genetic Diversity of Cultivated Rice', 724. See also Chang, 'Rice', 137.

[24] Van Driem, 'Domestications and the Domesticators', 185: Civáň et al., 'Origin of the Aromatic Group', 841. Others suggest Odisha and other locations in eastern India. Ray and Ray, 'The Birth of Aus Agriculture'.

[25] Hung, 'Prosperity and Complexity Without Farming'; Cobo, Fort and Isern, 'The Spread of Domesticated Rice'.

beginning of sedentary life, food security and vastly improved human living conditions is now widely questioned. There are many indications that mobile groups that derived their food from foraging, hunting, fishing or pastoralism ate better, were healthier and had more leisure time. The challenge is to explain why certain groups of early foragers in the ecologically rich setting of the Triangle chose to abandon their 'affluent' lifestyle at all to undertake the arduous work of agriculture – and why others decided against it.[26]

By Asian standards, rice cultivation appears to have developed late here.[27] But once people began to grow it systematically, it turned out to be a highly successful crop that became an essential staple for many groups and formed the basis of agricultural systems throughout the region since well before the beginning of the Common Era. Other staple crops included tubers (yam, taro, sago), millets and barley.[28]

Over time, the geography of rice became highly complex. As humans came to depend more and more on rice cultivation and derived most of their sustenance from it (this is when we can speak of 'agriculture'), they developed thousands of rice varieties (cultivars), carefully adapted to different seasons, soil conditions, intensity of rainfall, resistance to disease, taste preferences and so on. These varieties also diverged for the three main styles of cultivation: irrigated rice on rain-fed fields, shifting cultivation (also known as swidden, or slash-and-burn) and terrace cultivation in mountain regions. Currently, attempts are being made to protect this unique agrarian legacy, now under threat, by means of seed store banks.

Rice cultivars travelled across the region and diverse groups of cultivators preferred different strains. As a result, a regional differentiation in rice can be observed. The three original forms of cultivated rice (*indica*, *aus* and *japonica*) are all present in the Triangle today, often admixed, but with a distinct geographical preponderance of *aus* in Assam, Mizoram and the Chittagong Hill Tracts, *indica* in Manipur and adjacent areas in northwestern Myanmar, and *japonica* in Nagaland and Arunachal Pradesh.[29] In the floodplains all three types are well represented.[30]

---

[26] Scott, *Against the Grain*.

[27] The Triangle stands out as a major region of late adoption on the map in Fuller, Castillo and Murphy, 'How Rice Failed to Unify Asia', 713.

[28] Blench and Post, 'Rethinking Sino-Tibetan Phylogeny', 79–81; Pokharia et al., 'Late First Millennium BC to Second Millennium AD'. See also Taylor, 'Crop Distributions'.

[29] Chakraborty and Ray, 'Population Genetics Analyses'; Travis et al., 'Assessing the Genetic Diversity'; Wunna et al., 'Genetic Variation of Rice'.

[30] Rahman et al. suggest that rice cultivation first spread from Southeast Asia to the Bengal delta: archaeological finds show a preponderance of *japonica*. In recent times, however, *indica* and *aus* became dominant rice varieties in the delta. Rahman et al., 'Agricultural Systems in Bangladesh'.

Bamboo

Another plant that humans began to exploit was bamboo – a general term for over 100 different species of giant grass that grew abundantly across the region (Plate 3.3).[31] Bamboo makes an interesting contrast with rice because it resisted domestication and therefore it did not become a nucleus of agricultural production. Although it is possible to cultivate bamboo, for most of its association with humans it remained a forest product. In this way it stands for a large range of forest resources that sustained humans in this region from the earliest times – as they still do in many parts today.

Bamboo was an organism that early humans could exploit in many ways. It comes in many forms. Some species are long, thin and flexible, and others are sturdy, thick and durable. Their uses are manifold. It is likely that stone tools allowed early humans to fashion bamboo implements of various kinds.[32] Bamboo could be turned into offensive weapons for hunting or warfare – truncheons, javelins, knives, bows and arrows – or into fishing rods, looms and rafts.

Plate 3.3 Some varieties of bamboo

Source: Photo by Willem van Schendel.

---

[31] Banik, *Silviculture of South Asian Priority Bamboos*.
[32] Hazarika, 'Lithic Industries with Palaeolithic Elements', 55. See also Bar-Yosef et al., 'Were Bamboo Tools Made in Prehistoric Southeast Asia?'.

Split and cut in strips, bamboo could become a basket, mat, fence, razor-sharp stake (known as *panji*[33]) and a shelter – but also an elaborate animal trap, bird cage, rain hat, storage box, strainer, cordage and many other woven things. Hollow segments of bamboo stem could serve as food or water containers, cooking vessels, quivers or flutes. Bamboo could fuel a cooking fire. A burnt segment of bamboo could be used to predict the future.[34] And last but not least, bamboo shoots provided easily accessible food. It is no surprise that bamboo became crucially important in human survival and well-being, and that the region's cultures came to depend on it. The stunning versatility of bamboo may be why metal technology developed rather late here, even though Triangle populations were in contact with surrounding areas that used metal from much earlier times.

Bamboo was one of many botanic resources that the biodiverse rainforest environment provided. These ranged from fibres (cotton, rattan and lianas) to edibles (fruits, legumes, leafy vegetables, tubers and roots), dyes, poisons and medicines. Early inhabitants of the region depended for their survival on their enormous store of knowledge about the vegetal world around them. They foraged many plants and over time selected a number for cultivation.[35] Research into early associations between mobile humans and plants in the Triangle is still rare, but fragmentary evidence about surrounding regions suggests that plants have long been interchanged and taken to new destinations.[36] Both mango and citrus may have originated in the Triangle. Humans spread them and, in this way, they reached southern India by 1300 BCE.[37]

Exploiting animals

As humans developed their ecological engineering skills and expanded their environmental niche, they inevitably influenced the niches of other organisms. Their interactions with many different animal species changed in ways that would prove critical. Some animals were attracted to the new opportunities offered by human habitations. Clustered human bodies were great for mosquitoes, lice and flies. Human crops and food enticed rodents, jungle fowl and other birds, and these in turn attracted animals that preyed on them.

---

[33] Stewart, 'Notes on Northern Cachar', 645–6.
[34] Terwiel, *The Tai of Assam and Ancient Tai Ritual*, 99.
[35] Pokharia et al., 'Late First Millennium BC to Second Millennium AD'.
[36] Fuller and Harvey, 'The Archaeobotany of Indian Pulses'; Rahman et al., 'Wari-Bateshwar and Vikrampura'.
[37] Fuller et al., 'Across the Indian Ocean', 548–9.

Some of these animals adapted their behaviour to increase their advantage, gradually moving closer to humans and becoming integrated into human societies. Thus, dogs may have evolved out of wolves that followed hunting humans.[38] But increasing human–animal intimacy may also have grown out of human action. This could have happened accidentally, from a desire to manage overhunted prey animals, such as wild boars, water buffaloes and gaurs. But later it could also have been deliberate, with the intention to use animals in human pursuits, for example by taming elephants.[39] Irreversible domestication began with selective breeding and physical modification.

All along, human niche construction depended on the utilisation of wild animals. Hunters may have thought about their relationship with these animals in terms of reciprocity – wild animals being guided by forest spirits to 'give themselves' to the hunter.[40] The earliest known sites have yielded the remains of freshwater snails, serows (goatlike mammals), bats, rodents, crabs, porcupines, fish, birds, monkeys, wild boars, muntjac deer and so on.[41] These findings suggest that people gathered, trapped and hunted forest animals, and caught fish. They may also have collected animal products such as honey or eggs, as well as many other animal species such as insects and reptiles that have left no archaeological trace.

It was not until humans in this region settled down to cultivate crops that domestic variants of wild animals slowly came about and began to co-evolve with humans. Selective breeding for docility changed some red jungle fowl into chickens and wild boars into household pigs. Some water buffaloes became domesticated, and tame yaks grew out of wild forebears. Today, wild and domesticated varieties of chickens, pigs, water buffaloes, elephants and yaks still live in close proximity – and sometimes wild and domesticated individuals interbreed.[42] Humans began to

---

[38] Larson and Fuller, 'The Evolution of Animal Domestication'. The Triangle also was (and still is) home to wild dogs (dhole). For a description of three different types of wild dog, see Barbe, 'Some Account of the Hill Tribes', 387.

[39] Zeder describes these three pathways of prehistoric domestication as commensal, prey and directed. Zeder, 'The Domestication of Animals'.

[40] Several Triangle communities understood hunting in terms of reciprocity between female forest spirits and male hunters. If the spirits were sympathetic, they would direct game towards the hunters. Bareigts, *Les Lautu*, 140–3; Hmingthanzuali and Pande, 'Women's Indigenous Knowledge'; Myochit, *A Threatened Identity*, 67–8. Similarly, river spirits had to be placated before they would allow humans to take fishes from the river. Myochit, *A Threatened Identity*, 69. Ideas of animals 'giving themselves' have been described for many other hunter communities. Nadasdy, 'The Gift in the Animal'; Knight, 'The Anonymity of the Hunt'. See also Jalais, *Forest of Tigers*.

[41] Jamir, Tetso and Venuh, 'Recent Archaeological Investigation', 275.

[42] Hazarika, 'Understanding the Process', 210.

co-evolve with their domesticated animals and plants. They changed their behaviour and even some of their genetic makeup (Chapter 8).

However, many local animals could not be tamed or selectively bred to suit human needs. Goat-antelopes, muntjac deer, monkeys and many birds remained prey animals for human hunters. Humans could consider non-human hunters such as tigers, crocodiles, hyenas, jackals and rats as competitors for food, and they developed ways of dealing with these animals. For example, they could imagine these non-humans to be kinfolk; they could respectfully avoid them; or they could chase them away or kill them. A special case of domestication is provided by the mithun.

The mithun

One of the most unusual results of human–animal interaction – and unique to the Triangle – is *Bos frontalis*. This very large bovine, a distant relative of domesticated cattle, is known by many names across the region, with mithun or gayal most commonly used in English texts.[43] Its origins are disputed. Currently, most evidence points to it being a semi-domesticated form of the gaur (*Bos gaurus*), a massive wild bovine that is still found across South and Southeast Asia (Plate 3.4).[44] But there is also evidence to suggest that gaur and mithun are independent (sub)species that share an extinct common wild ancestor.[45] If so, contemporary mithuns may not be a product of domestication – selective breeding by humans. Instead, they could be seen as a species that entered the human niche of their own accord and co-evolved with humans for millennia.

Unlike gaurs, mithuns exist only in the Triangle (Plates 3.5 and 6.19; see also Map 8.2). Linguistic evidence suggests that early inhabitants saw them as a prototypical animal.[46] Mithuns developed a truly remarkable relationship with humans, quite unlike that of other domestic animals. They are free-ranging, take care of their own food and occasionally wander into human habitations. They are neither used as draught or plough animals nor kept for their milk. Their role in human societies has been largely ceremonial, to be bartered for goods or brides, or sacrificed (and consumed) during ritual occasions (Chapter 8).[47]

---

[43] For an early use of 'mithun', see Wilcox, 'Memoir of a Survey of Assam', 371, 374.
[44] Ahrestani, '*Bos frontalis* and *Bos gaurus*', 14; Prabhu et al., 'Complete Mitochondrial Genome of Indian Mithun'. For an early account, see Colebrooke, 'Description of a Species of Ox, named Gayál'.
[45] Baig et al., 'Mitochondrial DNA Diversity'.
[46] Blench, 'The Contribution of Linguistics', 103–4.
[47] For an overview, see Simoons and Simoons, *A Ceremonial Ox of India*.

Plate 3.4 A gaur (*Bos gaurus*)

Source: Photo by Willem van Schendel.

Plate 3.5 A free-ranging mithun (*Bos frontalis*)

Source: Photo by Willem van Schendel.

Long-distance connections

Early humans changed the environment in other ways as well. They were mobile and established contacts with other groups, sometimes far away. In this way ideas, goods and both human and non-human genetic material travelled over long distances. Technologies of toolmaking spread across the Triangle and beyond, domesticated rice travelled to new locations and humans carried certain species of bamboo across the region.[48] Some of these contacts developed into forms of exchange and trade. An example is the trade in semi-precious stone beads, which currently can be traced back to about 1000 BCE (Chapter 9). These and other goods followed various routes which criss-crossed the region and connected Yunnan, Myanmar, Assam and Bengal.[49] They were the forerunners of a dense web of trade routes that would develop in the centuries to come.

Long-term human history

We have seen that humans entered the region as an invasive species at least 40,000 years ago. They were successful in establishing a toehold in this complex biodiverse environment and very gradually began to have a stronger impact on it. Their ability to advance technologically was key. Tools made of stone and other materials, combined with sophisticated social skills, enabled them to innovate to the point that they began to manage other organisms which responded to their presence. Viewed on a world scale, cultivation of crops developed relatively late here, but by 1000 BCE rice had been domesticated and other crops were grown as well. This novel manipulation of the environment led to new interactions with various animal species, resulting in several of them also being domesticated. Agriculture and livestock management continued to coexist with food gathering, hunting and fishing. The Triangle had entered an uncharted trajectory in which humans increasingly occupied and altered space, and in which new relationships with animals and plants altered humans themselves.

---

[48] Banik, *Silviculture of South Asian Priority Bamboos*, 130.
[49] For maps of possible early trade routes, see Jamir and Vasa, 'Archaeological Evidence of Beads'. See also Jahan, 'Archaeology of Wari-Bateshwar', 140–1; and Moore, 'Carnelian in Myanmar'; Dussubieux and Pryce, 'Myanmar's Role in Iron Age', 609–10; Daniels, 'Nanzhao as a Southeast Asian Kingdom'; Bhattacharya, 'Old Routes, New Dreams'.

4

Livelihoods

Humans could increase their ecological footprint by domesticating the plants and animals that they found useful. They learned how to change these organisms by means of selective breeding – an early and effective form of genetic engineering. In this way, humans created new environmental niches for themselves that came to be known as agriculture and animal husbandry.

As human environmental manipulation in the Triangle reached a higher level, it began to take on many new characteristics. Older subsistence strategies based on hunting and gathering food strongly persisted, as did the mobile groups of people that typified this lifestyle. But they were now joined by groups that settled more permanently to practise specific forms of agriculture and animal husbandry. These forms largely depended on the terrain, much of which was mountainous, and the generous monsoon climate. Three broad types of Triangle livelihood began to take shape – and they survive today.

High-altitude life: Transhumance

The northern reaches of the Triangle include some of the highest elevations on earth. Here humans faced many problems of survival. In the high valleys on the southern face of the Himalayas, glaciers meet the wet South Asian monsoon, however, and here permanent human habitation was possible from at least 2500 BCE.[1] Thanks to greater control of animals and plants, a specific lifestyle took shape.

This lifestyle depended on the domestication of two high-altitude species: a bovine and a grass. Once humans were able to control and exploit the yak and barley, they knew how to survive just below the glaciers. The yak is a wild bovine that is perfectly suited to high altitudes. Current evidence suggests that yaks were first domesticated around 5000 BCE.[2] Today fragmented populations of wild

---

[1] Meyer et al., 'Holocene Glacier Fluctuations and Migration'.
[2] Qiu et al., 'Yak Whole-genome Resequencing'.

Livelihoods 53

yaks can still be found on the Tibetan Plateau but not on the eastern Himalayas.[3] Here yaks were domesticates that became essential to human survival (Plate 4.1).

It is thought that the first settlers of these alpine valleys came from the Tibetan Plateau and used fire to clear some of the natural vegetation of rhododendrons and junipers. They used the land to graze yaks (and possibly sheep) and to grow barley during the summer months. The ecological impact of grazing was distinct: some plants species were marginalised, and others flourished. Far from being a system 'in harmony with nature', signs of overgrazing were already noticeable thousands of years ago.[4] The importance of yaks revolved around their multiple usefulness. They provided dried dung for fuel, milk and meat for food, and hair and leather for clothing and shelter. They may also have been used as beasts of burden and as draught animals.

Barley is not a local plant but a non-native species introduced by humans. It may have reached these valleys from the northeast (via Tibet) or from the west (via sub-Himalayan India and Nepal). Indeed, the Triangle may have acted as a

Plate 4.1 Female yak with calf
Source: Photo by Willem van Schendel.

---

[3] Leslie and Schaller, '*Bos grunniens* and *Bos mutus* (Artiodactyla: Bovidae)'.
[4] Meyer et al., 'Holocene Glacier Fluctuations and Migration', 1229–30.

passage for barley from the west moving east into China.[5] Barley, with its short growing season and high tolerance for low temperatures, was well suited to cultivation in the harsh conditions of the high Himalayan valleys.

Barley and yaks allowed humans to co-create an entirely new niche for themselves – an economic system that combined pastoralism and agriculture, and probably also included foraging, fishing, hunting and trade. It is likely that the yaks moved to higher pastures in summer and returned to lower pastures in winter. This vertical livelihood practice is known as transhumance, or 'transhumant agro-pastoralism'. Later, sheep, goats and cows became part of the system. These would also move between winter and summer pastures, but at lower altitudes than the yaks. An important aspect was exchange with people living at lower altitudes. Pastoralists would barter yak products (milk, cheese, butter, dried meat) for agricultural produce and other essentials.

All along the northern rim of the Triangle, this livelihood turned out to be remarkably dependable over centuries. Even though it has declined in recent decades, it still survives in northwestern Arunachal Pradesh (India) and northern Bhutan.[6] Some contemporary pastoralists do not engage in agriculture at all and depend entirely on their yak herds, grasslands and – below the tree line – forests. They trade yak products as well as foraged items such as caterpillar fungus,[7] timber and herbal medicines, in exchange for various goods.[8]

Mountainside life: Shifting cultivation

The high alpine valleys covered only a small part of the Triangle. At lower altitudes, human manipulation of the environment took other forms. Here yaks could not survive and plenty of alternatives to barley were available. Early on, humans had learned that cutting down and burning forest vegetation produced ash to fertilise the soil. This knowledge led them to attempt to grow selected plants on these cleared patches of forest – the beginnings of agriculture.

---

[5] Liu et al., 'Journey to the East'; Lister et al., 'Barley Heads East'; Zeng et al., 'Origin and Evolution of Qingke Barley in Tibet'.

[6] Bora et al., 'Traditional Milk, Meat Processing and Preservation Techniques'; Namgay et al., 'Changes in Transhumant Agro-pastoralism'; Tshewang, Morrison and Tobias, *Bionomics in the Dragon Kingdom*; Moktan et al., 'Ecological and Social Aspects'.

[7] Foraged from alpine grasslands, caterpillar fungus (*Cordyceps sinensis*) currently fetches high prices. For its relationship with yak herding, see Wangchuk and Wangdi, 'Mountain Pastoralism in Transition'. See also Weckerle et al., 'People, Money, and Protected Areas'; Bawa and Kadur, *Himalaya*, 186–7.

[8] Mizuno and Tenpa, *Himalayan Nature*, 131–46; Mizuno, 'The Distribution and Management of Forests'; Singh et al., 'Paisang (*Quercus griffithii*)'.

Livelihoods

Across the region – lowlands, foothills and mountains – this practice, known as shifting (or slash-and-burn, or swidden) cultivation, began to flourish in many local variations.

Over time, in the lowlands and foothills, shifting cultivation would gradually be overtaken by other forms.[9] But it remained the dominant (and often only) form of cultivation on the steeper slopes (Plate 4.2), especially those with loose soil. Here shifting agriculture continued to be a very important form of human niche construction. The rugged landscape has given shifting cultivation its alternative name: mountain agriculture.

Where mountain agriculture was not very productive, its role remained marginal to hunting, fishing, foraging and animal husbandry. But in many places, it became productive enough to provide considerable sustenance. This type of agriculture did not tend towards monoculture; each field yielded a combination of crops that matured at different times, for example (sticky) rice, millet, taro,

Plate 4.2 Shifting cultivation in the Indo-Burma Arc
Source: Photo by Willem van Schendel.

---

[9] Low-lying, flood-prone land in Assam could be under shifting cultivation until the early twentieth century. For a description from the 1840s, see [Butler], *Sketch of Assam*, 22–3.

cotton, sesame, mustard, squash, ginger, opium,[10] forest bitter-berry, Ethiopian eggplant,[11] indigo and beans.[12] The interesting thing about this form of cultivation, from an environmental point of view, was that it included long periods in which humans willingly relinquished the niche that they had painstakingly created, giving other organisms an opportunity to flourish.[13] The main characteristic of this livelihood was its mobility – hence the name 'shifting cultivation'. After a few seasons, soil fertility would decline, so it made sense to clear a new field somewhere else. The old field would be left fallow for years, after which it might be reused. In this way the sparsely populated mountainsides became patchworks of primary rainforest, abandoned fields, secondary forest, newly cleared fields and human settlements. Settlements could move to a new location once they had exhausted the agricultural and forest resources in their immediate vicinity. This also enabled them to move for other reasons, for example, to escape more powerful groups or look for better hunting and foraging grounds. In other words, rather than constructing a permanent ecological niche for themselves, humans engaging in shifting cultivation followed a different strategy: intermittent niche construction.

Shifting cultivation depends on human labour and collaboration – no draught animals are used. As a result, settlements became tightly knit social units in which family groups would exchange labour, and work in teams, at certain periods in the agricultural cycle. The ecological conditions that allowed for shifting cultivation, and the semi-sedentary lifestyle that comes with it, shaped the development of specific social and cultural forms among these groups.

Valley life: Fixed-field cultivation

In flat areas such as river valleys, floodplains and level spots between mountains, shifting cultivation could be practised, but over time it was largely overtaken by a new form of agriculture on fixed fields. This form of cultivation required much more labour but also provided higher outputs. It needed, and could sustain, far higher concentrations of humans.

---

[10] Chouvy, 'Illegal Opium Production in the Mishmi Hills'; Kour, *A History of Intoxication*. See also Mills, 'The Mishmis of the Lohit Valley, Assam', 4, 11.

[11] Forest bitter-berry (*Solanum anguivi*) and Ethiopian eggplant (or bitter tomato; *Solanum aethiopicum*) are popular in the region. They are both thought to have originated in Africa.

[12] The number of crops in a single plot could be very high. For example, Domon et al. ('A Field Study Collecting Cultivated Crops', 347) noted 'sorghum, Job's tears, perilla, finger millet, pumpkin, lablab bean, rice bean, soybean, a tall chenopod ..., cassava, maize, yam ..., tomato, chili pepper, roselle, bitter gourd, cowpea, sponge gourd, taro, holy basil ..., *Elsholtzia blanda* ..., mustard, banana and ginger ... in addition to the staple crop, rice'.

[13] Delang and Li, *Ecological Succession on Fallowed Shifting Cultivation Fields*.

Livelihoods 57

For this form of cultivation, niche construction had to be more elaborate. It required landscaping on a much grander scale. On slopes in the foothills this could take the form of terracing – creating narrow strips of level land separated by stone dividers so that people could plant crops there (Plate 4.3). Terraces required much labour to create and maintain, and, in the Triangle, this was not possible on all slopes. Where slopes were very steep and the soil was loose, as in the Chittagong and Mizo Hills, the landscape was prone to erosion and frequent landslides. Here terracing was not possible and shifting cultivation remained the predominant form of cultivation.

On level land, fixed-field cultivation came into its own. The monsoon climate made it possible to grow different crops in different seasons. Most were rain fed but during the dry season (October–May) irrigation from the many rivers, streams and lakes could help. The abundance of monsoon rain was especially beneficial to rice, originally a swamp plant. About 2,000 years ago, humans began to create artificial swamp conditions by building field bunds to retain rainwater and puddling the soil. They also learned to raise rice seedlings in separate seedbeds and transplant them in the puddled fields. Simple irrigation techniques (channels, scoops, swing baskets and bamboo conduits) supplied additional water whenever it was needed – and such techniques survive today (Plate 4.4).

Plate 4.3 A terraced field in Arunachal Pradesh (India)
Source: Photo by Willem van Schendel.

Plate 4.4 Using a traditional wooden scoop to irrigate a rice field in Bangladesh
Source: Photo by Willem van Schendel.

Some wet rice fields have been cultivated for thousands of years, a feat that was made possible by both human and non-human labour. Ploughing the field before it was inundated was essential and this required draught animals. As a result, human niche construction based on fixed-field cultivation came with the introduction of bullocks and water buffaloes. Wild water buffaloes were indigenous to the Triangle and could be domesticated, and early on domesticated cattle were imported, probably from the west.

Wet-rice cultivation was the most intrusive form of human landscaping in the Triangle. It damaged the forest cover and created a niche in which only a few other organisms – frogs, fish, snakes, mosquitoes – could thrive. As human populations expanded, especially since the nineteenth century, this assertive form of human environmental manipulation came to destroy large swathes of lowland forest. In these highly engineered, human-dominated landscapes, rice fields supplanted numerous species of plants, mammals, birds, invertebrates and insects (Plate 4.5).[14]

---

[14] An illustration of the destruction of the lowland rainforest is provided by the remains of wild buffalo, tiger, elephant and gaur that have been collected from areas now completely dominated by irrigated rice agriculture. Hoque, 'Faunal Remains from the Peats'.

Livelihoods

Plate 4.5 A human-controlled landscape: wet-rice fields stretching to the horizon in Bangladesh
Source: Photo by Willem van Schendel.

These new livelihoods – transhumance, shifting cultivation and fixed-field cultivation – led to permanent differences in the pressure that humans put on the Triangle environment. The first (yak-barley) and the second (rice-millet) sustained relatively small populations. The third (cattle-rice) could provide sustenance for large populations. Thus, the river valleys and floodplains were able to feed larger populations than the foothills and mountains, but even they remained sparsely populated for a long time. Many river valleys were narrow, possibly making expansion of fixed-field agriculture cumbersome, and metal implements (such as metal-shod ploughs) arrived relatively late. In any case, it was not until the late nineteenth century that deforestation became rampant in the plains, and serious deforestation in the hills took off considerably later. Only very few patches can now be said to have 'experienced low human impact'.[15] Today population densities vary from below 20 per square kilometre in mountainous Arunachal Pradesh and Chin State (and considerably higher ones in other parts of the uplands) to over 1,200 per square kilometre in the largely denuded deltaic lowlands of eastern Bengal.

---

[15] Suarez-Rubio et al., 'Hkakabo Razi Landscape', 10. See also Faxon, 'After the Rice Frontier'.

As the three forms of agriculture spread across the region, they continued to coexist with hunting and foraging. It is often assumed that agriculture was technologically more advanced and more productive and that people were attracted to the higher standards of living it provided. This narrative of inexorable progress is now weakened by growing evidence to show that hunting and gathering provide better diets and health, and less back-breaking toil.[16] This raises the question of why populations shifted to these new livelihoods. Some suggest that growing numbers of mouths to feed prompted them to experiment with domestication and agriculture, which in turn led them down a one-way street of social differentiation, inequality and a sedentary lifestyle that allowed emerging state elites to 'capture' and exploit them. Whether this is what happened in the Triangle is unknown, but we do know that here a remarkable array of groups continued to depend wholly or largely on hunting and gathering. They lived in contact with agricultural groups and regularly traded foraged produce with them.

---

[16] See Cohen, 'History, Diet, and Hunter-Gatherers', 69:

> Small, mobile human groups living on wild foods enjoy relatively well-balanced diets and relatively good health ... [and] per capita intake of calories and of protein has declined rather than increased in human history for all but the privileged classes. The predominant direction of prehistoric and historic change in human stature has been a decline in size despite the 'secular trend' among some Western populations of the last century. Prehistoric remains of more sedentary and larger groups commonly display an increase in general infection and in specific diseases ... [and] signs of malnutrition.

Part II
Cosmologies

5

Stories of Human Origins

In Part I of this book, we outlined the geological history of the Triangle and the ways in which humans settled and survived in this complex environment. In this part of the book (covering Chapters 5–7) we turn to how they experienced their lifeworlds and gave meaning to them. They did so in various ways – actually, in so many ways that we must be very selective.

In cultural terms, this part will focus on the Triangle uplands, mainly because upland cultures help us comprehend the history of local world views best. These cultures were relatively lightly touched by external cosmologies that spread early in the lowlands of Assam, Bengal and Myanmar – and had a strong cultural influence there. Today we know these as Hinduism, Buddhism and Islam. Certainly, these traditions had their impact in the uplands as well (just as pre-existing cosmologies in the lowlands deeply influenced local forms of Hinduism, Buddhism and Islam); but this impact was minor and late, except in some localities.

Consequently, specific 'Triangle world views' persisted and were recorded in much more detail than those of the lowlands. This is not to say that these views did not change dramatically during the past century or so. First, colonial-era Christian missionary activity was intense in the uplands, and many inhabitants came to identify as Christians. They adopted the world view of that faith but inflected it strongly with their local beliefs, creating upland versions of Christianity. Second, new forms of education, rapidly rising literacy and improving infrastructure exposed them to many new ideas. Even so, the contours of the old world views have not been completely erased, and some are making a partial comeback (Chapter 8).

Triangle stories as historical sources

In this part of the book, we are concerned with how Triangle cultures thought of the place of humans and non-humans in the world. We explore how people in the region have understood their own histories, how they organised their narratives about the past and specifically how these narratives expressed a sense of the shared experience of all living creatures. This chapter explores ideas of human origins. The following chapters (6 and 7) deal with ideas about human–animal and human–plant histories, respectively.

What historical source material do we have to work with? As we explained in the Introduction, scholars working with non-European sources have long argued that they come across a range of ideas about time that are unknown in European texts and that these should be taken seriously to make historical theory globally inclusive.[1] They argue that time always is a human construct and that different groups have employed different 'temporalities' to think with. It can be misleading to suppose that we all inhabit a single time or that the assumptions underlying chronometric time are universally shared.[2] For many people, past and present, chronometric time was, and is, just one dimension of a more complex universe of time.

This is what we find in the Triangle, where the rhythms of human–non-human interactions were woven into cosmologies that pointed to multiple, non-chronometric understandings of time. These did not exclude each other but were intertwined, varied from place to place and were constantly reworked. Until very recently, these temporalities were transmitted by word of mouth.[3] Oral traditions were varied and rich, and it mattered how time was told, who told it and to what purpose.

Although these stories have often been dismissed as mere myths, we need to take them seriously for two reasons. First, they are full of references to past connections between humans, other animals, plants and the landscape, and, significantly, they have motivated, and still motivate, human behaviour towards other humans and non-humans. Second, these stories suggest some of the 'feel of life' in the Triangle during the very long stretch of time for which historical source material is scarce or completely lacking.[4] Although historical and archaeological research, and the use of 'proxy sources',[5] are whittling away at our ignorance about early times and non-literate societies, their reach is still very uneven. We need all the help we can get in deciphering the Triangle's past. Origin stories do throw some light on lived realities in the Triangle – how various communities perceived their relationships with non-humans.

---

[1] Sastrawan, 'Temporalities in Southeast Asian Historiography'.
[2] 'Viewpoints: Temporalities'.
[3] Singha, 'Wari Leeba'.
[4] Showren, 'Exploring Ethnohistory of Arunachal Pradesh'. See also Luce, *Phases of Pre-Pagán Burma*.
[5] Morrison, 'Conceiving Ecology'.

Triangle stories are historical sources that throw into sharp relief a core issue facing students of more-than-human history. When we talk about the entangled lives of humans and non-humans, how much agency do we attribute to each of these categories? Many Triangle stories present animals and plants as human-like actors who speak and behave like people and mingle with humans on an equal footing. This is clearly at odds with how most historians understand human–non-human relationships.

But such ideas do resonate with some scholarly debate in the social sciences. In this book we have chosen to speak of Triangle 'cosmologies', 'world views' and 'lifeworlds', rather than framing our analysis in terms of a currently popular theoretical concept, 'ontology'.[6] This notion – fiercely debated and variously applied in academic anthropology – is much less popular among historians and not well known among non-academic audiences. However, it emphasises an important point: the need to overcome the deep conceptual divide between nature and society. This divide is fundamental to most philosophical and scientific scholarship but not necessarily to other ways of being and acting in the world that reject a rigorous distinction between humans and non-humans. This is exactly the challenge that Triangle stories pose as sources for more-than-human history.

Therefore, this book can be read as a small contribution to a large experiment that we can sum up in a set of questions. First, how can we navigate between a conventional scholarly mindset that accepts only human agency and local source material that presents non-human agency as largely equivalent to human agency? And second, what are the limitations of more-than-human history? Can we ever push beyond our own human lifeworlds in our search to incorporate the lifeworlds of non-humans?

We approach these issues in a variety of ways. We are at pains to show that animals and plants have been agents in shaping human histories, but we do not ascribe intentions or human-level consciousness to them. On the contrary, in Chapter 2 we listed three advantages that set human consciousness apart from that of all other life forms: we humans have a genetic makeup that allows us to work together, share and connect by means of language; we advance technologically; and we transfer knowledge from one generation to the next, creating adaptable cultures.

This triple advantage has been crucial in shaping our entanglements with animals and plants, and it is the task of more-than-human history to explain how these entanglements have evolved over time. Cultural diversity plays a

---

[6] For some introductions to 'ontology', see Ingold (ed.), *What Is an Animal?*; Haraway, *When Species Meet*; Viveiros de Castro, *Cosmological Perspectivism*; Kohn, *How Forests Think*.

central role here: human groups create different ways of understanding their entanglements with animals and plants. In this book, we seek to show this by comparing various Triangle perceptions with each other as well as with scholarly narratives.

More-than-human history pushes the envelope and challenges human-centrism, but it is constrained by the complexity and variability of our own lifeworlds as well as by our current limited knowledge of – and limited capacity to identify with – non-human lifeworlds. As we develop the field, however, we will gradually be able to dismantle human-centrism further and tell stories in which humans, animals and plants play more equal parts. Throughout the book, our emphasis is on exploring this joint history of life forms and occasionally we venture further, making forays into how these life forms got entangled with inanimate entities such as water, mud and minerals.

Pushing the envelope implies searching for a language to express human–animal–plant entanglements in an open-ended way. We employ terms such as 'human–non-human', 'sentient beings' and 'non-human animals', without trying to theorise these as hierarchically fixed. Each of these terms helps us see certain aspects but none of them implies non-human intentionality.

Cultural variety

In this book we are keen to emphasise commonalities between humans as a species, but we must acknowledge that we humans show considerable intra-species diversity in our interpretation of the world and our place in it. The Triangle is an excellent site to explore this topic: it is a region of astonishing cultural variety. Hundreds of different languages are spoken here, and there are hundreds of distinct cultural communities.[7] Much of the best historical material is organised by community, so our sources usually refer to specific groups. In the following pages we mention over sixty communities. To help you locate them, Map 5.1 shows their approximate historical locations (but obviously not their geographical mobility over time). It is important to realise that this is just a small sample of the region's diverse cultures and that quite a few communities make no appearance at all.

Community names are contested. They change over time, there are differences between the names that community members and outsiders use, and the spelling varies.[8] Moreover, several names mentioned in Map 5.1 are umbrella terms that

---

[7] Post, 'Morphosyntactic Reconstruction'.
[8] For example, Adi/Abor, Aka/Hrusso, Bodo/Boro/Kachari, Garo/Mandi, Kacha/Kabui/Liangmei/Zeme, Kachin/Singpho/Jinghpaw, Mishmi/Taraon, Nyishi/Dafla, Pnar/Jaintia, Mara/Lakher, Mizo/Lushai and Mru/Mro.

Stories of Human Origins

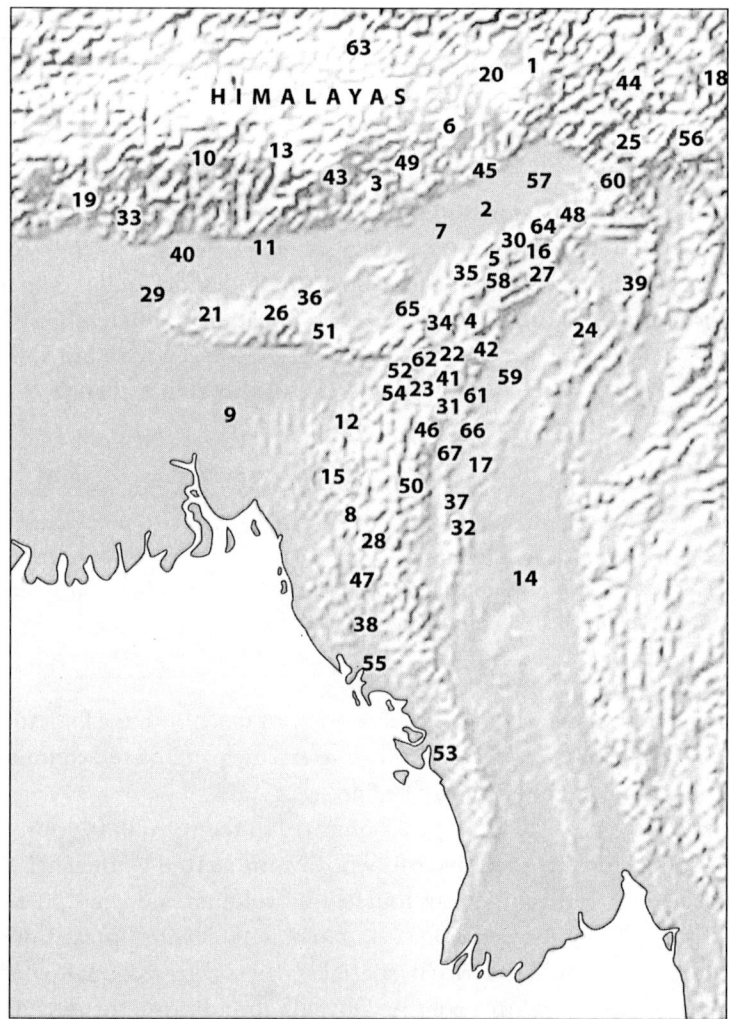

Map 5.1 Cultural groups mentioned in this book
Source: Authors.

Note: (1) Adi; (2) Ahom; (3) Aka; (4) Angami; (5) Ao; (6) Apatani; (7) Assamese; (8) Bawm-Zo; (9) Bengali; (10) Bhutanese; (11) Bodo; (12) Bongcher; (13) Brokpa; (14) Burmese; (15) Chakma; (16) Chang; (17) Chin; (18) Chinese; (19) Dhimal; (20) Galo; (21) Garo; (22) Inpui; (23) Kabui; (24) Kachin; (25) Khamti; (26) Khasi; (27) Khiam-niungan; (28) Khumi; (29) Koch; (30) Konyak; (31) Kuki; (32) Lautu; (33) Lepcha; (34) Liangmei; (35) Lotha; (36) Lyngam; (37) Mara; (38) Marma; (39) Maru; (40) Mech; (41) Meitei; (42) Meitei–Pangal; (43) Miji; (44) Mishmi; (45) Mising; (46) Mizo; (47) Mru; (48) Nocte; (49) Nyishi; (50) Pangkhua; (51) Pnar; (52) Poumai; (53) Rakhine; (54) Rengma; (55) Rohingya; (56) Singpho; (57) Sonowal Kachari; (58) Sümi; (59) Taman; (60) Tangsa; (61) Thadou; (62) Thangal; (63) Tibetan; (64) Wancho; (65) Zeme; (66) Zomi; (67) Zophei.

lump together many local identities (examples are Bhutanese, Chinese, Kachin, Kuki, Mizo), and we have broken down others (such as Naga, Arunachali) into some of their constituent identities.

Oral narratives

There is a rich variety of stories in the Triangle about how the world and human societies came about. People have certainly contemplated their 'deep history'. For any community, however, origin narratives are multi-layered and non-linear: they do not form a singular 'origin' text but are a compilation of different sets of stories that need not cohere. There are variations to each story, even within a particular community, but the main characters and events usually do not change.[9] As Verrier Elwin, an early field collector of these stories, explained:

> Stories, and the names of gods and heroes vary from place to place; the same informant may even pronounce a word, or use a name differently on two successive days. This is inevitable in a region where there is no fixed deposit of doctrine, no sacred books to carry traditions from one generation to another, and where the repositories of knowledge are human beings exposed to the inspirations of their dreams and fancies.[10]

In this chapter we present some of these stories, aware of both the limitations and the necessity to be very selective. The aim is to explore patterns and commonalities in how these stories describe human beginnings.

Stuart Blackburn provides a good example. In the year 2000, ethnographic fieldwork took him to the Apatani, who live in central Arunachal Pradesh (India), a region relatively lightly touched by colonial and even postcolonial interventions. This allowed him to work with 'living practitioners' of storytelling, who could be ritual specialists or professedly knowledgeable elders. The stories Blackburn collected give us an indication of the enormous range of themes that Apatani narratives deal with. These include the beginning of time, how and why things came to be, the relationship between animate and inanimate entities, the unseen world beyond the visible one and what happens at death.[11] As Blackburn observes, origin stories are important not only for what they tell us but also for how they can be used to draw linkages with communities beyond the region:

---

[9] For a detailed analysis, see Longkumer, *Reform, Identity and Narratives of Belonging*, 86–94.
[10] Elwin, *Myths of the North-East Frontier of India*, ix.
[11] Blackburn, *Himalayan Tribal Tales*.

Oral stories present a culture's reflection on itself, a commentary that has been abstracted from everyday life, passed down from generation to generation, and shaped according to local narrative conventions and taste ... as linguistic texts they may provide evidence of historical connections between cultures and the values they contain may suggest similarities between those cultures.[12]

Blackburn suggests that the many similarities in stories from the 'extended eastern Himalayas' make it possible to speak of a large 'culture area' (see also Chapter 8). In this culture area – which covers central Arunachal Pradesh, the Myanmar–India–Bangladesh borderlands and the uplands of mainland Southeast Asia and Southwest China – many communities share core ideas about the natural world.[13]

Oral narratives from the Triangle contain perceptions of time that differ markedly from the chronometric time of history-writing. A linear history of the region is impossible, just as it makes no sense to impose time periods on the entire region. For example, historians commonly invoke the 'colonial period' to structure their narratives but what does this mean? Colonial rule lasted some 200 years in the case of the Bengal delta but only a few years in the case of Arunachal Pradesh, parts of Nagaland, the southern Chin Hills and northernmost ('unadministered') Myanmar. For some areas, the 'colonial period' is a real misnomer because these did not experience colonialism at all. Yunnan and Bhutan were never colonised by Europeans, and other parts of the Triangle remained beyond state control until after the collapse of colonial rule.[14] As an article of the late 1940s put it:

> In the Himalayan tracts north of the Brah[m]aputra, administration has only been started since the end of the [Second World] War. Missions are banned from entry, and large tracts are still unexplored.[15]

---

[12] Blackburn, 'Oral Stories and Culture Areas', 420. See also Blackburn, *Himalayan Tribal Tales*, 213–49.

[13] Blackburn's careful delineation is much more helpful than that of early ethnographers, such as Hutton, who, recognising that similar stories existed in communities all over the world, drew bold parallels with stories from Africa, the Americas and other places. Hutton, 'Some Astronomical Beliefs in Assam', 113–31. See also Pau and Mung, 'Fragmented Tribes of the India–Burma–Bangladesh Borderlands'. Blench ('Ethnographic and Archaeological Correlates', 234) includes the Triangle in a proposed 'Mainland Southeast Asia' culture area that not only spans a linguistic convergence zone but also 'reflects a structural and psychological map of the many societies within the region'.

[14] Guyot-Réchard, 'Tour Diaries and Itinerant Government'; Guyot-Réchard, 'Tangled Lands'; Fürer-Haimendorf, 'The Morung System of the Konyak Nagas, Assam', 349; Lehman, *The Structure of Chin Society*, 40; Bezbaruah, 'Kami-Sabong Affairs, 1906–1916'; Means, 'Human Sacrifice and Slavery'.

[15] Stonor and Anderson, 'Maize among the Hill Peoples', 359. See also Young, 'A Journey from Yün-Nan'; Mills, 'The Mishmis of the Lohit Valley'; Blackburn, *The Sun Rises*, 43–8; Guyot-Réchard, 'Tour Diaries and Itinerant Government'.

Here the 'precolonial' period stretched into the mid-twentieth century; it is better described as the pre-state period. Consequently, across the Triangle, the inroads made by institutions of modernity and their impact on people's lifeworlds were extremely variable. As a result, for some communities today the old narratives are living entities, while for others they are either forgotten or a store of knowledge that comes to them through books and learning – ideas that are passed on, rather than lived by. Notwithstanding different levels of contemporary association and disassociation, these narratives do hold some sway over people's understandings of themselves, whatever the time distance may be.[16]

We are lucky that nineteenth- and twentieth-century British officials, missionaries and ethnographers – assisted by local interlocutors – recorded and translated many community stories of deep history in the Triangle. They usually categorised these stories as folklore – often to be discussed towards the end of their books, after dealing with topography and social organisation. Occasionally, the stories also appeared under the heading of religion. Colonial writings treated the region's stories as building blocks for the then budding Western discipline of folklore studies. At the same time, oral narratives were seen merely as quirks, showing the peculiarities of a particular community. Ethnographers were usually quite aware that recording these stories and 'reducing them to writing' homogenised them and sometimes forced upon them a continuity that perhaps was not recognised by the locals themselves. In addition, the Europeans who first translated these stories may have imposed their own cultural categories, or simply mistranslated some parts. Luckily, in several cases the text has also survived in the original language and many stories were recorded later, often by indigenous scholars.

The creation of the world

Origin stories are usually a combination of three strands.[17] The first explains the origins of the universe, celestial beings and the world. The second focuses on the origin of geomorphological features and nature as a whole: how the landscape, the traits of animals, the features of foliage and so on came to be. The third strand is concerned with the question of where we humans come from. It narrates the origins of a specific ethnic group, usually considered synonymous with the origins of humanity. Such stories often contain accounts of primeval migration and mobility.

---

[16] Pachuau, *Being Mizo*.

[17] Elwin provides many examples from Arunachal Pradesh. He distinguishes five traditions: the world arose from a primeval ocean, it was a macrocosm transformed from some great personage or tree, it was created by heavenly beings, it came from a cosmic egg or it was born of a universal mother. Elwin, *Myths of the North-East Frontier of India*, 3.

Stories of Human Origins

The deep history of a group usually starts with the 'beginning', the inception of the universe, the world. Some stories speak of a creator-deity. Among the Ao of Nagaland, this credit of crafting the world is given to Lachaba or Lizaba, although other deities are also acknowledged. After creation, Lachaba is said to have levelled the Assam plains, but when he came to the Naga Hills a water beetle – in some versions a cockroach – distracted him by shouting out that his enemies were going to attack him. This is why Lachaba left behind a jumble of hills in that region.[18]

Often, the creator of the universe was seen as a female force. The Kachin imagined an unnamed entity that was half-woman and half-bird. She brought forth two named spirits who produced lower spirits (*nat*s) as well as the birds, reptiles and wild animals. It was only later that the earth itself took shape, and another spirit shaped Kachinland with a hammer and a pair of tongs.[19]

Among the Mizo, it was Khuanu or Khuazingnu who created the earth.[20] Although not explicitly stated, the creator is considered to be female as the name carries the feminine suffix *nu*. Next to the creation of the material world, the most important explanation the Mizo required was for rainfall. According to local beliefs, the earth was green at the time of creation but became dry, so Khuanu had to open her windows to allow water to fall from the skies to relieve the parched earth.[21] However, the story continues, the earth was also full of stones, and soil had not yet formed. There was an 'ocean of excessive cold' (*tuihriam*) that had to be crossed to get to the mud that could be found there. After a conference of animals, it was the porcupine and the earthworm that came to the rescue. The porcupine was able to swim across because its quills helped it to withstand the cold and bring back a little mud. The earthworm ate some of this mud and defecated, thereby gradually increasing the amount. But the earth was still only a flat plain. A very tall tree – 'the tree-that-reached-the-skies' (*thingvantawng*) – was felled. As it landed on the earth, the undulations caused by its fall caused rivers, mountains and valleys to be formed.[22]

The Khasi of Meghalaya, too, believed in a creation story. The Supreme Being created Mother Earth, Ka Ramew, and her husband, U Basa. They had five children: Sun, Moon, Water, Wind and Fire. Only Moon is considered to be

---

[18] Mills, *The Ao Nagas*, 220; Smith, *The Ao Naga Tribe of Assam*, 79; Tzüdir, 'Appropriating the Ao Past in a Christian Present', 268. See also Myochit, *A Threatened Identity*, 32–3.

[19] Hanson, *The Kachins*, 109–12.

[20] Pachuau, 'Orality'; Zama, 'Origin Myths of the Mizo'. See also Pau, 'Rethinking Religious Conversion'.

[21] See also Duff-Sutherland-Dunbar, 'Abors and Galongs', 9.

[22] On the role of earthquakes in the creation of the world, see Hodson, *The Nāga Tribes of Manipur*, 127; Elwin, *Myths of the North-East Frontier of India*, 84–91.

male while the other children are all female.²³ Creation included the formation of 'great plains, vast forests and smooth rivers'. Afterwards, three of the goddesses – Fire, Water and Sun (Ka Ding, Ka Um and Ka Sngi) – came to earth to bury their mother. They each used their respective powers to do so. Sun, with her great heat, tried to destroy the body, but only ended up drying the rivers and withering the grass and forest leaves. Water then tried to accomplish the same task, but she only ended up flooding the land. Finally, Fire could accomplish the task of disposing of the remains of their mother as she caused a great fire, and the entire earth was in flames. The vast plains crumbled and changed their contours, and the mother was consumed. Fire thus left the earth with mountains, valleys and gorges.²⁴

The Ahom used animal and plant imagery to visualise the original deity and the creation of the world. The deity was 'suspended in the sky like a swarm of bees in a hive'. This deity created a spirit from whose navel the lotus sprouted and who created various animals. Among them were a pair of gold-tinted spiders who dropped their excrement, and this became the earth. The spiders then wove a web that rested on eight pillars, and this formed the heaven.²⁵

Unlike these ideas of creation, the Apatani and other Tani groups of Arunachal Pradesh did not believe in a creator-deity who formed the universe ex nihilo. Their idea was more closely related to a gradual evolution. Things came into being out of an inchoate mass (*kolyung-kolo* or *kami-komo*). Different forms developed through the powers of a force of non-descript gender (Pinii or Kolyung Pinii or Pinii Siyo). Not much is said about this stage, but the materialisation of the world is attributed to a female spirit, identified as Mother (Anii). Later she gave birth to Earth-Sky who, in turn, gave birth to the natural world. Therefore, the world emerged from a 'pro-creative, female body or earth'.²⁶ But this was not the end of the story. Once Earth-Sky was formed, she was continually infested with evil spirits that plagued her with diseases. A priest then had to be born to make sacrifices to the spirits to free the earth. Sacrifices of pig, dog, chicken, bamboo, thread, bamboo shaving and bitter leaves eventually rid the earth of these evil spirits. From different parts of Niikun (a primeval female force) then sprang nests for birds, the bottom of the sea, the lakes, the horizon, the roof of the world, the rocks and the mountains, forests, weeds and grass. From other spirits came celestial bodies such as the sun,

---

[23] Kharkongor, 'Khasi Myths and Matriliny'.
[24] Rafy, *Folk-Tales of the Khasis*, 24–5.
[25] Barua (ed.), *Ahom-Buranji*, 1–2. For a different reading of this Ahom text, see Terwiel, 'Myths Associated with Belief'.
[26] Blackburn, *Himalayan Tribal Tales*, 108.

moon and stars, and yet another spirit brought plants and vegetables to earth. Finally, Earth-Sky gave birth to the first human, Abo Tani (or Aabhu Thanyi[27]), and other humans.[28]

The beginning of the world forms an important aspect of most oral traditions. We have mentioned only a few, but these offer some insights into how some Triangle societies tried to grapple with the idea. Communities felt the need to explain the natural geography that they saw around them and how it may have been created. Animals, trees and spirits all played an active role in these stories. For most mountain communities, in particular, the contrast between the plains and the terrain that they inhabited had to be explained.

Natural phenomena

Origin stories also provide explanations for the occurrence of natural phenomena. The solar eclipse is a favourite. The Khasi understood that an eclipse was caused by the giant toad U Hynroh, a great magician, attacking the sun. The sun had given refuge to a beautiful girl named Ka Nam who had run away from the clutches of the giant toad. This celestial battle threatened the sun but was won with the help of humans whose loud drumbeats and shouts made U Hynroh retreat.[29] Another familiar story about the solar eclipse was that an animal ate the sun – a tiger in the case of the Ao and Sümi (Sema); a frog in the case of the Singpho; and a dog in the case of the Kabui Naga, Mizo and Meitei.[30] A particular understanding among the Angami was that an eclipse occurred because the eclipsed part of the orb had to repay the other part a loan of borrowed light.[31]

Other celestial phenomena receive mention in many of the region's narratives. As John H. Hutton pointed out, these are as diverse as the languages in the region.[32] Most groups have names for the sun, moon, Orion and Orion's belt, the Pleiades, the Milky Way and Venus, and – closer to earth – rainbows and parhelia. Very often a gender is assigned to these phenomena. Many groups (such as the Mising, Mishmi, Garo and Bongcher[33]) regard the sun as male and the moon

---

[27] Showren, 'Exploring Ethnohistory of Arunachal Pradesh'.
[28] Blackburn, *Himalayan Tribal Tales*, 110; Showren, 'Exploring Ethnohistory of Arunachal Pradesh'.
[29] Rafy, *Folk-Tales of the Khasis*. See also Elwin, *The Art of the North-East Frontier of India*, 123; Hanson, *The Kachins*, 119.
[30] In Garo stories this role is taken by a spirit. Playfair, *The Garos*, 88.
[31] Hutton, 'Some Astronomical Beliefs in Assam', 120. See also Elwin, *Myths of the North-East Frontier of India*, 29–58.
[32] Hutton, 'Some Astronomical Beliefs in Assam', 113.
[33] Sailo, *The Bongchers*, 32.

as female, whereas others (the Khasi, many Naga groups and the Nyishi) regard the sun as female and the moon as male.[34] According to the Mishmi, the sun and moon were husband and wife. The moon wanted some of the heat of the sun, but when she asked him, he was angry because he wanted the heat for all his children (humanity). He threw her into the pond and so the moon now has mud on her face.[35] According to Angami, on the other hand, the sun being womanly is afraid to go out at night, while the male moon is not afraid to do so (Plate 5.1).[36]

Besides the sun and the moon, which are usually seen as pairs (a couple, or siblings), there are stories woven around stars – and they frequently refer to human–animal relations. Orion and the Pleiades are the constellations that are most often given a name.[37] According to Parry, the Mara regard Orion's belt as two men carrying pigs who were turned into stars when the Great Darkness occurred.[38]

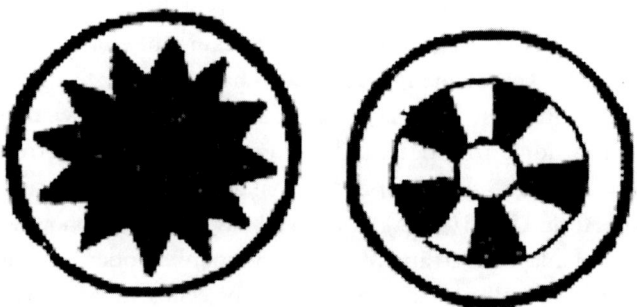

Plate 5.1 'Representations of the moon in Angami art, carved, and coloured black and white, on the barge-boards of houses.'

Source: Original caption from Hutton, 'Carved Monoliths at Dimapur', 58.

Note: This design also appeared in tattoos and is currently re-introduced as a fashionable identity marker. Krutak, 'Neo-Naga'. For an early depiction of the sun (c. 300 BCE) on a punch-marked coin from Bangladesh, see Ahmed (ed.), *Buddhist Heritage of Bangladesh*, 228.

---

[34] According to Hodgson, however, the Bodo of Assam believed the sun and the moon to be brothers. Hodgson, *Essay the First*, 168. See also Elwin, *Myths of the North-East Frontier of India*, 29–58.

[35] A somewhat similar story, from the Garo Hills – in which sun and moon are brother and sister – can be found in Playfair, *The Garos*, 86. See also Elwin, *Myths of the North-East Frontier of India*, 29–58; Hanson, *The Kachins*, 120.

[36] Hutton, 'Some Astronomical Beliefs in Assam', 117–18.

[37] For a story explaining the origin of the Great Bear, see Bhattacharjee, *Jamatia Folklore*, 233.

[38] Parry, *The Lakhers*, 494. Playfair mentions that Garo thought of Orion's belt as a pig being taken to the funeral meal of the mother of the moon. Playfair, *The Garos*, 86.

Stories of Human Origins

The story behind Orion's sword, on the other hand, was that once upon a time a mother was teaching her daughter how to weave and – as they were bent over – a tiger came and attacked them. The young men of the village came to their help, but just then an eclipse occurred and they were all turned into stars. The tiger became Awsichakeipa, more reddish in colour than the other stars – in other words, Mars. The Mizo detect other animals in Orion's belt and sword:

> There are eight stars, representing an owl, a rat's nest and six rat's holes. For a long time the rats used to come out of the holes, above which the owl sat in wait, and always got caught. One day the mouse said to the rat, 'You are very foolish. We always have a back door as well as a front door. If you make a back door like we do, the owl will not be able to catch you.' The rat took the mouse's advice, but as soon as he had finished his back way out the great darkness fell, and the owl and the rats' holes were all turned into stars [Plate 5.2].[39]

The Milky Way is often associated with winter. To the Mara it is the 'Rains and Dry Weather Boundary' (Sonatachhiarari), suggesting the onset of winter;[40] to the Mizo the 'Road to Winter' (Thlasik Kawng); to the Adi the 'Cold Weather Guide'; to the Mising the 'Winter and Summer Boundary'; and to the Ao Naga the 'Cold Weather-Rains Divider'. These names suggest a commonality of perception.

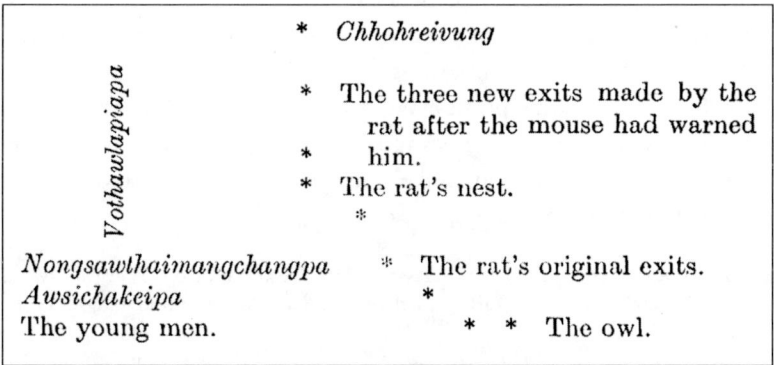

Plate 5.2 The stars of Orion's belt, as interpreted in stories of origin, with their names in the Mizo and Mara languages

Source: Parry, *The Lakhers*, 495.

Note: Chhohreivûng = the mound of earth created by a mouse digging a hole.

---

[39] Parry, *The Lakhers*, 494.
[40] Ibid.

But the Sümi Naga call it the 'Soul River'; the Angami refer to it as a 'Water Channel'; and the Garo call it the 'Hoofprints of the Buffalo', imagining it to be the tracks of a sacrificial buffalo that had escaped a funeral.[41]

In some Triangle communities, stories about celestial bodies have become distant memories, but for others these old narratives are very much alive and function as essential elements of contemporary spiritual life. An example is the Donyipolo movement, established in Arunachal Pradesh in 1968.

> In order to counter the spread of outside religions, the principal strategy of the Donyi-Polo [Sun-Moon] movement has been to promote a new religion of its own. Although it lacks a charismatic leader, Donyi-Polo is similar to other revitalisation movements in that it combines reinvented tradition with elements borrowed from the forces it opposes.... The movement has been developed into a formal 'religion' called 'Donyi-Polo-ism'. Oral myths have been smoothed into a coherent cosmology, with Donyi-Polo reigning like a creator-god.[42]

Somewhat similar revitalisation movements occurred elsewhere in the Triangle. Examples are the Seng Khasi, Heraka, Pau Chin Hau, Sanamahi, Rangfraa and Krama movements.[43] They, too, reoriented local cosmologies in response to competing cosmologies offered by Christianity and Hinduism. Today, the Donyipolo flag – a red sun on a white background – can be seen flying from houses that have joined the movement (Plate 5.3).

Whatever the exact details of the diverse origin stories, they frequently frame celestial bodies, eclipses and rainbows as powers that shaped life on earth – and as having their origins in some primeval animal kingdom inhabited by toads, dogs, frogs, tigers, pigs, rats, mice, buffaloes and owls. In addition, planets, stars, and sun and moon are credited with humanlike emotions, relationships and behaviour, as well as being linked to the changing seasons.

---

[41] Hutton, 'Some Astronomical Beliefs in Assam', 115. See also Hutton, *The Sema Nagas*, 251; Hutton, *The Ao Nagas*, 412; Duff-Sutherland-Dunbar, 'Abors and Galongs', 53; Playfair, *The Garos*, 87.

[42] Blackburn, *Himalayan Tribal Tales*, 48. See also Roy (née Chowdhury), 'The Donyi-Polo Cult of Arunachal Pradesh'; Stirn and Van Ham, *The Seven Sisters of India*, 43–9; Chaudhuri, 'The Institutionalization of Tribal Religion'; Showren, 'Exploring Ethnohistory of Arunachal Pradesh', 65; Scheid, 'Talom Rukbo and the Donyipolo Yelam Kebang'.

[43] Longkumer, *Reform, Identity and Narratives of Belonging*; Pau, 'Rethinking Religious Conversion'; Mahmud, *Ang Ing Mru Rung*; Uddin, 'Living on the Margin'; Singh, 'Religious Revivalism and Colonial Rule; Ara and Rashid, 'Tracking Local Dwelling Changes in the Chittagong Hills', 239–40; Barkataki-Ruscheweyh, 'Best of All Worlds: Rangfraism'.

Stories of Human Origins

Plate 5.3 The Donyipolo flag in Arunachal Pradesh (India), 2012
Source: Photo by Willem van Schendel.

Human origins

We have seen that the birth of the first human being is mentioned in the Apatani origin story. This is also the case in the Khumi origin story from the Chittagong Hill Tracts (Bangladesh). According to this community, the supreme deity created the world and the trees and creeping things – and then made a man and a woman out of clay. But at night a great snake would devour them, and each day the deity had to start all over again. Finally, the deity created a dog and made it watch the humans. At night the dog barked and scared the snake away, so the humans survived. This is the reason why, when a man is dying, his dogs begin to howl.[44] Among the Khumi, dogs remain ritually significant to this day, and they are never eaten.[45]

In other stories, such as those of the Mizo, the birth of the first humans is not explicit. But what most narratives have in common is a period when plants, animals

---

[44] Hutchinson, *Chittagong Hill Tracts*, 51. A century later, Uddin found the same story, with only minor variations. Uddin, 'Living on the Margin'. See also Uddin, 'In Search of Self'. On the supreme deity re-creating the first human, see also Myochit, *A Threatened Identity*, 33–5.

[45] Uddin, 'Living on the Margin', 36.

and humans could communicate freely with each other.⁴⁶ In the Mizo account, there was a time when all these life forms lived in peace. But soon animals and humans began to compete with one another, at which point a powerful being was asked to act as an adjudicator. This was Vanhrikpa (The Heavenly Louse Man), and it was because of his verdicts that plants and animals adopted their respective natures. However, the animals complained that humans were trapping too many of them, so Vanhrikpa asked the white ant (or termite) to eat the bowstrings of the traps. Humans then complained to Vanhrikpa that they could not trap any animals anymore, to which came the counsel to use the fibre of the sago palm (which the ant could not gnaw) for the traps. Bamboo, too, went to Vanhrikpa, complaining that its stem was so tall that when the wind blew, it broke very easily. Vanhrikpa advised it to tie strings at equal distances from each other, which would then turn into nodules. Hence bamboo with its segmented stem can now stand tall and strong against the wind.

Another important twist in the Mizo creation story is that of a period of chaos, also quite common in other stories in the Triangle. A thick mist of darkness covered the earth and strange transformations took place. Humans turned into birds and other creatures. Khuanu was saddened and therefore hid a human couple in a cave and covered it with a capstone. Several generations later Khuanu opened the capstone, and she was pleased to hear that the people had multiplied, so they were let out. It was said that they came out in such large numbers that they resembled winged ants emerging from the ground.⁴⁷

Thus, in the Mizo creation story, the rebirth of humanity occurred from a cave, underscoring an intimate connection between humans and the subsurface earth.⁴⁸ This is also asserted in other stories from the eastern rim of the Triangle, such as those told by the Chin, Bawm and Pangkhua.⁴⁹ The Thadou tell the story differently. According to them, humans were created in the subterranean world but one of them 'hunting porcupines in the [underground] jungle with his dog ... discovered a large hole' and this gave access to the uninhabited upper world. Defeating a snake and a lion that guarded the hole and removing its heavy cover, seven humans managed to reach the upper world and they became the ancestors of humanity.⁵⁰ The connection between those who stayed underground and the

---

⁴⁶ Lewin, *The Hill Tracts of Chittagong and the Dwellers Therein*, 95–6; Hutchinson, *Chittagong Hill Tracts*, 42; Shaw, *Notes on the Thadou Kukis*, 24–6; Elwin, *Myths of the North-East Frontier of India*, 95–136; Elwin, *The Art of the North-East Frontier of India*, 26–9; Bhattacharjee, *Jamatia Folklore*, 190–233.

⁴⁷ Zama, 'Origin Myths of the Mizo'.

⁴⁸ See also Lewin, *The Hill Tracts of Chittagong and the Dwellers Therein*, 95.

⁴⁹ Sakhong, *In Search of Chin Identity*, 1–10; Hutchinson, *Chittagong Hill Tracts*, 42.

⁵⁰ Shaw, *Notes on the Thadou Kukis*, 24–6.

Stories of Human Origins 79

Thadou above was never completely severed: earthquakes were thought to be caused by a subterranean ancestor shaking the earth to make sure that the Thadou were still alive.[51] Similarly, among the Ao the belief was that humanity emerged out of the earth at Lungterok (literally: Six Stones). Half of the stones were said to be male and the other half female. The different Ao clans each trace their origins to one of these six stones.[52]

Unlike many origin stories that tell us that humans emerged from beneath the ground, or out of a cave, the Khasi origin story speaks of humanity having come down from the skies and having spread far and wide in search of new agricultural land and better sources of livelihood.[53] Khasi stories begin with explaining the significance of a geological formation, the Sohpet Byneng Hill, a bare dome hill about 13 miles north of Shillong, the capital of Meghalaya. Its name means 'Centre of Heaven', or 'Navel between Heaven and Earth'. According to the story, after creation, heaven and earth were very near to each other, attached as they were by heaven's umbilical cord (in some versions this becomes a tree[54]). The cord was used as a ladder to move between heaven and earth. The earth was uninhabited but full of all kinds of trees and flowers, so heavenly beings found it a pleasure to visit earth. The land around Sohpet Byneng came to be cultivated by sixteen families who descended from heaven every day. One among them was extremely ambitious and did not want to be a subject of the Creator. Hence, on a day when only seven families had descended, the ambitious one cut the cord (tree) of communication between heaven and earth. This was how humankind came to live on earth. It is from these seven families – which the Khasi call the seven nests or seven roots (Ki Hinniew Skum) – that the nations of the earth came to be.[55] As soon as the cord was cut, it became shorter, and heaven ascended.[56]

Some stories from the northern Triangle emphasise the animal-like nature of the earliest humans. They were 'covered with hair', 'lived like deer in the forest' or 'like birds in nests high up in the trees'.[57] Originally naked, they eventually

---

[51] Shaw, *Notes on the Thadou Kukis*, 72. See also Hanson, *The Kachins*, 119–20.

[52] Ao, *The Ao-Naga Oral Tradition*, 1.

[53] There are some parallels here with the Ahom story of godlike humans descending from heaven by means of an iron ladder. Barua (ed.), *Ahom-Buranji*, 4–23. Tālish (*Tarikh-i Asham*, 89) mentions a ladder of gold. See also Myochit, *A Threatened Identity*, 32; Gros, 'Nature De-naturalised', 325.

[54] Stirn and Van Ham, *The Seven Sisters of India*, 98–9.

[55] Rafy, *Folk-Tales of the Khasis*, 6–7.

[56] Gurdon, *The Khasis*, 173. This account differs from the one in Rafy, *Folk-Tales of the Khasis*.

[57] Taken from Aka and Dhammai, Taraon Mishmi, and Wancho stories, respectively. Elwin, *The Art of the North-East Frontier of India*, 23.

discovered fire and began dressing in leaves and bark-cloth. Then deities or animals (for example, a spider, a fish, a snake) taught them how to weave clothes. Some of these animals could turn into humans (and back again), and they would marry human spouses.[58] Humans distanced themselves more from animals as they learned how to make implements and ornaments. But they still needed animal assistance: a woodpecker had to peck holes into the first bead-maker's beads, and an elephant and a crab taught the first ironmonger how to make knives and arrowheads.[59] Animals also played a crucial role in stories about the beginnings of agriculture. The Thadou in the eastern Triangle were convinced that rats had taught their ancestors how to grow rice, and the Kachin were certain that they had received rice from the sun spirit, but that an evil chameleon had shrank the rice to its present size.[60]

Stories from the southern Triangle echo some of these ideas but also add new ones. For example, Marma storytellers in the Chittagong Hills (Bangladesh) described an evolution from animals to humans. When the world was created, there were just two genderless animals that were naked but could speak. There was darkness, and they ate only the ashes of the burned earth. Then a cyclone came, and more rain, and the sun and the moon appeared. These animals knew only two days, one light and one dark, with no night separating them. Their bodies began to glow whenever they ate ashes. But then rice came out of the earth. As they ate it, blood started flowing through their bodies, their brains and intelligence grew, and they received gender features. They became fully human, cultivated the rice, covered themselves with leaves and started multiplying.[61]

Throughout the Triangle, people strongly felt that plants, animals and spirits played essential roles in the origins of humankind. Human lives were embedded in multispecies relationships that were forged in humanity's deep history and gave meaning to the present. Such relationships gave salience to community life, but they also stretched well beyond life on earth: they continued after death.

Death and the afterlife

Triangle stories contain many elements about the end of human lives, the passage from life to death, and what happens afterwards. These explain why extensive rituals surround this major life-cycle event. Despite distinct cultural differences

---

[58] Elwin, *The Art of the North-East Frontier of India*, 23–5.
[59] Ibid., 29.
[60] Shaw, *Notes on the Thadou Kukis*, 29; Hanson, *The Kachins*, 128.
[61] Bernot, *Les paysans arakanais du Pakistan Oriental*, 1:134–8. See also Hutchinson, *Chittagong Hill Tracts*, 51–2.

Stories of Human Origins

across the Triangle, there is a remarkable commonality in basic ideas.[62] There was a widespread presumption that everything that lives has an immaterial essence (a soul, sometimes more than one). This was not only articulated for humans but also for large mammals (such as tigers and bovines) and some plants (such as rice and maize), but vaguer for smaller animals and most plants.[63] Many communities believed that the souls of dead people – helped by correct funeral ceremonies – went to the abode of the dead.[64] Hunted animals would also go there, and funeral rituals prepared them for the journey.[65] This abode was variously imagined as the settlement of the dead;[66] a land of fertile fields, many mithuns and a happy family life;[67] a divine house with groves of areca palms;[68] a purgatory on a solitary peak;[69] the place where the pale ones lived[70] and so on. The abode of the dead could consist of different levels or sections, it could be underneath the earth or in the sky, or it could be linked to a specific feature of the local landscape – a mountain or a lake.[71]

It was a common belief that crossing to the abode of the dead was perilous. An old woman or man was waiting with a pellet bow, or a whip made of thorns, to shoot you down; a fearsome, questioning demon had to be distracted; a huge tongue would block the way; or monstrous caterpillars were ready to devour you.[72]

---

[62] Blackburn, *Himalayan Tribal Tales*, 218–19. See also Von Stockhausen, *Imag(in)ing the Nagas*, 352–7.

[63] De Maaker, 'Negotiating Life', 81; Parry, *The Lakhers*, 79, 267, 445–7; Marak, 'Rice from A·ba', 11. See also Gros, 'Nature De-naturalised'.

[64] Detailed descriptions of funeral ceremonies can be found in De Maaker, 'Negotiating Life'; Stack and Lyall, *The Mikirs*, 37–42; Playfair, *The Garos*, 102–13; Gurdon, *The Khasis*, 132–58; Aisher, 'Through "Spirits"', 383–9; Parry, *The Lakhers*, 399–429.

[65] For example, the *ai* ceremonies held for dead humans, tigers and gibbons. Shakespear, *The Lushei Kuki Clans*, 78–80.

[66] Parry, *The Lakhers*, 394–5; Sakhong, *In Search of Chin Identity*, 30–2; Pachuau, *Being Mizo*, 216–18; Hutchinson, *Chittagong Hill Tracts*, 50. See also Stack and Lyall, *The Mikirs*, 28; Barbe, 'Some Account of the Hill Tribes', 384.

[67] Blackburn, 'Die Reise der Seele', 87. See also Hutchinson, *Chittagong Hill Tracts*, 38.

[68] Gurdon, *The Khasis*, 105.

[69] Playfair, *The Garos*, 102.

[70] VanBik, *Proto-Kuki-Chin*, 239.

[71] Playfair, *The Garos*, 102–5; Shakespear, *The Lushei Kuki Clans*, 62–3; Parry, *The Lakhers*, 394–5; Myochit, *A Threatened Identity*, 36–7.

[72] Shakespear, *The Lushei Kuki Clans*, 61–5; Shaw, *Notes on the Thadou Kukis*, 43; Parry, *The Lakhers*, 397; Playfair, *The Garos*, 103–4; Sangma, 'Rites of Passage in the Garo Oral Literature', 223–4; Blackburn, 'Die Reise der Seele', 88; De Maaker, 'Negotiating Life', 111; Pachuau, *Being Mizo*, 217; Sakhong, *In Search of Chin Identity*, 31; Mahmud, *Ang Ing Mru Rung*, 57–8; Kipgen, 'The Enclosures of Colonization', 220; Myochit, *A Threatened Identity*, 37, 62.

Therefore, souls often needed a guide to make the journey. Once they passed this hurdle, however, they entered a new multispecies world: the abode of the dead was also home to animals and plants – some of them specific to the afterworld.[73] Souls usually took their lifetime achievements with them, as well as the souls of the wild animals that they had hunted and the domestic animals that they had sacrificed in their lifetime. Successful hunters and performers of animal sacrifices had an easier time making the crossing than others, and they could end up in a more comfortable section of the abode of the dead, surrounded by their former livestock and other creature comforts. Some stories speak of wives joining deceased husbands in the afterworld (or men finding spouses there) but it is often unclear if female souls (and children) could enter the afterworld on their own. As a result, it frequently comes across as a starkly male-oriented place.[74] Essentially, Triangle cultures imagined afterlife as resting on the same relationships between humans, non-human animals, plants and spirits as they experienced on this side of death.

Human mobilities

A final distinct feature of stories all over the Triangle is an insistence that humans came from elsewhere. Most groups believe that their ancestors originated somewhere else, often across the mountains, and migrated and settled in their current locations later. These stories usually differ from origin stories in that they are not told or performed in ritual settings. They are 'less like orally transmitted narratives and more like memorised historical records'.[75] Often, these stories provide some details on geography and chronology that could potentially be backed up by historical evidence.[76] With the exception of the Khasi (who claim to have descended from heaven at a named rock formation in the Khasi Hills[77]),

---

[73] Parry, *The Lakhers*, 395. See also Phayre, 'Account of Arakan', 709; Stewart, 'Notes on Northern Cachar', 632.

[74] Spielmann, 'Die Bawm-Zo', 112; Duff-Sutherland-Dunbar, 'Abors and Galongs', 77–8.

[75] See Blackburn, 'Memories of Migration', 17:

> For people without writing, such as the central Arunachal tribes, oral legends function less like performances and more like books, not to be read from cover to cover, but to be taken off the shelf for reference, for verification, for consultation, and for reflection. In sum, migration legends are less like orally transmitted narratives and more like memorised historical records.

[76] Ibid., 16–17. See also Luce, *Phases of Pre-Pagán Burma*; Ciin, 'A Study of Anthropological Perspectives', 11–12.

[77] Gurdon, *The Khasis*, 172. This account differs from the one in Rafy, *Folk-Tales of the Khasis*. See also Nongbri, 'Culture and Biodiversity'. Shaw (*Notes on the Thadou Kukis*, 26) describes both a migration story and an insistence on a local origin among the Thadou.

most communities have distinct ideas about their ancestors' journey. Typically, they imagine their community identities to have been formed before they migrated, so they project their current identities onto an ancient past.[78] What usually remains unexplained is why these migrations took place. Were people attracted to the rich ecology of the region, or the wealth of space for settlement? Were they escaping from disease, other groups, war or states?[79]

Communities as varied as Garo, Kachin, Brokpa and Apatani all claim migration from the north, from Tibet.[80] Their stories can be quite detailed:

> Apatanis view the past as a path, laid out along a sequence of imaginary places leading from the homeland to the present settlement in the Apatani valley. Migration is plotted along this path and through these places, where the ancestors stopped and lived for some time. The route proceeds from Wi (Spirit) Supung to Iipyo (Ancient) Supung, to Nyime (Tibet) Supung, to Hiising Supung (near the source of the Tsangpo [Brahmaputra] River), to Shango Supung and Mudo Supung (both in the Tsangpo valley). From there the ancestors crossed the mountains, forded rivers and came to Silo (Ziro) Supung, the valley where Apatanis live today.... The ancestors' journey along the migration path is particularly important because it reveals the two fundamental themes in Apatani oral tradition and culture. The first theme is differentiation.... Separation along the migration route give rises to the second theme: the resolution of potential conflict by alliance and exchange.[81]

According to this indigenous form of history-making, then, ancient Apatani mobility across different landscapes is well established. Moreover, this reading of the past remains of great significance because it shaped contemporary Apatani society in fundamental ways.

The Angami of Nagaland, too, believe in a migration story, although their story of where this migration started is not too clear. According to Khonyu Punyu, it started somewhere in the East (in the direction of Myanmar and Southeast Asia) and brought them to Makhel (now located in Manipur). From here they split up, but not before a covenant was made under a wild pear tree.

---

[78] Burling, 'Language, Ethnicity and Migration'.

[79] Scott, *The Art of Not Being Governed*. See also Daniels, 'Introduction'; Daniels, 'Blocking the Path'; Daniels, 'Nanzhao as a Southeast Asian Kingdom'.

[80] For detailed analysis of a number of migration stories, see Huber and Blackburn (eds.), *Origins and Migrations*; Playfair, *The Garos*, 7–14; Hanson, *The Kachins*, 15–26; Karst, 'Protected Areas and Ecotourism', 42; Blackburn, *Himalayan Tribal Tales*; Burling, 'Language, Ethnicity and Migration'. See also Duff-Sutherland-Dunbar, 'Abors and Galongs', 12–15; Mills, 'The Mishmis of the Lohit Valley, Assam'.

[81] Blackburn, *Himalayan Tribal Tales*, 110–11.

Some went to Khezhakheno and others to Kigwema and Viswema. Further dispersals brought them to their current locations in the Kohima district in Nagaland. Dispersal from Khezhakheno was said to be the result of a dispute between three brothers over a magic stone that could give them double the yield of rice placed on it. When the eldest brother prevented the youngest brother from using the magic stone, the latter set it on fire, which broke the stone into three pieces. Each brother took a piece and went in a different direction, although the stones no longer had their magic powers (Plate 5.4).[82] The Poumai Naga also trace their migration history through Makhel, from where different groups moved to

Plate 5.4 Migration history in stone: the pieces of the Khezhakheno stone, Nagaland (India)

Source: Photo by J. H. Hutton, c. 1920. See Hutton, *The Angami Nagas*, 19.

---

[82] Different accounts are found in Hutton, *The Angami Nagas*, 18–20; Punyu, 'Oral History of the Angami Nagas', 11–18; and Aier and Jamir, 'Re-interpreting the Myth of Longterok'.

new places, mostly in Manipur. One group, led by women who had been potters in Makhel, settled down in a place where they found the smell of the soil suitable for pottery. They called it Oinam (Village Discovered through Smell) and became the first of many generations of potters.[83]

Migration stories of many groups in the southern parts of the Triangle suggest an original home in the east or south.[84] Genealogies among the Thadou suggest that they moved south from the source of the Manipur River until they reached the sea, and then moved north again.[85] The Zophei (in Chin State, Myanmar) narrate that they moved because of a flood that destroyed their ancestral place, possibly in the Chindwin valley. The flood occurred when they had killed a large man-eating snake and water started pouring from its cave.[86]

Among the Chakma of the Chittagong Hill Tracts, there were conflicting ideas. They believed that

> they came originally from a country called Chainpango, or Champanugger. As to where this country is situated, accounts vary somewhat. By some it is said to be near Malacca; this would ascribe to them a Malay origin: while, on the other hand, there are many that assert that Champanugger is situated far to the north in the North-Western Provinces of Hindoostan.[87]

This idea of a western origin (and Hindu-Buddhist ancestors) became more prominent during the twentieth century, even though researchers have dismissed it as 'a myth'.[88] Be that as it may, the first firm indication that Chakmas were settled in the region that they still inhabit is over 500 years old. This suggests that stories about 'original' migration routes in the Triangle may, in many cases, refer to mobilities that took place centuries or millennia ago.[89]

---

[83] Gachui, 'An Oinam Poumai Potter at Work'.

[84] For example, the Marma-Chakma story in Hutchinson, *Chittagong Hill Tracts*, 54–5. A story among the Mech (in Assam and West Bengal) also points to an original home in the east – they were 'driven out of from the northeastern corner of India, Burma and Tibet (probably by the Chinese)'. Sanyal, *The Meches and the Totos*, 18–19. The Thadou in Manipur claimed to be from the south. Shaw, *Notes on the Thadou Kukis*, 16–18. See also Lainé, '*Phi Muangs*'; Myochit, *A Threatened Identity*, 18–19.

[85] Shaw, *Notes on the Thadou Kukis*, 28–39; for more recent migrations, see 44–7.

[86] Sakhong, *In Search of Chin Identity*, 6–7.

[87] Lewin, *The Hill Tracts of Chittagong and the Dwellers Therein*, 62.

[88] Hutchinson, *Chittagong Hill Tracts*, 95–6; Hutchinson, *An Account of the Chittagong Hill Tracts*, 21–2; Serajuddin and Buller, 'The Chakma Tribe'. See also Ray, 'Boundaries Blurred'; Ciin, 'A Study of Anthropological Perspectives', 11–12; Htwe, 'The Social Organization', 3–11.

[89] Jacquesson, 'The Linguistic Reconstruction of the Past'.

In these stories, animals are regularly mentioned as migrating together with humans. This is especially noteworthy regarding traditions among non-literate groups about 'lost scripts'.[90] Such tales insist that the group used to be literate in the past but lost the art of writing as a result of a calamity, often while travelling. There are three elements that commonly appear: the script was eaten by a dog, cow or another animal that accompanied the early migrants; the script was written on an animal skin that was eaten by people when they were famished; or the script was lost in water during a flood or as their ancestors crossed a river.[91] These stories underscore how Triangle communities imagined their histories as having been critically entangled with non-human actions.

Tentative patterns

What are we to make of the very rich variety of stories about how the world was created and how human societies in the Triangle came about? As people grappled with 'deep history', they developed a range of multi-layered narratives that coalesced into compelling theories of the world. These ideas emphatically 'humanised' animals and thereby highlighted the importance of past human–non-human linkages. They have nurtured many generations and they are deeply embedded in the Triangle's contemporary cultures and languages. For this reason alone, they are not to be dismissed as outdated folklore – defeated by more modern, rational understandings of history. As we shall see, today these narratives inspire intense feelings of belonging and community, shaping identities and fuelling future-oriented social movements all over the Triangle.[92]

Cosmological commonalities

Research into these stories has been far more detailed for some groups than for others, and comparative research is still rare. To help develop this field we suggest several patterns. There appear to be certain cosmological commonalities across

---

[90] Oppitz, 'Die Geschichte der verlorenen Schrift'; Aisher, 'Through "Spirits"', 81; Blackburn, *Himalayan Tribal Tales*, 116–17, 217–18; Sakhong, *In Search of Chin Identity*, 138; Hanson, *The Kachins*, 116–17.

[91] For examples of animals eating the script, see Bareigts, *Les Lautu*, 53; Brauns and Löffler, *Mru: Hill People*, 235–6; Sakhong, *In Search of Chin Identity*, 153; Chowdhury et al., 'Dietetic Use of Wild Animals', 29; Oppitz, 'Die Geschichte der verlorenen Schrift', 33; Duff-Sutherland-Dunbar, 'Abors and Galongs', 51; Hutton, *The Sema Nagas*, 299; Mills, *The Rengma Nagas*, 286. On script written on animal skin, see Hanson, *The Kachins*, 116–17; Grothmann, 'Migration Narratives', 136; Mills, *The Ao Nagas*, 207. On losing the script in water, see Gurdon, *The Khasis*, 10; Parry, *The Lakhers*, 501, 559; Blackburn, *Himalayan Tribal Tales*, 116–17.

[92] Karlsson, *Unruly Hills*, 3–6; Ray, 'Boundaries Blurred'.

the Triangle. There was a widespread idea that the universe was created and presided over by a faraway primary deity who generally had no direct dealings with humans. This deity was joined by a multitude of minor deities or spirits who did communicate with humans.[93] Human dealings with these spirits often reflected negotiation, exchange and a balance of power, rather than supplication, devotion and submission to higher authority.[94] The need to propitiate these spirits was felt on a daily basis and, as we shall see in Chapter 6, communication between spirits and humans usually took the form of animal sacrifices. There were other cosmological commonalities. One example is the sense that deep history was close by – it was of immediate relevance because it underlay everyday activities. Another was the conviction that the universe was sentient, and that stars and other celestial bodies were involved in events on earth, most notably the seasons. A third was the belief that the afterworld was crowded with spirits, animals and plants, just as life on this side of death was. And, last but not least, a fourth commonality was that Triangle cosmologies were multispecies cosmologies – they were grounded in the understanding that humans, plants, animals and spirits were partners in the world and that they shared a 'vital principle'.[95] If we wish to consider the Triangle as a 'culture area', we can take such commonalities as a starting point.[96]

Cosmological centres

Although there were strong commonalities across the region, the expression of these common beliefs took different forms. We suggest that it may be helpful to distinguish and compare four 'cosmological centres' – the North, the Eastern Rim, the Khasi and Jaintia Hills, and the Lowlands. For the North we have detailed recent studies that point to similarities in ideas about, among other things, a named original human being, migration from a more northerly ancestral home, specific ways of dealing with the spirit world and the mediating role of a sacrificial bovine, the mithun (about which more in Chapters 6 and 8).[97] The Eastern Rim is distinguished by stories about humans emerging from the earth, migration from

---

[93] Shakespear, *The Lushei Kuki Clans*, 61–91; Bareigts, *Les Lautu*, 133–61; Sitlhou, 'Land and Identity', 93–8; Longvah, 'Christian Conversions'.

[94] Ramirez, 'Enemy Spirits'; Sitlhou, 'Land and Identity', 121–2.

[95] Gros, 'Nature De-naturalised', 326. On spirits as ancestors of powerful families, see Shin, 'Descending from Demons'.

[96] Blackburn, 'Oral Stories and Culture Areas'; Pau and Mung, 'Fragmented Tribes of the India–Burma–Bangladesh Borderlands'. See also Huber, *Source of Life*. Another commonality was the story of a primeval flood or deluge.

[97] There are, of course, variations in the beliefs of the groups to the north of the Brahmaputra River, but the similarities (also, possibly, with the Garo of western Meghalaya) are worth exploring. See also Blackburn, 'Oral Stories and Culture Areas'.

an eastern ancestral home, a similar prominence of the mithun in sacrifices to the spirits and the putting up of memorial stones.[98] The Khasi and Jaintia Hills appear to be a distinct centre of cosmological ideas that do not link up with those of surrounding areas. For example, humans were thought to have descended from the heavens right there (so no migration narrative[99]), ancestor worship was prominent (with the clan ancestress underscoring a matrilineal descent system) and this related to a tradition of erecting memorial stones that appear to be much more ancient than in the Eastern Rim (Chapter 8). Finally, in the lowlands of Assam, Myanmar and Bengal (as well as the Manipur valley[100]), cosmologies have long been profoundly shaped by the influence of scriptural world views – although historians' reliance on textual and epigraphical sources may well have overplayed this influence and overlooked the historical contributions of persisting local cosmologies.[101] In a process that Doniger coined 'deshification', local (*deshi*) traditions absorbed Hindu (and by implication, Buddhist and Islamic) traditions to fit into local popular cultures.[102] Here locally inflected 'world religions' developed their own cosmologies, in which Islamic goddesses, Buddhist spirits and non-Vedic blood sacrifices played essential roles (Chapter 6).

These four centres were definitely not self-contained. Cosmological ideas radiated outwards and created complex fusions at the local level. For example, the Meitei of the Manipur valley in the Eastern Rim came under Bengali religious influence from the eighteenth century onwards. This led them to 'deshify' Hinduism (in the form of Vaishnavism, an already 'deshified' religious tradition in Bengal). Similarly, the Marma in the southern reaches of the Eastern Rim further 'deshified' the Arakanese form of Buddhism, and the Brokpa in the North did the same with the Bhutanese version of Buddhism.[103]

---

[98] For examples (Bawm-Zo, Pangkhua) from the southern part of the Eastern Rim, see Hutchinson, *Chittagong Hill Tracts*, 41–2. Ciin ('A Study of Anthropological Perspectives') contains stories of migration, reunification and elephant sacrifice.

[99] Nongbri, 'Culture and Biodiversity', 4.

[100] Although surrounded by uplands, the Manipur valley does not really fit the much-used upland–lowland binary. For a critique, see Jilangamba, 'Beyond the Ethno-Territorial Binary'.

[101] Sarma and Hazarika, 'Situating Northeast Indian Archaeology', 49; Ray, 'Boundaries Blurred'; Shin, 'Descending from Demons'.

[102] Doniger, *The Hindus*; Zakaria, *Pronomohi Bongomata*. Christianity – which spread much later, in some cases not until the 1970s (Myochit, *A Threatened Identity*, 3, 12, 21, 77–80) – was 'deshified' in the same way. For example, De Maaker, 'Have the Mitdes Gone Silent'; De Maaker, 'Aloof but Not Abandoned'.

[103] Parratt, 'The Religion of Manipur'; Charney, 'Literary Culture on the Burma-Manipur Frontier'; Hodson, *The Meitheis*, 95–103; Bernot, *Les paysans arakanais du Pakistan Oriental*; Karst, 'Protected Areas and Ecotourism'; Ray, 'Boundaries Blurred'. See also Terwiel, *The Tai of Assam and Ancient Tai Ritual*; Morey, *Turung*, 62–3, 66–70.

Triangle understandings of deep history

This overview of Triangle stories dealing with human origins shows that humans were convinced of their perpetual entanglement with the natural world – stretching from the very beginning of time all the way to the life hereafter. They constructed their history as a continual interaction with the animals, plants and sentient landscapes around them, as well as with the invisible world of supernatural beings. It is essential to understand this cultural foundation if we are to make sense of the social systems that evolved and the ways in which historical actors behaved.

These actors viewed the world differently than academically trained historians. They could never have accepted the scholarly tradition of setting 'human' history apart from 'natural' history by focusing only on human actors. The value of Triangle stories and their construction of the world is the challenge they pose to this scholarly tradition.

Scholars differ in their interpretation of these cosmologies, however. Some assert that we need 'a Copernican Revolution in the sciences of society and culture' to deal with this challenge.[104] They suggest that the key belief of these cosmologies is that all animate beings (including spirits) are members of a single 'cosmic polity'. There are hierarchies within this polity. Spirits form the top layer. They are the real owners of the human means of existence and dispensers of human prosperity.[105] Splitting this lifeworld up in segments such as 'culture' and 'nature' has no meaning:

> We scholars of a more skeptical or positivist bent are at liberty to demystify the apparent illusions of the Others. We can split up their reality in order to make society autonomous, expose the gods as fantasy, and reduce nature to things.... But if we do, it becomes much harder to know them better.[106]

Other scholars challenge this view. They feel that these cosmologies show that humans do recognise that they are a distinct species and therefore make some

---

[104] See Sahlins, 'The Original Political Society', 57:

> We need something like a Copernican Revolution in the sciences of society and culture. I mean a shift in perspective from human society as the center of a universe onto which it projects its own forms – that is to say, from the received Durkheimian, Marxist, and structural-functionalist conventions – to the ethnographic realities of people's dependence on the encompassing meta-person-others [gods, spirits, ancestors] who rule earthly order, welfare, and existence.

[105] For example, Montes, Kafley and Dema, 'Territory, Relationality and the Labour of Deities', speak of 'deity landlords' who claim territory and direct their human 'tenants' in Bhutan. See also Sitlhou, 'Land and Identity', 117, 122.

[106] Sahlins, 'The Original Political Society', 62.

distinction between 'nature' and 'culture', although in a very different and far less absolute way than 'skeptical and positivist' scholars do.[107] Despite these different positions, however, those who participate in this debate strongly agree that cosmologies cannot be ignored.[108] If we want to understand the complex history of the Triangle, we must engage with the world views that developed in the region, as well as with their transformations over time and their still vigorous presence in parts of the Triangle today.

Triangle understandings of deep history explain the present by selectively evoking powerful past experiences and events. They highlight how animals and plants have always co-constituted human societies. The evidence that these stories provide may not be chronometrically accurate or complete, but that is beside the point. What they do offer is a claim on the past and a charter for life. The period for which we lack conventional historical sources comes alive through them. Wondrous as these stories may seem, they are the only available help we have to see Triangle histories through local eyes. And they emphatically demand the inclusion of non-humans in the region's history. In the next two chapters we will first consider the role of human–animal relationships in Triangle histories and then that of human–plant relationships.

---

[107] Woodward, 'Gifts for the Sky People', 222; Aisher, 'Through "Spirits"'; Blackburn, *Himalayan Tribal Tales*, 74–7; Lyngdoh, 'Water Spirit Possession among the Khasis'; Longkumer, 'Spirits in a Material World'.

[108] Sahlins, 'In Anthropology'; Woodward, 'Gifts for the Sky People'; Varah, 'Situating the Humans Relationship'; Wouters, 'Relatedness'; De Maaker, 'Who Owns the Hills'.

6

Human–Animal Histories

In Chapter 5 we noticed that stories of human origins are full of references to a time when animals and humans could talk to each other, marry and have children together. In this chapter we focus on how people in the Triangle have understood animals to have contributed to human lifeworlds in more recent times. Close, long-lasting relationships with animals characterise most groups in the Triangle, not only in practical, instrumental terms but also in symbolic and emotional terms. These relationships have not been static; new meanings have been brought into them over time. In this chapter we consider how people imagined themselves to have family connections with certain animals, how they managed their fear of animals, how they distinguished between wild and domestic animals, and how they regulated hunting and sacrificing practices.

For humans around the world, animals have always been 'an essential part of our history, culture and existence'.[1] Ever since the appearance of modern humans, we have lived in close proximity to animals and have shared our lifeworlds with them. It is a relationship that is 'complex, intimate, reciprocal, personal' and, most importantly, 'crucially ambivalent'.[2]

Simplistic notions of so-called primitive societies being closer to, or one with, nature do not hold (Chapter 8). All societies – hunter-gathering, pastoral, agricultural and industrial – have associations with animals, but these vary.[3] Moreover, such societal relationships cannot be reduced to a single metaphor because individual and social attitudes are diverse and complex.[4] It is important not to romanticise the relationship between humans and nature in the case of societies that were technologically less sophisticated. In the Triangle, traditions such as

---

[1] Rowan (ed.), *Animals and People*, 9; cited in Morris, *Animals and Ancestors*, 20.
[2] Morris, *Animals and Ancestors*, 20.
[3] For example, Aiyadurai, 'Human–Animal Relations'.
[4] Morris, *Animals and Ancestors*, 20.

the sacred grove, or hunting rituals, have often been read as showing a profound spiritual union with nature. Humans in the Triangle did appear to be motivated by an understanding that their lifeworlds were entangled with those of all other living beings, but they also distinguished between themselves and non-humans.[5] What counted most for them was the absolute necessity to sustain relations of reciprocity with animals, plants and spirits. This endeavour pervaded their lifeworlds and religious imaginations. Taking proper care of human–non-human entanglements was a daily concern, but it did not hamper their construction of convenient niches for themselves. It is often assumed that colonial rule, Christianity and modernity destroyed what had been a pristine, sacred union, but this assumption needs to be carefully investigated.[6]

A history of human–non-human relations offers us many angles to consider. It comes with the need to highlight certain complexities of the region itself. Groups in the Triangle have been exposed to quite dissimilar kinds of religious and literate traditions as well as statist influence. Their lifeworlds, including their relationships with (non-human) animals, show historical diversity. In their symbolic universe some animals take precedence over others, and this differs across the region.[7] For example, the mithun came to play a very important role as an animal of sacrifice and a prestige item in the eastern and northern uplands but not in the lowlands or the western uplands. The symbolic importance of the mithun is often linked to similar importance being given to the largest forest bird, the hornbill, as we shall detail in Chapter 8. In the lifeworld of other groups – for example the Meitei, Khasi and Bhutanese[8] – the snake was a powerful presence.

Some animals have become symbolically more important over time. Today the rhinoceros is the emblem of Assam. It is Assam's 'state animal' and its image is everywhere: in advertisements for tea, petroleum and public events, and as a logo for public transport and sports clubs. In the past, however, it was actually the elephant that was the most highly valued animal in Assam, especially

---

[5] Emic hierarchies of humans–non-humans are explored by multispecies scholars such as Govindrajan, *Animal Intimacies*; Jackson, 'Colonial Conquest and Religious Entanglement'; and Lainé, *Living and Working with Giants*. See also Varah, 'Situating the Humans Relationship'; Woodward, 'Gifts for the Sky People', 222.

[6] Shah, *In the Shadows of the State*, 107–11; Karlsson, *Unruly Hills*, 83–4, 114–20; De Maaker, 'Have the Mitdes Gone Silent'; De Maaker, 'Aloof but Not Abandoned'.

[7] There are also striking commonalities, as Shakespear showed for an animal tale ('The Story of the Bat') that was found among communities in different corners of the Triangle. Shakespear, 'Tangkhul Folk Tales', 268–71.

[8] For Bhutanese beliefs in 'serpent beings' and poison gods taking the shape of snakes, see Tashi, 'Contested Past, Challenging Future'; Pommaret, 'The Community of Ngangla Trong', 22–3.

among the ruling classes. The rhino has very little archival presence, unlike the elephant.⁹ This was no doubt a result of the elephant's crucial role in warfare. In the seventh century, Xuanzang, a Chinese visitor, noted that war elephants were in use in Assam (Kamarupa): 'On the south-east of this country herds of wild elephants roam about in numbers; therefore, in this district they use them principally in war.'¹⁰

After settling in Assam in the thirteenth century, the Ahom rulers are said to have abandoned the horses they arrived with from the east because war elephants proved to be superior. Elephants became a key pillar of the Ahom state, which lasted into the nineteenth century (and they continued to be a pillar of the state during British colonial rule¹¹). The ownership of elephants came to signify status and power. They were exchanged at marriages and became trade items, and they were used to pay war indemnity and taxes. The Ahoms also embossed elephants on their coins and depicted them in a manuscript (Plate 6.1).

Plate 6.1 Eighteenth-century manuscript painting of elephants, Assam (India)

Source: Sukumar Barkaith, *Hastividyārnava*, c. 1740 CE.

Note: *Hastividyārnava*, by Sukumar Barkaith, is a manuscript on the management and maintenance of elephants in the royal stalls. See Ahmed, 'Elephants in Medieval Assam'; Lainé, 'Les éléphants sous la cour ahom'.

---

⁹ But see Daniels, 'Nanzhao as a Southeast Asian Kingdom', 199, for a reference to rhinoceroses and elephants from the upper Ayeyarwadi region being sent as tribute to the eighth-century Nanzhao state elite.

¹⁰ Beal (ed.), *Si-Yu-Ki*, 2:199.

¹¹ Saha, 'Colonizing Elephants'. See also Trautmann, *Elephants and Kings*.

Animals as kin

Several societies in the Triangle have stories that claim kinship ties between themselves and animals. Hutton informed us that all Naga regarded themselves as sharing a deep ancestry with the tiger. Thus, the Angami believed that the first spirit, the first man and the first tiger were the sons of one mother. But in time the tiger's ways deviated from those of the other two. Their mother was tired of the tiger's habit of eating his food raw (while man ate his food cooked and the spirit ate his smoke-dried). The tiger also treated her badly, whereas man and spirit treated her kindly. She came up with a plan to make sure that the siblings would live separately. She put a mark in the jungle; whoever would reach it first would stay in the village and the others would live in the jungle. Spirit and man collaborated. The spirit shot an arrow and the man shouted out loud that he had reached the mark. The tiger failed the test, and the jungle became its habitat. Thus, despite animosity between tigers and humans, the Angami clearly acknowledged that they were siblings. Whenever an Angami killed a tiger, he had to announce that it was not him but the gods who had killed it. Moreover, the village priest would declare a full day of abstention (*genna*) because an elder brother had been killed.[12]

All Naga groups recognised the relationship, although different groups had different understandings of their proximity to tigers. For a Chang subgroup it was taboo to touch the tiger, let alone kill it. They would eat the flesh of the leopard but not that of the tiger. The Angami would eat both, but the Sümi would abstain from them. The Sümi word *aynshu* could refer to a tiger or a leopard, and therefore neither species could be eaten.[13]

These practices were probably related to beliefs in the ability of tigers and humans to assume each other's form. Such animal–human transformations are known as lycanthropy. The Angami recognised the phenomenon but did not experience such transformations, whereas they were common in the Sümi area. Jan Ovesen details two kinds of beliefs about human–animal transformations in the Naga Hills. The first belief understood the soul of a tiger to take up residence in a person. This idea was common among the Ao and the Lotha. The second belief understood the soul of a person to settle in a tiger. It was common among the Sümi.[14] Among the Ao and Lotha, tiger-people (who could be male or female)

---

[12] Hutton, 'Leopard Men in the Naga Hills', 41.

[13] Hutton, 'Leopard Men in the Naga Hills'. See also Mills, 'The Were-Tigers of the Assam Hills'; Heneise, 'The Naga Tiger-Man'.

[14] This was also the case among the Garo, who believed that some human souls could embed themselves in tigers, snakes, rats and other animals while their bodies were sleeping. Other individuals actually transformed their bodies into tigers at night and went hunting in the jungle. Sangma, 'Shape-Shifting or Transformation Myth'.

were almost always linked to ritual healing powers. In the case of the Sümi, however, transformations were found especially amongst chiefly families and not linked to any magical powers. Generally speaking, tiger-people were not from marginalised sections of society.[15]

Besides Naga groups, there were several other groups in the Triangle that also viewed tigers and leopards as closely related to themselves and capable of transforming into humans. A subgroup of Chins claimed to be descended from the tiger and referred to it as 'my grandfather'.[16] The Mishmi of Arunachal Pradesh considered tigers to be their brothers, born of the same mother. Tigers were not to be killed except under extreme duress. The Mishmi story of human–tiger kinship is very similar to that of the Angami.[17] Two subgroups of the Bodo (Kachari), too, claimed close kinship with the tiger: the whole village would go into mourning on hearing the news of the death of a tiger.[18]

Respected and dreaded, tigers were not to be killed except if they posed an immediate threat to humans or livestock. If a tiger was killed, an expiatory ceremony had to be performed because even after death the animal had the power to cause illness or bad luck.[19] Many non-Naga groups banned the consumption of tiger meat,[20] and they credited certain humans with the ability to take on the appearance of tigers.[21] As Kyle Jackson suggests, the figure in the middle of Plate 6.2 could be an early depiction of such a dual 'tiger-person'.[22]

---

[15] Ovesen, 'Man or Beast'. See also Von Stockhausen, *Imag(in)ing the Nagas*, 344–5.

[16] Stevenson, *The Economics of the Central Chin Tribes*, 63. See also Parry, *The Lakhers*, 234; Bareigts, *Les Lautu*, 119–28; Boutry, Eh Htoo and Wunna, *Social Anthropological Study*, 41.

[17] Aiyadurai, '"Tigers Are Our Brothers"', PhD thesis. See also Jalais, *Forest of Tigers*, 74, 85.

[18] Endle, *The Kachāris*, 25, 28–9.

[19] For a detailed description of the 'tiger dance' performed to deflect a slain tiger's wrath, see Bareigts, *Les Lautu*, 119–28; Sakhong, *In Search of Chin Identity*, 76–9. See also Shaw, *Notes on the Thadou Kukis*, 43; Lehman, *The Structure of Chin Society*, 182–4; Haokip, 'The Petroglyphs of Indo-Myanmar Frontier'.

[20] For an early reference, see Van Schendel (ed.), *Francis Buchanan in Southeast Bengal (1798)*, 71.

[21] Parry, *The Lakhers*, xii, 84, 141–3, 234–6, 375–6, 542, 551–9. See also Shakespear and Hodson, 'Folk-Tales of the Lushais'; Bareigts, *Les Lautu*, 119–20; Chaudhuri, 'Guardian Spirits, Omens and Meat for the Clans'; Lyngdoh, 'Tiger Transformation'; Brighenti, 'Traditional Beliefs'.

[22] Jackson, 'Colonial Conquest and Religious Entanglement', 146–7.

Plate 6.2 Composition on a bamboo case, possibly showing a 'tiger-man', Chittagong Hill Tracts (Bangladesh), 1882

Source: Riebeck, *Die Hügelstämme von Chittagong*, Tafel 16.

In Mizoram the concept of were-tigers existed but apparently without an acknowledgement of human–tiger kinship.[23] Children were allowed to eat leopard and tiger meat, but not adults – the reason for this was unknown.[24] However, it was *thianglo* (inauspicious, taboo) to shoot a hoolock gibbon as this ape was a human prior to the Great Darkness (Chapter 5). Possibly this was the only animal in Mizoram that humans were not supposed to kill.[25]

Human–tiger kinship is just one example of how Triangle people expressed their intimacy and reciprocity with animals by invoking kin relations. In highland Bhutan people presumed kinship with yaks,[26] and in central Arunachal Pradesh the mithun was considered kin because it was known to have originated in a competition between siblings, resulting in one becoming human and the other a mithun.[27] Sometimes kinship and procreation overlapped. Among the

---

[23] The Thadou also had stories about were-lion(esse)s. Shaw, *Notes on the Thadou Kukis*, 110–12, 124.

[24] Shakespear, *The Lushei Kuki Clans*, 36.

[25] Ibid., 103. See also Shaw, *Notes on the Thadou Kukis*, 40; Aung, 'Social-Ecological Coevolution', 75.

[26] Wouters, 'Relatedness, Trans-species Knots'.

[27] Blackburn, *Himalayan Tribal Tales*, 119–22.

many stories about the origins of the mithun, one is that it was born out of brother–sister incest.[28] In Mizoram, there were stories of some animals having descended from humans (for example gibbons, elephants and certain birds). Conversely, in Nagaland some humans were considered to have descended from hornbills.[29]

Kinship by birth was one thing, but humans and animals could also be related through marriage. The Apatani story of two sisters, Biinyi and Biine, involves the good sister, Biinyi, marrying a snake that had shed its skin and become a man. He was a snake-man who returned to his snakeskin every night. Tired of this routine, Biinyi burned his skin and so the snake-man could no longer transform himself into a snake. This was the reason behind Apatani women not eating snake meat, while men are allowed to eat it.[30]

Kinship with animals implies that animals may behave in a human way. The Thadou represent the tiger as a simpleton who can easily be fooled by humans. Benglama is a typical human hero (the Mizo call their hero Chhura, the Tani groups Abo Tani, the Lotha Apvuho and so on). Clever Benglama was able to get himself out of what could have been a fatal encounter with a tiger. He told the tiger that there was a storm brewing and asked the tiger if he would tie him to a tree for security. Afterwards, the tiger could have him. In response, the tiger asked Benglama to tie him to the tree instead, to protect him from the storm. Benglama obliged, and so was able to get out of harm's way.[31]

Ideas of human–non-human kinship may also have played a role in naming some human groups after animals and plants. Among the Bodo (Kachari), some subgroups were known as animal folk (tiger, leech, mao fish, squirrel) and others as plant folk (jungle grass, sesame, jute, bamboo, fern).[32]

Animal power

There are numerous stories that highlight how animals can cause terror in humans. Take the story of U Thlen, an evil creature of supernatural powers from the Khasi Hills. It usually took the form of a snake. It was known for eating humans, so the people asked the deities for help to kill it. A spirit came to their rescue,

---

[28] Blackburn, *Himalayan Tribal Tales*, 119.
[29] Shakespear, *The Lushei Kuki Clans*, 93; Hutton, *The Angami Nagas*, 391–3; Parry, *The Lakhers*, xii, 138–9, 236.
[30] Blackburn, *Himalayan Tribal Tales*, 107–8. See also Shaw, *Notes on the Thadou Kukis*, 47–8.
[31] Shakespear, 'Tangkhul Folk Tales', 272. On the gullibility of tigers, see also Head, *Hand Book*, 35.
[32] Endle, *The Kacháris*, 25–8. Endle interprets these as totem names. See also Duff-Sutherland-Dunbar, 'Abors and Galongs', 10.

killed U Thlen and asked the people to eat every bit of the snake. But an old woman kept a piece, and U Thlen resurrected himself from it. He offered the old woman a bribe and, instead of informing the others, she succumbed to the promises of the malevolent snake to give her riches if it were not killed. Eventually, however, U Thlen began once again to demand human flesh, and the woman was then forced to employ henchmen (*nongshonoh*) to feed him. Some versions of the story include U Thlen's death in tormented writhing, causing gigantic earthquakes that changed the landscape forever. Even so, today some people still assume that there are keepers of U Thlen and that his murderers are active in the Khasi Hills.[33]

Shakespear reported a tradition from Mizoram where people thought that seeing the 'big snake' (*rûlpui*) was inauspicious. They were afraid to see it, or anything that represented it, because they could die from just looking at it. There were also said to be many places named Rûlpui. One had a big snake raised on a pole on one of its hills. The snake's shadow could fall on hills several miles away. It was called Rûlpui Thlen (big snake shadow), described as a deity. The fear was related to a love story between a girl named Chawngchili and Rûlpui, the snake. Upon hearing about their interspecies love, her father killed both the snake and his daughter, who was found to be carrying many snake children.[34] All except one were killed. The surviving one escaped and eventually settled in a village called 'Snake Feeding Hole' (Rûlchawm Kua), where the inhabitants fed it with goats and pigs and eventually children.[35]

There is an element of fear, too, in the relationship that the eighteenth-century Meitei rulers (the Ningthoujas) had with the snake deity that they regarded as their progenitor and worshipped as a god.[36] When it deigned to appear in the form of a snake, it was the duty of the presiding priestess to coax it on to a cushion and perform ceremonies to please it. If it appeared in diminutive form, it was a sign that the deity was in a good mood, but if it appeared in great size, the deity was displeased.[37] This godlike snake, Pakhangba, became a key representation of kingship in Manipur (Plate 6.3).

---

[33] Nongkynrih, 'U Thlen', 33–8; Nongbri, 'Culture and Biodiversity'; Tham, 'U Rngiew–The Dark One', 50; Lyngdoh, 'On Wealth and Jealousy'. For an interpretation stressing U Thlen's human origins, see Laloo, 'Re-reading Khasi Folktales'.

[34] For more on interspecies sexuality in origin stories, see Elwin, *Myths of the North-East Frontier of India*, 137–81; Shaw, *Notes on the Thadou Kukis*, 138.

[35] Shakespear, *The Lushei Kuki Clans*, 107–8. For another dreadful snake, see Sakhong, *In Search of Chin Identity*, 6–7.

[36] Parratt, 'The Religion of Manipur', 10; Parratt, *The Court Chronicle of the Kings of Manipur*.

[37] McCulloch, *Account of the Valley of Munnipore*, 17. Parratt points out that this may only refer to coronations. Parratt, 'The Religion of Manipur', 12.

Plate 6.3 The Manipur royal emblem: a coiled Pakhangba snake biting its tail

Source: Courtesy of Mrinashree Mairembam, Manipur State Museum.

Note: See also Beemer, 'The Creole City in Mainland Southeast Asia', 268–71.

The power of animals was also acknowledged in quite a different manner: they could portend the future. In the early seventeenth century, John Wade informs us, an advancing army in Assam wanted to know if it was propitious to build a particular bridge, so soothsayers studied a chicken's leg and decided that the omen was favourable.[38] In the Chin and Arakan Hills all important events that included journeys, raids, feasts, ceremonies or sacrifices involved consulting omens to find out if it would be auspicious or not. The most popular way was to kill an animal – a chicken, dog or larger animal – and check its liver, tongue or intestines; observe its nervous reaction on death; or study the position of the legs, or the

[38] Wade, *An Account of Assam, 1800*, 257.

direction in which the blood flowed. If the liver was congested or abnormal, it was an omen that the activity was not going to be fruitful. Breaking and studying an egg could also be effective.[39] There were other forms of divination as well, for example, reading the markings on a living python's skin.[40] In short, the power of animals to mediate between humans and their future was widely acknowledged across the Triangle. Divination was developed into a fine art that required considerable skill (Plate 6.4).

Plate 6.4 A Konyak Naga diviner examining a sacrificed pig, Nagaland (India), 1936

Source: Photo by Christoph von Fürer-Haimendorf. Original title: 'Divination using the sacrificed pig'. Reference PP MS 19/06/NAGA/0444. SOAS Library. © The Estate of Christoph von Fürer-Haimendorf, 1936. The Estate is currently (2015) represented by Nicholas Haimendorf, son of Christoph von Fürer-Haimendorf.

Note: See also Von Stockhausen, *Imag(in)ing the Nagas*, 343.

---

[39] Hughes, *The Hill Tracts of Arakan*, 21; Winston, *Four Years in Upper Burma*, 103; Lewin, *The Hill Tracts of Chittagong*, 91, 98; Gurdon, *The Khasis*, 116–19, 226–8; Brown, 'The Tamans of the Upper Chindwin', 316; Shaw, *Notes on the Thadou Kukis*, 40–1; Stevenson, *The Economics of the Central Chin Tribes*, 64; Terwiel, *The Tai of Assam*; Sitlhou, 'Land and Identity', 119–20; Sitlhou, 'Sacred Ecology and Ritual Practices'; Pau, *Indo-Burma Frontier*, 26. See also numerous examples in Mills, *The Rengma Nagas*; and Mills, *The Lhota Nagas*.

[40] Bower, *Naga Path*, 139–42. For a discussion of python spiritual power, see also Longkumer, *Reform, Identity and Narratives of Belonging*, 176–7.

Finally, the very sight of an animal could be inauspicious. In the Chin Hills the worst omen was seeing a snake, or – worse still – two snakes copulating. The person who saw this was not to return home or speak to anyone until the next sunrise.[41] And the slow loris (a tiny nocturnal primate) was 'in a class by itself ... [i]t brings the most grievous ill luck and is shunned completely' (Plate 6.5).[42]

In the Chittagong Hill Tracts (Bangladesh), seeing a kite or vulture was unfavourable, and so was finding the dead body of any animal on the road: 'they will go no further, but at once return home and stop all proceedings'.[43] Among the Mru, seeing a bear killed was a 'great sin'.[44] Seeing a mole, or hearing a gecko, or a nightjar or other bird, had the same effect in other parts of the Triangle.[45]

Plate 6.5 An 'ill-omened' animal: the slow loris
Source: Photo by Eric Hosking, 1966. See Van Schendel, Mey and Dewan, *The Chittagong Hill Tracts*.

---

[41] Carey and Tuck, *The Chin Hills*, 1:199. See also Hodson, *The Nāga Tribes of Manipur*, 137; Hanson, *The Kachins*, 138–9: Head, *Hand Book*, 44.

[42] Stevenson, *The Economics of the Central Chin Tribes*, 63 (for lists of 'ill-omened animals', see 62–4); Hanson, *The Kachins*, 138–9; and Jugli, Chakravorty and Meyer-Rochow, 'Tangsa and Wancho'.

[43] Lewin, *The Hill Tracts of Chittagong*, 70. See also Hutchinson, *Chittagong Hill Tracts*, 38.

[44] Chowdhury et al., 'Dietetic Use of Wild Animals', 31.

[45] Shakespear, *The Lushei Kuki Clans*, 102–4; Dey, *Bengal Peasant Life*, 8–9. See also Barman et al., 'Saving the Greater Adjutant Stork'.

The evil power of animals could also be more distant. For example, the Tangsa blamed accidents and unnatural deaths on gibbons. 'Whenever an incident happens, villagers go and hunt a gibbon, kill it, cut its body into pieces and throw them away.'[46] They also feared to bring hornbills home 'as they were considered to possess ill-causing spirits'.[47]

The fearsome power that humans ascribed to certain animals shaped human behaviour in many ways. Propitiating ceremonies; cancelled hunting trips, wedding dates and military attacks; and abandoned journeys were just a few of the immediate human responses that animals could trigger. Ideas about animal power also had a deeper impact on Triangle lifeworlds, food habits, livelihoods and identity politics (Chapter 8).

Animals: Wild and domestic

People in the Triangle differentiated sharply between wild animals and their domesticated counterparts. Many communities expressed this distinction linguistically: they had separate vocabularies for these two categories. The Sümi call wild animals *tagashi* (wild/jungle flesh) and domestic animals *tikishi* (house flesh).[48] Among the Mizo animals are called *sa* (flesh) and wild animals are *ram sa* (wild flesh).[49] In Nyishi and Apatani stories, the fundamental difference between humans and spirits is conveyed by their attitude to animals:

> Whenever Abo Tani [the first human] killed an animal in the forest, Doji [the leader of the spirits] was unhappy because he was the spirit of the forest. But if Doji was unhappy, Abo Tani was happy. They were total opposites. Abo Tani hunted all sorts of animals – deer, boars, rats, birds and monkeys. They were wild to Abo Tani, but to Doji they were domestic, almost like his relatives. At the same time, Doji hunted dogs, cows and mithuns, which were domestic to Abo Tani.[50]

This distinction reflected wider ideas in Triangle societies about how to distinguish between the realm of spirits, plants and wild animals and that of humans.[51] As we have seen, this distinction was bridged by imagining a primeval kinship

---

[46] Jugli, Chakravorty and Meyer-Rochow, 'Tangsa and Wancho', 5, 22. See also Shaw, *Notes on the Thadou Kukis*, 76–7.
[47] Jugli, Chakravorty and Meyer-Rochow, 'Tangsa and Wancho', 8.
[48] Hutton, *The Sema Nagas*, 90.
[49] See also Gros, 'Nature De-naturalised', 329.
[50] Blackburn, *Himalayan Tribal Tales*, 74–5. For similar reasoning among the Nyishi, see Aisher, 'Through "Spirits"'.
[51] Bareigts (*Les Lautu*, 114) points out that for this reason, among the Lautu, 'no wild animal may enter the village alive; it has to be killed before crossing the village gate'. See also Jalais, *Forest of Tigers*, 86–8.

Human–Animal Histories

between humans and some wild animals (and spirits). The realm of wild animals was pictured as a hierarchical entity, just like human society. Thus, the tiger was widely seen as the lord of the jungle, just as the human male was regarded as its opposite, the lord of the village and its domestic animals. Significantly, the tiger was considered to have a soul; he was a (non-human) person.[52]

Domestication created a different relationship between humans and animals. Domestic animals were not seen as kin, but humans sometimes did personalise the relationship. In recognition of the individuality of their dogs and pigs, Lotha gave them names, and so did Mru (but they never gave them names used for human beings).[53] Lotha treated dogs very well, especially hunting dogs. These were never eaten and, when they died, they were given a decent burial. When pups, piglets and calves were born, Lotha observed special rituals of abstention (*genna*).[54] The Nyishi also gave names to their mithuns, especially female ones.[55] The Lautu (or Lutuv) of the southern Chin Hills sacrificed chickens to the souls of their other domestic animals by invoking the soul of the mithun, the highest-ranking domestic animal: 'Oh female mithun! May the villagers speak well of you. Don't get hurt, don't sprain your legs, be well, may your prosperity be manifold and assured … and wherever you go, may your journey be good. I call your soul with a chicken.'[56]

The cultural boundary between wild and domestic was well established but it was not impermeable. Wild elephants were regularly caught and tamed, and sometimes domestic elephants interbred with wild ones. The same happened in the case of domestic chickens and wild jungle fowl, domestic and wild pigs, and water buffaloes and yaks.[57]

Hunted animals

If we want to understand more-than-human histories in the Triangle, probably no practice is more revealing than hunting. It is an ancient pursuit that was depicted in the earliest surviving works of art (Plate 6.6). Importantly, hunting was not a solitary affair.[58] Many colonial-era researchers remark on an intense love of

---

[52] Woodward, 'Gifts for the Sky People', 222. The notion of non-human personhood has become of great interest to social theorists, but it has not yet caught the attention of many historians. For introductions, see Ingold (ed.), *What Is an Animal*; Haraway, *When Species Meet*; Viveiros de Castro, *Cosmological Perspectivism*; Kohn, *How Forests Think*.
[53] Brauns and Löffler, *Mru: Hill People*, 131.
[54] Mills, *The Lhota Nagas,* 61–2. See also Duff-Sutherland-Dunbar, 'Abors and Galongs', 45.
[55] Simoons and Simoons, *A Ceremonial Ox of India*, 49, 63.
[56] Bareigts, *Les Lautu*, 158–59 (our translation). See also Myochit, *A Threatened Identity*, 41.
[57] Hazarika, 'Understanding the Process', 210.
[58] For example, Mills, *The Lhota Nagas*; Myochit, *A Threatened Identity*, 67–71.

Plate 6.6 Elephant hunt: terracotta plaque from Bhasu Vihara, Bogra (Bangladesh), c. tenth century CE

Source: Photo by Department of Archaeology, Government of Bangladesh.

Note: See also Ahmed (ed.), *Buddhist Heritage of Bangladesh*, 133.

hunting, both in the hills and in the plains. They give detailed descriptions of how communities undertook hunts, which animals they hunted, and the equipment and methods they used.

Almost all people in the Triangle ate meat and, consequently, hunting was a very important source of sustenance. Meat certainly was not the only thing that made wild animals vital to humans. Most hunted animals were 'multi-purpose': they also provided humans with medicines, adornment, clothes, floor covering and more. Take bears: their meat was eaten, their fur was turned into hats or coats (Plate 6.7) and their gall bladders served as a medicine, often traded to China (Chapter 10). The rhinoceros provided meat, but its tough skin was also much sought after as the best material for shields, and its horn was greatly valued for medicinal purposes.[59] And many wild animals – from reptiles to birds to mammals – were hunted for their fat, feathers, hair, bile, blood, bone, horn, tongue and skin. These wild-animal products were (and still are) used as medicines all over the Triangle.[60]

---

[59] M'Cosh, *Topography of Assam*, 45; Stewart, 'Notes on Northern Cachar', 645; Carey and Tuck, *The Chin Hills*, 1:214; Shaw, *Notes on the Thadou Kukis*, 148.

[60] Betlu, 'Indigenous Knowledge of Zootherapeutic Use'; Chinlampianga, Singh and Shukla, 'Ethnozoological Diversity of Northeast India'; Chowdhury et al., 'Dietetic Use of Wild Animals'; Jugli, Chakravorty and Meyer-Rochow, 'Tangsa and Wancho'; Kikon and McDuie-Ra, *Ceasefire City*, chap. 4.

Plate 6.7 A Mising hunter with bow, arrow, bear-fur hat and mithun-hide shield, Arunachal Pradesh (India), 1954

Source: Photo by Verrier Elwin. Courtesy of Ashok Elwin.

What makes hunting key to understanding Triangle lifeworlds, however, is its spiritual dimension. For most communities, hunting was much more than a functional activity. Hunting was as emotional and sanctified as it was instrumental.[61] A comparative study of hunting in the Triangle is long overdue; here we can only touch lightly and anecdotally on some aspects (see also Chapter 9).

---

[61] Bareigts, *Les Lautu*, 113–31; Stirn and Van Ham, *The Seven Sisters of India*, 119–31.

It is through the rules and ceremonies surrounding hunting that we best appreciate the lifeworlds of people in the Triangle. These practices reveal that for them the separate realms of animals and humans were nevertheless deeply connected, in the present as well as in the afterworld. There were definite variations in the meaning of hunting, however. Various Naga groups regarded the hunt as being closely related to fertility: the hunted animal's power was channelled towards the fertility of the group. Among the Khiamniungan Naga, a man who had killed a tiger could wear its image indelibly tattooed on his skin.[62] The Chin and Mizo, on the other hand, understood hunting primarily as an avenue to gaining social status in the present and in the afterlife.[63]

The importance of hunting could also vary over time in relation to changing human beliefs. After many Meitei took to Hinduism in the eighteenth century, hunting became less popular. Even so, Meitei commonly organised themselves in so-called tiger clubs to protect themselves from the many tigers and leopards that roamed the Manipur valley. Here status and romance were also at stake. There were stories of rewards to hunters, as in the popular pre-Hindu epic of Khamba and Thoibi, in which a heroic tiger slayer was allowed to marry Thoibi, a princess (Plate 6.8).[64]

The hunter-hero

Successful hunters were highly valued and often given special honours. For example, among the Mizo they could achieve the much-coveted status of *thangchhuah*. This title was only bestowed upon someone who had killed an elephant, a bear, a gaur, a wild boar, a barking deer and a sambar deer. It was even better to have killed a viper, a flying lemur and a hawk as well.[65] Strangely, killing a tiger was not a requisite, even though there was no taboo and killing a tiger called for an elaborate ceremony (see later). It was also possible to earn this highly prestigious title by giving several feasts for the entire village, each one lasting many days. These feasts included the killing of domestic animals: pigs, goats and, most importantly, mithuns. Being a *thangchhuah* ensured that a man, upon death, would be able to enter Pial Ral (The Land Beyond) and not be shot down by its gatekeeper.[66]

---

[62] Krutak, 'Tattoos der Tigerjäger und Krieger', 54.

[63] Simoons and Simoons, *A Ceremonial Ox of India*, 158–9.

[64] Hodson, *The Meitheis*, 46, 150; Shakespear, 'The Pleasing of the God Thangjing'.

[65] Shakespear, *The Lushei Kuki Clans*, 64. For a slightly different set of required animals among the Chin, see Stevenson, *The Economics of the Central Chin Tribes*, 62.

[66] See also Shaw, *Notes on the Thadou Kukis*, 75–6; Sakhong, *In Search of Chin Identity*, 30–2, 62–3; Kipgen, 'Forests, Ecology', 220. The road to Pial Ral passed through Rih Dil, a small lake. Today an international border divides this more-than-human spiritual geography. The vast majority of Mizo live in India, but the lake is 3 kilometres across the border in Myanmar.

Plate 6.8 Killing the tiger, Manipur (India)

Source: Photo by Recky Maibram.

Note: Undated painting in the temple of Ibudhou Thangjing (a pre-Hindu deity), site of the annual Khamba-Thoibi dance in Moirang (Manipur). The scene depicts the contest between the hero, Khamba, and his nemesis, Nongban, to kill a ferocious wild tiger in front of the king's entourage. See Hodson, *The Meitheis*, 134–51; Raina, *Khamba Thoibi*, 64–78; Singh and Dhanamanjuri, 'The Legendary Ballad', 100.

Mang Hnin, a chief in the nearby Chin State, composed a song that conveyed the hunter-hero's self-esteem and confidence in the hereafter:

> When I consider the forest of my hunt, I will lie in peace,
>
> For I am not an ordinary hunter.
>
> Let the large gaur march in front of me into the next world.[67]

The killing of animals reflected spiritual convictions. In many communities, hunting required elaborate rituals to placate spirits, ensure success and restore animal–human–spirit reciprocity.[68] Killing a wild animal generally required a follow-up sacrifice to be made, often to ensure that the killer could gain possession of that animal's spirit in the afterlife. Among the Mizo this ceremony was called *ai*, 'to obtain power over'. Performing the *ai* ceremony meant that the animal's

---

[67] Sakhong, *In Search of Chin Identity*, 63.
[68] Aisher, 'Through "Spirits"'; Aiyadurai, '"Tigers Are Our Brothers"', PhD thesis, 66–8.

spirit could pass into the 'settlement of the dead' – and he who performed the *ai* ceremony would have power over the animal thus hunted. If a man was killed in a raid, an *ai* ceremony was also performed; it required the sacrifice of a mithun and a pig.[69]

The Mishmi believed that wild animals were owned by a mountain spirit, *ngolo*, who delivered the animal to the hunter. Consequently, *ngolo* had to be appeased by giving it an offering after a successful hunt, but also by following a proper code of conduct. Otherwise, hunters could be hurt in an expedition or fall victim to serious illnesses. The code required that during the hunt animals were identified by a specific code name, different from the name used in general conversation. The elephant's code name was 'the one having a tail on both sides' and the musk deer's name was 'meat of the high mountain'.[70]

The Nyishi had very similar ideas. They felt that wild animals were protected and reared by spirits. Before and after the hunt, it was important to make a ritual offering to these spirits, not just for large game but also for other animals, such as (flying) squirrels, snakes, and birds (Plate 6.9).[71] The Lautu held a ceremony twice a year to ensure that there would be game to hunt. They invoked the forest spirit who oversaw wild animals:

> Oh mistress, we, your priests, offer you this sow and request you to call the wild animals. With your help, may the game with the beautiful antlers and tusks arrive ... from the rivers, the fog, the rocks, the steep cliffs – make them come in their hundreds, in their tens.[72]

Hunting and gender

Hunting was a man's job – we have not come across examples of female hunters. As a Chin proverb had it: 'to a man: war, the hunt, and the feast – to a woman: work in the house and the fields'.[73] The rewards to men were manifold. Hunters could engage in intense male bonding, enjoy the excitement of the chase, earn social prestige and provide food and animal products for the community. Village boys would

---

[69] Shakespear, *The Lushei Kuki Clans*, 78–9. See also Shaw, *Notes on the Thadou Kukis*, 154; Sakhong, *In Search of Chin Identity*, 31.

[70] Aiyadurai, '"Tigers Are Our Brothers"', PhD thesis, 69; Aiyadurai, '"Tigers Are Our Brothers"', 309. See also Lehman, *The Structure of Chin Society*, 173. Garo use respectful descriptions rather than the word for elephant – they speak of 'the big one', 'grandparent', and 'uncle from the hills' – and for tiger – described as 'the one who does not wash his face'. Sur, *Jungle Passports*, 126–8.

[71] Aisher, 'Through "Spirits"', 237. See also Gros, 'Nature De-naturalised', 328–9.

[72] Bareigts, *Les Lautu*, 140–3 (our translation).

[73] Stevenson, *The Economics of the Central Chin Tribes*, 62.

Plate 6.9 Children holding up a giant flying squirrel, Chin Hills (Myanmar), 1920s

Source: Photo by G. E. Harvey, 1920s. Original caption: 'The large flying squirrel, 26" across the "wings" and 4 ft in length, Haka Dist.' © Pitt Rivers Museum, University of Oxford. Accession Number: 1998.314.383.2.1.

meet hunters who returned home to respectfully carry their guns and the game that they had bagged (Plate 6.10). Many Triangle masculinities were shaped around hunting; it was an activity that they deeply loved and identified with.[74]

At the same time, this division of labour excluded women from an important opportunity to gain status in society. A place in the afterlife was open only to those who could hunt. Although a few women did have high status in this life because they were village chiefs or wives of hunting heroes (*thangchhuah*[75]), non-hunters had little presence in the afterlife. Among the Kuki in Manipur, however, a woman could perform a ceremony that paralleled the male *ai* ceremony following the killing of wild animals. This female-oriented ceremony, known as *chang ai*, or 'victory over rice', would give praise for a series of especially abundant harvests. As one woman explained:

> This auspicious occasion [*chang ai*] used to be celebrated with pomp and grandeur by slaughtering mithuns and pigs for the public feast, because from that day onwards the performer and her family would be accorded the privilege to enter 'peogal', meaning the land of eternal bliss after death.[76]

---

[74] Mills, *The Lhota Nagas*, 65; Mahmud, *Ang Ing Mru Rung*, 44.
[75] Lorrain, *Dictionary of the Lushai Language*, 447.
[76] Kipgen, 'Forests, Ecology', 219–20. See also Shaw, *Notes on the Thadou Kukis*, 74–5; Kamkhenthang, *Folk Songs of the Thadou*, 3; Sitlhou, 'Land and Identity', 129.

Plate 6.10 Boys proudly carrying a hunter's trussed-up barking deer and guns into their village, Chin State (Myanmar), 2013

Source: Photo by Tyler Chapman. Copyright © 1998–2020, RFA. Used with the permission of Radio Free Asia, 2025 M St. NW, Suite 300, Washington, DC 20036. https://www.rfa.org.

Note: See also Bareigts, *Les Lautu*, 114–18.

Gender differences permeated not only the practice of hunting but also women's more distant relationship with wild animals. When Mishmi hunters returned home after a successful hunt, they had to follow certain practices. Among these were a prohibition to have sex, or receive food from a menstruating woman, and the injunction that the meat had to be cooked by men, outside the main house.[77] Mishmi women were not allowed to eat any meat of wild animals (except rats, fish and big birds) for fear of retaliation by the spirit protecting wild animals.[78]

Eating wild animals

Once a successful hunting party returned home, there were strict rules for who was to receive which portion of the meat. Among the Lotha the meat was

---

[77] Aiyadurai, '"Tigers Are Our Brothers"', PhD thesis, 66–70; Aiyadurai, 'Human–Animal Relations, 29. See also Duff-Sutherland-Dunbar, 'Abors and Galongs', 46; Hutton, *The Sema Nagas*, 57; Ramirez, 'Enemy Spirits, Allied Spirits', 23–4.

[78] Aiyadurai, '"Tigers Are Our Brothers"', PhD thesis, 36, 56. See also Rowlatt, 'Report of an Expedition into the Mishmee Hills', 491.

divided between the person who threw the first spear, the second spear, the owner of the hunting dog and so on.⁷⁹ In some communities, the chief extracted a portion as tax.⁸⁰

As we have seen, many communities considered the eating of certain animals (for example, tiger) forbidden for the whole community. There were spiritual reasons for food avoidance but also medical ones. Some meat was considered harmful to the body. The Lotha absolutely forbade the meat of the great hornbill because the bird made a croaking sound and therefore people eating its meat would die of hiccoughs.⁸¹ The Sümi, on the other hand, did not eat hornbill meat because whoever did would develop sores on their feet like the scutes on the bird's feet. People who wore hornbill feathers as a headdress during a ceremony could not eat wild vegetables because they would develop the same symptoms.⁸²

Displaying wild animals

The skulls of wild animals were widely understood to be sacred objects, and they were hung on racks on the outer walls of houses all over the Triangle.⁸³ As the abode of the spirit that protected hunters, the skull rack was a distinctly male space.⁸⁴ In 1889–90 invading British forces came upon Fo Lyan Sôn, a powerful man in the Chin Hills, and they recorded his sense of pride and self-esteem:

> At the lower east gate there was a spot where the skulls of all tigers killed were buried. This animal appears to be regarded with some superstition, and its skull is never hung on the walls of the houses like other trophies of the chase. The Head Chief, Fo Lyan Sôn, seventy years of age, received the party at his house, which was clean and well-built. The walls of the vestibule were crowded with skulls; in front, those

---

⁷⁹ Mills, *The Lhota Nagas*, 65.

⁸⁰ Shakespear, *The Lushei Kuki Clans*, 52–3; Shaw, *Notes on the Thadou Kukis*, 65–6; Stevenson, *The Economics of the Central Chin Tribes*, 68–9; Haokip, 'Identity, Conflict and Nationalism', 189; Sakhong, *In Search of Chin Identity*, 37: Zou, 'The Past of a Fringe Community', 213: Myochit, *A Threatened Identity*, 68–9. Among the Taman, the 'spirit-keeper' was entitled to a portion. Brown, 'The Tamans of the Upper Chindwin', 307.

⁸¹ Mills, *The Lhota Nagas*, 77.

⁸² Hutton, *The Sema Nagas*, 92.

⁸³ Some groups also, separately, displayed human skulls. These were symbols of martial prowess rather than hunting prowess. As headhunting was an 'intra-species' practice between humans, it falls outside the scope of this book. However, for images of human skull racks, see, for example, Jacobs et al., *The Nagas*.

⁸⁴ Aisher, 'Through "Spirits"', 125, 165, 228; Aiyadurai, '"Tigers Are Our Brothers"', PhD thesis, 70–2, 78, 96, 99, 161, 178; Simoons and Simoons, *A Ceremonial Ox of India*, 49–50; Mahmud, *Ang Ing Mru Rung*, 44. See also Young, 'A Journey from Yün-Nan to Assam', 167, 170; Mills, 'The Mishmis of the Lohit Valley', 3.

of seven elephants, and behind, closely packed, others of bison, sambhur, mythun, wild boar, buffalo, bear, monkey, &c. The old man said that the whole were of his own shooting, and boasted that he had himself accounted for 1,070 wild animals of different kinds.[85]

The ritual importance of even small animal heads was obvious: 'All the skulls of larger animals killed by [a Naga] are religiously kept, from that of an otter to that of an elephant, while even the heads of small birds may often be seen nailed to his house.'[86] These skulls were important reminders of a man's hunting prowess but also of his guaranteed entry into the best possible afterlife (Chapter 5). Therefore, among the Bawm-Zo, men were reportedly buried together with their animal skulls.[87] Today racks of hunted and sacrificed animal skulls are still on display (Plate 6.11).[88] In many communities these skulls have lost their sacrality but they remain decorative and nostalgic status symbols.

Wild animals and human inequality

Hunting could be used as a tool to maintain and underline social inequality within communities. Only men (and sometimes only seasoned warriors) were allowed to adorn themselves ceremonially with wild-animal ornaments, such as wild boar's tusks, bear or gibbon fur, ivory armlets, hornbill tail feathers and leopard skin (Plate 6.12; see also Plate 8.5).[89] Hats made of red panda fur were a mark of distinction among the Mishmi and, among the Konyak, a person's status determined the kind of meat they could eat.[90] Commoners were allowed all types of meat, except tiger, but the elite abstained from eating goat and bear.[91] In many communities, men were allowed meat that was denied to women.[92]

Clearly, the Triangle's human history has been structured by hunted animals in many ways. Hunting gave status to men, provided food and other things, shaped group identities and linked the human and spirit worlds. Wild animals were considered to be in a category that was clearly separate from the animals that were closest to humans on a daily basis – domestic animals.

---

[85] Reid, *Chin-Lushai Land*, 123–4. Bareigts (*Les Lautu*, 118–28) explains the spiritual dangers of bringing a tiger skull into a village.
[86] Hutton, *The Angami Nagas*, 158.
[87] Barbe, 'Some Account of the Hill Tribes', 384.
[88] For an image of a rack of water buffalo skulls in a Nocte village in Arunachal Pradesh, see Kolkman and Blackburn, *Tribal Architecture in Northeast India*, 228.
[89] Mills, *The Lhota Nagas*, 13; Fürer-Haimendorf, *The Konyak Nagas*, 13.
[90] Mills, 'The Mishmis of the Lohit Valley', 3.
[91] Fürer-Haimendorf, *The Konyak Nagas*, 58–9.
[92] Aiyadurai, '"Tigers Are Our Brothers"', PhD thesis, 36, 56.

Plate 6.11 Skulls of gaur, wild buffalo, mithun, deer and other animals on display near the India–Myanmar border, Mizoram (India), 2012

Source: Photo by Willem van Schendel.

Plate 6.12 Men wearing hats adorned with fur, boar's tusks and feathers, Upper Chindwin Valley (Myanmar), 1935

Source: Photo by Henry C. Raven. Original caption: 'Men wearing traditional costume, Hahti to Singkaling Hkamti, Myanmar, March 1935.' Image # nnc-m36v47-vhc-n016, American Museum of Natural History Library.

Domestic animals

In Chapter 3 we saw how, thousands of years ago, humans and animals in the Triangle began sharing their intimate spaces. There were various routes to domestication. Animals could colonise human spaces (rodents, lice), they could join human activities (wolves following human hunters) or they could be actively confined by humans (wild boars, jungle fowl, bovines, elephants). Selective breeding gradually altered these animals, resulting in domestic dogs, chickens, pigs and so on. It mostly fell to women to care for domestic animals (Plates 6.13 and 6.14).

Plate 6.13 A woman with her pigs, dog and chicken, probably in Chin State (Myanmar), 1920–30

Source: Photo probably by G. E. Harvey. Original caption: 'Young woman, wearing neck ornaments, with baby on her back in a sling. Behind her are bundles of thatching plant material on a stilted rack. In front of her pigs and chickens eat out of a wooden trough. A dog stands beside her. A house is just seen on far left.' © Pitt Rivers Museum, University of Oxford. Accession Number: 1998.314.635.2.

Plate 6.14 Pig feed being cooked in a separate 'pig kitchen', Mizoram (India), 2011
Source: Photo by Willem van Schendel.

Triangle humans came to depend on domestic animals for food (meat, eggs and, in some areas, milk and yak cheese), hides and more. What interests us here, however, is their symbolic importance. Domestic animals represented wealth that was exchanged between humans, and they were enormously meaningful for human exchanges with the spirit world – as sacrifices.

Animal exchange and trade

Domestic animals could be important partners in fostering relationships between communities. They were a means through which networks of exchange developed, as they travelled between communities when marriages were arranged, peace pacts were made, war captives were freed or ransoms had to be paid.[93] Exchanges could

---

[93] Lewin, *Progressive Colloquial Exercises*, 80; Shakespear, *The Lushei Kuki Clans*, 47–8; Head, *Hand Book*; Simoons and Simoons, *A Ceremonial Ox of India*, 50–5. Pau (*Indo-Burma Frontier*, 172, 182) reports that 'the northern Chin/Zo used a mithun, [but] the southern Chin/Zo took an oath with a tiger's skull to observe the peace'.

be commercial, for example, when mithuns were used as currency to obtain bells from Tibet,[94] or when people traded dogs to be sacrificed or eaten (Plate 6.15).[95]

An important example of reciprocity was the movement of mithuns between communities in Arunachal Pradesh. The Nyishi combined shifting cultivation with animal husbandry. They reared goats and common cattle for their meat, and pigs and mithuns as sacrificial animals. Throughout the eastern Himalayas, mithuns were the highest-ranking animals for sacrifice, and this created a problem for the Apatani who lived nearby. They practised wet-rice cultivation on permanent, irrigated fields. Although they valued mithuns highly, they could not allow them around their fields because this would lead to the destruction of their

Plate 6.15 Travelling dog traders, northern Myanmar, 1920s

Source: Photo by James Henry Green. Original caption: 'Maru dog traders.' James Henry Green Charitable Trust, Royal Pavilion & Museums Trust, Brighton & Hove.

Note: See also Hanson, *The Kachins*, 56; Shaw, *Notes on the Thadou Kukis*, 86.

---

[94] Simoons and Simoons, *A Ceremonial Ox of India*, 54–5. See also Duff-Sutherland-Dunbar, 'Abors and Galongs', 35; Mills, 'The Mishmis of the Lohit Valley', 4.

[95] For images of dog sacrifices, see Brauns and Löffler, *Mru: Hill People*, 164; Mahmud, *Ang Ing Mru Rung*, 55–6. See also Terwiel, *The Tai of Assam*, 35–6; Boutry, Eh Htoo and Wunna, *Social Anthropological Study*, 27; Myochit, *A Threatened Identity*, 61. On current debates about eating dog meat, see Kikon and McDuie-Ra, *Ceasefire City*, chap. 4.

crops: mithuns are semi-domesticated and free ranging. Instead, they placed their mithuns in the care of a Nyishi who, in return, would get every third or fourth calf born to that animal.[96] There was also a trade in mithuns from Arunachal to Bhutan, in exchange for common cattle moving in the opposite direction.[97]

Animals as sacrifice

Animal sacrifice was an important aspect of Triangle lifeworlds, and in some areas this continues to be the case.[98] Previously, in parts of the Triangle, there was a tradition of headhunting or human sacrifice as well. Although this tradition has attracted much comment and produced a considerable literature, we will not be concerned with it here, simply because this was a human-to-human (or intra-species) activity in which non-humans were not immediately involved.[99] Human sacrifices did, however, reflect the lifeworlds of the groups that practised them, just as animal sacrifices do – they are all blood sacrifices. In other words, they should be understood as 'part of a single ritual system ... sacrifice entails the death or destruction of a valued being or object which is presented to nonhuman beings in return for immaterial gifts of blessing, power, or grace'.[100]

Animal sacrifices brought the region together in many ways.[101] They even became inscribed in the landscape. The name of the Patkai mountains that lie between northern Myanmar and Assam is derived 'from the Ahom words *pat*, meaning "cut", or "sacrifice", and *kai*, meaning "chicken"'.[102] In most of the Triangle uplands the quintessential and highest-ranking sacrificial animal was

---

[96] Simoons and Simoons, *A Ceremonial Ox of India*, 65. See also Tarr and Blackburn, *Himalayan Tribal Tales*, 43–53.

[97] Simoons and Simoons, *A Ceremonial Ox of India*, 26, 97, 189.

[98] Bareigts, *Les Lautu*, 133–61. The ritual killing of animals may not always be understood as a 'sacrifice' to the spirit world, as the annual festival of village purification among Garo exemplifies. To remove the pollution of the past year, men go out to hunt a langur (or, failing that, a squirrel). The priest hits each village house with its body to absorb the pollution and finally disposes of it in the forest, together with last year's pestles, brooms and rice-cooking sticks. De Maaker, 'Negotiating Life', 68.

[99] Zou, 'Raiding the Dreaded Past'; Kar, 'Heads in the Naga Hills'.

[100] Woodward, 'Gifts for the Sky People', 226, 218–19. See also Bareigts, *Les Lautu*, 129–31; Urban, *The Power of Tantra: Religion*, 241–245; Kar, 'Heads in the Naga Hills', 352; Myochit, *A Threatened Identity*, 37–46. Hunted animals could be treated in similar ways as headhunted humans. Von Stockhausen, *Imag(in)ing the Nagas*, 81.

[101] For a story from Arunachal Pradesh explaining the invention of animal sacrifice, see Ramirez, 'Enemy Spirits, Allied Spirits', 16–17.

[102] Terwiel, *The Tai of Assam*, 39.

the mithun – and especially the mithun bull.¹⁰³ It was not butchered for the provision of meat but only sacrificed during ritual feasting. The religious and social significance of these 'feasts of merit' was enormous, as revealed by lasting commemorative symbols: wooden posts or stones showing mithun horns, skulls hung on house walls or decorative wooden 'horns' on the roof of a feast-giver's house (for details and illustrations, see Chapter 8).

Mithun sacrifices marked marriages or deaths, times of illness or misfortune, trade deals, peace treaties and friendship pacts.¹⁰⁴ They were 'religious, social and economic action'.¹⁰⁵ And they established status in society. As many as forty mithuns could be sacrificed in a single ceremony, and such lavishness required a sufficiently prosperous person, usually a chief, to host the sacrifice.¹⁰⁶ At the same time, the sacrifice and the feasting that followed ensured the redistribution of wealth. Sacrifices were concurrently individual, in that they offered prestige to the giver, and communal, in that they distributed wealth, status and well-being within a community.¹⁰⁷

In the case of the Naga, mithun sacrifices were related to fertility and reproduction. Both human ancestors and spirits had the 'life-substance' (*aren*) that can bring about human and crop fertility and productivity. To acquire this life-substance, humans had to exchange it for a sacrificed mithun. Nyishi, on the other hand, exchanged their mithuns for divine protection. They believed that the world is inhabited by spirits, malevolent or benign, who must be propitiated. Tamün was a particularly evil spirit, who required a major mithun sacrifice to obtain his protection.¹⁰⁸

Mithun sacrifices involved references to many other animals, showing how the animal kingdom resonated in Triangle lifeworlds. Nyishi senior priests wore mantles of tiger, leopard or clouded leopard hide (without the head, tail or legs) because during the ceremony 'the priest *is* a tiger'. They also carried a fan made of the tail feathers of a bird of prey and two long drongo tail-rackets. Ordinary people used fans made of hornbill wings. The feathers were a medium to make

---

[103] Simoons and Higham, 'More on Higham's Study', 405; Simoons and Simoons, *A Ceremonial Ox of India*. In the Bhutan uplands the top sacrificial animal was the yak. Tashi, 'Contested Past, Challenging Future', 19, 228; Wouters, 'Relatedness, Trans-species Knots', 28.

[104] Head, *Hand Book*; Jimo, 'Text, Knowledge and Representation'. Sometimes humans wore special ceremonial dress during sacrifices. Von Stockhausen, *Imag(in)ing the Nagas*, 95.

[105] Woodward, 'Gifts for the Sky People', 221. See also Chowdhury et al., 'Dietetic Use of Wild Animals', 29.

[106] Fürer-Haimendorf, *The Konyak Nagas*, 60.

[107] Sakhong, *In Search of Chin Identity*, 46–81.

[108] Stonor, 'Notes on Religion and Ritual', 6–7.

contact with the spirit world: they summoned spirits. In the Triangle, the spiritual properties of tail feathers were widely acknowledged. Naga used the tail feathers of the great hornbill on ceremonial occasions, as did the Mishmi with the tail feathers of Sclater's monal.[109]

Humans sacrificed many other animals as well.[110] The elaborate community sacrifices of the Ahom included elephants, horses, deer, buffaloes and many smaller animals.[111] Some animal sacrifices required a (semi-)permanent material sign. The Nyishi believed that animals larger than a fowl required the setting up of an altar of tall leafy bamboo. On it, emblems made of thin wood were placed, each linked with a particular spirit: a flying hornbill, a trident, a square and more.[112] The Konyak and many other groups marked the sacrifice of a mithun by erecting forked Y posts (see Plate 8.10 for an example from the Chittagong Hill Tracts). The number of such posts depended on the number of animals sacrificed. The posts were said to symbolise the animals themselves – they honoured them. Priests requested the animals: 'Do not grieve; in your place, we erect these posts; in the future mithan will be as numerous as the eggs of insects.'[113]

Animal sacrifice and different religious traditions

There was never a sharp boundary between local religions and other cosmologies that developed in the Triangle, notably the ones we now call Hinduism, Buddhism and Islam. Local deities embedded themselves in the rituals of these broader religions and there were constant negotiations about how these related to the gods of these faiths. Some rituals involved animal sacrifices. For example, the Mech of Assam and northern Bengal did not make images of deities but did use the Hindu term 'puja' for their ceremonies, at which blood and meat of beheaded animals (pigs, goats, chickens, ducks and pigeons) were offered to various deities.[114]

---

[109] Stonor, 'Notes on Religion and Ritual', 10–12.

[110] For the role of pig and chicken sacrifices in rituals related to agricultural production and rain, see Sakhong, *In Search of Chin Identity*, 48–51. See also Stack and Lyall, *The Mikirs*, 30–4; Hanson, *The Kachins*, 154–5, 162–3; Terwiel, *The Tai of Assam*.

[111] Terwiel, *The Tai of Assam*, 48–54.

[112] Stonor, 'Notes on Religion and Ritual', 16–18.

[113] Fürer-Haimendorf, *The Konyak Nagas*, 60.

[114] Sanyal, *The Meches and the Toṭos*, 1:67–8, 74; for animal sacrifices by the Toṭo, see 2:41–2. Writing about Assam and northern Bengal, Hodgson remarked: '[The Páni Kocch] eat no tame animal without offering it to God (the gods).... There are no images. The gods get the blood of sacrifices; their votaries, the meat ... no Bodo or Dhimál will touch flesh the blood of which has not been offered to the gods.' Hodgson, *Essay the First*, 146–7, 161. Sacrificial animals included pigs, buffaloes, goats, pigeons, ducks and chickens (and eggs). Ibid., 168, 170, 173–4, 179.

Similarly, Islamic ideas have influenced devotion among the Bodo (Kachari) of Assam. They worship several gods, one of which is Nawab Badshah – a Muslim god – with chicken sacrifices.[115] In southern Bengal these complexities play out in shrines where three deities are jointly venerated. The first is Bonbibi, a powerful Muslim goddess of the forest who was raised by deer. The second is Dokkhin Rai, a Hindu deity who is half man-half tiger, and to whom duck and goat sacrifices are made.[116] And the third is Ghazi Khan, another Muslim deity, sometimes depicted as riding a tiger.[117]

Hindu practices in the Triangle have a long and specific history of animal sacrifice, thought to have derived from local pre-Hindu rituals. The earliest local Hindu texts, dating to the tenth and sixteenth centuries CE, describe the pre-Hindu inhabitants as having 'shaven heads and yellow skins' and being 'strong, ferocious, ignorant and addicted to meat and liquor'.[118] These texts went straight against Vedic ritual because they deemed both wild and domestic animals acceptable as sacrifices.[119] The wild animals included tortoise, bird, crocodile, fish, monkey, mongoose, wild boar, rhinoceros, lizard, lion, yak, rabbit, tiger, jackal and elephant. The domestic animals listed were buffalo, bull, sheep and he-goat.[120]

Assam's chief Hindu temple Kamakhya is constructed on two earlier strata reaching back to 200 BCE. It has been suggested that it was previously a sacred site (possibly a graveyard) of a local religion.[121] Today, daily rituals at this temple are focused on the bloodthirsty, menstruating mother goddess Kamakhya. These rituals are inconceivable without animal sacrifices offering blood to her – notably water buffaloes, goats, pigeons and fish (Plate 6.16). Here,

---

[115] Ali, 'Islam in the Hill Areas', 6.

[116] Mitra, *Mangrove Forests in India*, 340.

[117] Jalais, *Forest of Tigers*, 68–75. See also Jalais, 'People and Tigers', 82–5.

[118] Quoted in Shin, 'Yoni, Yoginīs and Mahāvidyās', 7.

[119] *Kalika Purana* (c. tenth century CE) and *Yogini Tantra* (c. sixteenth century CE) were composed in or near Assam. Borkataky-Varma, 'Red: An Ethnographic Study', 188.

[120] Kakati, *The Mother Goddess Kāmākhyā*, 65; Urban, *The Power of Tantra: Religion*, 62–3; Urban, 'The Womb of Tantra', 238.

[121] The Khasi and Garo, still living nearby, have a tradition of animal sacrifice to honour the dead – and so did the Koch and Bodo (Kachari). Kakati, *The Mother Goddess Kāmākhyā*, 37; Rosati, 'The Goddess Kāmākhyā', 142, 147; Shin, 'Yoni, Yoginīs and Mahāvidyās'; Hodgson, *Essay the First*, 147; Endle, *The Kachāris*, xvii–xviii, 29, 41, 82; Sharma, 'Territories of Belonging', 179–82.

sacrifice to the goddess includes a number of clearly non-Vedic and impure animals (for example, buffaloes), offered in extremely non-Vedic ways (such as bloody beheading). Many of these sacrificial traditions ... owe far more to the indigenous, pre-Hindu religions of the northeast hills than to any Vedic rite.[122]

What makes the long-term influence of local religions on these Hindu practices even more evident is the fact that – against prescriptions in Hindu texts – sacrificial animals are ritually beheaded, and their heads offered to the deity.[123] Plate 6.17 shows a large wild buffalo skull, daubed with vermillion powder, on the outer wall of another important Hindu shrine in Guwahati, the capital of Assam.

In Cooch Behar and Assam, Shiva worship also required sacrifices of buffaloes, pigs, he-goats, pigeons, ducks and roosters; and goat sacrifices continue

Plate 6.16 Goats about to be sacrificed, Kamakhya temple, Guwahati, Assam (India)
Source: Photo by Willem van Schendel.

---

[122] Urban, *The Power of Tantra: Religion*, 52; see also 57–72. The snake goddess Manasa is also thought to have originated in snake worship – and U Thlen stories – in the neighbouring Khasi Hills (169–70). See also Smith, *The One-Eyed Goddess*; Borkataky-Varma, 'Red: An Ethnographic Study'.

[123] Urban, *The Power of Tantra: Religion*, 64–7.

Plate 6.17 Buffalo skull on the Ugrotara temple in Guwahati, Assam (India), which was established during Ahom rule in 1725

Source: Photo by Willem van Schendel.

Note: See also Urban, *The Power of Tantra: Religion*, 240–1; Urban, 'The Womb of Tantra', 240–1.

to be practised at Shiva temples in Assam.[124] A similar influence of local religions predating Hinduism can be detected in Tripura. Today goats, eggs and buffaloes are sacrificed here in an important Hindu temple, much like in the Kamakhya temple in Assam.[125]

Although the teachings of Buddhism forbid the killing of animals, in the Triangle many of those who consider themselves Buddhists practise animal sacrifice. In Bhutan, pre-Buddhist traditions of sacrificing chickens, pigs, yaks and sheep were intended to ensure 'vitality, fertility, and abundance of wealth'. They were gradually abolished by government decree and finally formally discontinued in 2013.[126] The Lepcha of Sikkim, whose traditional beliefs are described as

---

[124] Kakati, *The Mother Goddess Kāmākhyā*, 21. See also Terwiel, *The Tai of Assam*, 41–2.

[125] The Tripura Sundari (or Matabari) temple in Udaipur, established around 1500 CE. See Stirn and Van Ham, *The Seven Sisters of India*, 163.

[126] Tashi, 'Contested Past, Challenging Future', 19, 138; Miyamoto, Magnusson and Korom, 'Animal Slaughter and Religious Nationalism'.

'Buddhist-shamanic', continue to practice ritual blood sacrifices of fishes, chicken, pigeons and bullocks'.[127] The Buddhist Khamti of the northeastern India–Myanmar borderlands placate their three most powerful guardian spirits with goats, chickens and ducks.[128] And the Buddhist Marma of the Chittagong Hill Tracts sacrificed pigs, goats and chickens (and previously cows), and offered the heads to their deities.[129]

For those in the Triangle who became Muslims, animal sacrifices carried over easily. In Islam, the annual Feast of Sacrifice (Eid ul Adha, or Qurbani Eid) requires the sacrifice of goats, sheep, cows, buffaloes or camels – not by beheading but by draining blood from the body. The ritual shedding of blood and sharing of meat as an expression of devotion to Allah became a core celebration in local forms of Islam.[130] It became not only a marker of piousness, however, but also a celebration of social inequality. 'The days preceding the Eid-ul-Azha become a podium for self-aggrandisement which is performed and established through the comparisons made among sacrificial animals ... the acquisition of expensive, super-sized cows provides heightened prestige to the family.'[131] A few people reach for even more powerful status symbols and import camels as sacrificial animals (Plate 6.18).[132]

Local forms of Islam in the Triangle are strongly influenced by pre-Islamic and Sufi traditions. Pre-Islamic beliefs about the power of animals to act as conduits between humans and the spiritual world became embedded in local Sufi devotion. Certain wild animals – crocodiles, monkeys, turtles, pigeons and fishes – are believed to channel the charisma of deceased Sufi spiritual guides (*pir*). Devotees visiting their very popular shrines venerate (but do not sacrifice) the animals that live there.[133] The influence of local cosmologies can also be traced in buffalo sacrifice: among Sufi Muslims in lowland Chittagong, sacrificial buffaloes apparently 'first came as gifts of pilgrims from the Chittagong Hill Tracts'.[134] Local forms of Islam also include worship of 'Muslim deities', such as the cholera goddess Ola Bibi. During an annual festival, as well as during outbreaks of cholera,

---

[127] Torri, 'In the Shadow of the Devil', 158.
[128] Lainé, '*Phi Muangs*'. See also Terwiel, *The Tai of Assam*.
[129] Bernot, *Les paysans arakanais du Pakistan Oriental*, 2:497, 596–619. See also Zakaria, 'A Grammar of Hyow', xxvi, 18, 447, 474, 641; Htwe, 'The Social Organization', 62–5.
[130] Bertocci, 'A Sufi Movement in Bangladesh', 18–20.
[131] Akhtar, 'The Wrong Kind of Sacrifice'.
[132] Harder, *Sufism and Saint Veneration*, 62.
[133] Mukul, Rashid and Uddin, 'The Role of Spiritual Beliefs'; Khan, *Protected Areas of Bangladesh*, 22; Uddin, 'In the Company of *Pirs*'; Van Schendel, *A History of Bangladesh*, 76–7, 293.
[134] Harder, *Sufism and Saint Veneration*, 64.

Plate 6.18 Sacrificial camels on the road in northern Bengal (India), 2005
Source: Photo by Willem van Schendel.

Ola Bibi is invoked with sacrifices of beheaded goats and fishes.[135] Another Muslim deity, Manik Pir, is believed to have a special relationship with animals: he is the patron saint of cattle.[136]

Christianity was a relative latecomer in the Triangle. Initially, there was quite some resistance against the teachings of Christian missionaries who forbade animal sacrifices. As one village chief told a missionary in 1901: 'School I want, but the Heavenly Jesus I don't want. If we do not sacrifice chickens and pigs we die. Therefore, I don't want Jesus custom.'[137]

Nevertheless, as more inhabitants of the Triangle began to identify as Christians, animal sacrifices and feasts of merit lost their former cosmological connotations or were integrated into the new faith. For example, chickens continued to be sacrificed to propitiate field spirits before an agricultural field was used, but now a Christian priest could officiate, and the offerings could be made in the name of the Christian god.[138] And certain Christians also believed in – and sacrificed goats

---

[135] Ferrari, 'Devotion and Affliction', 38, 42.
[136] Mukharji, 'Lokman, Chholeman and Manik Pir'.
[137] Quoted in Sakhong, *In Search of Chin Identity*, 138.
[138] Aung, 'Social-Ecological Coevolution', 73–4, 86–7, 99. See De Maaker, 'Who Owns the Hills', 363–4, for rice offerings among Christian Garo.

and chickens to – powerful non-Christian deities.¹³⁹ Remarkably, the connection between animal sacrifice and feasting was not lost either. Occasions such as Christmas, harvest festivals and weddings are still accompanied by the ceremonial killing of mithuns and other domestic animals, their meat being shared among large groups of people (Plate 6.19; see also Chapter 8).¹⁴⁰ People now experience animal sacrifice more as a social, community-oriented act than as a religious one.

Plate 6.19 A mithun to be ceremonially killed at a Christian wedding in Mizoram (India), 1959

Source: Photographer unidentified, V. Thangzama collection.

---

[139] Lyngdoh, 'An Interview with a Goddess'.
[140] Brauns and Löffler, *Mru: Hill People*, 130. They describe mithuns as being considered rare, expensive 'luxury animals' in the Chittagong Hill Tracts. See also De Maaker, 'Have the Mitdes Gone Silent', 137; Aung, 'Social-Ecological Coevolution', 74, 99.

In short, animals-as-sacrifice have been important to the inhabitants of the Triangle as powerful tools to communicate with the spiritual world, or, more precisely, various spiritual worlds. Historically, blood sacrifices in the Triangle have been integral to both community religions and Hinduism, Buddhism and Islam. In recent times, Christian and Buddhist authorities have pushed back against animal sacrifices, but they have not been able to eliminate them completely.

Triangle styles of sacrifice have always focused on the sacred meaning of animal heads and the importance of sacrifice by beheading. The heads were offered to deities and often preserved. This form of sacrifice was anathema to scriptural Hinduism, Buddhism and Islam alike, and yet it persisted among Triangle inhabitants who thought of themselves as Hindus, Buddhists and Muslims – as the examples of the Kamakhya temple, the Marma and Ola Bibi demonstrate.

Evidently, this regional ritual spoke so intensely to Triangle spirituality that it became integrated into cosmological and social orders that developed later, even though these orders formally disapproved of it. Animal sacrifices signify the cultural specificity of the Triangle – and they underline how 'world religions' such as Hinduism, Islam, Buddhism and Christianity get inflected in any given locality.[141]

Human–animal interactions

In this chapter we have explored how people in the Triangle incorporated the animals around them into their cosmologies. They created a cultural universe in which animals could be kinfolk, fearsome adversaries, wild or domestic, companions and essential assistants in accessing the invisible realm of spirits and the afterlife. All over the Triangle, humans developed sophisticated regulations that permitted the killing of animals during the hunt or the sacrifice. Human lifeworlds were saturated with beliefs, visions and emotions about animals.

Inevitably, this chapter has been no more than a quick tour, indicating some commonalities and changes over time. The literature in the footnotes helps to fill in details and contexts, but a lot of broader comparative research needs to be done. We will now move to Chapter 7, which considers the role of human–plant relationships in Triangle cosmologies.

---

[141] Doniger, *The Hindus*. See also Zakaria, *Pronomohi Bongomata*; De Maaker, 'Have the Mitdes Gone Silent'.

7

Human–Plant Histories

In Chapter 6 we explored historical relationships between humans and several non-human animals. We will now turn to historical connections between humans and plants, once again focusing our attention on symbolic aspects as well as on changes over time.

In the Triangle, humans have always been surrounded by thousands of different plant species. The meeting point of three biodiversity hotspots, the Triangle boasts a wide range of landscapes and a lush monsoon climate. It is a verdant place and home to an astounding diversity of plant life. And yet, the significance of this diversity for human history has been insufficiently explored. It has remained largely invisible, taken for granted as a backdrop to human life. We need to overcome our tendency towards 'plant blindness' – the misguided anthropocentric ranking of plants as inferior to animals.[1]

Plants were always absolutely vital for human life, not only as sources of nourishment, but also because of their cultural significance. Numerous interspecies relationships connected humans and plants in the Triangle from the earliest times. One way of putting it is to say that plants are deeply implanted in the region's imagination. Another is to state that humans have always constructed their cultures around plants.

How did the natural environment of the Triangle frame the lifeworlds of its people? How did they think about forests, plants and trees? How did plants figure in Triangle cosmologies? And how did plants shape human cultures? The answers cannot be as explicit as in the case of animals because the role of plants is often less clearly articulated in historical stories and practices. Even so, we can suggest several plant contributions to human cultures in the Triangle. We will first look at notions of ancient sacred connections between humans and plants, and the role of plants in ceremonial life. Then we will briefly consider

---

[1] Wandersee and Schussler, 'Preventing Plant Blindness', 82. See also Gagliano, Ryan and Vieira (eds.), *The Language of Plants*; Margulies et al., 'Illegal Wildlife Trade'.

ideas about the healing powers of plants and, finally, how humans interacted with plants as domestic companions.

Origin stories and plants

Stories about the origins of the universe do not dwell much on plants, and yet there is a givenness about their role. In Chapter 5 we encountered stories among the Khasi and Mizo about enormous trees that, at the beginning of time, used to connect the earth and the sky. The power of such ideas continues to be remarkable: a large piece of sacred wood, said to have been part of the original earth-sky tree, is still being preserved in a Khasi village. Wrapped in bamboo, it forms the central pole of the house of the priestess in Smit village.[2] In Apatani stories, a spirit brought plants and vegetables to the earth. The Khumi believed that a deity created the world, trees and creeping things, before fashioning humans. And the Angami story of original migration featured a covenant signed under a wild pear tree.

In origin stories the forest is an all-pervasive presence. These stories provide a charter for humans to deal with the environment. Alexander Aisher and Stuart Blackburn argue that the Nyishi and Apatani divide the world into two parallel worlds inhabited by spirits and humans.[3] Forests and mountains came to be the abode of spirits, and the lower terrain and cleared land came to be human places. These stories are full of references to how humans should behave towards the spirits and their territory, and which placating rituals are required when entering the forest. This approach was based on an understanding of exchange relationships connecting humans, animals, plants and spirits. Humans were guests in the forested domain of spirits. This attitude ensured a conservative exploitation of the forest and its resources and, in certain cases, a prohibition to enter forests at all. Such forests became known as sacred groves.

Sacred groves

Various communities across the Triangle have long maintained sacred groves. Here human interference was prohibited for spiritual reasons. Often, these forested areas were thought to be inhabited (or protected) by treasured or fearsome supernatural beings and, therefore, out of bounds for mere humans. This is not to say that these were 'untouched' virgin forests, representing an original biodiversity. It is quite possible that they were manipulated for religious reasons to make them more suitable for their supernatural inhabitants.[4]

---

[2] See image in Stirn and Van Ham, *The Seven Sisters of India*, 98–9.

[3] Aisher, 'Through "Spirits"'; Blackburn, *Himalayan Tribal Tales*.

[4] Although this point has not been explored for the Triangle, it is addressed in Tomalin (*Biodivinity and Biodiversity*, 155–63) and Sivaramakrishnan ('Ethics of Nature in Indian Environmental History', 1285). See Allison, 'Deity Citadels'.

Today, hundreds of sacred groves can still be found in the Triangle, some quite small but others more extensive. Thus, in Meghalaya State (India) alone some 80 groves cover an area of 260 square kilometres.[5] Although they were not maintained for consciously environmental reasons (a desire to 'protect nature'), they did act as a refuge for many rare species. In some cases, however, a conservationist urge has been read into the location of sacred groves: among the Khasi these are often around the headwaters of rivers and at vulnerable sites, such as the rain-eroded hillsides of Cherrapunji.[6]

Over time, attitudes towards the groves have been changing. Some have been described as 'places of resistance and resilience' to geopolitical forces.[7] But the sanctity and integrity of others are no longer respected, particularly in areas where traditional religions are in decline or have been abandoned.[8] This opened the way not only for community exploitation for firewood and wild vegetables but also for outsiders entering the groves in pursuit of scientific knowledge, commercially valuable species, eco-tourism or bio-piracy (acquiring ownership by means of plant patents).

Outside the sacred groves, the worlds of spirits and humans were in constant communication as well. We have seen how stories comprised instructions to hunters who entered forests to propitiate the spirits that protected wild animals. The same was true for humans entering the forests to disturb the vegetation and clear plots for cultivation. Such instructions form the basis of complex agricultural rituals that are still being practiced in many parts of the Triangle.[9] To maintain a good relationship between humans, spirits and crops, offerings are made at various points in the agricultural cycle. Quite often, these plant-oriented practices involve animal sacrifices.[10]

Ceremonial plants

Plants without any nutritional value could nevertheless become very important items of consumption. This was the case with an odd pair: a palm tree and a forest creeper. Neither the areca palm (*Areca catechu*) nor the betel vine

---

[5] Khan, Khumbongmayum and Tripathi, 'The Sacred Groves'. See also Medhi and Chakrabarti, 'Traditional Knowledge'; Karlsson, *Unruly Hills*, 106–14; Allison, 'Deity Citadels'.

[6] Nongbri, 'Culture and Biodiversity', 14.

[7] Allison, 'Deity Citadels', 3.

[8] Karlsson, *Unruly Hills*, 3–6; Ormsby, 'Analysis of Local Attitudes'; Mishra et al., 'Effects of Anthropogenic Disturbance'; Khumbongmayum, Khan and Tripathi, 'Sacred Groves of Manipur'; Khatoon, 'Natural Resources and Biodiversity'; Aung, 'Social-Ecological Coevolution'.

[9] For example, Htwe, 'The Social Organization', 54–6.

[10] For example, Brauns and Löffler, *Mru: Hill People*, 109–18, 141–4.

(*Piper betle*) is native to the Triangle.[11] They arrived by human agency many centuries ago – nobody knows when – and developed into key cultural icons. In many communities, the areca nut (also known as the betel nut) and fresh leaves of the betel vine acquired potent ritual connotations. Grown in homesteads, gardens or forests, their cultivation can require specific ceremonies.[12] They are often consumed as a stimulant, together with an animal product (lime, made from crushed mollusc shells). Offering them to visitors as a sign of respect became a standard everyday practice, and they also became indispensable in innumerable essential rituals, such as worship of major deities, divination and life-cycle events (notably marriage, divorce and death).[13] There were also ideas about their role in the afterlife. Among the Khasi,

> it is believed that the spirits of the dead, whose funeral ceremonies have been duly performed, go to the house or garden of God, where there are groves of betel-nut trees; hence the expression for the departed, *ula lam kwai ha ung u blei* (he who is eating betel-nut in God's house), the idea of supreme happiness to the Khasi being to eat betel-nut uninterruptedly.[14]

Areca nuts and betel leaves were also linked to romance. A young man would offer them to a girl and, by accepting the offer, she could signal her romantic interest in him.[15] In some cases, humans also endowed areca nuts with magic sexual meanings.[16] Finally, the cultural power of areca nuts and betel leaves was underlined when some Christians in the Triangle began to discourage their use. Dubbed 'crops of vice', their consumption was discouraged, together with that of tobacco and alcohol (Plate 7.1).[17]

---

[11] Both are from Island Southeast Asia, where the habit of their joint consumption appears to have originated. They may have arrived overland with early migrants, possibly the forebears of the Khasi (as Ludden suggests), or by sea via the Bay of Bengal. Zumbroich, 'The Origin and Diffusion of Betel Chewing'; Ludden, 'Cowry Country', 78; Hoogervorst, 'Tracing Maritime Connections', 760–1. See also Young, 'A Journey from Yün-Nan to Assam', 160.

[12] Khan, 'The Nishorgo Support Project', 72.

[13] For a few examples, see Endle, *The Kachāris*, 82, 86, 89, 96; Terwiel, *The Tai of Assam*, 2:30; Sharma et al., 'Medico-religious Plants'; Meitei and Marak, 'A Study on Megalithic Burial Stones', 163; Ahmed and Singh, 'Traditional Knowledge System'; Jugli, Chakravorty and Meyer-Rochow, 'Tangsa and Wancho of North-East India', 21; Khan, 'The Nishorgo Support Project'. See also Tālish, *Tarikh-i Asham*, 94, 98–9. For a story linking the birth of areca nut, betel vine and tobacco to human death, see Sawian, *Khasi Myths*.

[14] Gurdon, *The Khasis*, 105.

[15] Fürer-Haimendorf, 'The Morung System', 362; Brauns and Löffler, *Mru: Hill People*, 178.

[16] Garigliano, '"A Very Naughty Place!"', 68; Borkataky-Varma, 'Red', 188.

[17] Zhimomi, 'Christianity and Politics in Nagaland', 111; Cairns, 'The Alder Managers', 44; Longkumer, 'Rice-Beer, Purification', 453; Ross, 'Development of Local Theology', 108.

Plate 7.1 Crops of worship, sociability or vice? Areca nuts and betel leaves for sale in Assam (India)

Source: Photo by Willem van Schendel.

In the same way, humans gave ceremonial and sacred meanings to many other plants that they found in, or imported into, the Triangle. For example, rituals of circumcision and death among the Meitei–Pangals (a Muslim group in Manipur) required the spines, charcoal, leaves and seeds of several local plants.[18] When the Thadou made a peace deal, they swore an oath of friendship on two specific plants.[19] Many groups needed holy basil (tulsi, *Ocimum sanctum*), bel (*Aegle marmelos*), sijou (siju, *Euphorbia spp.*[20]), mango, ginger, banana and other plants for their daily, seasonal or lifecycle ceremonies.[21] Some plants were important to ward off malevolent deities. Others could help in

---

[18] Ahmed and Singh, 'Traditional Knowledge System'.

[19] Shaw, *Notes on the Thadou Kukis*, 43; see also 67–8.

[20] The ritual importance of this plant crossed religious, temporal, and geographical boundaries. It was as essential to the cult of the snake goddess Manasa in lowland Bengal around 1500 CE (Sen, *Vipradāsa's Manasā-Vijaya*) as it was to Boro practices around 1900 CE (Endle, *The Kachāris*, 30, 36–7, 86).

[21] For example, Trant, 'Notice of the Khyén Tribe', 264; Trant, 'Report on a Route', 1146; Sharma et al., 'Medico-religious Plants'.

predicting the future.²² And certain plants were ritually taboo – people could not use them.²³

Medicinal plants

Human–plant relations went far beyond the ceremonial and sacred – they always stretched into the realm of human well-being. Spirituality and healing were inseparable.²⁴ Throughout the Triangle, humans saw plants as preservers and restorers of health, so healthcare depended heavily on plants. Over the centuries, Triangle societies developed complex understandings of the healing capacities of roots, leaves, flowers, fruits and stems, and they knew how to prepare numerous medicines. Medical practices were mobile and various. They were shared and compared; and they were transmitted orally from one generation to the next – until over the past century and a half they came face to face with other medical approaches and were marginalised as 'folk medicine'.²⁵

Generally speaking, practitioners of Western medicine have long been dismissive of these regional health systems, but recently this has begun to change because they have come to suspect that many Triangle plants have eminent curative properties. This has given rise to a recent outpouring of research on these properties.²⁶ Many of these studies make little effort to analyse the Triangle

---

[22] Dalton, *Descriptive Ethnology of Bengal*, 12; Endle, *The Kacháris*, 30, 36–7, 82; Playfair, *The Garos*, 18; Shaw, *Notes on the Thadou Kukis*, 83–4; Sharma et al., 'Ethnobotanical Studies'; Medhi and Borthakur, 'Sacred Groves and Sacred Plants'; Sharma and Pegu, 'Ethnobotany of Religious'; Singh, 'Plants Associated in Forecasting'; Zomi, 'Marriage Practices of the Zou Tribe'; Singh, Singh and Sharma, 'Ethnobotanical Studies'; Pangging, Sharma and Sharma, 'Ethnobotanical Study of Plants', 2019; Tashi, 'Contested Past', 94, 151, 152, 159–60, 175.

[23] Lyngdoh, 'An Interview with a Goddess', 69.

[24] See examples in Sharma et al., 'Medico-religious Plants', 790–4; De Maaker, 'Have the Mitdes Gone Silent'. See also Shaw, *Notes on the Thadou Kukis*, 156.

[25] In a slightly different context Mukharji argues that 'these humbler, relatively obscure, mostly oral traditions were never given the same social, political, or epistemic status [as elite medical traditions]. Instead, from the second half of the nineteenth century, they were increasingly swept into a residual category called "folk medicine"'. Mukharji, 'Dis-locating Subaltern Therapeutics', 135.

[26] For example, Thu et al., 'A Review of Common Medicinal Plants'; DeFilipps and Krupnick, 'The Medicinal Plants of Myanmar'; Ong et al., 'Ethnobotany of Wild Medicinal Plants'; Chakraborty et al., 'North-East India an Ethnic Storehouse'; Sarmah et al., 'Traditional Medicobotany of Chakma Community Residing'; Wiart, *Medicinal Plants of Bangladesh*; Rahman et al., 'Medicinal Plant Diversity'; Wangchuk and Tobgay, 'Contributions of Medicinal Plants'.

healthcare systems themselves, instead offering lists of explored plants and their applications. But some help us in understanding the larger cultural contexts.[27]

Triangle healthcare traditions varied. Some were influenced by ideas in the wider Asian environment, such as those now often known as Sowa-Rigpa, Ayurveda, Unani, Desana, Bethitzza or Vezzadara medical knowledge.[28] Others were inspired by locally developed perceptions of plant–animal–human–spirit connections. In all of them plants were acknowledged as healing organisms that could come to the rescue when humans faced illness, pain or misadventure. Animals and minerals were also involved in healing, but hundreds of plant species dominated the medical landscape. For example, over 800 different medicinal plants were reportedly being used in Meghalaya alone.[29]

Knowledge of the causes of illness and the (plant) remedies to fight them was often in the hands of medical specialists who observed, advised, administered and offered support. Sometimes they would first try the effectiveness of medicinal plants on animals before giving them to humans.[30] These people could have certain privileges, such as being entitled to enter sacred groves to collect plants. Both women and men could become specialists by means of family connections or personal skill and talent.[31] The roles of these specialists – *maibi-maiba* (Meitei), *ojha* (Chakma), *gunial* (Garo), *thempu* (Thadou), *nyubu* (Nyishi), *kobiraj* (Assamese and Bengali) and so on – reflect the meanings of healing in their respective spiritual worlds. In English texts, these specialists are variously referred to as healers, herbalists, doctors, medicine (wo)men, priest(esse)s and shamans. They could be wholly beneficial 'life-givers' – as the Mizo term *ti-damtu* indicates[32] – but some could use plants to harm other people.[33]

---

[27] Even in studies of marginalised therapeutical traditions in South Asia that are mindful of the power relations between dominant and subaltern traditions, the traditions of the Triangle are usually excluded or marginalised. See Hardiman and Mukharji (eds.), *Medical Marginality in South Asia*.

[28] Yeshi et al., 'An Integrated Medicine of Bhutan'; Wangchuk, Yeshi and Jamphel, 'Pharmacological, Ethnopharmacological, and Botanical Evaluation'; Latt et al., 'Traditional Medicine and Diabetes Care'; Ong and Kim, 'Medicinal Plants for Gastrointestinal Diseases'; Mukharji, 'Dis-locating Subaltern Therapeutics'; Coderey, 'Myanmar Traditional Medicine'.

[29] Lyngdoh, Syiem and Mao, 'Pattern of Traditional Medicine'.

[30] Albert, 'Medical Pluralism', 91–3, 147.

[31] Ibid., 87–90. See also Biswas et al., 'Inherited Folk Pharmaceutical Knowledge'; Singh, Rallen and Padung, 'Elderly Adi Women of Arunachal Pradesh'; Ramashankar, Deb and Sharma(eds.), *Traditional Healing Practices*; Stirn and Van Ham, *The Seven Sisters of India*, 95–107.

[32] Lorrain, *Dictionary of the Lushai Language*, 495.

[33] Take the *ara* plant among the Garo in Bangladesh: 'A kind of plant that is grown and tended by a ko-bi-raj or gu-ni-al (herbal doctor) and that is said to be used to kill people.' Burling, *The Language of the Modhupur Mandi*, 5.

Plant-based healing was not without other risks either, as the Zeme Naga story of Herakandingpeu demonstrates. This renowned ancestral healer cured people (and animals) with plantain leaves, grass and roots like ginger, but never sacrificed an animal. This behaviour enraged the gods who were craving blood. They killed Herakandingpeu, and his vast plant knowledge died with him. The only thing that he had taught other people was the healing power of ginger. Since then, people were forced to sacrifice animals to the gods.[34]

Finally, plants themselves could pack danger. 'Certain medicinal plants are categorised as *dikgi*. The Garo attribute a set of characteristics and powers to them (beneficial and/or harmful) that must be controlled. These plants are a double-edged sword: they can help people and/or hurt them.'[35] In short, plant-based remedies had to be applied judiciously. Medicinal plants were powerful organisms that could save (or ruin) a person's health. Their application only made sense if accompanied by human knowledge derived from careful observation of the environment and an inherited comprehension of the world order.

For several generations now, these healthcare systems have been in decline. New ways of thinking about illness and health gained ground but they did so very unevenly. They reached some groups and regions much earlier than others. Today, the availability of scientific medical knowledge and institutions – and the affordability of treatment and drugs – are still patchy and highly skewed against poor, illiterate and rural populations. Many people in the Triangle continue to rely to a greater or lesser extent on the ideas and treatments of their forebears.

Remarkably, the fact that 'scientific medicine' has become more sensitive to plural medical practices has boosted Triangle healing traditions. A flurry of studies appeared that labelled Triangle practices as 'ethno-medical', 'ethno-pharmacological' and 'ethno-botanical'. Institutes of 'folk medicine' were established and researchers began surveying the wisdom of traditional healers. States officially recognised traditional healers' knowledge as 'intangible cultural heritage'. The Indian government created a North Eastern Institute of Folk Medicine in the Triangle 'to strengthen and develop traditional health practices for the benefit of the nation, with special focus on the North Eastern region'.[36] Myanmar's government created a Department of Traditional Medicine.[37]

---

[34] Longkumer, *Reform, Identity and Narratives of Belonging*, 102–3. See also Bower, *Naga Path*, 137.

[35] Claquin Chambugong, 'Sociocultural Conceptions', 202.

[36] This institute was established under the Ministry of Ayurveda, Yoga and Naturopathy, Unani, Siddha, Sowa Rigpa and Homoeopathy (AYUSH) in 2008. It is located in Pasighat, Arunachal Pradesh.

[37] Coderey, 'Myanmar Traditional Medicine'.

And Bhutan's government has a Department of Traditional Medicine Services, with a Division of Local Healing and Spiritual Health. Thus, Triangle healthcare knowledge became of more than regional interest as governments and entrepreneurs woke up to the economic value and possibility of patenting plants and genetic material. Today medical pluralism and struggles over vegetal property rights are transforming the relationships between humans and medicinal plants in the Triangle.

Companion plants

The plants whose ceremonial and medicinal meanings we have explored so far were important partners of humans in the Triangle. But there were many more plants that did not have primarily ceremonial or medicinal roles to play. These companions could be wild or domestic specimens.

Among the wild companion plants there were many that were traded (or bartered) between humans in different ecological zones, thereby enlarging the livelihood portfolios of these communities. Among these plants were rattan, yams, timber, bamboo, fuel wood and forest fruits, in return for salt, metal goods, fish paste, beads and so on. Some reached distant markets. An example is agarwood, a costly fragrant resin that is used in perfumes, incense and medicines. It develops in the heartwood of some trees of the *Aquilaria* family in response to a fungus infection. Agarwood from the Triangle found its way to customers as far apart as ancient northern India; sixteenth-century Japan; nineteenth-century Turkey, Arabia, Persia and Europe; and twentieth-century China.[38]

Another wild plant that became of great global commercial interest in the nineteenth century was *Ficus elastica*, or the India rubber tree.[39] Humans could harvest latex from this tree, but it was also a companion in a very different way. Its strong aerial roots could be trained across rivers to fashion living root bridges for humans to cross. If well maintained, such bridges were long-lived, and several still exist in Meghalaya.[40]

Tea was another companion plant that became of global commercial interest in the nineteenth century. It grew wild in the northern Triangle and was also cultivated by some groups who processed tea leaves to make an infusion.[41]

---

[38] López-Sampsoni and Page, 'History of Use'; Barden et al., *Heart of the Matter*, 10, 17–26, 38; Mohamed (ed.), *Agarwood*. See also Tālish, *Tarikh-i Asham*, 84–5. Today, wild *Aquilaria* trees are increasingly threatened, and tree plantations are taking over.

[39] Kar, 'Historia Elastica'; Majumdar, 'The Colonial State and Resource Frontiers'; Zou, 'Riverine Bazaars'.

[40] Ludwig et al., 'Living Bridges'.

[41] This practice continues today. Lungphi, Singh and Das, '"Phalap-Khah"'.

In the early 1820s, Europeans became aware of tea growing in the Triangle.[42] This would lead to the emergence of a highly profitable agro-industry that spread tea seeds and served consumer markets around the world (see Plates 10.1 and 10.11).[43] But not all wild plants were innocuous companions – some could be lethal.

Poisonous plants

The Triangle offered humans a range of plants that contained poisonous substances. Several became essential partners in political, social and economic life. Many different types of poison were used but a favourite was derived from aconite, a tuber that grows at high altitudes in the eastern Himalayas.[44] The Triangle is thought to have exported aconite poison to different parts of India from very early times; it is mentioned in the Atharva Veda, a collection of texts that predate 1000 BCE.[45] The regional aconite trade across the Triangle is well documented.[46]

In the Triangle, poison-tipped arrows were widely used in warfare. Among upland communities, success in war often depended on mastery in handling bows and poisoned arrows.[47] And poisoned arrows may have played an important role in how upland communities were able to repel lowland states – before the advent of firearms.

Plant poisons also afforded humans ascendancy over animals. Poisoned arrows could bring down elephants, bears, tigers and smaller animals, without hunters having to get close to their prey.[48] Today, plant poisons continue to be used in the

---

[42] Bruce, *An Account of the Manufacture*; Sharma, 'British Science'; Sharma, *Empire's Garden*.
[43] Karlsson, 'Introduction', 10.
[44] The two most frequently used varieties were *Aconitum ferox* and *Aconitum lethale*. There are also reports of arrow poisons being made from rotting meat, for example, Parry, *The Lakhers*, 50–1.
[45] Bisset and Mazars, 'Arrow Poisons in South Asia', 8–9.
[46] Rowlatt, 'Report of an Expedition', 489; [Butler], *Sketch of Assam*, 30; Mills, 'The Mishmis of the Lohit Valley', 6; Duff-Sutherland-Dunbar, 'Abors and Galongs', 47–8; Dunbar, *Frontiers*, 127–8.
[47] For example, Pemberton, *Report on Bootan*, 157; Hughes, *The Hill Tracts of Arakan*, 40; Waddell, 'Note on the Poisoned Arrows of the Akas', 59; Brinckmann, 'The Táng Era "Annals of Yúnnán"', 64; Young, 'A Journey from Yün-Nan to Assam', 158; Millington, *On the Track of the Ábor*, 106–7; Fürer-Haimendorf, *The Naked Nagas*, 134; Ardussi, 'Bhutan before the British', 218. On poisoned wells, see Butler, *Travels and Adventures*, 113; Hutton, *The Angami Nagas*, 153. Arrows could also be made of poisonous bamboo. Dunbar, *Frontiers*, 127–8; Aisher, 'Through "Spirits"', 351.
[48] For example, Trant, 'Notice of the Khyén Tribe', 268; Trant, 'Report on a Route', 1149–50; Phayre, 'Account of Arakan', 705; Wilcox, 'Memoir of a Survey of Assam', 338; Butler, *Travels and Adventures*, 89; Stewart, 'Notes on Northern Cachar', 642–3; Shakespear, *The Lushei Kuki Clans*, 196–7; Hanson, *The Kachins*, 83; Kingdon Ward, *In Farthest Burma*, 122–3; Hutton, *The Angami Nagas*, 378; Srivastava, *The Gallongs*, 37–8.

hunt and to catch birds,[49] and many different poisons are used in rivers to stupefy fish (Plate 9.2).[50] Some are harmless for humans, but others can harm or kill them, so there were strict rules for how to handle them.[51] Even so, poisonings did occur, either by accident (for example, eating rhododendron-blossom honey[52]) or on purpose (murder or suicide).[53] Finally, cattle had to be steered away from toxic plants.[54]

Knowledge of plant poisons was an essential means of empowerment that humans passed down through the generations. It increased their ability to protect themselves from human and animal predators, and to enrich and diversify their diets. The human–toxic plant partnership shaped warfare, hunting and fishing during millennia. And even today, when firearms are commonplace and industrial poisons are available, poisons from wild plants are still widely used as cheap and effective alternatives, especially in the Triangle uplands.

Agricultural crops

Although wild plants were important companions, most companion plants were domesticated varieties, notably agricultural crops. As agriculture developed in the Triangle (Chapter 3), crops became highly meaningful organisms to those who tended them. People turned into guardians, managers and protectors of these plants, and human societies evolved to suit plant requirements. The rhythms of vegetal growth took over human lives. Crops became daily companions. Both nurturing and demanding, they could be stern – but unintentional – taskmasters, driving human labour and creating gendered work patterns. Human–crop relationships ran deep. And they were

---

[49] Roy (née Chowdhury), 'The Donyi-Polo Cult of Arunachal Pradesh', 117–18; Tag and Das, 'Ethnobotanical Notes on the Hill Miri Tribe', 82; Sarmah et al., 'Indigenous Technical Knowledge', 53; Aiyadurai, *Hunting in a Biodiversity Hotspot*, 26; Rethy, 'Ethnobotanical Studies', 63; Namsa et al., 'Ethnobotany of the Monpa Ethnic Group', 6; Yumnam and Tripathi, 'Ethnobotany', 158–9; Kalita et al., 'Diversity and Traditional Uses', 758–61.

[50] For example, Yumnam and Tripathi, 'Ethnobotany', 158–9; Boko and Narsimhan, 'Rapid Survey of Plants Used', 274–5; Ahsan and Khan (eds.), *Red List of Bangladesh*, 209; Imchen and Joglekar, 'Traditional Fishing Practices', 386–7. See also Peal, 'Notes on a Visit', 31; Playfair, *The Garos*, 49; Hanson, *The Kachins*, 77, 83; Gurdon, *The Khasis*, 50; Hutton, *The Angami Nagas*, 89–90; Hutton, *The Sema Nagas*, 84, 87; Mills, *The Lhota Nagas*, 70–2, 125; Mills, *The Rengma Nagas*, 106–8; Parry, *The Lakhers*, 163–4.

[51] Kolkman and Blackburn, *Tribal Architecture*, 182, 185.

[52] Kingdon Ward, *In Farthest Burma*, 81–2; Bailey, *China–Tibet–Assam*, 126–7.

[53] Hutton, *The Angami Nagas*, 230; Hutton, *The Sema Nagas*, 232; Mills, *The Lhota Nagas*, 82; Burling, *The Language of the Modhupur Mandi*, 142, 144, 162, 266.

[54] Pemberton, 'Abstract of the Journal', 268; Penjore, *On the Mule Track to Dagana*, 36.

multidimensional because economic and social life was structured by the requirements of complex combinations of crops.

Significantly, plants came to dominate Triangle constructions of time. People divided the year into four to six seasons that corresponded to the weather and the agricultural cycle. The new year was often considered to begin with the dry season around April, followed by the hot and rainy seasons, the autumn and the cold season. In upland agriculture three distinct slack periods occurred after clearing a field, weeding it and harvesting the various crops. Rituals also followed a seasonal pattern, with feasts of merit often taking place in the cold season.[55] Christians in Mizoram linked agriculture to their new religion when they chose the slack period following weeding (*favâng âwllên*) as the time to hold their large congregational gatherings. Among Inpui Naga Christians in Manipur, the word for heaven (*lozaan nu*, 'place of rest') also refers to the slack season. The rhythm of crops shaped human behaviour and ideas in sometimes unforeseen ways.

Cultivating a mountain field

In mountain agriculture (or shifting multi-cropping), pieces of forest were periodically cleared for cultivation. The selection process involved observing the terrain and reading it for unlucky signs. Trees could communicate danger. For example, a tree with a bulbous top or another protuberance could be a warning sign not to select a particular site. And if two tree boughs were heard rubbing together, this could denote the presence of a hostile spirit.[56] Animal sacrifices (chicken, goat, pig or mithun[57]) were essential at this point. If the omens signalled that the spirits were willing to have the plot used for agriculture, the cultivators could go ahead.[58] They burned the vegetation, cleared the tree stumps, constructed a field hut and made further sacrifices to secure a good harvest.[59] Some communities burned all plots at the same time, followed by a day of mourning for the animals and spirits that had perished in the fire.[60] Planting specific flowers around the field hut could keep spirits at bay. For example, the Mizo believed that amaranth flowers 'dazzle the eyes of the evil spirits so much that they cannot see human beings standing near the plants'.[61]

---

[55] Ara and Rashid, 'Between the Built and the Unbuilt', 6.
[56] Shakespear, *The Lushei Kuki Clans*, 101–2.
[57] Bareigts, *Les Lautu*, 78, 81–2, 88, 141–3, 157–8; Myochit, *A Threatened Identity*, 54–6.
[58] De Maaker, 'Who Owns the Hills'.
[59] Aung, 'Social-Ecological Coevolution'; Bareigts, *Les Lautu*, 81.
[60] Sitlhou, 'Land and Identity', 116–17. See also Marak, 'Rice from *A·ba*'.
[61] Lorrain, *Dictionary of the Lushai Language*, 558. See also Dokhuma, *Hmanlai Mizo Kalphung*, 14.

After these tasks were done, the sowing of multiple crops could begin (Plates 7.2 and 7.3). Usually dibble sticks were used to make holes in which a mix of seeds was deposited, but sometimes seeds were sown broadcast. The field hut provided shelter during overnight stays that were necessary to safeguard the crops. Constant vigilance was required to ward off marauding animals, such as wild boars, monkeys, deer, birds – and sometimes even mithuns that love to eat maize. Planting ginger around the field hut was thought to keep tigers away. Cultivators held frequent ceremonies to placate the spirit world: they understood their crops to be temporary invaders into the forest realm of wild vegetation.[62]

Plate 7.2 Women sowing a freshly burned field, Chittagong Hill Tracts (Bangladesh)
Source: Photo by Lorenz G. Löffler. See Brauns and Löffler, *Mru: Hill People*, 85.

---

[62] There are many descriptions of the agricultural processes, ceremonies, beliefs and interpretations of dreams involved. For examples see Mills, *The Lhota Nagas*, 45–59; Mills, *The Rengma Nagas*, 75–89; Gurdon, *The Khasis*, 39–48; Shaw, *Notes on the Thadou Kukis*, 77–8; Brauns and Löffler, *Mru: Hill People*, 109–25; Aisher, 'Through "Spirits"'; De Maaker, 'Negotiating Life', 64–78; Gupta, 'Jhum Cultivation Practices'; Mahmud, *Ang Ing Mru Rung*, 24–7, 31, 33; Marak, 'Rice from *A·ba*'; Aung, 'Social-Ecological Coevolution', 73–4, 86–7, 99, 121–9.

Plate 7.3 A man with a dibble planting rice and cotton, Chittagong Hill Tracts (Bangladesh)
Source: Photo by Lorenz G. Löffler. See Brauns and Löffler, *Mru: Hill People*, 111.

Cultivating a mountain field was hard work because the field needed constant care. The various crops that were planted would grow at different speeds and labour requirements would peak at certain times. This was especially pressing in the case of rice. Rice plants had to be watched carefully because, in the early stages, other plants ('weeds') would outgrow them. So these unwanted plants had to be removed to give space to the rice – to help the rice to construct its niche. It was common for three weedings to be done before the rice plants were strong enough to outgrow competing vegetation. Weeding was very labour intensive and usually beyond the capacity of single households, so communal weeding teams were formed to help out.

There were several models. One consisted of groups of teenage boys who were sent around the fields to help, their participation being ensured by penalties. This model was linked to communities with institutions known as 'boys' clubs' or 'bachelors' dormitories'.[63] A second model was for unmarried boys and girls to form voluntary teams, working the fields in pairs and sometimes in larger groups. These teams were (and still are) strictly reciprocal – working each other's fields by turns, in exchange for a meal or rice beer.[64] This model connected back-breaking agricultural work to feelings of freedom, harmony, friendship and romance, and it has been described as effectively functioning as a dating system.[65] A third model was reciprocal assistance arranged among groups of young men. They sometimes put up stones to mark their lasting friendships. This is how four friends in Mizoram expressed their fond memories of collective weeding, twenty years previously: 'Difficult to forget are these slopes that we weeded and cultivated with one heart – as if we were Chawngtinleri's children' (Plate 7.4).[66] In this case, as in the other forms of communal weeding, crops and weeds together gave shape to human institutions, relationships and emotional attachments.

Finally, harvesting the staple crops (maize, millets, rice) required further sacrifices to the spirits.[67] Among the Lautu, this was also a moment in which plants were believed to show agency. The crop (which had a soul) had to be mollified

---

[63] Stack and Lyall, *The Mikirs*, 11–12. Such organisations have been reported among upland communities all over the Triangle. They had many more community uses – standing army, dancing group, schooling – and were crucial institutions.

[64] The morals of reciprocity were expressed in a story of three co-weeding animals (a pig, a jungle fowl and a monkey) in Parry, *The Lakhers*, 537–8. See Kipgen, 'Significance of LAWM'; and Sitlhou, 'Land and Identity', 304–7, for detailed descriptions of co-weeding groups in Manipur.

[65] Nunthara, *Impact of the Introduction*, 53–4; Nunthara, *Mizoram*, 107–8; Dokhuma, *Hmanlai Mizo Kalphung*, 14.

[66] Chawngtinleri is a spirit chieftainess in charge of all forest animals. She is very beautiful, takes possession of hunters and then blesses them by leading them to animals to hunt. Hmingthanzuali and Pande, 'Women's Indigenous Knowledge'.

[67] These could include a ritual to lead insect and pest spirits away from the fields, so that they would not return later. Myochit, *A Threatened Identity*, 58–9.

Plate 7.4 'Our memorial to collective weeding': a commemorative stone erected by four friends in Mizoram (India) in 1965

Source: Photo by Robert Laltinchhawna.

with prayers (and harvesting had to be carried out in silence) because the crop could reduce or expand its size at the very moment of reaping, or even afterwards.[68]

In lowland areas of the Triangle, agriculture was carried out on permanent, often irrigated fields. Here mono-cropping (growing a single crop) was the age-old model, with rice dominating during the main season and subsidiary crops sometimes occupying the same land afterwards. This model required different

---

[68] Bareigts, *Les Lautu*, 83–6, 145–6. See also Sitlhou, 'Land and Identity', 122–8; Sitlhou, 'Sacred Ecology'.

Human–Plant Histories

labour inputs and produced an altogether different dynamic. Here humans and plants co-produced institutions, relationships, temporalities, culinary traditions and emotional attachments that were unlike those in the mountains. Such ultimately plant-based social and cultural distinctions persist today. But there are also practices that link agricultural communities in the lowlands and uplands. One of them is the extensive use of bamboo.

The meanings of bamboo

Bamboo is one of the most versatile companion plants in the region. In Chapter 3 we saw that from the earliest times bamboo has been an essential ingredient of Triangle cultures. It provided tools, weapons, fishing rods, musical instruments, looms, containers, utensils, and basketry. It could be used to construct houses and fences. As fuel it kept the kitchen fires going. It facilitated movement across rivers because it could be made into bridges and rafts (Plate 7.5).[69] And humans turned its shoots into favourite fermented foods (Chapter 8). It was a companion plant that grew wild, but some varieties were grown in forests or near homesteads.

Plate 7.5 Bamboo and rattan bridge in Mizoram (India), 1960s

Source: Photographer unidentified, Lalhruaitluanga Ralte collection.

Note: See also Parry, *The Lakhers*, 127–9.

---

[69] For an early description of the type of rattan bridge that people cross, hanging suspended in loops, see Wilcox, 'Memoir of a Survey of Assam', 385–6, 397, 418. See also Rowlatt, 'Report of an Expedition', 482; Duff-Sutherland-Dunbar, 'Abors and Galongs', 21–3.

Not surprisingly, bamboo became culturally significant. It figured in origin stories,[70] it was essential in a great many religious ceremonies and it was frequently used to construct ritual altars (Plate 7.6). People also used it to predict the future.[71]

In Apatani cosmology, a particular variety of bamboo played a central role. It was seen as magically expanding, journeying horizontally through ritual space. In this way it could reach ancestors and spirits to summon them to feasts. This 'ever-expanding bamboo' was a potent emblem of growth, but it also

Plate 7.6 Bamboo and other plants used in egg-topped altars, Arunachal Pradesh (India), 2012

Source: Photo by Willem van Schendel.

---

[70] Elwin, *Myths of the North-East*, 101, 195, 232.
[71] Reghunathan, 'Sunshine on Faith', 144; Singh, 'Plants Associated in Forecasting', 191.

symbolised fertility. This was most explicit during a festival in which groups of men with 'erect bamboo phalluses' engaged in erotic playmaking (Plate 7.7).[72]

The largely bamboo houses of various Triangle communities were constructed to fit cosmological beliefs and were often 'not permanent, but fleetingly constructed'.[73] The layout of houses built by the Chakma of Bangladesh, for example, reflected the union of male and female energies.[74]

Bamboo has been an essential companion to humans all over the Triangle for as long as we can reconstruct. It has shaped people's lives and cultures in endless ways. Although overwhelmingly beneficial, it also had its darker sides. Bamboo could cause terror in some localities when it flowered gregariously, leading to 'bamboo

Plate 7.7 A 'phallic joker' with his bamboo pole, Arunachal Pradesh (India), 2005

Source: Photo by Michael Aram Tarr.

Note: See also Tarr and Blackburn, *Himalayan Tribal Tales*, 146.

---

[72] Blackburn, *The Sun Rises*, 99–101, 109–10, 281; Endle, *The Kachāris*, 34; Bower, *The Hidden Land*, 95; Fürer-Haimendorf, *The Apa Tanis*, 139; Tarr and Blackburn, *Through the Eye of Time*, 143, 145–6; De Maaker, 'Negotiating Life', 30.

[73] Ara and Rashid, 'Between the Built and the Unbuilt'.

[74] Chakma, 'The Androgynous House'. See also Parry, *The Lakhers*, 67–71; Laha, 'Bamboo Uses for Housing'; Stirn and Van Ham, *The Seven Sisters of India*, 51–63; Ara and Rashid, 'Between the Built and the Unbuilt'. Detailed descriptions of bamboo-house design can be found in Kolkman and Blackburn, *Tribal Architecture*.

famines' among humans (Chapter 8). The resulting distress migration was an example of plant- or animal-induced human mobility.

Enduring staple crops

Companion plants followed many different historical trajectories. For some we know fairly exactly when they arrived in the Triangle: high-yielding varieties of rice were introduced in the 1960s and the Hevea (or Pará) rubber tree (*Hevea brasiliensis*) in the late nineteenth century. For others – potato, tomato, chili pepper, papaya, pineapple – we know that they arrived in the decades and centuries after 1500 CE (Chapter 10). Most staple crops go back much further, however. Currently we have evidence that rice and barley may have become companion plants some 4,000 years ago (Chapters 2 and 3), and tubers (yam, taro, sago) and millets (notably Job's tears) are thought to be endemic species that became staple foods much earlier.[75]

There is one staple food, however, whose origins are a puzzle: maize. The Triangle is home to several varieties of maize that differ strikingly from the maize varieties that spread from Mexico and the Caribbean to Asia as part of the 'Columbian exchange' in the centuries after 1500 CE (Chapter 10).[76] The origin of these 'primitive' maize varieties is disputed, and it has even been suggested that they travelled from the Americas (possibly Peru) across the Pacific to eastern Asia in ancient times.[77] These older varieties have long been important in mountain agriculture because they are fast growing. They can be used as 'catch crops' – crops that can be harvested before the main rice crop matures, thereby staving off seasonal hunger.[78] Today these 'ancient' or 'primitive' maize varieties (popcorns, green maize used as a fresh vegetable and brewing maize) continue to be grown, often in combination with millets, and they are still distinct from the newer, post-1500 varieties known as 'field maize'.[79]

---

[75] According to Thadou history-telling, the first humans emerged from the subterranean world with millet and Job's tears, and rats later taught them how to cultivate rice. Shaw, *Notes on the Thadou Kukis*, 29.

[76] Crosby, *The Columbian Exchange*.

[77] Stonor and Anderson, 'Maize among the Hill Peoples'. For a general study of maize whose author dispels several theories about its origins (but apparently did not have access to the Stonor and Anderson article), see Bonavia, *Maize*. See also Taylor, 'Crop Distributions by Tribes'; Johannessen and Parker, 'Maize Ears Sculptured', 176–9; Bhatt et al., 'Isozyme Diversity'; Rathod et al., 'Characterization of Mimban Maize Landrace'.

[78] Lorrain, *Fifty Years in Unknown Jungles*, 116; Aisher, 'Through "Spirits"', 378.

[79] Stonor and Anderson, 'Maize among the Hill Peoples', 403. See also Bareigts, *Les Lautu*, 75–6. For the first mention of (field) maize in seventeenth-century Manipur and Bhutan, see Ahmed and Singh, 'Traditional Knowledge System', 384; Dorji, Tamang and Vernoy, *The History of the Introduction*, 20.

The dispute about whether this 'ancient' maize actually reached Asia before 1500 CE focuses on genetic properties. It is worthwhile, however, to introduce a cultural element into this discussion that has not been given much attention. How do Triangle people view the history of maize in their region? They make a clear distinction between the 'ancient' varieties and the ones that arrived later. The former are deeply entangled in their world views, origin stories and ritual practices, and the latter much less so. This can be read as evidence of a long presence of these 'ancient' varieties in the Triangle, although it does not constitute proof of pre-1500 dispersal.

Still, there are remarkable cultural assertions. The Nyishi believe that the daughter of the Sun (who married the first human) 'cast and spread the seeds of maize, rice, millets and human seeds', which does suggest that maize arrived very early on.[80] In similar vein, the 'Kacha Naga' were said to have a tradition that 'they first emerged from a cave in their area, and brought their old established crops with them, maize being among them'.[81] Furthermore, unlike other crops introduced after 1500 CE, maize is credited with a soul – rice being the only other plant so credited.[82] Special dances and an annual festival have traditionally marked the maize harvest. Maize is also known to share its name with a prominent spirit, have its own tutelary deity and be especially effective in keeping powerful spirits contented – close connections with the spirit world that (other) 'Columbian exchange' plants do not enjoy.[83] Whatever the date of their introduction, these 'ancient' maize varieties clearly became deeply embedded in the cultural universe of the Triangle.

Plants clothing human bodies

In the Triangle, stories about the earliest humans describe them as originally being naked and then covering their bodies with leaves and bark-cloth.[84] Later, deities or animals taught them how to weave and use woven fabrics as clothes (Chapter 5).[85]

---

[80] Aisher, 'Through "Spirits"', 277.

[81] Stonor and Anderson, 'Maize among the Hill Peoples', 363. On humanity having first emerged from a cave, see Chapter 5.

[82] Parry, *The Lakhers*, 79, 267, 445–7; De Maaker, 'Negotiating Life', 81. But see Playfair, *The Garos*, 80; Bareigts, *Les Lautu*, 145–6; Sitlhou, 'Land and Identity', 119, 122–8; Sitlhou, 'Sacred Ecology and Ritual Practices '.

[83] Aisher, 'Through "Spirits"', 126; Stonor and Anderson, 'Maize among the Hill Peoples', 362; Allison, 'Enspirited Places, Material Traces', 202.

[84] For use of bark-cloth, see also Wilcox, 'Memoir of a Survey of Assam', 333.

[85] See Hutchinson, *Chittagong Hill Tracts*, 51–2; Elwin, *The Art of the North-East*, 23–5; Bernot, *Les paysans arakanais du Pakistan Oriental*, 1:134–8.

Three different plants emerged as textile companion plants, or main suppliers of human clothes: cotton, jute, and silk. Cotton figures in many stories about the beginnings of the world. Among Apatani women, cotton is seen as a gift from the ancestor spirit whose body is the source of the natural world and who presides over women's material culture. Her hair became cotton thread. According to tradition, women had unsuccessfully tried to weave with the hair of monkeys, flying squirrels, rats and sheep, and even bird's feathers. But only with the hair of the spirit, which became cotton thread, could they make shawls to cover human bodies. Cotton was also an early trade item, which Apatani (valley dwellers who cultivated rice but little cotton) acquired from mountain-dwelling neighbours in exchange for rice.[86]

Other textile plants also came with sacred connotations. For example, a Bodo subgroup identified with the jute plant. Known as jute folk, 'on occasions of great religious ceremonials its members were bound to chew a certain quantity of jute'.[87] Silk – actually, a plant–animal co-production by specific trees and silkworms feeding on their leaves (Chapter 8) – was also surrounded with sacred beliefs. In Assam, women producing silk from leaves and Muga silkworms (a variety endemic in the northern Triangle) needed to appease the 'sylvan diety, locally known as Phi-thun of the feeding yard, by offering eggs, fowls and rice-beer'.[88]

Gendering plants

Human interaction with forests and crops was so intimate and enduring that these sentient non-human assemblages came to play a major role in structuring and diversifying human cultures and social arrangements. An example is the contribution of agricultural crops to the differential gendering of Triangle cultures. In upland agriculture, women worked alongside men in the mixed-crop fields, although their tasks there might differ. For example, among the Kuki in Manipur, 'only men [were] entitled to wield guns – to hunt, and the axe – to slash down the trees in the jhum field. All other tasks involved in the jhumming cycle [were] either done jointly or by women alone'.[89] In lowland agriculture, women were often ritually barred from certain rice-field tasks (such as ploughing) or from working in the fields altogether (as was the case among Muslim women in Bangladesh). Cropping patterns also imposed seasonal rhythms on societies,

---

[86] Blackburn, *Himalayan Tribal Tales*, 122–5, 144–5, 151.
[87] Endle, *The Kachális*, 25.
[88] Borthakur, 'Ethnobiological Wisdom', 234.
[89] Jhum is a regional term for shifting cultivation. Kipgen, 'Forests, Ecology and Traditional Knowledge', 216.

Human–Plant Histories 149

determined settlement patterns, produced dissimilar labour regimes, influenced diets and health, and gave rise to food preferences that became the bedrock of various local cuisines. Abundant food-crop harvests in consecutive years could

Plate 7.8 Bamboo art: tassels dangle from ceremonial scaffolding as Mru men play enormous bamboo mouth organs during a feast in the Chittagong Hill Tracts (Bangladesh)

Source: Photo by Claus-Dieter Brauns. See Brauns and Löffler, *Mru: Hill People*, 210.

also enhance a woman's status by allowing her to throw a 'feast of merit' for her village and attain a coveted honorific (Chapters 6 and 8).[90]

But food crops were just one set of gendering plants. There were many others. Cotton supplied fibres that allowed weaving to emerge as the region's predominant – and predominantly female – art form (Chapter 8). And bamboo gave rise to the region's inimitable – and predominantly male – art of basketry, as well as architecture, ceremonial art and musical instruments (Plate 7.8).[91] In short, even the gendering of art forms in the Triangle was co-produced by plants and people.

Human–plant interactions

This brief overview of some human–plant relationships may indicate the complexities of how human lifeworlds were shaped by plants. Forests, trees and plants figured prominently – but often unobtrusively – in Triangle cosmologies. As fellow living beings, plants were significant others that were included in relations of mutuality, co-dependence and care. Humans found plants, like animals, indispensable for communication with the divine, and they credited some plants with a soul.

In other words, humans in the Triangle were not suffering from 'plant-blindness' – ranking plants as inferior to animals – by any means.[92] On the contrary, they would routinely subordinate animal lives to plant lives when they sacrificed animals to persuade spirits to make crops grow well, or to celebrate a successful harvest. They were also well aware of the power of plants to give life or take it away. Plant power was deeply rooted in the beliefs, visions and emotions that energised Triangle cosmologies.

---

[90] Kipgen, 'Forests, Ecology and Traditional Knowledge', 219–20.

[91] Fraser and Fraser, *Mantles of Merit*; Jacobs et al., *The Nagas*; Young, 'A Journey from Yün-Nan to Assam', 166–7; Parry, *The Lakhers*, 71–2; Elwin, *The Art of the North-East*; Bareigts, *Les Lautu*, 71–4; Brauns and Löffler, *Mru: Hill People*; Stirn and Van Ham, *The Seven Sisters of India*, 65–75; Shaha and Mithun, *Behind Products*; Mang, 'Ethnographic Textile Art', 35–7; Kolkman and Blackburn, *Tribal Architecture*; Ara and Rashid, 'Between the Built and the Unbuilt.

[92] Wandersee and Schussler, 'Preventing Plant Blindness'; Gros, 'Nature De-naturalised'; Margulies et al., 'Illegal Wildlife Trade'.

Part III
More-Than-Human Histories

8

Cultural Geographies

In Part II of this book ('Cosmologies' – Chapters 5–7), we looked at more-than-human histories as expressed and experienced by Triangle people themselves. The chapters provided a bird's-eye view of how they narrated the origins of the universe and human societies, how they understood the passing of time and how they imagined relationships between humans, animals, plants and the spirit world. There was considerable variation in these accounts but also what we have called 'cosmological commonalities' (Chapter 5).

We now turn our attention to how these ideas interacted with numerous new ways of thinking that affected the Triangle during the past century and a half. We begin Part III with a chapter on cultural geographies, the spatial dimensions of more-than-human histories. The chapters that follow (Chapters 9–11) are concerned with quite rapid change over the past several generations, as humans intensified their exploitation of the Triangle's natural resources. We will trace how this led to ecological devastation, attempts at conservation and new forms of human–non-human conflict.

In this first chapter of Part III we are concerned with how the Triangle can be understood as a number of alternate spaces, each based on human–non-human interactions. We explore how the interplay of microorganisms, animals and plants created spatial patterns that changed over time with human and non-human mobilities. Some of these cultural geographies are rooted in Triangle ideas and traditions, and others in the imagination of outsiders. The ways in which these cultural geographies changed are often related to struggles between proponents of these different perspectives.

'Civilisation'

The idea of the Triangle as the antithesis of something else is deeply rooted. Students of the earliest surviving South Asian writings have remarked upon a distinction in those writings that is still part of everyday thinking. This is 'the opposition between the settled agricultural community (*grāma*) and the alien outside sphere of the jungle (*araṇya*)'.¹ The two domains were seen as interdependent and complementary. They exchanged products and services but were culturally distinct. These writings in Sanskrit (an Indo-European language) elevated the settled life of agriculturists and their rulers over that of inhabitants of the jungle.

Such ideas probably did not enter the Triangle until about the fourth century BCE, when speakers of Indo-European languages arrived in Bengal and Assam. They described the languages of the local inhabitants of these heavily forested regions as 'vile' (*āsura*).² Their name for people from the Triangle was *kirāta*. In various early Sanskrit texts, *kirāta* were described as 'living on fruits and roots, clad in skins, fierce with their weapons, cruel in their deeds' and 'with hair done in pointed top-knots, pleasant to look upon, shifting like gold, able to move under water, terrible, veritable tiger-men'.³

A familiar cultural hierarchy was beginning to take shape. Self-proclaimed civilised people, who lived settled lives based on growing domesticated plants and tending domesticated animals, distinguished themselves from forest dwellers. They imagined these others to be in close communion with undomesticated nature and possibly less fully human.⁴ Quite similar ideas were behind old Chinese, Tibetan and Burmese distinctions between themselves and the 'barbarians' living in the Triangle.⁵ Among the stories that circulated about the Triangle uplands were tales of some inhabitants supposedly being completely naked and living in trees like monkeys.⁶ These ideas about civilisation and its antithesis received a boost when Europeans rose to dominance during colonial times. Their ideas about 'civilisation' also excluded forest dwellers, and they often framed them as being 'wild', 'savage' and 'children of nature' (Plate 8.1).⁷ Thus, a book about the Garo of Meghalaya

---

¹ Heesterman, *The Inner Conflict of Tradition*, 118.
² Roy, *Roots of Bengali Culture*, 4. See also Van Schendel, *A History of Bangladesh*.
³ Chatterji, *Kirāta-Jana-Kṛti*, 26–38.
⁴ Bhattacharya and Pachuau (eds.), *Landscape, Culture, and Belonging*.
⁵ Fiskesjö, 'China's Animal Neighbours'; Wellens, 'Migrating Brothers'; Mayilvaganan, Khatoon and Bej (eds.), *Tawang, Monpas and Tibetan Buddhism*, 29, 59; Scott, *The Art of Not Being Governed*; Ma, 'Salt and Revenue in Frontier Formation'; Daniels and Ma (eds.), *The Transformation of Yunnan*; Daniels, 'Nanzhao as a Southeast Asian Kingdom'; Huber, *The Cult of Pure Crystal Mountain*, 128–52; Blackburn, 'Memories of Migration'; Brinckmann, 'The Táng Era'.
⁶ Phayre, 'Account of Arakan', 703; Lewin, *The Hill Tracts of Chittagong*, 89 (for his own ideas about civilisation, see 115–18); Van Schendel (ed.), *Francis Buchanan in Southeast Bengal (1798)*, 93; Van Schendel, 'A Politics of Nudity'.
⁷ For nuances, see Wouters, 'Reconfiguring Colonial Ethnography'. For examples, see Ludden, 'History Outside Civilization'; Van Schendel, Mey and Dewan, *The Chittagong Hill Tracts*, 237–52; Sharma, *Empire's Garden*; Guite, 'Colonialism and Its Unruly'; Jhala, *An Endangered History*, 124; Lainé, '*Phi Muangs*', 253.

Cultural Geographies 155

Plate 8.1 A photo of people in the Chin Hills (Myanmar), 1920s; the original caption reads: 'Group of wild Chins'

Source: 'Gruppe von wilden Tschin's'. An undated image by an unidentified photographer, thought to be from the 1920s. From the collection of the former Anthropological Society of Berlin. Ident. Nr. VIII C 20337 (P 15780), Ethnologisches Museum, Staatliche Museen zu Berlin.

(India) described them as 'wild, jolly animals', living in 'a den of wild beasts, and still wilder men'.[8]

In the post-colonial cultural geography of the Triangle, such ideas continue to play. For example, they have become the stock-in-trade of the tourism industry, which promises an escape from civilisation and an intimate encounter with 'nature'. As one tour operator informs us:

---

[8] Carey, *A Garo Jungle Book*, 6, 34.

Scattered across the state, the tribes of Arunachal send out the message of strong bond with nature. These humble tribes reflect how gratitude and caring for Mother Nature can bring unsurpassed happiness and prosperity in one's life as well as land. *Tour My India*'s tribal tour packages ensure to include this experience of bonding with nature and of course interacting with the tribal men and women to get a better perspective towards simple lives.[9]

This cultural frontier runs as a fault line through the Triangle. People imagining themselves to be more civilised and distant from 'nature' are concentrated in towns and cities, and in the agrarian lowlands of Assam, Bengal, Arakan and central Myanmar.[10] And over time, many people living in the forested foothills and uplands have come to internalise the 'Othering' image: they now think of themselves as 'tribal' or 'indigenous'. In other words, the narrative of civilisation defines inhabitants of large parts of the Triangle in negative terms, as not-yet-civilised and not-yet-distanced-from-nature. It is a cultural geography that is hierarchical and often racialised.[11] Deeply entrenched and deeply problematic, it is a powerful engine propelling current political, social and psychological conflicts throughout the region.

Microbes, enzymes and cultures

Other cultural geographies seek to understand the inhabitants of the Triangle, and their relationships with the non-human world, in neutral or positive ways. We will give brief examples. First, we consider the relationship of humans with the tiniest non-humans. These did not figure in Triangle cosmologies because for centuries people were unaware of them. We enter the world of microbes and the human intestinal tract because these minute organisms produced spatial patterns among Triangle humans. The region straddles two cultural frontiers, both dealing with food, or, more precisely, with dairy and fermentation.

---

[9] 'Arunachal Tribal Tour Packages', Tour My India, https://www.tourmyindia.com/states/arunachalpradesh/tribal-tour-packages.html (accessed 19 August 2020). Another explains: 'Much of the traditional lifestyle [of the Chittagong Hill Tracts, Bangladesh] is still preserved – tribal kings, village headmen and a self-sustaining, natural lifestyle. All in a rich, still pristine foothill ecological environment.' See 'Hilltract and Tribal Tours', Bangladesh Ecotours, https://bangladeshecotours.com/ourtours/hilltracttribaltours/ (accessed 19 August 2020).

[10] For the way in which educated urban Christian Garo view their rural, non-Christian counterparts, see De Maaker, 'Performing the Garo Nation'.

[11] Wouters and Subba, 'The "Indian Face"'; McDuie-Ra, *Debating Race in Contemporary India*. See also Shah, *In the Shadows of the State,* on 'eco-incarceration'.

Dairy

The Triangle presents a frontier between dairy-rich and dairy-restricted cuisines. Around the world there are striking differences in the consumption of milk and milk products, and various theories seek to explain these. Most theories point to a remarkable geographical variation in the genetic ability of humans to digest lactose, a milk sugar. Those whose gut produces enough of the necessary enzyme (lactase) can process dairy products, but those whose gut lacks this enzyme cannot. The latter are said to suffer from lactose intolerance, which leads a mix of gut bacteria that process the lactose, causing flatulence, intestinal cramps and diarrhoea.[12]

All new-born mammals produce high levels of lactase to digest the lactose in their mother's milk, but these levels go down rapidly after weaning. The persistence of lactase production in some human populations is the result of a genetic mutation that is likely to have occurred at the time when people had domesticated cattle. 'The interactions between the human body, milk, and our microbes were likely established during [the] later parts of the Neolithic Revolution and played a key role in establishing some components of the modern human microbiota.'[13] Human bodies and the microbes they hosted changed, and human cultures began to adapt and co-evolve.[14] Dairying began in Mesopotamia at least 6,000 years ago, spreading rapidly. Mutated individuals could digest milk without problems, and today they make up almost half of humankind.

The extent to which the human gut microbiome[15] actually determined culinary choices and the human use of domestic animals is moot.[16] What is clear, however, is that the Triangle traditionally showed a striking culinary pattern. To the west, in South Asia, were vast areas of milk consumption, and to the east, in Southeast and East Asia, equally vast areas of milk avoidance.[17] The boundary between these two zones snaked through the Triangle. Milking domestic animals and consuming dairy was common in the Brahmaputra valley and eastern Bengal, as well as in the northern Himalayan fringe with strong Tibetan cultural influence.

---

[12] Itan et al., 'A Worldwide Correlation'. A seventeenth-century text on Assam appears to describe this reaction. Tālish, *Tarikh-i Asham*, 90–1.

[13] Weyrich, 'The History of the Human Microbiome', 239.

[14] On gene-culture co-evolution, see O'Brien and Laland, 'Genes, Culture, and Agriculture'.

[15] The human microbiome is the entire mass of microorganisms living in the human gastrointestinal tract. They interact constantly with their human host and play an important role in the absorption of nutrients and the synthesis of enzymes and vitamins.

[16] Huang, 'Hypolactasia and the Chinese Diet'; Itan et al., 'A Worldwide Correlation'; Burke, *The Indian Field Shikar Book*, 49.

[17] Simoons, 'The Geographic Hypothesis'.

But the extensive uplands covering the eastern half of the Triangle, as well as Arakan in the south, were dairy avoiding (Map 8.1).[18] Here domestic cattle and goats were used for their meat and hide, and they were important as sacrificial animals, but generally not milked.[19]

European colonial travellers and officials in the Triangle were mostly lactose-tolerant individuals. As they were keen to augment the supply of dairy for their own consumption, milk products became more widely available.[20] Today, food habits have changed throughout the Triangle and the consumption of dairy products has spread and increased everywhere. For many, however, the old culinary preferences continue to be relevant. The contours of these two subregions of the Triangle – milking and non-milking – are still noticeable.

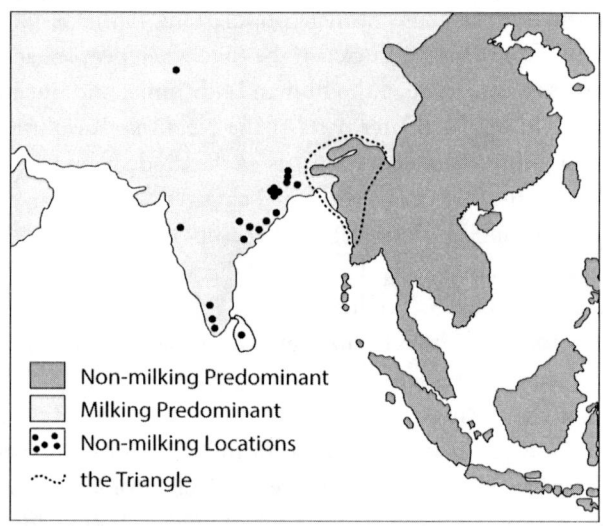

Map 8.1 Traditional areas of milking and non-milking (after Simoons, 'Dairying, Milk Use', 63)

Source: Authors.

---

[18] For details and a map, see Simoons, 'The Traditional Limits', 580. Jonathan Saha included a reproduction of this map in Saha, 'Milk to Mandalay', 4. See also Simoons, 'Dairying, Milk Use'; Brauns and Löffler, *Mru: Hill People*, 130.

[19] One European writer alleged that mithun milk 'is drunk by a few, but by most of the natives it is regarded as excreta'. Burke, *The Indian Field Shikar Book*, 49.

[20] See Saha, 'Milk to Mandalay', on British annoyance at the difficulty of procuring milk in colonial Myanmar, how they imagined the dairy geography of Myanmar and how they devised spatialised dairy policies.

Fermentation

The second example of human–microbe interaction – and how it has shaped Triangle cultures – is a distinct fondness of fermented foodstuffs. Fermentation is a common and ancient tradition of preservation all over the world. Many different microbes and fungi can be involved in fermenting food, beverages and medicines, and this means that fermented foodstuffs are, by definition, multispecies products.

What makes the Triangle special is the astonishing variety of fermentation practices as well as the number of plant- and animal-based foods and medicines produced. These fermented products are made of soybean, vegetables, herbs, fruits, fish, meat, animal fat, tea, tobacco and – in milking areas – milk.[21] Perhaps the best-known fermented products from the Triangle are bamboo shoots,[22] fish paste,[23] fermented soybean[24] and alcoholic drinks (Plate 8.2).[25] Each comes in many different local forms. Alcohol made of rice, millet or maize has been closely connected with local cosmologies, which often also included animal sacrifices and feasts of merit – thereby tying microbes, cereals, humans, sacrificial animals and spiritual beings into webs of human–non-human interdependency reaching back many centuries.

With the rise of puritanical forms of Christianity in parts of the Triangle, however, this interdependency came under attack. Church organisations framed

---

[21] A detailed overview of regional fermentation processes as well as a historical exploration of the earliest fermentation practices can be found in Tamang, *Himalayan Fermented Foods*. See also Teron, 'Ethnic Food Plants'; Das et al., 'Diversity of Traditional'. For the broader Asian context, see Owens (ed.), *Indigenous Fermented Foods*; Tamang (ed.), *Ethnic Fermented Foods and Alcoholic Beverages*; Tamang (ed.), *Ethnic Fermented Foods and Beverages*.

[22] Kikon, 'Bamboo Shoot in Our Blood', and her film *Seasons of Life* ('Seasons of Life', Bangalore International Centre, 22 August 2020, https://bangaloreinternationalcentre.org/event/seasons-of-life/ [accessed 4 January 2022]). See also Kikon, Menangnichet and Kikon, 'Taste So Good!'.

[23] Muzaddadi, 'Naturally Evolved Fermented Fish Products'; Hossain et al., 'Production Procedure'.

[24] Das et al., 'Dietary Use of Algae', 300; Sitlhou, 'Food Culture and Identity'.

[25] The many different alcoholic beverages in the region are made by fermenting rice, millet, maize, barley or palm juice, and they vary from light beers to very strong liquors. Moore and Pauk ('Nyaung-gan') present indications that the manufacture goes back to the Bronze Age. For overviews, see Tamang (ed.), *Ethnic Fermented Foods and Alcoholic Beverages*, 30–3, 73–90; and Tamang (ed.), *Ethnic Fermented Foods and Beverages*, 1–104, 349–537, 583–619. Some case studies are Bareigts, *Les Lautu*, 92–102; Aisher, 'Through "Spirits"'; Longkumer, *Reform, Identity and Narratives of Belonging*, 129–34; Longkumer, 'Rice-Beer, Purification'; Teron, 'Hor, the Traditional Alcoholic Beverage'; Bhatt, Malav and Ahlawat, '"Jumin", a Traditional Beverage'; Tarr and Blackburn, *Through the Eye of Time*; Miyamoto, 'Contesting Values of Brewing'. See also Hodgson, *Essay the First*, 188–9.

Plate 8.2 Drinking home-made alcohol in the Chin Hills (Myanmar), 1920s

Source: Photo by G. E. Harvey. © Pitt Rivers Museum, University of Oxford. Accession Number: 1998.314.387.2.1.

alcohol consumption – which many in the Triangle actually considered 'a gift from god'[26] – as morally reprehensible, and they pushed state authorities to outlaw it. Inevitably, this led to a decline in the cultivation of the varieties of rice, millet and maize that had been grown specifically for alcohol production. Today 'it would probably raise eyebrows to see a "good Baptist" with his jhum fields full of Job's tears!'.[27] Among these largely Christian communities, however, non-Christians continue to exist, and they keep alive the know-how of producing alcohol from local plants.[28]

The Triangle is united in its remarkable appreciation of the aromas of fermented food and drink. Even so, there are specific subregional fermentation practices and products that serve as powerful identity markers for many local cultures within the Triangle. It can be argued, however, that they all contribute to a distinct Triangle 'microbial terroir'[29] and a 'transethnic culinary identity'.[30]

---

[26] Longkumer, 'Rice-Beer, Purification', 448–9.

[27] Job's tears (adlay) is a cereal from which alcohol can be distilled. Cairns, 'The Alder Managers', 468.

[28] De Maaker, 'Negotiating Life'; Cairns, 'The Alder Managers', 233; Longkumer, 'Rice-Beer, Purification'.

[29] Felder, Burns and Chang, 'Defining Microbial Terroir'.

[30] Kikon, 'Bamboo Shoot in Our Blood'.

Pathogens

The relationship between humans and microorganisms went way beyond food. Bacteria, viruses and parasites affected human health. Fear of disease led Triangle humans to adopt distinct forms of spatial behaviour. Malaria is a case in point. It is not a 'local' disease but caused by a mosquito-borne parasite, an invasive species. The malaria parasite was a very early immigrant into the region. Malaria originated in Africa and travelled to Asia with the predecessors of modern humans. As these became extinct, malaria adapted to become a specialised disease of modern humans. Textual evidence of malaria in Asia is available from about 1000 BCE and it appears that the disease was most prevalent in areas that grew rice. Malaria must have had an impact on the cultural geography of human life in the Triangle ever since.[31] In the Triangle, some communities may have sought to escape the mortal danger of malaria – as well as attacks by other communities[32] – by moving out of the valleys and into cooler air. They became mountain-ridge settlers who ventured into the valleys only during the day, when mosquitoes were less active.[33] In this way, a tiny organism became an important architect of human society. But even on the mountain ridges people were not out of reach of microbes. Outbreaks of contagious diseases such as measles, dysentery, influenza, smallpox or cholera (and rinderpest among mithuns) occurred regularly and they affected human behaviour as well. When epidemics struck, people would block all entrances to their settlements, perform special rituals, abandon their settlements, flee to the jungle or attack settlements from which the disease was thought to have originated.[34] In this manner, microorganisms co-determined human life chances as well as the spatial distribution and mobility of humans across the region.

Plant geographies

Microbes were hardly the only organisms that gave spatial shape to human cultures in the Triangle (we will hear more about them in Chapter 9). Innumerable plants also played a huge role. They were used as foodstuffs, medicines, clothing,

---

[31] Green and Jones, 'The Evolution and Spread'. See also Daniels, 'Nanzhao as a Southeast Asian Kingdom', 200–2.

[32] Hanson, *The Kachins*, 38; Haokip, 'Escape Agriculture, Foraging Culture'; Young, 'A Journey from Yün-Nan to Assam', 162.

[33] In the southern Triangle these culturally very diverse groups were collectively categorised as *toungtha* (children of the hills). Lewin, *The Hill Tracts of Chittagong*.

[34] Ibid., 78; Hughes, *The Hill Tracts of Arakan*, 38; Shakespear, *The Lushei Kuki Clans*, 76; Head, *Hand Book*, 41, 47; Hutton, *The Angami Nagas*, 179, 192; Parry, *The Lakhers*, 455–7, 468–9; Stevenson, *The Economics of the Central Chin Tribes*, 24; Stonor, 'Notes on Religion', 8–9.

decoration and much more (Chapters 3 and 7). In terms of cultural geographies, three stood out: bamboo, rice and 'textile plants'.

Bamboo

The Triangle depended on its many varieties of bamboo to such an extent that observers have sometimes described it as a 'bamboo culture'.[35] The spatial distribution of bamboo across the region varied and this variation was highly relevant in the case of the so-called 'bamboo famines'. These occur roughly twice a century, when all specimens of two types of bamboo blossom and then produce fruits at the same time. In the southern Triangle, where ecologically rich bamboo-dominated forests (and these two varieties) are common, this could lead to human famines and social dislocation because bamboo rats would proliferate and – having finished the bamboo fruits – would eat the crops that humans relied on (see Plate 8.3).[36] Such famines shaped human behaviour in southern parts of the Triangle – and could have severe political consequences there[37] – but they did not occur in northern and western parts of the region.

Rice

Rice – which generally co-appears with bamboo in the Triangle – is especially significant geographically because of a distinction between varieties that are sticky (glutinous) and varieties that are not. When cooked, the grains of sticky rice are tender and stay together, whereas non-sticky ones are dry and do not cohere. Sticky-rice varieties (which can vary in their stickiness) are the result of a mutation that may have occurred in early domesticated rice in mainland Southeast Asia. It became very popular in diets from Japan to the Himalayas.[38] In the Triangle, sticky rice can be found everywhere. It is often preferred for breakfast, dessert, snacks, rice powder and the manufacture of rice liquor.[39] It is prominent in the

---

[35] Spate, *India and Pakistan*, 75.

[36] One variety (*Melocanna baccifera*) flowers gregariously roughly every fifty years and another (*Bambusa tulda*) every thirty years. For details on these species, and their local names, see Banik, *Silviculture of South Asian*, 211–33, and 85–100. The natural rhythms underlying mast flowering have been theorised by means of the 'predator satiation hypothesis', Janzen, 'Why Bamboos Wait So Long to Flower'. See also Singleton et al. (eds.), *Rodent Outbreaks*; Platt et al., 'Notes on *Melocanna baccifera*'; Kimmerer, *Braiding Sweetgrass*, 16–21; Fava and Colombo, 'Remote Sensing-Based Assessment'.

[37] For example, the bamboo famine of 1960 triggered a twenty-year war of independence in Mizoram. Pachuau and Van Schendel, *The Camera as Witness*, 295–358.

[38] Fuller, Castillo and Murphy, 'How Rice Failed to Unify Asia', esp. the map on 719.

[39] Asada, 'Cultivation of Glutinous Rice'; Dipti, Bari and Kabir, 'Grain Quality Characteristics of Some *Beruin* Rice'; Roy et al., 'Genetic Diversity Analysis of Specialty Glutinous', 3.

Cultural Geographies

Plate 8.3 Victims of a bamboo–rodent–human encounter: famine refugees, Mizoram (India), 1882

Source: Riebeck, *Die Hügelstämme von Chittagong*.

Note: See also Van Schendel, Mey and Dewan, *The Chittagong Hill Tracts*, 62; Nag, *Pied Pipers in North East India*; Sridhara and Rajendran, 'Gregarious Bamboo Flowering'.

eastern highlands but less so in the western lowlands where tastes gravitate more towards non-sticky varieties. In areas of South Asia further west beyond the Triangle, diets do not favour sticky rice. In other words, the Triangle marks the western boundary of Asia's ancient sticky-rice zone, just as it marks the western boundary of dairy avoidance. Internally, its culinary geography graduates from high sticky-rice and low dairy consumption in the east to low sticky-rice and high dairy consumption in the west.

Textile plants

From the earliest times humans have used plant fibres (such as cotton, hemp and jute) to clothe themselves, and they have used vegetal dyestuffs (such as indigo, hibiscus and turmeric[40]) to colour their clothes. Such 'textile plants' came in many forms, and they were geographically significant. Some could be found all over the Triangle, but others were used only in specific parts of the region. The most common textile plant was cotton. It grew almost everywhere, in lowlands

---

[40] Sutradhar et al., 'Short Communication'; Hmingthanzuali and Pande, 'Women's Indigenous Knowledge', 136.

and uplands alike, and was widely used for as long as we can reconstruct.[41] Even so, there were cotton geographies across the Triangle. These were not linked to an uneven spread of the plant itself, but to how humans in different parts of the region used it. Cotton developed an especially close relationship with women. It was they who processed the crop and wove cotton into textiles, predominantly for clothes (Plate 8.4). Importantly, weaving was not merely utilitarian. Quite the contrary: weavers created distinctive styles and patterns, and these expressed group aesthetics, symbolic meanings and identities. In other words, weaving had spatial dimensions: it produced aesthetic and symbolic geographies. All over the Triangle, cotton clothes became the 'social skin' by which people could easily recognise one

Plate 8.4 A Bawm-Zo weaver at her loom, Chittagong Hill Tracts (Bangladesh)

Source: Photo by Amiya Kanti Chakma. Courtesy of Niaz Zaman.

Note: See also Chakma and Zaman, *Strong Backs Magic Fingers*, 117.

---

[41] Cotton did not grow in high mountains, so lowland cotton was traded to these regions. Rowlatt, 'Report of an Expedition', 489. On ancient cotton trade routes between India and China, see Dale, 'Silk Road, Cotton Road'; Bhattacharya, 'Old Routes, New Dreams', 317–18.

Cultural Geographies   165

another's provenance, region and status.⁴² Today, such textile geographies continue to be extremely meaningful.⁴³

Some textile plants were more prevalent in certain parts of the Triangle than in others. For example, jute geographies differed from cotton ones. Jute was an important crop in low-lying areas with an abundance of water to soak the plant. In a process known as retting, waterborne microbes dissolve the jute bark to free the fibres. Historically, jute fibres had many uses, including being woven into clothing for poor people in the Triangle lowlands.⁴⁴ Another old textile geography was also based on multispecies complexity. The Brahmaputra valley and surrounding hills are the natural habitat of several trees that can host caterpillars of a specific moth. Unlike the much better-known silkworms (that feed on mulberry leaves and have a geographical spread way beyond the Triangle), the Muga moth is exclusively cultivated in this section of Triangle.⁴⁵ It produces a very durable glossy golden thread ('Muga silk') that became an icon of Assamese textiles and Assamese culture.⁴⁶

Textile plants were important because they clothed the people in the Triangle – but also because they linked them to wider geographies. Ancient trade networks connected the Triangle with neighbouring regions and further afield. Two-millennia-old texts reveal that Triangle cotton fabrics were sought after as tribute and trade goods, and that Triangle people were intermediaries in the overland westward trade of Chinese silk all the way to northern India and Afghanistan.⁴⁷ In the same period, cotton textiles were already being traded overseas, via the Bay of Bengal, to Southeast Asia, China and the Mediterranean world.⁴⁸

---

⁴² Turner, 'The Social Skin'; Von Stockhausen, *Imag(in)ing the Nagas*, 380–93; Pachuau, 'Sartorial Matters'; Horam, 'Weaving Resistance and Identity'. See also Shaw, *Notes on the Thadou Kukis*, 91–2; Luce, *Phases of Pre-Pagán Burma*, 96.

⁴³ Fraser and Fraser, *Mantles of Merit*; Jacobs et al., *The Nagas: Society, Culture*; Mang, 'Ethnographic Textile Art'; Chakma and Zaman, *Strong Backs Magic Fingers*; Wettstein, *Naga Textiles*; Varsangzuali, 'Evolution of Mizo Dress'; Kharsyntiew, 'Youth Fashion and the Identity'.

⁴⁴ Sen (ed.), *Eastern Bengal Ballads*, vol. 3, part 1, 157, 203.

⁴⁵ The production of other Triangle silks (*tassar* and *eri*, made from the cocoons of different moths) is not as restricted to the Triangle as the production of Muga.

⁴⁶ Vadarajan, 'Silk in Northeastern and Eastern India'; Phukan and Chowdhury, 'Traditional Knowledge and Practices'; Zethner, Koustrup and Barooah, *South Asian Ways of Silk*, 49–55, 130.

⁴⁷ Chatterji, *Kirāta-Jana-Kṛti*, 33, 35, 37.

⁴⁸ Huntingford, *The Periplus of the Erythraean Sea*, 55.

Such wider geographies were never static. They changed in response to changes in demand. The period of European imperial expansion brought a major transformation. Raw cotton, jute and silk (as well as dye plants such as indigo) became highly valued 'raw material' for textile factories in Europe. In this way they powered technological innovation, cultural change and further expansionism in that part of the world.

It often goes unnoticed how plants played a critical role in enabling industrialisation and new lifestyles halfway around the globe, as well as transforming landscapes in the Triangle itself. Smallholders planted jute, cotton and indigo on their fields, and plantations of tea, rubber and teak destroyed vast areas of forest. These new plant geographies demonstrated the power of plants to organise people. Labourers from China and central India, managers from Scotland, lawmakers from England, and moneylenders from western India arrived in the Triangle to assist selected plants in making the best possible niches for themselves. Triangle societies and cultures would bear the long-term imprint of these imperial entanglements.

Animal geographies

In Chapter 6 we have seen that animals, like plants, have always been essential for human survival in the Triangle – as sources of food, medicine, and clothing, as well as for protection, transport, and companionship. Just as textile plants provided fibres for human clothing, the fur and skin of certain animals also created textile geographies within the Triangle. For example, people in the high mountains fended off the winter cold by wearing clothes made of yak, goat and sheep wool; hats and coats made of bear and fox fur; and shoes and boots made of wool and leather. Such materials were not necessary at lower altitudes, so animal-derived clothing tended to be concentrated in the colder uplands. Animals were essential in shaping other human cultural geographies in the Triangle as well, as the following brief examples will show.

Sea snails

For millennia, the Triangle was of central importance in a huge sea-snail trade. Local inhabitants never actually encountered these snails themselves but their remains – tiny shiny whitish shells – were very familiar to many. The shells came from the Maldives in the Indian Ocean, which exported enormous quantities of these cowries (or *kauri*s) across Asia and Africa where, used as coins, they fed into local financial markets. Described as 'the first global money', cowries arrived by sea and moved inland across practically all the Triangle and, beyond it, to Yunnan.[49]

---

[49] Yang, *Cowrie Shells and Cowrie Money*, 249.

The historical importance of this human–animal geography has led scholars to emphasise that, from very early days, the Triangle was intimately connected with the much wider world. For example, a cowrie found in an archaeological site on the eastern edge of the Triangle was dated to about 12,000 years ago, and the Dian kingdom in Yunnan (third century BCE) was well known for its spectacular bronze cowrie containers.[50] Scholars offer the terms 'cowry country' and 'cowrie (money) world' as a new perspective on this animal-driven human topography. David Ludden describes the 'Cowry Country' of several centuries ago as follows:

> It stretched overseas from the Maldives (a string of coral islands off the western coast of the Indian peninsula), along rivers of deltaic Bengal, and across tropical mountains of Burma and Yunnan, connecting agrarian frontiers of Mughal India with Qing China and Indian Ocean trade networks. In the watery parts of its commercial space, merchant ships sailed the Bay of Bengal and Sylheti boatmen sailed the Meghna River, where Sylhet was the pivotal inland port, in northern Bengal, at the base of the mountains (now in Meghalaya). Above Sylhet, Khasia traders hiked jungle pathways connecting lowland Bengal with highland Burma. Cowry Country included the so-called Southwestern Silk Road and Horse and Tea Road, winding through China, Tibet, Nepal, Burma, Bengal, and North India.[51]

For Bin Yang, the 'cowrie (money) world' includes even wider Afro-Eurasian spaces:

> It could serve as an alternative to purely land-based regional studies or ocean-based analysis, since this world crossed both boundaries and connected lands with the oceans.... The cowrie money world consisted of the large land masses and vast bodies of water that cowrie money linked, lubricated and combined into a commercially and culturally intertwined world. This world crossed, traversed and transcended various boundaries of topography, people, culture, religion and society.[52]

Within the Triangle, cowries were put to many different uses. As small change they facilitated monetary exchange, they became significant as decorative status goods (Plate 8.5), and they served ritual and funerary purposes. Some subregions – such as Sylhet, Nagaland and Yunnan – became deeply invested in cowries, whereas

---

[50] Moore, 'Archaeology of the Shan Plateau'; Cremin, 'Seeing Dian through Barbarian Eyes'; Beal (ed.), *Si-Yu-Ki*, 2:207; Cole, 'Heirloom Beads', 16–17; Pryce et al., 'A First Absolute Chronology', 693; Yang, *Cowrie Shells and Cowrie Money*, 96; Brinckmann, 'The Táng Era', 90.
[51] Ludden, 'Cowry Country', 75.
[52] Yang, *Cowrie Shells and Cowrie Money*, 259. See also his maps on 260–3.

Plate 8.5 Two men wearing cowries-encrusted aprons as part of their ceremonial warrior's costumes, Nagaland (India), 1954

Source: Photo by Verrier Elwin. Courtesy of Ashok Elwin.

Note: The costumes of these men, identified as Western Rengma Naga, also included the following animal products: hornbill feathers, bear-fur hats, shoulder sashes made of goat's hair, mithun(?)-hide shields and conch-shell necklaces. See also Kanungo, 'Naga Ornaments and the Indian Ocean'; Jacobs et al., *The Nagas*, 273.

others – the Chin Hills, Arunachal Pradesh and the Chittagong Hill Tracts – were much less involved.[53] The subregional trajectories of the cowrie trade, the cultural importance of the shells, and variations over time remain to be mapped and explained. They have been explored most thoroughly for Yunnan, where

---

[53] But see Dalton, *Descriptive Ethnology of Bengal*, table XIII. Among the Chin, black and white beads were in use as currency in debt exchanges. Moore and Myint, 'Beads of Myanmar (Burma)', 59.

cowries were clearly important.[54] Here the shells symbolised 'social status, power, and probably wealth' to the Dian people, as demonstrated by the elaborate cowrie containers found in elite tombs.[55] In other periods, and in other Triangle locations, cowries could carry much less cultural weight. Thus, the use of cowries as small change is well documented for Bengal but in sixteenth-century northern Bengal (Cooch Behar) cowries apparently were not used as such: a visiting Englishman reported that 'their smal mony is almonds, which oftentimes they vse to eat'.[56] And in the nineteenth century, the Mru of the Chittagong Hill Tracts seem to have had no use for cowries except for deciding on the name of a newborn child.[57] Cowrie-driven cultural geographies waxed and waned and, as the Triangle cowrie trade declined over time, such geographies became less important. But today they continue to be visible and aesthetically meaningful in various parts of the Triangle.[58]

Hornbills

Another animal that shaped human cultural geographies was the hornbill, a huge forest bird. As a meeting place of three global biodiversity hotspots, the Triangle boasts an extraordinary variety of local ecosystems (Chapter 1) and it is home to many different bird species. The hornbill has been described as a 'charismatic species'.[59] Hornbills have been important to humans because of their meat (which some groups eat, and others shun[60]), fat (used as a medicine), feathers (used as decoration and for arrows), and craniums and beaks (used as decoration). The human–hornbill relationship has powerful symbolic meanings. People in various parts of the Triangle have attributed magical powers to these birds and seen them as sacred symbols of the upper world, courage, splendour, freedom and fraternity.[61] In some cases, people believed that they themselves were descended

---

[54] Yang, *Cowrie Shells and Cowrie Money*, 64–123.

[55] Ibid., 96.

[56] Ryley, *Ralph Fitch, England's Pioneer*, 113. However, in the seventeenth century cowries were reported to be in use in adjacent Assam. Tālish, *Tarikh-i Asham*, 84; Qadri, *Pre-Colonial Northeast India*, 32.

[57] Lewin, *The Hill Tracts of Chittagong*, 93. In the Arakan hills cowries were reportedly used for ornamental purposes. Trant, 'Report on a Route', 1144.

[58] A parallel ancient animal geography involves the conch shell (*Turbinella pyrum*), traded from the south Indian coast to Bengal. It is important in Hindu and Buddhist rituals as well as for ornaments in many upland communities. Cole, 'Heirloom Beads', 17.

[59] Aiyadurai and Banerjee, 'Bird Conservation from Obscurity to Popularity', 905.

[60] Brauns and Löffler, *Mru: Hill People*, 123.

[61] For example, Hanson, *The Kachins*, 37; Elwin, *The Art of the North-East Frontier of India*, 143–4; Woodward, 'Gifts for the Sky People', 225; Guite, 'Representing Local Participation', 301.

from hornbills.⁶² The use of beaks and feathers – notably the large tail feathers of the Great Hornbill (Plate 8.6)⁶³ – was not just decorative; it was gendered, linked to status and ceremonies, and controlled by complex rules (Plate 8.5).

Plate 8.6 A hornbill beak tops the ceremonial hat of a man in Arunachal Pradesh (India), 1954

Source: Photo by Verrier Elwin. Courtesy of Ashok Elwin. © National Anthropological Archives, Smithsonian Institution.

Note: The man is identified as belonging to the Galo group, Koyu village, Subansiri district. Original caption: 'Man Wearing Hat Decorated with Great Indian Hornbill (*Dichoceros Bicornis*) Beak (Symbol of Valor) Used During Ceremonial Dances, 1954.' See also Wilcox, 'Memoir of a Survey of Assam', 333.

---

⁶² Hutton, *The Angami Nagas*, 391–3; Parry, *The Lakhers*, xii, 138–9, 236.
⁶³ Five different species of hornbills are found across the Triangle, from lowland forests to Himalayan ones: the Great, Wreathed, Austen's Brown, Rufous-Necked and Oriental Pied.

In recent times the cultural geography of human–hornbill relations changed in three important ways. First, relentless hunting and trapping began to cause real concerns about the survival of these birds. In 2001 a remarkable initiative made synthetic hornbill beaks available to adorn ceremonial headgear in Arunachal Pradesh. Replacing real beaks by fibreglass or wooden ones turned out to be a success (Plate 8.7), just as chicken or duck feathers were acceptable instead of traditional hornbill feathers.⁶⁴

Second, hornbills became pawns in human identity politics as various Triangle groups claimed the bird as an emblem of authenticity. For example, the state of Arunachal Pradesh (India) adopted it as its 'state bird'. Both the Chin State (Myanmar) and the Chin National Front feature the bird on their flags. And the Zomi Re-unification Organisation (which seeks to reunite the Zo people in Myanmar, India and Bangladesh) claims the hornbill as its 'sacred and noble' national bird.⁶⁵

Plate 8.7 A man wearing ceremonial headgear adorned with a synthetic hornbill beak, Arunachal Pradesh (India), 2014; original title: 'A fake hornbill bopia hat that never loses its orange flair (Photo by Magnus Lidén, modelled by Prof. Tana Showren).'

Source: Photo by Magnus Lidén, 2014.

Note: See also Bawa and Kadur, *Himalaya*, 130–1; Stirn and Van Ham, *The Seven Sisters of India*, 40.

---

⁶⁴ Aiyadurai, 'Wildlife Hunting', 69; Blackburn, *The Sun Rises*, 94; Pangging et al., '*Byopa*: A Traditional Headgear of Nyishi Tribe'.

⁶⁵ 'The Hornbill Emblem', Zogam, http://zogam.org/hornbill-emblem (accessed 4 January 2022). See also Chakraborty, 'Identity and Virtual Spaces', 177.

Third, the hornbill was recruited as a crowd-puller, notably for two new state-sponsored 'hornbill festivals', started in the 1990s and the 2010s, respectively. Both are intended to boost tourism by staging (and commodifying) 'authentic' indigenous cultures. Here the hornbill serves as a commercial symbol of exoticism and closeness to nature. The oldest and largest of these festivals is organised by the government of Nagaland and has been the object of much scholarly scrutiny (Plate 8.8).[66]

Another hornbill festival (organised by the Forest Department of Arunachal Pradesh) is oriented more towards eco-tourism and the protection of wildlife. Each day is named after a different hornbill species, and its logo highlights the

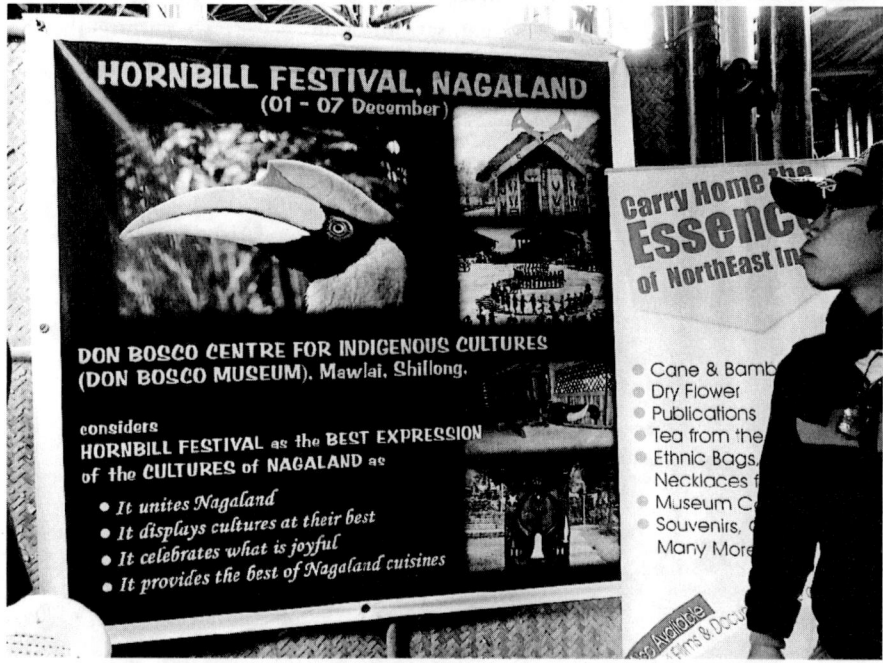

Plate 8.8 A visitor eyeing a poster at the Hornbill Festival in Nagaland (India), 2012

Source: Photo by Willem van Schendel.

Note: The festival is held annually at the 'Naga Heritage Village', established by the government of Nagaland.

---

[66] For example, Kikon, 'Operation Hornbill Festival 2004'; Longkumer, 'Who Sings for the Hornbill'; Longkumer, '"As Our Ancestors Once Lived"'; Longkumer, 'Representing the Nagas'; Thong, *Colonization, Proselytization, and Identity*, 25–32.

Cultural Geographies   173

intimacy of human and bird (Plate 8.9, see also Plate 8.7). The cultural geographies of the human–hornbill bond are complex, overlapping and rapidly changing.[67]

Mithuns

The spatiality of human–non-human entanglement in the Triangle is also thrown into sharp relief by the mithun.[68] We introduced this large bovine in

Plate 8.9 Logo of the annual Pakke Paga Hornbill Festival

Source: Pakke Page Hornbill Festival (@PakkePagaFestival), 'Home', https://www.facebook.com/PakkePagaFestival/ (accessed 28 August 2020).

---

[67] For developing hornbill-focused eco-tourism across the border in China, see Zheng et al., 'Flocking of Hornbills Observed'. In 2020, Tripura State inaugurated its first hornbill festival.

[68] The term 'mithun' or 'mithan' is widely used for this species (*Bos frontalis*) in English-language literature. According to Simoons and Simoons, this word may be of Mon-Khmer origin, just as the other term for it, 'gayal', may be of Bengali origin. The (semi-)domestication of the species is likely to have originated with groups speaking Tibeto-Burman (or Trans-Himalayan) languages. Currently, many of these groups use forms of the word 'sia' to refer to mithuns. Simoons and Simoons, *A Ceremonial Ox of India*, 225–7. See also Bareigts, *Les Lautu*, 88.

Chapters 3 and 6 (see Plates 3.5 and 6.18). In cultural-geography terms it is remarkable for several reasons. Its natural habitat is confined to the Triangle – it is a truly endemic species. It thrives in the Triangle's hills and mountains but not in the lowlands or highest Himalayan elevations (Map 8.2). Its habitat crosses the boundaries of the three global biodiversity hotpots that meet in the Triangle (Plate 1.4). And finally, it plays a crucial role in the cultural history of the Triangle uplands. For this reason, it is a quintessential Triangle creature – and the mountainous regions have been described as 'Mithun Country'.[69]

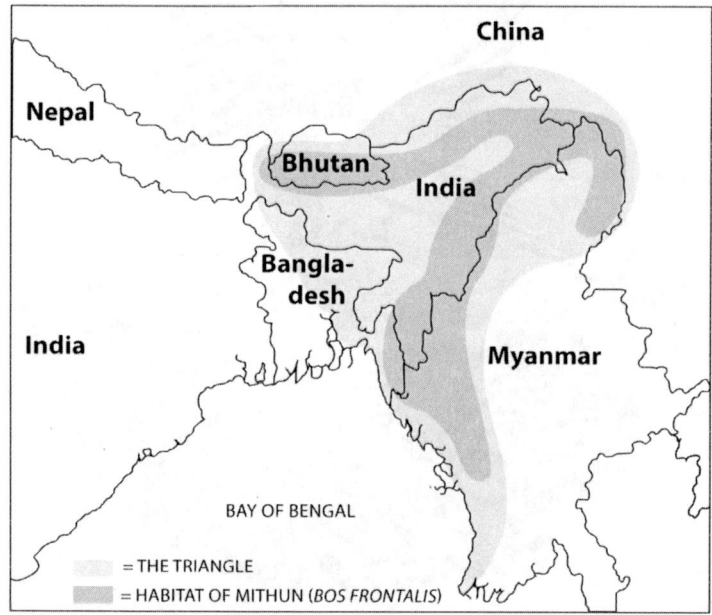

Map 8.2 Habitat of the mithun (dark grey), shown within the Triangle (light grey) (after Simoons and Simoons, *A Ceremonial Ox of India*, 6–7)

Source: Authors.

---

[69] Simoons and Simoons, *A Ceremonial Ox of India*, 9. They distinguish a northern and a southern subregion within Mithun Country (37–8). It should be noted that the mithun habitat does not extend to the (Garo, Khasi and Jaintia) mountains of Meghalaya. Here the most highly valued sacrificial animals were bulls. In Bhutan, mithuns were regularly imported for crossbreeding from neighbouring Arunachal Pradesh: 'A pure Mithun called *Bamen* (western Bhutan) and *Mencha* (eastern Bhutan) bull is a very precious animal for a Bhutanese herder, and this animal will be given utmost respect and care and will not be put to any kind of work except for siring local cows.' Namgay, 'Transhumant Agro-pastoralism', 24.

In human cultures across the Triangle uplands, mithuns, like hornbills, play an important role – but, unlike hornbills, they are semi-domesticated. They roam freely in the forests and, craving salt, occasionally enter human settlements.[70] Humans have established individual ownership claims, however, and therefore they consider mithuns livestock.[71] These animals provide humans with meat, hides and horns, but their material uses are eclipsed by their immaterial, symbolic ones.

The true value of mithuns is their cultural role. As we have seen in Chapter 6, they were of core importance in various local cosmologies – sacred animals that were not butchered but only sacrificed during ritual feasting. The enormous religious and social significance of these 'feasts of merit' was often indicated by memorial objects. These could be commemorative posts or large stones that showed mithun horns; the animal's skull mounted on the wall of the person(s) who had donated it; or conspicuous wooden 'horns' on the roof of the donor's house (Plates 8.10 and 8.11).[72] These feasts were strongly male-dominated – although parallel 'feasts of merit', initiated by women, were not unknown (Chapter 6).[73]

These complex practices were essential to many communities across the region. The rules governing them, and the significance attached to them, varied but always involved the distribution of a wealthy donor's largesse, animal sacrifices, communal eating, drinking alcohol and the erection of wooden posts or stones.[74] The frequent occurrence of memorial stones has given rise to a conception of the uplands as a space of 'monumentalist' or 'megalithic' practices. It has been suggested that the Triangle forms the western (and largest) collection of megalithic sites of a 'Southeast Asian Megalithic Complex'. But the Triangle may also be understood as a separate complex because of its physical distance from megalithic practices in mainland Southeast Asia, and because of the unique

---

[70] An early description can be found in Lewin, *The Hill Tracts of Chittagong*, 104–5.

[71] Haokip ('Escape Agriculture, Foraging Culture') describes this as 'the art of "half-tamed" and "half-looked-after" animal husbandry'.

[72] Stuart Blackburn identifies the bond between humans and sacrificial animals in 'feasts of merit' as one of the elements of his cultural geography of the 'extended eastern Himalayas', which partly overlaps with the Triangle. Blackburn, 'Oral Stories and Culture Areas'. See also Myo, *Customary Law*, 5–17; Trant, 'Report on a Route', 1146–7; Head, *Hand Book*, 31–5; Shakespear, 'Tangkhul Folk Tales', 273–81; Stevenson, *The Economics of the Central Chin Tribes*, 47–9, 118–47, 156–63; Brauns and Löffler, *Mru: Hill People*, 225–40; Jacobs et al., *The Nagas: Society, Culture*, 77–81; Tzüdir, 'Appropriating the Ao Past'; Myochit, *A Threatened Identity*, 37–46, 71–2; Pau, 'Rethinking Religious Conversion', 6; Von Stockhausen, *Imag(in)ing the Nagas*, 258–9, 286–7; various contributions to Wunderlich, Jamir and Müller, 'Hierarchy and Balance'; Wunderlich et al., 'Societies in Balance'.

[73] Kipgen, 'Forests, Ecology and Traditional Knowledge', 219–20.

[74] Mithun sacrifices could also have military significance. For example, they were used as a mechanism to ensure solidarity during the Kuki-Anglo War of 1917–1919. Kipgen, 'Resistance, War Council and Formation of Militia'.

Plate 8.10 Villagers, holding a spear for mithun sacrifices, stand in front of a horned memorial post, Chittagong Hill Tracts (Bangladesh), 1961

Source: Photo by David Sopher. See Van Schendel, Mey and Dewan, *The Chittagong Hill Tracts*.

Note: Mithuns are now rare in this area; see Chowdhury et al., 'Dietetic Use of Wild Animals', 31. For a different style of wooden posts in southern Chin State, see Myochit, *A Threatened Identity*, 29, 40; Aung, 'Social-Ecological Coevolution', 210. See also Von Stockhausen, *Imag(in)ing the Nagas*, 70, 292–7.

megalith-mithun connection.[75] Megalithic practices in the Triangle overlap to a large extent with the natural habitat of mithuns, traditionally the prime sacrificial animals during these feasts. But the erection of large stones did not occur all over mithun habitat, nor was it confined to it. Among a Naga group in Myanmar, for example, mithuns were sacrificed during feasts of merit, but reportedly neither stones nor sacrificial posts were erected.[76] Conversely, the Khasi and Jaintia Hills in eastern Meghalaya (India) are famous for their many – and very old[77] – megaliths,

---

[75] See map in Loofs, *Elements of the Megalithic Complex*, x; Janowski, 'Stones Alive!'. See also Thakuria, 'Hollowed Monoliths of North Cachar'; Jamir, 'Affinities of Naga Megaliths'; Sarma and Hazarika, 'Situating Northeast Indian Archaeology', 42; Von Stockhausen, *Imag(in)ing the Nagas*, 298–7; Wouters, *In the Shadows of Naga Insurgency*, 156–7; Haokip, 'The Petroglyphs of Indo-Myanmar Frontier'; Wunderlich et al., 'Societies in Balance'.

[76] Steen, 'Material Culture of the Langsing Nagas'.

[77] The dating of megaliths in the Triangle is difficult. Currently, the megalithic tradition in the Khasi and Jaintia hills is thought to reach back to the first century BCE. In other parts, surviving megaliths appear to point to more recent origins, but still several centuries ago. Wunderlich, Jamir and Müller, 'Hierarchy and Balance', 18–19; Robinne, 'Memorial Art'; Sarma, 'Ethnoarchaeology of the Karbi Megaliths', 359; Hazarika et al., 'The *Raj Sabha* at Silchang'.

Plate 8.11 A precolonial memorial stone on the India–Myanmar border; among the depictions are mithuns and hornbills

Source: Photo by Willem van Schendel.

Note: For details on memorial stones in this area (Vangchhia, Mizoram), see Singh, 'New Discoveries of Petroglyphs in Vangchhia'; and Malsawmliana, 'A Typological Classification'.

and yet there are no mithuns in Meghalaya.[78] Here megaliths were linked primarily to commemorative and funerary rituals. In lower hills where mithuns cannot survive, water buffaloes, bulls, pigs, goats and chickens took their place as sacrificial animals.[79] In Bhutan, too, megaliths occur without a connection with mithun sacrifices.[80]

---

[78] Mawlong, 'History Etched in Stone'; Mitri, 'Exploring the Monumentality'. For feasts of merit among the Bodo of Assam, see Hodgson, *Essay the First*, 165, 170.

[79] Brauns and Löffler, *Mru: Hill People*; Gros, 'Cultes de fertilité chez les Drung du Yunnan (Chine)'; Hazarika et al., 'The *Raj Sabha* at Silchang', 362; Lyngdoh, 'An Interview with a Goddess', 60, 66, 70.

[80] Penjore, 'Digging the Past'.

As we saw in Chapter 6, during the twentieth century more and more Triangle inhabitants became Christians. As a result, ritual feasting lost its former cosmological connections – but the connection between mithun sacrifice and feasting was not lost.[81] It remained linked to Christmas and weddings, occasions that did not require the erection of memorial stones.[82] Even so, ceremoniously killing domestic animals, feeding large groups of people and erecting memorial stones remained a prominent cultural complex.[83] Today it is more common for social organisations than wealthy individuals to organise these feasts and sometimes put up megaliths to commemorate various events. In this way, ceremonial feasting and megalithism continue to tie humans, animals, stones and the spiritual world together in a very specific way (Plate 8.12).[84]

Plate 8.12 Two contemporary megaliths in a Manipur village; one celebrates the golden jubilee of an ethnic organisation (1997) and the other that community's formal renaming under the Indian constitution (2012)

Source: Photo by Willem van Schendel.

---

[81] For contemporary practices of stone worship among non-Christians, see Dutta, 'V-Shaped Columns'. See also Hazarika et al., 'The *Raj Sabha* at Silchang'; Playfair, *The Garos*, 96–7; Bezbaruah, 'Ethnography to Archaeology'; and Woodward, 'Gifts for the Sky People', 227–9; De Maaker, 'Have the Mitdes Gone Silent'; Sarma, 'Ethnoarchaeology of the Karbi Megaliths'.

[82] Pachuau and Van Schendel, *The Camera as Witness*, 77–81. See also Tzüdir, 'Appropriating the Ao Past', 284–5.

[83] Blackburn, 'Oral Stories and Culture Areas'.

[84] Devi, 'Manipur Megaliths'; Sarma, 'Ethnoarchaeology of the Karbi Megaliths'. A similar human–animal–stone–spirit connection is expressed in another art form: rock art. See Malla and Bezbaruah (eds.), *Cultural Ecology*.

Animal symbols of self-identification

Today, however, the symbolic value of mithuns goes well beyond their sacrificial uses and feasts of merit. Like hornbills, they have been repositioned as modern symbols of Triangle authenticity and identity. The mithun motif appears everywhere: as 'state animal', on signboards and clothes, in trendy tattoos and so on (Plates 8.13–8.15).[85]

In contemporary identity politics, the mithun motif is often combined with that other powerful regional image, the hornbill. The logo of Zomi National Day

Plate 8.13 The official seal of the state of Nagaland (India)

Source: 'Basic Facts on Nagaland State Logo or Emblem', Nagaland GK, 12 November 2019, https://nagalandgk.com/nagaland-state-logo/ (accessed 4 January 2022).

---

[85] Mo Naga, a contemporary tattoo artist, has introduced mithun heads in his art. Mithuns were not traditionally used in tattoos, but they did figure on Naga men's shawls. 'Mo Naga: Tattoo Revival in India', *Lars Krutak*, 9 February 2019, https://www.larskrutak.com/mo-naga-naga-tattoo-revival/ (accessed 4 January 2022); Krutak, 'Neo-Naga', 54. Among the southern Mara (Lakher) and Mizo, however, 'young men are fond of having *mithuns*' heads tattooed on their chests' but these were 'said to have no particular meaning'. Parry, *The Lakhers*, 58; Shakespear, *The Lushei Kuki Clans*, 12. See Mang, 'Ethnographic Textile Art', 32, for women's tattoos featuring other plant and animal motifs (banana bud and rooster's tail feathers).

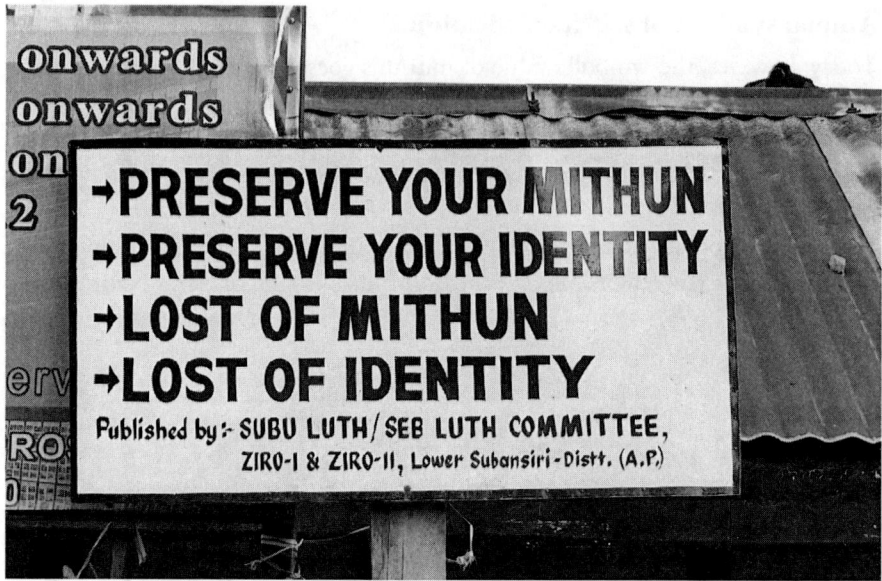

Plate 8.14 A signboard linking animal and human identities, Arunachal Pradesh (India), 2012

Source: Photo by Willem van Schendel.

Plate 8.15 Men at a village gathering in Nagaland (India), 2011

Source: Photo by Willem van Schendel.

Cultural Geographies

displays both (Plate 8.16), and so does the entrance to a neighbourhood in an India–Myanmar border town (Plate 8.17). In both images the mithun–hornbill motif is combined with human symbols of masculine power: a spear and guns.

Plate 8.16 Zomi National Day, Manipur (India), 2018

Source: Photo by Joy Ngaihte.

Note: The speaker is the president of the Zomi Re-unification Organisation.

Plate 8.17 Entrance gate to an urban neighbourhood, Manipur (India), 2012

Source: Photo by Willem van Schendel.

Animal symbols of self-identification are even more conspicuous in the Naga Heritage Village, a tourist attraction newly established by the government of Nagaland. It showcases imitation bachelors' dormitories (*morung*) of different ethnic groups. Their façades display an abundance of animal symbols. In Plate 8.18 we see a tiger eating a deer (left-hand pillar); hornbills and a human skull (central panels); a lion, a human figure and a mithun head (central pillar); and a monkey riding an elephant (right-hand pillar). Here animals are employed in tourist art to convey an exotic version of Naga identity: colourful and appealing, but also sanitised. It lacks the intense concern with fertility that characterises real dormitory art, and which an observer in the 1930s described like this: 'Sexual motifs are frequent; the private parts of the human figure are strongly

Plate 8.18 Konyak bachelors' dormitory, Naga Heritage Village, Nagaland (India), 2020

Source: Photo by Joy L. K. Pachuau.

Note: Fürer-Haimendorf gave this description of Konyak dormitories in 1938:

> The carvings represent men and women in various positions, tigers, elephants, hornbills, gibbons and occasionally other wild animals, but hardly ever domesticated animals such as the mithun (*Bos frontalis*), buffaloes, cows, pigs, or chickens. Some *morung*, however, are not entitled to have carvings of tigers or human figures. A favourite motif for the inner, but seldom for the outer, post is an elephant's head with the trunk flanked by two small human figures, usually a man and a woman with a child. The tiger, which may be either on the outer or the inner post, is invariably running downwards. All these carvings are very naturalistic, though the artists' capacity varies, of course.... The carvings may or may not be painted. In Wanching all carvings, the posts, the stamping boards, and the log-drum are painted in red, black and white. Kongan prefers white, and in Wakching only one *morung*, the Balang, has painted carvings. (Fürer-Haimendorf, 'The Morung System', 351)

See also Von Stockhausen, *Imag(in)ing the Nagas*, 366–73.

emphasized and the penis is often shown in a state of erection. Representations of coitus are also found and one Wakching *morung* even contains the carving of a man having intercourse with an elephant.'[86]

Although the message from tourist art is ambiguous, the new meanings given to the human–mithun connection are politically highly significant. 'Many Nagas, like the mithun, are raging. The raging mithun symbolizes the indomitable Naga spirit.'[87]

Not only is the mithun now a powerful symbol of upland self-confidence, but it also upends the civilisation discourse that has long marginalised the Triangle. By adopting an endemic animal as their emblem, upland communities have turned their presumed 'closeness to nature' into a badge of honour. Rejecting the connotations of being uncivilised and primitive, they proudly display traditional Triangle aesthetics and claim an organic connection with non-humans. In the twenty-first century, the intentional use of animal symbols communicates cultural self-confidence, modernity, interethnic solidarity and political defiance.

Interspecies labour relations

Our final example of spatial entanglement between humans and non-humans concerns animals that labour for humans. When Triangle humans tried to lighten their own workload, they learned that several animal species allowed themselves to be recruited for certain tasks. Oxen could be used for levelling and ploughing agricultural land; otters for fishing; dogs for hunting; yaks for carrying loads; and elephants for riding, heavy lifting and warfare (Plate 10.10).[88] Each of these interspecies labour relationships had its own spatial connotations and limitations. Yak labour was restricted to the Triangle's northern rim, animal traction was not used in mountain agriculture in the India–Myanmar borderlands, and fishing with trained otters was practised in rivers and coastal areas.

An interspecies labour relationship that deeply affected human life across the Triangle was the emergence of long-distance transport by pack animals. From the first millennium BCE, humans learned to employ ponies, horses,

---

[86] Fürer-Haimendorf, 'The Morung System', 351. See also Fürer-Haimendorf, *The Konyak Nagas*, 18, 23–7; Elwin, *The Art of the North-East Frontier of India*, 141; Jacobs et al., *The Nagas: Society, Culture*, 26–31, 164–5, 200–1, 210.
[87] Lotha, *The Raging Mithun*, i.
[88] On elephant labour, see Shell, 'Elephant Convoys beyond the State'; Lainé, 'Les éléphants sous la cour ahom'; Lainé, 'Conduct and Collaboration'; Lainé, 'Travail Interespèces et conservation'; Lainé, '*Phi Muangs*'; Lainé, *Living and Working with Giants*'.

and mules – probably originating from Tibet[89] – to carry large loads across the rugged mountains, thereby linking the Triangle's river valleys on both sides of the mountain-top watersheds as never before. Over time a specific geography of transport and markets developed, with mule caravans from Yunnan becoming a familiar sight in the uplands. As these caravans moved across a dense network of regional bridle paths (sometimes referred to as the Southern Silk Road), they connected numerous communities, affected population movements, crossed political boundaries and unified the Triangle as a trading world.[90] They extended across all parts of the Triangle in which river transport was not feasible, except in the mountains of Arunachal Pradesh and northernmost Myanmar where the steep terrain was too harsh for mules. For many centuries, pack animals completely dominated long-distance transportation in most of the Triangle uplands. In this way, the joint labour of horses, ponies, mules and muleteers created an embodied regional infrastructure.[91]

It was a time-bound infrastructure, however. It was seasonal, pulsating with life during the dry months but almost disappearing during the annual rains. It also responded to periods of political and economic uncertainty, always bouncing back, and reconfiguring itself after periods of strife, risk and danger. The heyday of this interspecies labour system lasted a long time. It did not come to an end until technological change caught up with it in the second half of the twentieth century. Since then, more extensive road building has allowed motorised traffic in many parts – but even today mule caravans still supply some areas where these roads do not go (Plate 8.19).[92]

Caravans rarely reached the Triangle lowlands. Here transportation was taken over by boats and carts. Today, even though motorised transport has made enormous headway, animal transport continues to be used all over the lowlands. Oxen, water buffaloes and horses, guided by humans, can still be seen hauling carts stashed with goods or people (Plates 8.20 and 8.21).

---

[89] Clarence-Smith, 'Breeding and Power in Southeast Asia'; Chakravarti, 'Early Medieval Bengal', 201–3.
[90] Yang provides maps of this network during different historical periods. Yang, 'Horses, Silver, and Cowries'. See also Ma and Ma, 'The Mule Caravans'; Cederlöf, 'Tracking Routes'; Van Schendel, 'Fragmented Sovereignty'; Carter et al., 'Tracing the Trade of Heirloom Beads'.
[91] For a parallel embodied infrastructure of elephants and humans, see Shell, 'Elephant Convoys beyond the State'. See also Barua, 'Animating Capital'.
[92] Gros, 'Nature De-naturalised'. See also Einzenberger, 'Contested Frontiers', 151; Smyer Yü and Dean (eds.), *Yunnan–Burma–Bengal Corridor Geographies*.

Plate 8.19 A mule caravan crossing a road in Mizoram (India), 2000

Source: Photo by Willem van Schendel.

Plate 8.20 Ox labour in Guwahati, Assam (India), 2012

Source: Photo by Willem van Schendel.

Plate 8.21 Horse carts being loaded in Bangladesh, 2003
Source: Photo by Willem van Schendel.

Horses, ponies and mules were especially versatile companions. They were very important as pack animals, but they provided humans with labour of many other types as well, especially as riding horses.[93] For example, they served in cavalry warfare, hunting and, in one small region within the Triangle, as mounts in a signature sports game (Plate 8.22).

The dynamism of spatial imaginations

The sometimes rapidly changing cultural geography of human–non-human relationships is a reminder that spatial imaginations are never static. The spatial frameworks that we have surveyed include microbes, plants and animals. All these frameworks are mutable and change over time with human and non-human mobilities. Some (like the cowrie and mule connections) endure for centuries but then fade away, while others (like fermented food or sticky rice) persist

---

[93] On human–mule relationships in the Triangle during World War II, see Webb et al., 'More-Than-Human Emotional Communities'.

Plate 8.22 Polo players and their ponies in Manipur (India)

Source: Photographer and date unidentified. 'Polospieler aus Manipur'. Ident. Nr. VIII C 14809, Ethnologisches Museum, Staatliche Museen zu Berlin.

and even move with Triangle people to wherever they settle in faraway places.[94] In addition, new spatial frameworks are coming up all the time – for example, the idea of 'biodiversity hotspots' (Chapter 1), the new field of Trans-Himalayan studies,[95] or the creation of wildlife sanctuaries, which we will explore in Chapter 10.[96] The result is a layered and dynamic ensemble of overlapping spaces, some anchored primarily in Triangle imaginations and traditions, and others in imaginations originating outside the Triangle. As human–non-human geographies emerged and vanished, their temporality shaped the complex history of the Triangle, underlining that humans are forever yoked to their many non-human companions.

---

[94] McDuie-Ra, *Northeast Migrants in Delhi*, 100–1, 153–6; Sitlhou, 'Food Culture and Identity'.
[95] Smyer Yü, 'Introduction: Trans-Himalayas'.
[96] Aiyadurai and Banerjee, 'Bird Conservation from Obscurity to Popularity'.

9

Exploiting Natural Resources

The past 150 years have seen a remarkable acceleration of human interference in the Triangle's environment. Current practices are widely studied but too rarely with due awareness of the historical dimension. Understanding how this acceleration came about is crucial because the exploitation of natural resources is nothing new – it is the human condition. One of the main concerns today is to explain how humans came to choose so many practices that prove to be unsustainable. This chapter introduces some pieces of this complicated puzzle.

We have seen how an innate ability to manipulate the environment powered early human attempts to upgrade their habitat, often at the expense of other organisms (Chapter 2). Uniquely advantaged by their genetic makeup, humans could work together, communicate by means of language and accumulate knowledge from generation to generation. In the Triangle, as elsewhere in the world, humans proved to be superior ecosystem engineers. From uncertain beginnings, tens of thousands of years ago, they grew into the region's dominant species, imagining themselves increasingly in control of the area's future. Over time, their ecological footprint burgeoned.

The domestication of certain plants and animals created agriculture and animal husbandry, and these allowed human populations to maintain themselves and even expand (Chapter 3). As human numbers increased, especially since the nineteenth century, human landscaping overwhelmed forests, swamps and waterways. Highly engineered landscapes – agricultural fields and orchards; irrigation systems, dams, roads and railways; villages and towns – connected humans across the region and beyond. Throughout history, however, the region's basic characteristics moulded human options. Its destiny was shaped by deep geological association, a wet monsoon climate and enormous biodiversity. Numerous rivers connected the vertical landscape and provided a range of ecological opportunities at close range.

Beyond agriculture and animal husbandry, however, human manipulation of the environment took many forms. In this chapter, we focus on these practices. Most have a history going back many centuries, but some are of more recent origin. We begin with how people's relationship with plants and animals changed. The second section of the chapter deals with how people exploited inanimate resources.

Foraging undomesticated plants and animals

Our species has been foraging wild produce and animals from the earliest days of our arrival in the Triangle. These pursuits have sustained countless generations up to the present day. People depended on foraging in forests and wetlands, but also in the domesticated landscapes dominated by agriculture and urban living.

In relatively sparsely populated parts of the Triangle, forests continued to be essential for human survival well into the twentieth century. They provided medicines and poisons, building and clothing materials, fibres and dyes, and indispensable food resources. Some foraged forest products were traded from the earliest recorded times, and over astonishingly long distances. Himalayan spikenard (or muskroot), a plant whose roots yield an intensely aromatic oil, was used as an expensive medicine and perfume in ancient Egypt and the eastern Mediterranean. It was mentioned in the Bible, as was cassia, an aromatic leaf produced in the Triangle, used in cooking and ointments.[1]

Over time, the number of communities that depended solely on foraging declined because most added agricultural practices to their livelihood strategies. For many, however, foraging remained hugely relevant. For example, in the 1940s an observer of hill villages in the eastern Triangle noticed: 'At least half, and perhaps more, of the Naga diet is of uncultivated plant foods. The women gather a great variety of tubers, bulbs, seeds, fruits, and greens. Some of these are eaten immediately after gathering; others are dried and stored.'[2] Today, foraged food and medicine continue to be essential in many rural communities.[3] Across the region, important wild food items include mushrooms, bamboo, climbing wattle, stink beans, Chinese sumac, lichens, wild taro, wild banana and wild ginger (Plate 9.1). Foraged medicines vary from orchids to herbs, ferns, vines and trees – the range

---

[1] According to a source from the first century CE, cassia leaves (*Cinnamomum tamala* – widely known in the Triangle as *tejpata* and in ancient Europe as *malabathrum*) were dried and prepared locally, sold in bundles and exported via the delta. Huntingford (ed.), *The Periplus of the Erythraean Sea*.

[2] Steen, 'Material Culture of the Langsing Nagas', 275. See also Angami et al., 'Status and Potential'.

[3] Thang, 'The Dynamics of Natural Resources'.

Plate 9.1 Next to a fast-flowing river, women are cleaning bamboo shoots that they have collected in the forest, Mizoram (India)

Source: Photo by M. S. Dawngkima (Dadonga).

of foraged plants is enormous, and for most no English names exist.[4] As we have seen, today considerable research is being done into the properties of wild foods and medicinal plants.[5]

The enduring presence of foraging is often overlooked. For many poorer people – both rural and urban – it remains an essential livelihood strategy.[6] Today, landless people who depend on seasonal labour often turn to it during lean times. Take the fruit-bat hunters in the lowlands, who demonstrate that a forested environment is not a prerequisite for successful foraging. In their human-engineered landscape of intensively cultivated agricultural fields they cannot survive on day labour, so seasonally they hunt fruit bats that are attracted to village

---

[4] Many of these plants have no common English names, for example, *Alocasia fornicate* or *Amomum dealbatum*. For a list, see Kar et al., 'Wild Edible Plant Resources'. See also Tsering et al., 'Medicinal Orchids of Arunachal Pradesh'; De et al., 'Tribal Life in the Environment'; Terangpi, Engtipi and Teron, 'Utilization of Less Known Plants'; San et al., *Study on Distribution*; Ayam, 'Ethnomedicine of Wild Plants of Ziro'; Faruque et al., 'Qualitative and Quantitative Ethnobotanical'.

[5] The boundaries between foraging and domestication are often vague and locally specific. Arora, 'Plant Genetic Resources of Northeastern Region'. See also Angami et al., 'Status and Potential of Wild Edible Plants'; Rahman, 'Indigenous Knowledge of Herbal Medicines'; Kabir et al., 'A Survey of Medicinal Plants'; Das, 'Dietary Use of Algae'; Khomdram et al., 'Local Knowledge'; *Medicinal Plants of Myanmar*.

[6] For hunting by relatively well-off urban men, see Kikon and McDuie-Ra, *Ceasefire City*, chap. 4.

date palms and fruit trees. They also hunt rabbits, squirrels, foxes, mongooses and other small animals that live around the villages. And they catch eels, snails, fish and turtles in rice fields, ponds and lakes. In this way they tide over periods of scarcity. These seasonal foragers catch all these animals mostly for self-consumption but sell some to generate a little income.[7]

Today, hunting and gathering remain essential to sustain delicately balanced urban and rural lifestyles. Across the Triangle, children can be seen in city parks and open spaces collecting dry leaves and branches for cooking fires. Boys with slingshots go out to shoot birds. Women gather roadside herbs. Men set traps for small animals. And in some places the very poorest must rummage through trash bins and garbage dumps for edibles and reusable items. Throughout the region, millions are continuously scouring their human-manipulated environment for useful resources, as they have done for generations. And this includes drinking water collected from streams, wells and water points.

In some urban settings, hunting could also take another shape. In Dimapur, Nagaland's largest city, male college students and retired government officials would go hunting in nearby forests. Such 'masculine leisure trips' were neither for sustenance nor simply a form of sport. They involved emotional encounters between humans, animals and spirits, and they highlighted the 'inter-species relationships that persevere in the urban environment'. Even in the twenty-first-century city, 'hunting remains a central trope of Naga identity', a way of connecting with memories of a rural past, and a form of male bonding.[8]

Another form of foraging is fishing. The region's many water bodies provide natural conditions for an astonishing variety and abundance of fish species.[9] Early on, humans learned to catch fish by using rods, traps, nets, weirs, harpoons, rafts, boats and poison (Plate 9.2) – and they still do so.[10] Catching fish could be turned into a full-time profession, so communities of fisherfolk emerged to supply fish to non-fishing groups. Some fisherfolk engaged the help of non-human assistants: they trained semi-domesticated otters to drive fish into their nets.[11]

---

[7] Nahar et al., 'Hunting Bats for Human Consumption'. See also Khan, *Protected Areas of Bangladesh*, 33–4.
[8] Kikon and McDuie-Ra, *Ceasefire City*, chap. 4.
[9] Pardharasadhi, 'Ecological Biogeography'; Allen, Molur and Daniel (comp.), *The Status and Distribution*, 26; IUCN Bangladesh, *Red List of Bangladesh*, vol. 5.
[10] For examples, see Woodthorpe, 'Explorations on the Chindwin River', 212. See also Yumnam and Tripathi, 'Ethnobotany: Plants Use in Fishing'.
[11] Mountfort and Hosking, *The Vanishing Jungle*, 225, 227–8.

Plate 9.2 Fishing with a poisonous creeper in Assam (India), c. 1946; upstream men are beating the plant, and downstream boys are trying to catch the stupefied fish

Source: Hangrum village, North Cachar, Assam, India. Photo by Ursula Violet Graham Bower. Courtesy Pitt Rivers Museum, Oxford.

Note: See also Hanson, *The Kachins*, 77; and illustrations in Mills, *The Lhota Nagas*, 70–1.

Much fishery is simply a matter of garnering, but fish breeding – a form of animal husbandry – also has a long history, especially since the times that humans began to dig ponds in their settlements. These were used primarily to store water for human consumption, washing and bathing – but they also doubled as fishponds and sources of leafy greens (Plate 9.8).

The region's waterways sustained the livelihood of other professional gatherers as well. Traders would cut bamboos in upriver forests and float them downstream in large rafts. There bamboo served as raw material for house construction, agricultural instruments, fishing gear, basketry, paper, furniture and much more. It is a trade that is still very much alive (Plate 9.3).[12]

Rivers also developed into important routes for other trade goods sourced from forests. For example, the Chindwin River, which drains the eastern slopes of the Triangle, has long been used to transport foraged teak and rattan to the towns and cities of Myanmar.[13]

---

[12] Baldizzone and Baldizzone, *Caravanes de bambous*.

[13] Woodthorpe, 'Explorations on the Chindwin River', 200; Pau, *Indo-Burma Frontier*, 189–90.

Exploiting Natural Resources

Plate 9.3 Enormous rafts of bamboo from state forests on their way to a paper mill in Chandraghona (Bangladesh), 1964

Source: Photo by Keith Sandercock. See Van Schendel, Mey and Dewan, *The Chittagong Hill Tracts*.

Note: At the time Bangladesh was East Pakistan.

Hunting, or foraging the undomesticated environment for animals, was an essential survival skill. Excavations in a large cave in Nagaland (India) – thought to have been occupied by hunter-gatherers in the fifth millennium BCE – yielded remains of deer, gibbon, wild boar, serow (goatlike mammal), porcupine, squirrel, bats, rodents, birds and many smaller animals.[14] Over time, the figure of the hunter took on a special role throughout the Triangle, becoming a key emblem of masculinity and power in many local cultures (Chapter 6). Early depictions show men heroically attacking large prey (Plate 6.6). Hunting could develop into an elite pastime (Plate 9.4), but in many communities hunting was indispensable as a source of food and for ritual purposes, and it was hemmed in by various restrictions.[15] Men would hunt in groups to kill larger game (Plate 9.5).[16]

---

[14] Jamir, Tetso and Venuh, 'Recent Archaeological Investigation', 275. See Chapter 3.

[15] Janaki, Pandit and Sharma, 'The Role of Traditional Belief Systems'; Aisher, 'Through "Spirits"'; Aiyadurai, '"Tigers Are Our Brothers"', PhD thesis; Stevenson, *The Economics of the Central Chin Tribes*, 62–71; Jackson, 'Colonial Conquest and Religious Entanglement'.

[16] Aiyadurai, Singh and Milner-Gulland, 'Wildlife Hunting by Indigenous Tribes'; Aiyadurai, 'Wildlife Hunting and Conservation in Northeast India'; Hlawndo, 'A Study of the Cultural Factors', 73–6 ; Chowdhury et al., 'Dietetic Use of Wild Animals', 31. For an account of hunting as an elite pastime, see Cooch Behar, *Thirty-Seven Years of Big Game*.

Plate 9.4 Horsemen with dogs hunting deer, eighteenth-century temple relief in Assam (India)

Source: Photo by Willem van Schendel.

Note: Bishnudol (an Ahom temple) in Sibsagar. See also Das, 'Terracotta Sculptures', 426–7.

Plate 9.5 A party of hunters returning to their village, Assam (India), c. 1946

Source: Laisong village, North Cachar, Assam, India. Photo by Ursula Violet Graham Bower. Courtesy Pitt Rivers Museum, Oxford.

Exploiting Natural Resources 195

Traditional hunting tools included blowpipes and darts, bows and (poison-tipped) arrows, pellet bows and spears (Plate 6.7). Traps were also extensively used for small animals, such as squirrels and birds, as well as for large ones, such as tigers and bears.[17] In recent centuries the arrival of firearms critically changed power relations between humans and wild animals. This was an important transformation because hunting success was so essential for local men to build up a reputation and climb the social ladder (Chapter 6). Hunting with guns made it easier to kill big game (Plates 9.6 and 9.7), and colonial policies further transformed local hunting practices by offering large cash rewards for the corpses of tigers, bears and leopards – animals that had rarely been hunted previously. But in some areas of northern Burma, another effect of colonial policies was noted. 'The tiger and the leopard, with many smaller species of the *Felidæ*, are distressingly abundant, and in many localities on the increase, as the inhabitants have been practically disarmed.'[18]

Plate 9.6 Hunter with tiger and shotgun in Mizoram (India), c. 1923

Source: Photo by Charles Dennis Balding, Darth[l]alang, Mizoram (then Lushai Hills). © The British Library Board (Balding collection/Photo 498/3(24)).

---

[17] Needham, 'Squirrels and Marriage', in Elwin (ed.), *The Art of the North-East Frontier*, 292–3; Shaw, *Notes on the Thadou Kukis*, 88–9; Parry, *The Lakhers*, 146–61; Kauffmann, 'Die Fallen der Thadou-Kuki in Assam'; Htwe, 'The Social Organization', 57–8. On hunting with pellet bows and spears in Chin State c. 1970, see Banks, 'Innovation in a Zanniat Chin Village', 39.

[18] Hanson, *The Kachins*, 36

Plate 9.7 Hunter and friends proudly posing with a wild gaur in the Chittagong Hill Tracts (Bangladesh), 1970

Source: Photographer unidentified, Mizo National Front (MNF) collection.

Note: The hunter, Pu Hrangthanga Colney, shot the animal in Tuisen Chhantlang, East Pakistan (now Bangladesh).

At the same time a market opened up for rhinoceros horn, which was thought to have medicinal properties and fetched fabulous prices.[19] These innovations led to the emergence of local trophy hunters – an 'animal gold rush'[20] – and the disappearance of many species from the region: the last Sumatran (two-horned) rhinoceros was killed near the Myanmar–Bangladesh border in 1966.[21] This depletion of trophy animals closed the historically important avenue for Triangle men to enhance their position in local society by hunting big game.

---

[19] Jackson, 'Colonial Conquest', chap. 3.
[20] Ibid., 141.
[21] Mountfort and Hosking, *The Vanishing Jungle*, 230–1.

Although in many mountainous parts of the Triangle men still hunt with guns, the era of the heroic hunter is over. It is remembered with nostalgia, as walls bedecked with animal skulls bear out (Plate 6.11).

Human-centred history is often 'about how human beings have learned to control Mother Nature's wild, impulsive ways by replacing them with our own orderly, efficient, and thus more trustworthy ways of going about being fed, housed, and properly looked after'.[22] But human manipulation of the Triangle environment took many forms and the persistence of foraging points to a less anthropocentric understanding. Plants, animals and people are in constant interaction and shape each other's behaviour. People took responsibility for the survival of some local plant or animal populations (such as rice, or mangoes, or pigs) but not for 'wild' ones. The former became 'domesticated' – but these species can also be said to have domesticated the behaviour of the people involved. Likewise, 'undomesticated' species and people influenced each other's behaviour in an 'interactive matrix of species and harvesting tactics'. It makes little sense to categorise people as either 'foragers' or 'farmers' because most humans combined subsistence practices from both domains.[23] Human attempts to construct their niche and harvest other species were always multiple, interdependent and open ended.

Resources from the earth's surface and below

It was not only living organisms that provided humans with resources to better themselves. The very terrain of the Triangle offered humans many opportunities to improve their grip on their environment. Human niche construction also involved growing control of many inanimate resources – some of which turned out to be more plentiful than others. We will have to be selective here and briefly introduce two examples from the earth's surface (water and mud) and two from below the topsoil (semi-precious stones and fossil fuels).

Water

We have seen that the Triangle is an exceptionally well-watered region but with marked seasonal differences. Between June and October heavy rains fall, glaciers melt, rivers swell and parts of the Triangle get flooded. During the winter months very little rain falls, mountain peaks freeze and small water courses dry up.

---

[22] Terrell et al., 'Domesticated Landscapes', 359.
[23] Ibid., 323. To overcome the focus on 'domesticated landscapes', they propose a model ('the provisions spreadsheet') that embraces all human subsistence practices (351–9).

But there is always plenty of water in mountain springs and larger rivers, especially in the Triangle's main thoroughfare, the vast Brahmaputra River.

Finding drinking water has never been a really serious issue. Even so, some inhabitants had to invent technologies to access water. For those who lived in settlements on hilltops this could be a problem. Living in these locations had the advantage of being able to see an enemy approach as well as avoiding an unseen enemy, malaria, which especially plagued the forested valleys. But water could be scarce up there, so it had to be brought up from below. Downhill, underground water currents would spill out to form springs, waterfalls and waterways. An effective technology was found with the help of plants: using segments of stout bamboo, carried in large baskets. This was women's work and carrying up the water-filled bamboos was hard daily labour. This practice, which allowed humans to extend their environmental niche to water-deprived hilltops, continued well into the twentieth century (Plate 9.8).

In level areas, the urge to retain water in the dry season led to long-term changes in the landscape. Humans began to excavate ponds. Some were enormous and required a great collective effort to make (Plate 9.9).[24] Many more were small affairs dug to supply a single family or a cluster of dwellings. Today, square or rectangular ponds are a fixed feature all over the alluvial parts of the Triangle landscape. Non-humans have taken advantage of them, too. Frogs, fishes, insects, birds and many other animals have created their own habitats in and around the ponds.

In the late twentieth century the use of surface water for consumption declined as people learned more about hygiene and new technologies spread. In many places tube wells were installed, or trucks supplied water that customers stored in large household water barrels. In some places piped water became available. But today women can still be seen carrying water up from wells and water points, now no longer in giant bamboos but in jerry cans or plastic containers.

Water was also an important resource for irrigated rice cultivation. Here, too, technologies changed over time. Today, age-old (and relatively cheap) ways of moving water from waterways to rice fields (Plate 4.4) coexist with lift pumps and deep tube wells. In agricultural communities, irrigation water connected humans to their rice crops. The apportioning of this natural resource could become a perennial social and political issue among rice cultivators.

Soon after electricity came to the Triangle, plans were made to use streaming water to generate it. An early example is the proposal to exploit the hydropower of the Karnaphuli River, which flows from the Indo-Burma mountain range to the Bay of Bengal. In 1906 a plan was launched to dam this river to supply the city of Chittagong with electricity. The plan was deemed too expensive at the time, but

---

[24] For very large pre-tenth-century ponds in the northwestern Triangle, see Jahan, 'Bhitargarh'.

Exploiting Natural Resources

Plate 9.8 Women engaged in a daily chore: carrying water-filled bamboos up to their hilltop households, Mizoram (India), 1932

Source: Photo by Barbara Angus; used by kind permission of the Angus Library and Archive, Regent's Park College, Oxford, UK.

Note: See also Hanson, *The Kachins*, 79; Hmingthanzuali and Pande, 'Women's Indigenous Knowledge'.

Plate 9.9 Jagannath Dighi, one of several huge ponds in Udaipur, Tripura (India), that date back to the seventeenth century

Source: Photo by Willem van Schendel.

half a century later it was underway. A large dam was constructed in the tiny hill village of Kaptai (Bangladesh) (Plate 9.10). When it was completed, it created an enormous lake, which flooded many villages and agricultural fields. It was later described as a major ecological disaster.[25] A visiting World Wildlife Fund team cited the verdict of the local forest manager:

> Most of the best forested valleys were drowned and although the water rose slowly, considerable loss of wildlife occurred. Many Elephants, Tigers and various species of deer which escaped drowning were unable to retreat across the 3,000-foot ridge of the Lushai Hills to the east, and therefore moved either north to Assam or west across the Kassalong River into Tripura.... Under present plans, an additional thousand acres per annum were to be taken from the reserve for planting Teak. A monoculture of Teak, however desirable commercially, is a death-knell to wildlife conservation. No species of deer or monkey can find food in such vegetation, and they are forced to abandon the area. In the absence of deer, Tigers and Leopards turn to preying on cattle and goats around the villages and are therefore soon shot.[26]

---

[25] Van Schendel, Mey and Dewan, *The Chittagong Hill Tracts*, 197–217.
[26] Mountfort and Hosking, *The Vanishing Jungle*, 105–6; Van Schendel, Mey and Dewan, *The Chittagong Hill Tracts*, 143–8.

Plate 9.10 The Kaptai hydroelectric project in 1964, Chittagong Hill Tracts (Bangladesh)

Source: Photo by Keith Sandercock. See Van Schendel, Mey and Dewan, *The Chittagong Hill Tracts*.

The Kaptai hydroelectric project was a precursor of many later schemes to construct dams across rivers in the Triangle. Many were hotly contested because of the massive ecological fallout of such heavy-handed forms of human niche construction.

Mud

In addition to water, the earth's surface provided another crucial resource: its topsoil. It was essential for plant growth and agriculture, of course, and humans learned how to treat it to facilitate cultivation. They shaped the soil by means of embankments, contours, terraces and irrigation channels; fallowed it by means of animal-drawn ploughs; levelled it by means of harrows; manured it; and left it to recuperate after cultivation.

The soil had many non-agricultural uses as well. Where stones were available, these could be used to build walls and construct shelters for people and animals. In many parts of the Triangle, however, stones were hard to come by, especially in the river valleys and the vast delta. Here road building, house construction and cement manufacture created a demand for stones from hillside quarries and riverbeds, and these became trade items. The river valleys and the delta consisted of very thick layers of alluvial silt, and mud was – and continues to be – a key building material of wattle-and-daub huts and courtyard stoves (Plate 9.11). From early times humans also learned to use fire to turn mud into bricks. Brick walls and roads grace archaeological sites around the region. Today many brickyards dot the countryside around the growing cities, revealing that sand and

Plate 9.11 Women repairing a mud hut in Bangladesh, 1988

Source: Photo by Willem van Schendel.

clay have become very valuable commodities. Their extraction, like that of stones, is increasingly understood to be environmentally damaging (Plate 9.12).[27]

Pottery was another form of baked mud. Currently we can date the oldest potsherds in the Triangle to around 1000 BCE (Chapter 3), but just beyond its eastern reaches much older pottery has been found.[28] Histories of where people settled could be bound up with where good mud for pottery was available.[29] Pottery continues to be a living craft.[30] And mud lay at the basis of another important art form: terracotta. Sculptures, ornamental plaques and other objects

Plate 9.12 Removing sand and clay from the Brahmaputra, 2008
Source: Photo by Willem van Schendel.

---

[27] Chhibber, *The Mineral Resources of Burma*, 287–309; Padmalal and Maya, *Sand Mining*; Seddiky, 'Poverty and Social Vulnerability'; Biswas et al., 'The Drivers and Impacts of Selling Soil'; Ahmed et al., 'Environmental Sustainability Assessment'.

[28] Sharma and Singh, 'Luminescence Dating'. For earlier pottery, from nearby northern Myanmar, see Hudson and Lwin, 'Earthenware from a Firing Site'; and Pryce et al., 'A First Absolute Chronology'. Wheel-turned pottery has a long tradition, and handmade pottery continues to be made and traded in the Triangle. Both men and women are known to have been potters (Hazarika, 'Neolithic Pottery', 79–107). For Naga women collecting pottery clay from pits, see Vasa, 'Experimenting'. See also Von Stockhausen, *Imag(in)ing the Nagas*, 378–9.

[29] Gachui, 'An Oinam Poumai Potter'.

[30] For example, Marak, 'Women and Clay'.

have been recovered from various archaeological sites across the region (Plate 6.6).[31] Terracotta art has remained a living tradition ever since.

Water and mud are just two forms in which humans exploited the earth's surface to make their lives easier and safer. Locally, the earth's surface yielded other highly useful materials as well: salt (from salt marshes, salty lakes or upland salt springs[32]); gold (from some rivers[33]); and iron (from granite outcrops[34]). But most of the Triangle's mineral wealth was found below the surface.

Quarrying and mining

As toolmaking gradually improved in the Triangle, it became possible to explore what lay beneath the earth's surface. Sand and limestone could be quarried.[35]

---

[31] For example, Barman, 'Early Medieval Archaeological Landscape'; Das, 'Terracotta Sculptures'.

[32] Van Schendel (ed.), *Francis Buchanan in Southeast Bengal*, 10–12; Wilcox, 'Memoir of a Survey', 322; Hamilton, *An Account of Assam*, 47; Pemberton, 'Abstract of the Journal', 270, 274; Phayre, 'Account of Arakan', 710; M'Cosh, *Topography of Assam*, 61–2; Barbe, 'Some Account of the Hill Tribes', 386; Stewart, 'Notes on Northern Cachar', 595; *Selections of Papers*; Morris, 'The Vernay-Hopwood', 654; Stevenson, *The Economics of the Central Chin Tribes*, 676–7; Saikia and Amin, 'A Study on the Salt Production'; Haokip, 'Salt Land and State Monopoly'; Zhao, 'Chapter 1: Salt, Grain and the Change'; Haokip, 'The Petroglyphs of Indo-Myanmar'.

[33] Sometimes in quantities that could sustain professional communities of gold washers, for example, the Sonowal Kachari, who filtered gold from alluvial sands in the Subansiri, Brahmaputra and Burhi-Dihing Rivers, and the gold washers of the upper Chindwin and Uyu Rivers. Tālish, *Tarikh-i Asham*, 83–4; Qadri, *Pre-Colonial Northeast India*, 32; Hamilton, *An Account of Assam*, 46–7; Grant, 'Mode of Extracting', 148–9; Pemberton, *Report on the Eastern Frontier*, 28, 81–2, 126–7; Pemberton, 'Abstract of the Journal', 270–1; M'Cosh, *Topography of Assam*, 57; Woodthorpe, 'Explorations on the Chindwin River', 208–9; Allen, *Assam District Gazetteers*, 198–201; Brown, *Burma Gazetteer*, 36; Hanson, *The Kachins*, 76; Lambert, 'From the Brahmaputra', 318–19; Burma Frontier Areas, *Report Submitted to His Majesty's Government*, 207–10; Lintner, *The Kachin*, 153–4; Saikia, *The Unquiet River*, 126–32; Daniels, 'Nanzhao as a Southeast Asian Kingdom', 198, 202.

[34] Blench ('The Contribution of Linguistics', 106–7) uses linguistic evidence to suggest that knowledge about iron and iron smelting reached the Triangle relatively late, and from China, not India. Thakur ('Iron in the History') suggests that iron use spread from Kachin areas to Arunachal Pradesh and mentions creation stories in Meghalaya involving iron-working gods. See also Hamilton, *An Account of Assam*, 47; W. C. [William Cracroft], 'Smelting of Iron', 150–1; Wilcox, 'Memoir of a Survey', 322, 373, 383; Trant, 'Report on a Route', 1149; Yule, 'Notes on the Iron'; Oldham, 'On the Geological Structure', 1:201–7; Hooker, *Himalayan Journals*, 2:510–12; Prokop and Suliga, 'Two Thousand Years of Iron Smelting'.

[35] Limestone had been traded from the Khasi Hills to the plains (by Khasi and 'Armenians, Greeks, and low Europeans') well before the 1770s, when Robert Lindsay established himself as a major lime merchant in the region, supplying Calcutta. Lindsay, *Lives of the Lindsays*, 3:174–80. For a later description of the lime industry, see Oldham, 'On the Geological Structure', 180–5. For postcolonial developments, see Karlsson, *Unruly Hills*, 201–7.

Exploiting Natural Resources

Over time, shallow pits that gave access to subterranean treasures developed into more elaborate mines. The region became known for its amber and semi-precious stones (carnelian, jade) that could be traded over long distances. In some parts, seams of coal were discovered and exploited. In others oil was found near the surface. There were also naturally occurring gas vents, but this resource could not be harnessed effectively until much later.[36] Uranium and nickel are among the Triangle's most recently exploited mineral resources.[37] The history of mining is long, as two brief examples will show: semi-precious stones and fossil fuels.

Semi-precious stones

We have seen that the primeval collision of the Indian and Eurasian tectonic plates pushed up the mountains of the Indo-Burma Arc (Chapter 1). The eastern slopes of this battered landscape are particularly rich in mineral resources that humans found interesting. Archaeological evidence points to the early use of, and trade in, semi-precious stones for decorative and ritual purposes. Although it is not possible to show that there is an unbroken tradition, many of these stones are still in use. Take carnelian, a reddish-brown stone that was quarried, fashioned and traded here from at least 500 BCE. It was sought after in the form of beads, amulets and pendants, and it may have been traded across the Triangle as well as into Yunnan.[38] There were other sources of carnelian in the region, for example in Arakan,[39] and in Meghalaya, where 'Lynngam males wear bead necklaces, the beads being sometimes of cornelian [sic] gathered from the beds of the local hill streams'.[40] Carnelian ornaments are still in use. They are notably documented among the Nagas.[41] Current supplies no longer derive from the region, however, and it is thought that imports of carnelian beads from western India are centuries old.[42]

---

[36] Francis Buchanan visited a 'burning rock' and a 'burning-well' in the late eighteenth century and gave a detailed description. Van Schendel (ed.), *Francis Buchanan in Southeast Bengal*, 18–22.

[37] Uranium prospecting began in the early 1960s and by 1974 exploitable quantities were found in Meghalaya. Dwivedi, 'Possibility of New Uranium Discoveries'; McDuie-Ra, *Civil Society, Democratization*; Sirnate, 'Students versus the State'; Karlsson, *Unruly Hills*, 173–201. On nickel, see Einzenberger, 'Frontier Capitalism and Politics'.

[38] Moore, 'Carnelian in Myanmar'; Moore and Myint, 'Beads of Myanmar (Burma)'; Jamir and Vasa, 'Archaeological Evidence'; Jahan, 'Archaeology of Wari-Bateshwar'; Wilcox, 'Memoir of a Survey', 373; Carey and Tuck, *The Chin Hills*, 1:173; Rayhan, 'Prospects of Public Archaeology', 8–9; Shaw, *Notes on the Thadou Kukis*, 20, 72–73; Rahman et al., 'Agricultural Systems in Bangladesh', 5; Georjon et al., 'Late Neolithic'.

[39] Parry, *The Lakhers*, 42–3.

[40] Gurdon, *The Khasis*, 23.

[41] Kanungo, 'Ornaments of the Dead'.

[42] Cole, 'Heirloom Beads', 16.

A second semi-precious stone from the eastern edge of the Triangle was jade (or jadeite[43]). This opaque or translucent stone was not much traded within the region, but it was highly sought after in China, where it was of ancient and enduring cultural significance. The Triangle jade mines are said to produce the highest-quality jadeite in the world. These mines may have been in operation since before the eighth century CE. Considerable trade with Yunnan (and further China) picked up in later centuries and large-scale extraction developed in the eighteenth century. Mining continues today, now mostly on an industrial rather than an artisanal scale, and it powers a brisk jade trade to customers in China.[44]

Amber is the third valuable resource from the eastern edge of the Triangle. Technically it is not a stone but a plant product. Amber is ancient, fossilised resin, but it is treated as a gemstone. According to Chinese sources, amber has been mined in the upper reaches of the Chindwin River since at least the first century CE.[45] Many in the Triangle have worn it as jewellery and used it for ritual and medical purposes. For example, an early-twentieth-century observer noted that, among the Mizo, 'both sexes are fond of necklaces; those of amber are most valued, and any that have histories attached to them fetch prices which to us seem absurd'.[46] Triangle amber has also been traded to China for many centuries, and today it has a worldwide market.[47] Apparently, the main technique, digging pits with fairly simple shovels and bamboo implements, has changed little since it was first described in the 1830s (Plate 9.13).[48]

Triangle amber is not only sought after for its beauty. It is also of intense interest to scholars of ancient life forms and truly deep environmental history.

---

[43] The term 'jade' actually refers to two minerals: jadeite and nephrite. Jadeite is usually more appreciated because it is rare, translucent and displays the most sought-after green hues. Chhibber, *The Mineral Resources of Burma*, 23–84; Chang, 'Guanxi and Regulation in Networks'.

[44] Møller, *Spectral Jade*; Lintner, *The Kachin*, 161–81; Prasse-Freeman, 'Necroeconomics'.

[45] Zherikhin and Ross, 'A Review of the History'; Hanson, *The Kachins*, 75–6; Chhibber, *The Mineral Resources of Burma*, 85–94; Cruickshank and Ko, 'Geology of an Amber Locality'; Møller, *Spectral Jade*, 90–1, 139–43, 157–9; Brinckmann, 'The Táng Era', 94–5.

[46] Shakespear, *The Lushei Kuki Clans*, 13–14. See also Lewin, *The Hill Tracts of Chittagong*, 78, 103; Dalton, *Descriptive Ethnology of Bengal*, Plate II; Hanson, *The Kachins*, 48; Zahulha, 'Thihna Chhuana'; Banks, 'Innovation in a Zanniat Chin Village', 341. Similarly, among the Thadou, carnelian beads were easily 'valued at 5 to 10 mithuns' in the early twentieth century. Shaw, *Notes on the Thadou Kukis*, 73.

[47] Rippa and Yang, 'The Amber Road'.

[48] Pemberton, *Report on the Eastern Frontier*, 131; Pemberton, 'Abstract of the Journal', 269–72, 274–5; Griffith, *Journals of Travels in Assam*, 1:77; *Blood Amber*.

Plate 9.13 Mining amber in northern Myanmar

Source: Photographer unidentified. From: 'Amber Is Myanmar's New Gold', *Ancient Artifacts*, 1 July 2018, https://psjfactoids.blogspot.com/2018/07/amber-is-myanmars-new-gold.html (accessed 12 May 2021).

Trapped within the amber are the remains of many different insects, scorpions, dinosaurs, birds, spiders, snails, frogs, fungi, conifers and flowering plants that inhabited the Triangle some 99 million years ago. And new 'amber species' are being discovered all the time; by 2020 over 1,500 had been identified.[49]

The semi-precious stones that humans found in the eastern Triangle not only enthused them but also led them to change the landscape. They dug mines and created pathways and markets to facilitate trade. With a rapid increase in the demand for these gemstones, production methods became industrial and environmentally more damaging. The deleterious effects were especially noticeable in the denuded forests and polluted rivers of the mining areas.[50]

---

[49] Ross, 'The Remarkable Palaeodiversity'; Ross, *Burmese (Myanmar) amber taxa*.
[50] The same is true of gold mining in the same area. Papworth et al., 'The Impact of Gold Mining'; Tun, Wongsasuluk and Siriwong, 'Heavy Metals'.

Fossil fuels: Coal, oil and gas

The jumbled terrain of the Triangle holds other treasures for humans as well: fossil carbon fuels, which are the remains of ancient plants. Wherever humans found these, they were quick to use them to their advantage. This was easiest in the case of coal if it appeared near the surface. Early colonial prospectors eagerly explored coal seams in Meghalaya, upper Assam and northern Myanmar,[51] and it was not long before commercial coal production took off in two forms: artisanal and industrial. Both survive today. Artisanal coal production developed in upland Meghalaya and Nagaland, where local landowners dug pits to mine coal. They sold their produce mainly to lowland consumers.[52] In colonial upper Assam, on the other hand, coal

Plate 9.14 Coal tubs leaving the Tipong colliery, Arunachal Pradesh–Assam border (India), 2004

Source: Photo by Willem van Schendel.

---

[51] *Selections of Papers*; Woodthorpe, 'Explorations on the Chindwin River', 212; Chhibber, *The Mineral Resources of Burma*, 114–31.

[52] Oldham, 'On the Geological Structure', 185–201, provides an early description. For recent developments, see Karlsson, *Unruly Hills*, 65–70, 208–15; Vakkayil and Canato, 'Muddling Through'; McDuie-Ra and Kikon, 'Tribal Communities and Coal'; Kikon, *Living with Oil and Coal*.

mining was in the hands of industrial corporations that worked on a grand scale. They exploited both deep mines (Plate 9.14) and vast coal fields (Plate 9.15). Making use of the rapidly spreading railways, they were able to market their coal all over India.

Fossil fuels come in other forms as well. In the eastern half of the region large reserves of oil and natural gas can be found.[53] Some of these have been exploited commercially for generations, providing energy for new lifestyles, changing the landscape and causing human migrations. British prospectors discovered oil as soon as they took control of Assam. The first report dates from 1828, and by the late nineteenth century oil wells and a refinery had come into production.[54]

Plate 9.15 Working the Makum coalfield, Assam (India), 2004
Source: Photo by Willem van Schendel.

---

[53] Brahma, Sircar and Karmakar, 'Hydrocarbon Prospectivity'; Shetol et al., 'Present Status of Bangladesh Gas Fields'; Laishramcha, 'Hydrocarbon Extraction'; Kikon, *Living with Oil and Coal*.

[54] Jack, 'The Development of the Petroleum Industry'; Imperial Institute, *Petroleum*, 18–21; Evans, 'The Oilfields of India and Burma'; Birney, *The Story of the Assam Railways*, 9, 44–9; Saikia, 'Imperialism, Geology and Petroleum'.

Oil wells were well known across the border in Myanmar, too, and they continue to be exploited today.[55] Natural gas seeps were also known in eastern Bangladesh, but systematic gas explorations did not commence here until the early twentieth century. From 1950 these large reserves could be exploited commercially. The environmental effects of gas exploitation were considerable.[56]

The limits of exploitation

Utilising natural resources comes naturally to humans. Human life simply would be unsustainable without such behaviour. As we have seen, from the very beginning humans in the Triangle supported themselves by means of foraged plants, animals and inanimate matter. And today this is still the case. Entire livelihoods are based on extracting bits of the natural environment, from bamboo to jade, from wildlife to water, and from petrol to fish and greens.

However, by the late twentieth century it had become increasingly evident that such livelihoods are not sustainable. First, the resources on which they rely are finite. Some (big game and gold) have already been largely depleted and others (fossil fuels) are non-renewable and will run out in the foreseeable future. Even resources that once seemed inexhaustible (such as sand and water) are now in ever shorter supply. Second, extractive pursuits have proved to be unsustainable because of the destruction of natural habitats, pollution and increased risks to human health. All over the Triangle there is a growing awareness of environmental degradation and crisis. This is what we will explore in the next chapter.

---

[55] Durkee and Gerrard, 'An Integrated Oil Industry Runs'.
[56] Rashid, 'The Exploration of Natural Gas'; Gardner et al., 'Field of Dreams'.

10

Dealing with Environmental Decay

Ever since their arrival in the Triangle, humans have been busy expanding their ecological niche and so make their lives easier and more sustainable. They found solutions to many of the problems they faced. Unlike other living beings, they were masters of technological innovation and began to think of their trajectory in terms of 'progress'. That trajectory also involved the human niche becoming a more unequal place: some people lived lives of relative comfort while others struggled to survive. Historians have long paid attention to these two aspects. They have routinely understood human technological progress in glorious and self-gratulatory terms, such as 'civilisation' and 'development'. And they have described human inequalities in terms of 'social differentiation', 'poverty', 'exploitation' and 'backwardness'.

What most scholars have only recently focused on, however, are the knock-on effects of human niche construction beyond the human sphere, and how to write adequate histories of the region that take into account the connectedness of human and non-human histories. It was only with quickening environmental degradation in the late twentieth century that this became imperative. In this chapter we look at how, during this 'Great Acceleration' in humanity's impact on the world,[1] human niche construction ultimately went haywire, causing serious ecological devastation. The following chapter ('The Elephant Strikes Back') will consider the ways in which non-human actors and processes have begun to curb human niche construction.

In Chapter 2 we saw how, early on, humans emerged as the world's 'ultimate ecosystem engineers'.[2] Their advantage over other organisms (microorganisms, plants and animals) is threefold. They have an innate ability to work together and connect by means of language; they create new technologies to alter their

---

[1] MacNeill and Engelke, *The Great Acceleration*.
[2] Arroyo-Kalin et al., 'Civilisation and Human Niche', 106; Jones et al., 'Positive and Negative Effects of Organisms'; Odling-Smee, Laland and Feldman, *Niche Construction*.

environment; and they have highly adaptable cultures that transfer accumulated knowledge from one generation to the next. These three qualities kick-started a process of incessant habitat upgrading, allowing humans to restrict the availability of resources to non-human organisms.

By the mid-twentieth century, as the number of humans in the Triangle steadily grew, their environmental impact began to speed up and its adverse effects on other organisms became more noticeable. In this chapter we look at some aspects of environmental manipulation that are particularly relevant to life in the Triangle today: species migration, environmental awareness, conservation and the fate of the commons.

Human-aided species migration

Forests once carpeted almost the entire region except for its highest mountain tops. Today there are no pristine, untouched forests left in the Triangle. We can understand forests as dynamic assemblages of microorganisms, plants and animals that adapt to long-term fluctuations in temperature and rainfall. Vegetation studies in the Triangle show that the human presence began to affect this dynamism from about 10,000 BCE. Soil samples dating to this era contain charcoal and cereal pollen, indicating forest clearance by humans.[3] *Homo sapiens* were beginning to show their manipulation skills. They curbed the habitats of other forest organisms by setting fire to forests, hunting and gathering, introducing new species and, later, letting domesticated livestock graze in the forests. Initially this must have had a very marginal impact, but some signs of overgrazing were already noticeable thousands of years ago.[4]

Wittingly or unwittingly, humans added new elements to the natural environment in which they found themselves, and they eliminated elements that could not withstand human interference. Human-aided species migration was an important component, but it has not been studied in detail for the Triangle. Nevertheless, to get a sense of the antiquity and complexity of species migration into and out of the Triangle, we can begin by distinguishing four phases.

Plants have travelled with humans from the earliest times. Cereals are a case in point. The Triangle is home to some cereal crops that are today still used in mountain agriculture, notably two local millets, *raishan* (*Digitaria cruciata* [Nees] A. Camus) and Job's tears (or adlay; *Coix lacryma-jobi*).[5]

---

[3] Basumatary et al., 'Late Pleistocene Palaeoclimate'. In Nagaland, cultivation left its ecological mark from 6000 BCE. Nienu, 'The Prehistoric Archaeology', 120.
[4] Meyer et al., 'Holocene Glacier Fluctuations', 1229–30.
[5] Singh and Arora, 'Raishan (*Digitaria sp.*)'; De Wet, 'Millets', 117; Das, 'From Millet to Rice'.

Several other cereals were brought here by humans. Important early arrivals were barley from the west and sticky (glutinous) rice from the east, both reaching the Triangle before the first millennium BCE (Chapters 3 and 4). The development of agriculture meant that these, and a selection of other plants that humans found useful, became unbelievably widespread. On the other hand, an important early export from the region is the citron. It has its origin in the eastern Himalayas and is the ancestor of most cultivated citrus fruits worldwide. Millennia ago, it travelled west to Africa and the Mediterranean.[6] Similarly, the mango is thought to have originated in the Triangle and spread to south India and beyond by the second millennium BCE.[7]

The dynamics of human-aided species migration across Eurasia and Africa changed markedly by the sixteenth century when humans connected the natural wealth of these spaces with that of the Americas. In this second phase, numerous plants and animals began to spread from the New World to the Old, and vice versa, a process now known as the Columbian exchange. The chicken (a descendent of the Triangle's jungle fowl[8]) and the rat found a new home in the Americas, just as many American species entered the environment of the Triangle. Among these were plants that are now widely thought of as authentically local. Chili pepper (capsicum), tomato, potato and okra were integrated into local cuisines. Papaya, guava and pineapple came to be seen as much-prized local fruits. And tobacco smoking became a widespread custom. But it was not only cherished crops that made the trip from the Americas to the Triangle. Various other plants ('weeds') invaded the region's forests, and some were extremely effective in creating niches for themselves. Notable newcomers that humans now think of as pervasive pests were bitter vine (*Mikania micrantha*), the giant sensitive plant (*Mimosa diplotricha*) and shrub verbena (*Lantana camara*).[9]

Human-aided species migration sped up in the third phase, which coincided with colonial rule. This phase saw the blossoming of eco-engineering – the purposeful manipulation and transfer of species to supply European markets. For example, humans transferred tea seeds from the Triangle to many parts of the colonised world, while tea monoculture destroyed vast expanses of forest in Assam (Plate 10.1). Similarly, a hunger for tropical hardwood led to an all-out assault on teak trees in the eastern Triangle.[10] Teak was also imported into parts of the

---

[6] Talon, Caruso and Gmitter Jr., *The Genus Citrus*.
[7] Fuller et al., 'Across the Indian Ocean', 549.
[8] Lawler, 'Dawn of the Chicken Revealed', 1411.
[9] Hiremath and Sundaram, 'Invasive Plant Species'; Dorjee, 'Assessing the Risk'; Rai and Singh, '*Lantana camara* Invasion'.
[10] Bryant, 'Burma and the Politics of Teak'; Sharma, *Empire's Garden*.

Plate 10.1 A tea plantation in Assam (India)
Source: Photo by Willem van Schendel.

Triangle where it was not indigenous: plantations were set up in the Chittagong Hill Tracts despite local protests.[11] Ornamental rhododendrons spread from their Triangle home to all corners of the world, just as decorative water hyacinth (a native of Brazil) began to choke the Triangle's waterways.[12] Himalayan tahrs (wild goats) were introduced to other British colonies, notably New Zealand and South Africa. And rat infestations on Caribbean islands, Hawaii and Fiji led sugar planters there to import small Indian mongooses.[13] In this period, humans also spread some species unintentionally, for example the cholera microbe (*Vibrio cholerae*), which is thought to have been an endemic species in the low-lying parts of the Triangle. The first known cholera outbreak to spread pandemically across the world originated in Jessore (Bangladesh) in 1817.[14]

---

[11] Rasul, 'Political Ecology'.
[12] Iqbal, 'Fighting with a Weed'; Saikia, *The Unquiet River*, 278–80.
[13] Hays, 'Small Indian Mongoose'.
[14] Hamlin, *Cholera*; Kotar and Gessler, *Cholera: A Worldwide History*; Ferrari, 'Devotion and Affliction'. For a description of an epidemic in seventeenth-century Assam, see Tālish, *Tarikh-i Asham*, 207–9.

Dealing with Environmental Decay

The fourth phase of human-aided species migration began after decolonisation and is continuing today. In this period, ideas about 'development' led to environmental engineering and the introduction of many new species to the Triangle, a region with high climatic suitability for alien species.[15] Fish breeders introduced tilapia, pangasius and rainbow trout, and soon these were found in water bodies all over the region.[16] Plantations of *Hevea* rubber (originally from Brazil, Plate 10.2) spread, sidelining the local variety of rubber (*Ficus elastica*, 'India rubber'), which was less suitable for commercial production (but spread worldwide as an ornamental plant).[17] Policymakers planned to import oil palms (*Elaeis guineensis*, originally from West Africa) for the large-scale production of palm oil.[18] And new varieties of rice, developed in international research stations,

Plate 10.2 A rubber plantation in Meghalaya (India)
Source: Photo by Willem van Schendel.

---

[15] Adhikari, Tiwary and Barik, 'Modelling Hotspots'.
[16] Laskar, Bagra and Das, 'Invasion of Rainbow Trout'; Barua, Khan and Reza, 'The Status of Alien Invasive Species'.
[17] Troup, *The Work of the Forest Department*, 39–40; Kar, 'Historia Elastica'; Majumdar, 'The Colonial State'; Chakraborty et al., 'Recognizing the Rapid Expansion'; Rasul, 'Political Ecology', 159–60.
[18] Srinivasan, 'Oil Palm Expansion'.

caused concern because their monoculture threatened the survival of many local varieties.

There were also very localised introductions. For example, a pair of langurs released in a Bangladesh village over a century ago went on to produce a large population that became problematic for humans living there.[19] And an entirely new human–lemon–elephant relationship sprang up around a national park in Assam as a result of a lemon-planting project meant to rehabilitate people after political strife in the 1990s.[20] Political strife could also lead to the smuggling of valuable biota as a source of income for rebel groups.

In some cases, wildlife smuggling contributed to human-aided migration of species out of the Triangle. For example, the global pet trade dispersed Burmese pythons to Florida, where they spread in the wild.[21] Conversely, the pet trade also brought exotic animals into the Triangle, for example, macaws, iguanas and a kangaroo.[22]

Seen in a long-term perspective, the human impact on the flora and fauna of the Triangle has been momentous. Human actions halfway around the globe (for example, the sea journeys that led to the Columbian exchange five centuries ago), as well as local human actions, brought many new species to the Triangle and spread local species all over the world. The environment of the Triangle was always in flux, and, over time, human interventions became a major driver. Many consequences of species introductions were unanticipated and unintended. By the twenty-first century, an understanding of these consequences led to a reassessment of more-than-human histories and an environmentalist approach.

Environmental awareness

Loss of the Triangle's natural forest cover is associated with the earliest human presence, but for a long time the effects were so marginal that they raised little concern. The retreat of forests became more noticeable with the expansion of agriculture, from its uncertain beginnings to its triumphant proliferation. It was an uneven process across the Triangle. Fixed-field agriculture in the lowlands depended on the permanent removal of woodlands but shifting cultivation in the uplands coexisted with periodic forest regeneration (Chapter 4).

---

[19] Khatun, Ahsan and Røskaft, 'Attitudes of the Local Community'.

[20] Kikon and Barbora, 'The Rehabilitation Zone'.

[21] Rees and Rodda, 'Burmese Python'; Willson, Dorcas and Snow, 'Identifying Plausible Scenarios'.

[22] Parashar and Hussain, 'Assam Forest Officials Seize Kangaroo'; Guha, 'Illegal Trade of Exotic Animals'.

It is only in the past few centuries that humans began to perceive their manipulation of the environment less as a triumph and more as a problem. The depletion of the upland forests was long masked by the fact that it can be difficult to distinguish between shifting cultivation and old-growth forests: what at first sight appears to be forest may be currently uncultivated agricultural fields and tree plantations. As a result, mountains and hill slopes look far more forested than they really are, and land-use studies may sharply overestimate the extent of old-growth forests.[23] Even in the lowlands – now covered in permanent agricultural fields – many forests were not cleared until the early twentieth century.

Slowly an environmental awareness began to influence human–non-human relationships. But this did not happen before human actions had unmistakably changed the biological contours of the Triangle and restricted the habitats of many other species. This process had started tens of thousands of years ago, when the first humans prevailed over their competitors and threats to their niche. They eradicated their cousins (*Homo erectus* – if these were still around at the time[24]) and predators such as wolves and hyenas.[25] Humans are likely to have played a role in the early elimination of prey animals, hunting them to extinction, although species extinctions have many different causes.[26]

During the twentieth century, numerous animals and plants became rare or disappeared from the Triangle.[27] Often this was a direct effect of human pressure on forest and wetlands habitats. Agriculture expanded as never before, eating into forested areas – as did human settlements, roads and railways. Dams created reservoirs that submerged large areas, blocked rivers and devastated wildlife.[28] Watercourses became polluted with fertilisers, pesticides and human waste. As human landscaping took over, many non-human habitats were lost or progressively compromised.

In addition to deforestation, human activities also targeted specific species. Hunting for food, skins, feathers, pet-keeping or medicinal uses threatened the

---

[23] Kurien, Lele and Nagendra, 'Farms or Forests'; Nandy and Das, 'Comparing Tree Diversity'.
[24] Dennell and Petraglia, 'The Dispersal of *Homo sapiens*'.
[25] Wolves are still occasionally reported in the Triangle's northern fringes. Jamtsho and Katen, 'Livestock Depredation'; Talukdar et al., 'Mammals of Northeastern India', 18083.
[26] Ahrestani and Sankaran (eds.), *The Ecology of Large Herbivores*; Faith et al., 'Plio-Pleistocene Decline'.
[27] Choudhury, 'The Status of Endangered Species'; Khan, *Protected Areas of Bangladesh*, 11–23; IUCN Bangladesh, *Red List of Bangladesh*, vol. 1.
[28] Mountfort and Hosking, *The Vanishing Jungle*, 105–6.

survival of species as varied as gibbons,[29] songbirds, hornbills, pygmy hogs, otters, snow leopards,[30] sloth bears, takin, red goral,[31] gharial crocodiles,[32] golden cats,[33] sal trees and agarwood.[34] Harvesting wild species for profit has a very long history, from the ancient export of elephants and ivory to colonial-era trade in rhinoceroses and teak for European markets.[35] The commodification of wildlife continues today, creating 'lively capital' and serving customers around the world.[36] In the Triangle it targets species such as freshwater turtles (for meat and use in traditional medicine, or as pets[37]), tokay geckoes (as medicine and aphrodisiac[38]), pangolins (for their scales[39]), rhinoceroses (for their horn), tigers (for their skin, teeth, and bones[40]) and orchids (for ornamental and medicinal use[41]).

Other species declined sharply because humans purposely destroyed their habitat. An example is the greater adjutant (*Leptoptilos dubius*), a large stork that used to be widely distributed from Pakistan to Cambodia. Most humans despised it for its carrion-eating habits. They cut down the trees in which it nested and drove it almost to extinction. Around 1900 there were hundreds of thousands, but today only around a thousand survive worldwide. Their chief nesting site is in Assam, where people considered the bird to be unclean, messy and a bad omen. A creative conservation campaign recently managed to give village women a sense of guardianship. It linked the bird to their weaving practices and local festivals, and it raised their hopes of future income from eco-tourism. The women's protection helped the number of greater adjutants to expand once more (Plate 10.3).[42]

---

[29] Choudhury, 'The Distribution, Status'; Kumar et al., 'Population, Behavioural Ecology'.
[30] *Out in the Cold*.
[31] Qiu and Bleisch, 'Preliminary Assessment', 42.
[32] Saikia, 'Indian Gharial'; Saikia, 'A Study on the Salt Production', 154, 280. For an early description and the habit of eating its meat, see Tickell, 'Extracts from a Journal', 89.
[33] Khan, *Protected Areas of Bangladesh*, 39.
[34] Saikia and Khan, 'Homegardens of Upper Assam'.
[35] Pachuau and Van Schendel, *The Camera as Witness*, 183–5; Van Schendel, *A History of Bangladesh*, 50–1. See also Duff-Sutherland-Dunbar, 'Abors and Galongs', 4.
[36] Barua, 'Animating Capital'; 2020. See also Moore, 'The Rise of Cheap Nature'.
[37] Kuchling et al. ('The Softshell Turtles'), who report that shells of Chindwin turtles are bartered for China-made thermos flasks.
[38] Datta, 'Selling of Tokay Gecko'; Yadav, 'Illegal Wildlife Trade Victim'; Das, Choudhury and Nonglait, 'Zootherapy among the Ethnic Groups'.
[39] Aisher, 'Scarcity, Alterity and Value'; Nijman, Zhang and Shepherd, 'Pangolin Trade'.
[40] Saif et al., 'Local Usage of Tiger Parts'.
[41] Hanson, *The Kachins*, 38, 75; De et al., *Commercial Orchids*; San et al., *Study on Distribution*; Gale et al., 'Quantifying the Trade'; Wong and Liu, 'Wild-Orchid Trade'.
[42] Barman et al., 'Saving the Greater Adjutant Stork'.

Dealing with Environmental Decay 219

Plate 10.3 A greater adjutant in Assam (India)

Source: Photo by Willem van Schendel.

Even though the Triangle still abounds with flora and fauna, it is now recognised that human activity has wiped out, or severely endangered, many non-human species. Quite a few species are making a last stand here. Among the large mammals, hunting and habitat loss has driven one-horned rhino, tiger, clouded leopard, snow leopard, elephant, wild buffalo, pigmy hog and sloth bear close to extinction.[43] The same is true of many smaller mammals, birds,[44]

---

[43] For 'perhaps the last viable population of tigers in China' in the Triangle's mountainous northern edge near Namcha Barwa, see Qiu and Bleisch, 'Preliminary Assessment', 42; Li et al., 'Camera-Trap Surveys'.

[44] For example, the white-bellied heron, endemic to Bhutan, Northeast India and Myanmar. Menzies, Rao and Naniwadekar, 'Assessing the Status'.

amphibians, fish, reptiles, invertebrates and insects, as well as numerous categories of plants.[45] An iconic case is the endemic pink-headed duck, not seen since the 1930s.[46]

Exploring wildlife

Awareness of what had been lost came with an understanding that the environmental resources of the Triangle were actually very incompletely known. Some scientific explorations had been mounted in colonial times, for example, a 'Chindwin expedition' to northern Burma, organised on behalf of the American

Plate 10.4 A man holding a grey peacock pheasant, upper Chindwin region (Myanmar), 1935

Source: Photo by Henry C. Raven. Image # nnc-m36v47-vhc-f021, American Museum of Natural History Library.

Note: See also Hasinoff, *Confluences*, 55–6; Sailo, 'Ecological Studies'.

---

[45] Mir et al., 'A Comprehensive Checklist'; Bawa and Kadur, *Himalaya*; Huda and Jahan, 'Assessment of Conservation'.

[46] Tordoff et al., 'The Historical and Current Status'; Hume, 'A High Price to Pay'; Khan, *Protected Areas of Bangladesh*, 21. See also Burke, *The Indian Field Shikar Book*, 193–4.

Dealing with Environmental Decay

Museum of Natural History in 1935.[47] These explorers, in search of biological specimens, encouraged locals to bring samples to their camps (Plate 10.4).

Explorations became more frequent and systematic in the late twentieth century, especially after the Triangle was acknowledged to be the meeting point of three biodiversity hotspots of worldwide importance (Chapter 1). These explorations were partly scientific endeavours involving wildlife specialists and environmental scientists, partly commercial ventures to discover plants and animals that could be sold for profit and partly legal affairs in pursuit of claiming plant patents for companies or states.[48]

Accelerated exploration led to the rediscovery of many species. In 2015 researchers in the Khasi Hills rediscovered two tree species that had been thought extinct for almost 100 years.[49] The hispid hare, long considered to have vanished from the Triangle, was also rediscovered,[50] as were a bird (the Mishmi wren-babbler[51]), butterflies[52] and various plants.[53]

The number of *newly* discovered species – some very rare – is much larger, and growing fast.[54] These species were, of course, often known to local inhabitants, but scientists had not encountered them before. They include species as varied as fishes,[55] birds,[56] insects,[57] snakes,[58] frogs,[59] scorpions,[60] geckoes,[61] flying squirrels,[62]

---

[47] The Vernay-Hopwood Chindwin Expedition. See Mayr, 'The Birds of the Vernay-Hopwood'; Carter, 'The Mammals'; Hasinoff, *Confluences*. For a list of early explorations, see Thwin et al., 'Ornithology of Northern Myanmar'; Renner et al., *Avifauna of the Southeastern Himalayan*, 17–8.

[48] De et al., *Commercial Orchids*, 35–9.

[49] Mir et al., 'Rediscovery of *Magnolia rabaniana*'; Mir, Upadhaya and Roy, 'Rediscovery, Distribution'. See also Mir, Roy and Upadhaya, 'Taxonomy, Recollection'; Chen, Jin and Shui, 'Rediscovery and Amended Descriptions'.

[50] Gopinathan, 'Ecology and Conservation'.

[51] King and Sonahue, 'The Rediscovery and Song'; Aiyadurai, '"Tigers Are Our Brothers"', 134.

[52] Choudhury, 'Rediscovery of Two Rare Butterflies'.

[53] For example, Chen, Jin and Shui, 'Rediscovery and Amended Descriptions'; Tiwari et al., '*Impatiens cyclosepala*'.

[54] Thompson, *The Eastern Himalayas*; Thompson et al., *Hidden Himalayas*.

[55] Vishwanath, 'Diversity and Conservation'; Kullander et al., '*Laubuka tenella*'; Kullander and Britz, 'Description of *Danio absconditus*'; Chen, Qin and Chen, '*Oreoglanis hponkanensis*'.

[56] Aiyadurai and Banerjee, 'Bird Conservation'.

[57] Balkenohl, '*Trilophidius gemmatus*'.

[58] Mirza, Sanap and Kunte, 'A New Species of Green Pit Vipers'.

[59] Biju et al., 'Frankixalus'; Howlader et al., 'A New Species of Microhyla'.

[60] Mirza et al., 'A New Species of the Genus'.

[61] Al-Razi, Maria and Hasan, 'First Record'.

[62] Saha, 'A New Genus'.

monkeys[63] and deer[64] – as well as mushrooms[65] and numerous plant species.[66] In this way, scientists learned about many non-human companions that have histories reaching back long before humans ever made it to the Triangle. The unprecedented urgency of searching for as yet unknown species – before they vanish forever – sank in, and environmental movements flourished across the Triangle.[67]

Plate 10.5 A baby leaf muntjac (*Muntiacus putaoensis*); this tiny deer species was first encountered in northern Myanmar in 1997 and later also found in Nagaland and Arunachal Pradesh (India)

Source: Photographer unidentified. 'Leaf Muntjac', Odd Animals, https://oddanimals.com/leaf-muntjac/ (accessed 20 June 2021).

Note: See Amato, Egan and Rabinowitz, 'A New Species of Muntjac'.

---

[63] Geissmann et al., 'A New Species of Snub-Nosed Monkey'; Liedigk, Yang and Roos, 'Evolutionary History'; Sinha et al., '*Macaca munzala*'.

[64] Amato, Egan and Rabinowitz, 'A New Species of Muntjac'; Datta et al., 'Discovery of the Leaf Deer'.

[65] Hosen and Li, '*Phylloporus gajari*'.

[66] For example, Kine, Lindsay and Kluge, '*Selliguea kachinensis*'; Jiménez-Meijias and Noltie, 'Carex drukyulensis'; Zhou, '*Coelogyne victoria-reginae*'; Adit, Koul and Tandon, 'Twelve New Additions'.

[67] Yhoshü, 'Nagaland Conservationist'; Van Schendel, *A History of Bangladesh*, 293–9.

Dealing with Environmental Decay 223

They recognised that human landscaping has destroyed many natural habitats and needed to be reined in. Plates 10.5–10.10 show some species that scientists have discovered during the past 30 years.

Plate 10.6 The high-altitude Arunachal macaque (*Macaca munzala*) was discovered in Arunachal Pradesh (India) in 2004; it also lives across the border in Bhutan

Source: Photo by Krushnamegh Kunte.

Plate 10.7 The black (or Myanmar) snub-nosed monkey (*Rhinopithecus strykeri*), first identified in Kachin State (Myanmar) in 2010

Source: Photo by Yin Yang.

Plate 10.8 This orchid (*Spathoglottis jetsuniae*) was discovered in Bhutan in 2017

Source: Photo by Kezang Tobgay. See Gyeltshen et al., 'New Species Discoveries'.

Plate 10.9 A new snakehead fish (*Channa bipuli*) from Assam (India), discovered in 2018

Source: Photo by Beta Mahatvaraj. See Praveenraj et al., '*Channa bipuli*'.

Plate 10.10 A new species of bush frog (*Raorchestes rezakhani*), found in Sylhet (Bangladesh) in 2019

Source: Al-Razi, Maria and Muzaffar, 'A New Species of Cryptic Bush Frog'.

Conservation

Awareness of the deleterious effects of human niche construction came early in some parts of the Triangle. In Chapter 7 we came across sacred groves, which humans set aside as dwelling places of spirits that should not be disturbed. In some cases, the establishment of these groves may have emerged from an urge to protect river headwaters or ecologically degraded sites.[68] Quite different religious motives prompted the establishment, from the 1780s onwards, of some animal sanctuaries in the lower Chindwin area, on the Triangle's eastern edge. Here forest-dwelling Buddhist monks came under the influence of Hindu teachers from Manipur as well as Buddhist scriptures that prohibited the consumption of certain kinds of meat and warned against the taking of life. These monks were instrumental in having ponds dug to provide protection to turtles and fishes and in persuading the Burmese royal court to set aside several forested village territories as animal sanctuaries.[69]

---

[68] Nongbri, 'Culture and Biodiversity', 14.
[69] Charney, 'Demographic Growth', 236–7.

During colonial rule, new conservation measures came into being. These were not modern versions of sacred groves – forest lands that humans could not touch – by any means. On the contrary, they are best understood as novel forms of human niche construction, in which powerful humans denied less powerful humans access to certain areas. These new forms included scientific forestry and wildlife sanctuaries, both based on state coercion.

Scientific forestry

As the British Indian state pushed its way into most of the Triangle, it claimed large parts of the territory as state property and turned these into the domain of its powerful Forestry Department. An intricate system of 'reserved', 'protected' and 'unclassed' forests was devised. When a forest was designated a reserved forest, it would thereupon, 'together with all the produce thereof and animals or things found therein, be deemed to be the property of the Government'.[70] Although some hill forests were to be protected because of their 'indirect effects' on climate, rainfall, water storage and the prevention of denudation (and 'without any reference to their commercial value'), most forests were to be brought under 'efficient management'. The main purpose was the 'supply of valuable timbers for commercial purposes, such, for example, as the teak forests of Burma [and] the sál forests of … North-Eastern India'.[71] The Forest Department viewed the forests as standing stocks of a key commodity, timber. Triangle timber was in great demand beyond the region, for railway sleepers, tea boxes, shipbuilding, house construction, furniture, railway carriages and much more. Some forests were expressly set aside as 'fuel wood reserves' for the expanding railways.[72] Both human and animal labour was employed in this extraction of natural resources in service of the imperial endeavour (Plate 10.11).

At first the Forest Department focused on timber extraction, but it soon realised that it was depleting the forest resources.[73] This led to a gradual move towards 'scientific forestry' and a more sustainable exploitation of various forest produce – not just timber, but also firewood, bamboo, leaves, fruits, fibres, grass, gums, resins, barks, and animal and mineral products.

---

[70] The Burma Forest Act, 1902, in *The Burma Code*, 484; *The Assam Code in Two Volumes*, vol. 1.

[71] Troup, *The Work of the Forest Department*, 2–6. See also Sivaramakrishnan, 'The Politics of Fire'; Singh, *The Last Frontier*, 38–49; Karlsson, *Contested Belonging*; Wary and Singh, 'Sal Timber Trade'; Weil, 'Conservation, Exploitation'.

[72] Aung et al., 'The Environmental History'.

[73] Karlsson, *Contested Belonging*; Saikia, *Forests and Ecological History*.

Dealing with Environmental Decay   227

Plate 10.11 Humans, elephants and bullocks felling timber for tea boxes in Assam (India), 1903 or earlier

Source: Photo by Bourne and Shepherd. NAA INV 04423901, Photo lot 161, Emma A. Koch photograph collection of India, South Asia, and Australia, National Anthropological Archives, Smithsonian Institution, Washington, DC.

Forest management also included the establishment of teak and rubber plantations within reserved forests.[74] The Triangle's forests had become a bundle of valuable commodities, state property and a highly profitable colonial enterprise.[75] This would later be described as an 'imperial onslaught' on the region's forests.[76]

By and large, local people were barred from these areas. Frequently, shifting cultivators were ejected and forest produce, water courses and pastures were declared out of bounds for them. They became the Triangle's first 'conservation refugees'.[77] For the first time, access to forests became encoded in written law

---

[74] Troup, *The Work of the Forest Department*, 14–15, 18; Ghosh and Ghosal, 'Historical Geography'.
[75] Troup, *The Work of the Forest Department*, 63; Weil, 'Conservation, Exploitation', 334.
[76] Karlsson, *Contested Belonging*, 74.
[77] See Chakma, 'Conservation Refugees'; Dowie, *Conservation Refugees*.

and forest dwellers were turned into mere claimants. For example, in reserved forests, 'the practice of shifting cultivation shall be deemed a privilege subject to control, restriction and abolition by the Local Government'.[78] As a result, local livelihoods were severely restricted and this gave rise to intense struggles over rights and access.[79] The Forest Department was a dauntingly powerful adversary – for example, it owned more than half the territory (or 52,000 square kilometres) of Assam in the early twentieth century.[80] The ethos of the Forest Department comes through in this colonial civil servant's account of the Chittagong Hill Tracts in the 1870s:

> When the Pax Britannica was extended to those wilds and intertribal warfare ceased, the population increased so much that if not checked they would soon have burnt every bit of forest off the hills. Dr. Schlich, the head of the Forest Department, calmly proposed that the whole Mugh [Marma] and Chakma population should be removed from their native hills! He did not say where they were to go. He simply said, in the true departmental spirit, 'These people destroy the trees, therefore let them be sent away.'[81]

Vertical conservation

The colonial period ushered in a clash between two forms of conservation that we can call horizontal and vertical. Before colonial rule there had certainly been forms of reservation and exclusion, but these tended to be among social equals. For example, Kuki villages were surrounded by a 'reserve forest called *meilam* (literally fire way) or *ujok* (preserved trees) beyond which was the cultivated zone and at the outer circle was their hunting ground'.[82] The village hunting ground was a 'deep-forested area [that] was literally preserved for wild animals and birds to flourish and from which they procured their meat.... This "hunting ground" could be shared between two adjoining villages in times of peace, whilst a demarcation line

---

[78] The Burma Forest Act, 1902, in *The Burma Code*, 480.
[79] Bryant, *The Political Ecology*; Saikia, 'Making Room Inside Forests'; Karlsson, *Unruly Hills*, 127–72; Banerjee et al., *The Creation of West Bengal*.
[80] Saikia, 'Making Room Inside Forests', 156.
[81] Beames, *Memoirs of a Bengal Civilian*, 282. See also Guha, 'The Prehistory of Community Forestry'.
[82] 'The *meilam*, as the name connotes, was mainly a buffer against turbulent wild fire. Besides, it was preserved for procuring wild fruits and vegetables, dead wood, and as a grazing ground for domesticated animals. It was literally the "garden" of the village community.' Guite, 'Colonialism and Its Unruly', 1201. See also Bareigts, *Les Lautu*, 110; Sitlhou, 'Land and Identity'.

Dealing with Environmental Decay

was drawn during conflict'.[83] Thus, the hunting ground acted as both a larder and a buffer zone. The size of hunting grounds was flexible, expanding in times of political turmoil and shrinking in times of peace.[84] In many parts of the Triangle similar systems of flexible forest use existed, or still exist, with their own forms of 'horizontal' sharing or exclusion between communities.[85]

Such arrangements were completely ignored by the 'vertical' system based on the colonial state's arrogation of property rights. In the early colonial period this led to warfare with communities such as the Kuki, usually described in colonial records as tribal 'raids' and British 'punitive expeditions'.

This struggle over resources between locals and forest officials did not end with decolonisation but continues to this day.[86] The practices underlying scientific forestry and wildlife sanctuaries endure. Even though the Forest Departments of independent India, Bangladesh and Myanmar have allowed more local input in forestry, the vertical–horizontal clash persists.[87] The Triangle forests remain arenas in which state-connected humans seek to impose their specific brand of niche construction on less powerful humans. Resistance usually takes surreptitious forms – such as (in official parlance:) poaching, pilfering, clandestine grazing and illegal settlement – but the emergence of environmental activism has led to an increase in more visible, confrontational tactics.[88] For example, in the Chin State, resistance against the Myanmar Farmland Law (which states that shifting cultivation should be eradicated and that such land is considered 'empty' and unoccupied) forced a temporary halt to a mining project on agro-forestry land.[89]

Wildlife sanctuaries

In addition to scientific forestry, wildlife sanctuaries were developed as another form of vertical conservation. They had their roots in colonial hunting practices. Hunting as a pastime was nothing new. Aristocrats in South Asia had practiced it for centuries (sometimes reserving areas for themselves[90]), but in the mountainous

---

[83] Guite, 'Colonialism and Its Unruly, 1201–2.
[84] Ibid., 1203.
[85] For example, Boutry, Htoo and Wunna, *Social Anthropological Study*, 16; Thang, 'The Dynamics of Natural Resources'; Singh, *The Last Frontier*, 125–33.
[86] Thang, 'The Dynamics of Natural Resources', 50–3.
[87] Lainé, 'Effects of the 1996'; Lainé, '*Phi Muangs*', 241, 254; Aung, 'Social-Ecological Coevolution'. See also Faxon, 'After the Rice Frontier', 19–20.
[88] Cusack et al. ('Measuring the Intensity of Conflicts') present a model of 'conservation conflicts'.
[89] Mark, '"Fragmented Sovereignty"'.
[90] Cooch Behar, *Thirty-Seven Years of Big Game*; Mani, 'Guns and Shikaris', 180–212.

areas of the Triangle this was not the custom. Here, hunting for food was regulated by local communities.[91]

Colonial rule introduced new ideas about human–animal relations[92] and gave elite Europeans privileged hunting rights, partly in game reserves.[93] This was a form of inequitable niche construction that was similar to the tree-oriented reserve forests, and sometimes the two overlapped. Set aside for the use of colonial officers, administrators and planters, game reserves were devoted to the killing of trophy game.[94] Locals were keenly aware of the inequity. For example, the Thadou in Manipur understood that colonial game laws were introduced because 'the Sahebs want to [hunt] game and catch fish and so this preservation has been brought in to avoid having too many blank days while so doing'.[95] For these Sahebs, hunting was an 'incredibly important aspect of masculine identity':

> [The] contest against a wild animal tested the mettle and skill of the European hunter, but also testified to the innate notion of British fair play through the skilful and 'sporting' nature of the hunt.... Unlike lower-caste Indians or lower-class British poachers who merely hunted for food, the true hunter's reward was the challenge of man against beast and the glory symbolised by a mounted ... head or ... stretched-out pelt.[96]

In their pursuit of thrills, adventure and confirmation of their masculinity, privileged European hunters (with servants in tow) criss-crossed the Triangle (Plate 10.12). They compared their prowess by measuring the size of the animals they had killed – and especially the size of 'trophy skulls' or 'record heads', which they obsessively recorded, reported and displayed.[97] The colonial authorities encouraged the manipulation of forest ecosystems by declaring some animals to be 'vermin'

---

[91] Guite, 'Colonialism and Its Unruly'; Aiyadurai, Singh and Milner-Gulland, 'Wildlife Hunting by Indigenous Tribes'; Velho and Laurance, 'Hunting Practices'. See also Talukdar and Gupta, 'Attitudes towards Forest and Wildlife'.

[92] Saha, 'Among the Beasts of Burma'.

[93] Mani, 'Guns and Shikaris'; Amin, 'Hunting for Meaning'; Pau, *Indo-Burma Frontier*, 50. The term is still in use, see Khan, *Protected Areas of Bangladesh*, 35–6.

[94] For example: 'In the four years ending in March 1941 no less than 168 wild elephants and 84 tigers were shot in the reserved forests alone.' Birney, *The Story of the Assam Railways*, 2. For an overview of trophy species, see Lydecker, *The Game Animals of India*; Evans, *Big-Game Shooting*.

[95] Shaw, *Notes on the Thadou Kukis*, 90.

[96] Beattie, 'Plants, Animals and Environmental Transformation', 233. For examples of hunter's memoirs, an established genre, see Wood, *Shikar Memories*; and Nicholls, *Assam Shikari*. For views on 'the Indian poacher,' see Stebbing, *The Diary of a Sportsman*, 241–55.

[97] For detailed lists, see Burke, *The Indian Field Shikar Book*.

Dealing with Environmental Decay

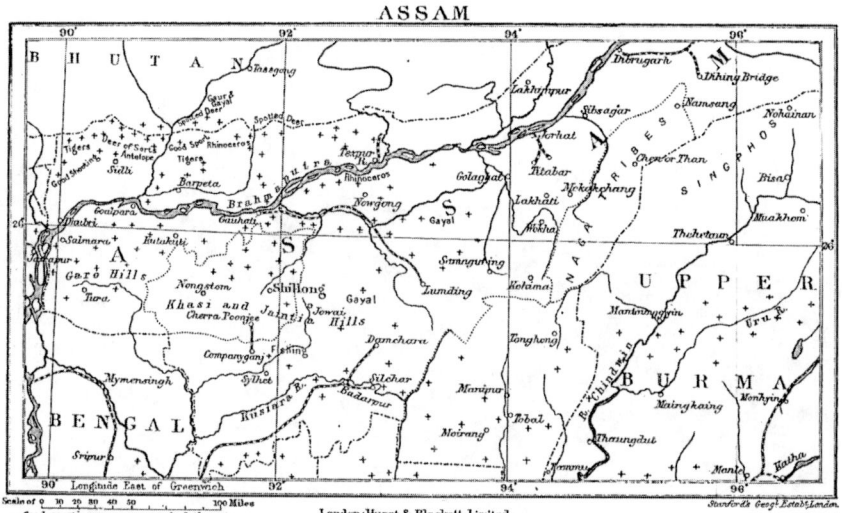

Plate 10.12 Hunting map of the northern Triangle (1900), showing 'good sporting areas' (marked +) and game animals such as tiger, mithun (gayal), spotted deer, gaur, antelope and rhinoceros

Source: Pollok and Thom, *Wild Sports*, 425.

Note: For an indication of the abundance of game in the southern Triangle in the same period, see Carey and Tuck, *The Chin Hills*, 1:218–20.

and 'game destroyers'. They offered cash rewards to kill these species – bears, tigers, leopards, wild dogs, wolves, cobras and many more – and, as a result, hunting them became a commercial enterprise.[98] Local hunters and European 'sportsmen' alike freely victimised wildlife – until they realised, by the late nineteenth century, that they were exterminating both 'game destroyers' and trophy game at an alarming rate (Plate 10.13).[99] This first became evident in the case of elephants, which were hunted and killed as trophies as well as for their ivory. But they were also captured alive as a status symbol, as well as for their military use and labour power. The Elephant Preservation Act of 1879 was an early legal response to growing fears about the decline of this very valuable resource.[100]

---

[98] Singh, *The Last Frontier*, 49–50; Pachuau and Van Schendel, *The Camera as Witness*, 183–5; Jackson, 'Colonial Conquest', 135–51.

[99] Burke (*The Indian Field Shikar Book*, 126–7) did not see it that way. He blamed the decline of wildlife on 'active measures for preservation in several large areas ... the ever-increasing efficiency in firearms, the increase in native professional shikaries [hunters], and the extension of cultivation'.

[100] Nongbri, 'Elephant Hunting'; Singh, *The Last Frontier*, 49.

RESULT OF FORTNIGHT'S SPORT (ASSAM).
From a Photo by P. Burges, Esq.

Plate 10.13 'Result of a fortnight's sport (Assam)': heads of rhinoceros and wild buffalo, and mounted skins of tiger, leopard and bear

Source: Pollok and Thom, *Wild Sports*, 447.

Gradually, the European male self-image of intrepid sportsmen-adventurers began to morph into that of naturalists-conservationists. Hunting-oriented game reserves – not long ago described as 'unhealthy and tiger-infested'[101] – were converted into conservation-oriented sanctuaries and national parks, run by the Forest Department. Game laws and a licence system attempted to regulate big-game hunting.[102] But it was a slow and uneven process: it was not until 1962 that tiger shooting was prohibited in northern Bengal.[103]

Among the first wildlife reserves in the Triangle were Kaziranga in Assam (proposed in 1905, established in 1908) and Pidaung in Kachin State (proposed in 1908, established in 1918).[104] They were to serve the needs of big-game animals, rather than those of local people, who were regularly evicted and who were

---

[101] Birney, *The Story of the Assam Railways*, 59–60.
[102] Gee, 'The Wild Life Reserves'; Burke, *The Indian Field Shikar Book*, 297–406.
[103] Mallick, 'Past and Present Status', 749.
[104] Rookmaker, 'Lady Curzon'; Yin, 'Wild Life Preservation'.

increasingly framed as 'enemies of nature'.[105] By elevating certain non-humans over local humans, conservationists set in motion a dynamic that continues today: ideological and physical clashes between conservationists – claiming to speak for non-humans or 'nature' – and local populations who feel that their rights, legitimate wishes, interests and ideas about human–non-human interactions are being ignored.

Today the Triangle hosts dozens of wildlife sanctuaries, national parks, reserves, eco-sensitive zones, eco-parks and protected areas. Some cross the national borders.[106] In several parks, conflicting interests have been defused by allowing 'local communities' more involvement.[107] It is important to realise that such communities need not be old or deeply rooted. Triangle populations have always been mobile. For example, most humans who were living around the periphery of the Namdapha Nature Reserve in eastern Arunachal Pradesh had moved there from Bangladesh, and smaller groups of settlers were from Myanmar, Nepal, India and Bhutan.[108]

Despite recurrent upbeat policy pronouncements about community involvement, the role of residents is usually quite limited and can be more cosmetic than real, especially in the face of local or transnational commercial interests.[109]

---

[105] Saikia, *Forests and Ecological History*, 13. See also Hazarika and Kalita, 'Conservation and Livelihood Conflict'; Daniels, 'Environmental Degradation'. In parts of the Triangle, the Forest Department allowed some existing villages within forests to continue under the *taungya* forestry system. Bryant, *The Political Ecology*; Ghosh and Ghosal, 'Historical Geography of Forestry'; Chowdhury (ed.), *Forest Conservation*.

[106] For example, Manas National Park in Assam (India) and Royal Manas National Park in Bhutan, and Namdapha National Park in Arunachal Pradesh (India) and Hukawng Valley Wildlife Sanctuary in Myanmar, currently planned to be expanded to Chinese border regions (Uddin et al.,'Integrating Geospatial Tools') and the Gaoligongshan National Nature Reserve in Yunnan (China) and Kachin State (Myanmar). See Yang et al., 'Identifying Transboundary Conservation Priorities'; Shakya et al., 'Mapping of the Ecosystem'. For a list of sanctuaries in Bangladesh, Northeast India, Bhutan, Myanmar and the Namcha Barwa region of Tibet, see Mukul, 'Biodiversity Conservation Strategies'; Khan, *Protected Areas of Bangladesh*; Dikshit and Dikshit, *North-East India*, 252; Tshewang, Morrison and Tobias, *Bionomics in the Dragon Kingdom*; Yin, 'Wild Life Preservation'; Qiu and Bleisch, 'Preliminary Assessment'; Li et al., 'Camera-Trap Surveys'.

[107] Letro and Wangchuk, 'Monpa, the Early Settlers'; Allendorf et al., 'Community Attitudes toward Three Protected Areas'; Allendorf and Yang, 'The Role of Ecosystem Services'; Smadja, 'Belonging, Protected Areas'; Chowdhury and Koike, 'An Overview on the Protected Area System'; Barbora, 'Riding the Rhino'.

[108] Arunachalam et al., 'Anthropogenic Threats', 251.

[109] Khan, 'The Nishorgo Support Project'; Chowdhury (ed.), *Forest Conservation*; Nath, Jashimuddin and Inoue, *Community-Based Forest Management*; Cao et al., 'Analysis of Management Effectiveness'.

In several sanctuaries, conservation has become militarised. This is especially noticeable in sanctuaries that have been commodified as tourist destinations. The foremost example is Kaziranga National Park in Assam (Plate 10.14):

> Concern for the [rhino], much of it advertised via electronic and print media, has welded together a particular idea of conservation, tourism and regional sentiments that disregard the impoverishment of the agriculturalists living along the fringes of the park.... [Kaziranga has] become the site of serious contestations about the idea of conserving nature in colonised spaces, leading to the outright militarisation of the park and celebration of the killings of rhino poachers among a class of people who have little ties to the local economy, but are very vocal in the public sphere ... the production of a narrative of the poacher-as-terrorist ... has become a convenient lens for furthering the militarisation of the parks, as has been done in other parts of the world, notably in Africa.[110]

Plate 10.14 Tourists on elephants, armed forest guards and a rhinoceros in Kaziranga National Park, Assam (India)

Source: Photographer unidentified.

Note: See also Khan, *Protected Areas of Bangladesh*, 33.

---

[110] Barbora, 'Riding the Rhino', 1146, 1156, 1158. See also Karlsson, *Contested Belonging*, 106–46; Smadja, 'A Chronicle of Law Implementation'; Saif, Rahman and MacMillan, 'Who is Killing the Tiger'; Jalais, *Forest of Tigers*, 196–201.

Dealing with Environmental Decay

For people living in and around these sanctuaries, the forest remained an essential resource, partly for subsistence, but in some cases primarily for trade.[111] Thus, a survey of fifteen villages in the northernmost national park of Myanmar (abutting the China–India–Myanmar border meeting point) found that agriculture was the predominant occupation, but that hunting was the most important source of livelihood, followed by collection of non-timber forest products.[112] There was a high demand in nearby China for specific animal parts, notably the gall bladders of bear, macaque, civet, takin and various species of deer; the musk of musk deer; and the skins and antlers of various species.[113] Local hunters reported that a number of species that they had previously hunted for trade – otter, clouded leopard, porcupine and pangolin – were no longer to be found.[114] The trade in wild animal parts was often in the hands of cross-border networks. A study of hunting in the Jaintia Hills (Meghalaya, India) found that 'meat and other valuable parts of the hunted animals viz. pelt, organs with medicinal values were reported to be sold to dealers from Assam and Bangladesh using local networks'.[115]

The tragedy of the Triangle's commons

Areas set aside for the conservation of wildlife can be understood as a new variety of human niche construction. Over millennia humans have been concerned with manipulating their environment to increase their collective survival, a process that generally involves the destruction of non-human habitats. Wildlife conservation introduced a fundamentally new logic, however, because now humans curtailed their own niche and offered certain non-human species better habitats in an attempt to ensure their survival.

But this was hardly a collective decision by *Homo sapiens*. On the contrary, the emergence of wildlife conservation in the Triangle was an illustration of the 'tragedy of the commons' as it involved a clash of multiple forms of governance.[116] As we have seen, communities across the region have long had rules to share

---

[111] Mukul, 'Biodiversity Conservation and Ecosystem Functions'.
[112] Rao et al., 'Hunting for a Living'. Some of these were also used locally, for example, animal gall bladders in Assam. Betlu, 'Indigenous Knowledge'. See also Min, 'Impacts of Wildlife Trade'.
[113] For a price list of various wildlife body parts, see Rao et al., 'Hunting for a Living', 162–3. On trading musk from Assam to north India in the seventeenth century, see Tālish, *Tarikh-i Asham*, 84–5; Qadri, *Pre-Colonial Northeast India*, 32–3. See also Mills, 'The Mishmis of the Lohit Valley', 5.
[114] See also Qiu and Bleisch, 'Preliminary Assessment'.
[115] Goswami, 'Forest Cover', 82–3, cf. 72, 85a.
[116] Frischmann, Marciano and Ramello, 'Tragedy of the Commons after 50 Years'.

natural resources among members. These regulated (not necessarily equal) access, use and boundaries.[117] Such rules were contextual: Kuki, Mishmi, Garo and other Triangle communities developed forms of governance that varied noticeably.[118] And the rules would change over time.[119]

Colonial rulers largely disregarded these community rules and sought to establish their own form of governance based on state and private property rights, encoded in written law. Partly unaware of pre-existing communal property rights, and partly in direct defiance of such rights, colonial minds settled on a narrative that reproduced a worldwide trend in creating state-run protected areas managed as islands (or fortresses[120]) of conservation. This was the 'Yellowstone model' – Yellowstone Park in the United States was the world's first 'national park', created in 1872.[121] It was based on two assumptions. First: it was inspired by the nineteenth-century Romantic movement that contrasted the brutality of technological progress and industrialisation with the beauty, wildness and fragility of the natural world. Second: it held that natural resources that were not explicitly privately owned were therefore in the public domain and state property. Consequently, to ignore community commons and define areas of spectacular wildlife as being out of bounds for locals were entirely fitting acts of stewardship. Indeed, they were noble and 'conscious act[s] of self-restraint for the greater good'.[122] Bureaucrats and conservation experts were put in charge and locals were removed and excluded. This model of state annexation of commons has become dominant across the Triangle (Plate 10.15).[123]

---

[117] 'Commons involve some form of communal ownership (community property rights, public property rights, joint ownership rights). As a consequence, access to the resource is restricted to the members of the relevant community, under more or less restrictive conditions, and nonmembers can be excluded.' Frischmann, Marciano and Ramello, 'Tragedy of the Commons after 50 Years', 221.

[118] Guite, 'Colonialism and Its Unruly'; Aiyadurai, '"Tigers Are Our Brothers"', PhD thesis; Velho and Laurance, 'Hunting Practices'; Talukdar and Gupta, 'Attitudes towards Forest and Wildlife'; Daniels, 'Environmental Degradation'; De Maaker, 'On the Nature of Indigenous Land'; De Maaker, 'Who Owns the Hills'; Thang, 'The Dynamics of Natural Resources'. See also Kikon and McDuie-Ra, *Ceasefire City*, chap. 4.

[119] Aiyadurai, Singh and Milner-Gulland, 'Wildlife Hunting by Indigenous Tribes'.

[120] Aisher and Damodaran, 'Introduction'.

[121] For a defence of the model, see Wuerthner, 'Yellowstone as Model'.

[122] Locke and Heuer, 'Yellowstone to Yukon', 121.

[123] Annexation of commons was not new in the Triangle, but annexation in the name of conservation was. Apart from private land grabbing, the region had seen state-organised dispossession of large tracts for timber production, tea plantations, and railway and road construction. Such dispossessions were legalised by declaring land to be waste land, as in the Waste Land Grant Rule of 1838, which enabled the colonial government to hand out more than a quarter of all land in the Brahmaputra valley to tea planters. Sharma, *Empire's Garden*.

Dealing with Environmental Decay

Plate 10.15 A notice cautions locals in Ziro, Arunachal Pradesh (India), that an alliance of state and conservation organisations has taken charge of the environment

Source: Photo by Willem van Schendel.

Note: These include the Government of India (GOI), the United Nations Development Programme (UNDP), the G. D. Pant Institute of Himalayan Environment and Development (GDPIHED) and the Nature Care and Disaster Management Society (NCADMS). The notice was put up by the local Biodiversity Management Committee (BMC).

State control of large chunks of the landscape in the name of conservation was, however, not purely for the protection of endangered nature. Bureaucrats, politicians, forest officials, rebel groups and military personnel often saw an opportunity to enrich themselves by privately extracting forest resources or allowing (international) corporations to do so. They gave these activities a gloss of legality by issuing permits for felling trees, quarrying stones, harvesting agarwood or removing sand.[124]

What made conservation such a revolutionary innovation in human niche construction worldwide was that it was no longer simply a case of humans versus other organisms. Now it was humans versus humans as well. Conservationists'

---

[124] Barden et al., *Heart of the Matter*, 22–5; Rasul, 'Political Ecology'; Singh et al., 'Conservation Strategies'; Mukul et al., 'Comparing the Effectiveness'; Dutta and Suykens, 'Constellations of Power and Authority'; *State of Corruption*; *The Croatian Connection*.

claims on territories were a threat to the livelihoods of people dependent on their natural resources – whether local inhabitants or non-resident traders. As a result, conservationists came to see local people as problems, and local people came to see certain forms of wildlife as emblems of state oppression. New battle lines were drawn, based on class, community, networking, residence and diverging understandings of nature.

Such 'vertical conservation', rooted in colonial practices, gets support from the postcolonial states and international conservation bodies. It is sometimes referred to as 'green grabbing'.[125] But in some corners of the Triangle another pattern of biodiversity conservation can still be observed. In these areas, the state arrived very late and therefore made few inroads, or found strong opposition, or ruled indirectly. As a result, community ownership of territory survived. The most manifest example is Arunachal Pradesh.[126] Until the very end of colonial rule, this large, mountainous and sparsely populated region was relatively lightly touched by outside powers, and today both the Indian state (which administers it) and the Chinese state (which calls it 'South Tibet') claim it.[127] In these mountains, forms of communal ownership survived, and local people retained some of their rights to regulate the collection of fuelwood, timber and other forest products; graze their livestock; and parcel out plots for shifting cultivation. These rights were never inviolate, however. They were progressively eroded by, first, the establishment of a patchwork of state-run protected areas and, second, large infrastructural projects, notably dams and roads.[128] In Bhutan (which has not been a colony) conservation took a similar route. Its forest laws declared all non-private forest land to be government-owned forest reserves, and it introduced a system of zoning and user permits. It has tended towards more community participation than in other parts of the Triangle, but with mixed results.[129]

State control of natural resources led to pushback from several directions. For example, regional, national and international anti-dam movements focused on the destructive effects of large dams on natural habitats, biodiversity and

---

[125] Fairhead, Leach and Scoones, 'Green Grabbing'; Einzenberger, 'Contested Frontiers', 157–9, 168–72.

[126] On Chin State, see Thang, 'The Dynamics of Natural Resources'; Mark, '"Fragmented Sovereignty"'; on Manipur, see Sitlhou, 'Land and Identity'.

[127] Guyot-Réchard, *Shadow States*.

[128] Khatoon, 'Natural Resources'. See also Tiwari et al., 'Institutional Arrangement'; Harriss-White, Mishra and Upadhyay, 'Institutional Diversity'; and, on Meghalaya, Karlsson, *Unruly Hills*; Goswami, 'Forest Cover'.

[129] Rinzin et al., 'Nature Conservation and Human Well-Being'; Wang, Curtis and Lassoie, 'Farmer Perceptions of Crop Damage'; Tshewang, Morrison and Tobias, *Bionomics in the Dragon Kingdom*; Allison, 'Spirits and Nature'; Karst, 'Protected Areas and Ecotourism'.

human livelihoods.¹³⁰ Wildlife traders sought to create alliances with compliant state personnel or continued their business by illegal means. There were also many less highly publicised local responses, such as by the Mishmi, an ethnic group living close to where the borders of India, China and Myanmar meet. Activists among them began to claim an ecological, conservational identity for the group by insisting on naming specific non-human species 'Mishmi': the Mishmi teeta (a plant), the Mishmi takin (a mammal¹³¹), the Mishmi wren-babbler (a bird), the Mishmi monal (a bird) and the Mishmi beetle (an insect). As Kati, one of these activists, pointed out:

> Why do these animals have the name 'Mishmi' attached to them? This has something to do with our people. Someone has given the credit of wildlife preservation to our community. Because of our Mishmi community, these species are surviving.¹³²

Claiming an ecological identity for the community challenges two external impositions. The first is that the conservation of nature is the domain of states, professionals, and enlightened elites – and that locals need to be taught the values of biodiversity and sustainability.¹³³ The second is that the naming of non-human species is the preserve of scientifically trained outsiders – and that locals have no say in this. Remarkably, the latter challenge has had some effect, with 'Mishmi' designations now appearing in professional writings.¹³⁴

Environmental subjectivities

We have seen that vertical conservation introduced a coercive form of wildlife protection based on the state claiming to own the habitat. The response to this claim engaged with issues of ownership and rights, but it ran much deeper than that because vertical conservation also implied a crushing assault on Triangle cosmological orders. It sought to brush aside deeply rooted ideas about

---

[130] *Stop Damming the Chindwin*; Baruah, 'Whose River Is It Anyway'; Islam and Islam, '"Environmentalism of the Poor"'; Kipgen, 'The Enclosures of Colonization'; Kirchherr, Charles and Walton, 'The Interplay of Activists'; Sharma, 'Dam, "Development"'; Joy et al. (eds.), *Water Conflicts in Northeast India*; Ete, 'Hydro-dollar Dreams'; Yu, Xiangxue and Middleton, 'From Hydropower Construction'.

[131] For an early description, see Rowlatt, 'Report of an Expedition', 493.

[132] Quoted in Aiyadurai, '"Tigers Are Our Brothers"', PhD thesis, 138–9.

[133] For a study taking the perspective of locally grounded human–animal interactions by recognising the sociability and affinity between humans and animals, see Kikon and Barbora, 'The Rehabilitation Zone'.

[134] Li, Huang and Jiang, 'Spatiotemporal Occurrence'.

human–plant–animal–spirit connections and replace these by a scientific discourse grounded in a stark opposition of nature and human culture. Triangle traditions had also set humans apart from the realm of animals and plants but with a strong emphasis on exchange, reciprocity, kinship, negotiation and entanglement. In the conservationist perspective on the world, humans were understood to act upon nature but not be entangled in such relations of reciprocity.

Despite having the full force of successive states and generations of professionals behind it, however, the assault turned out to be only partly successful. Triangle cosmologies were resilient. Multispecies lifeworlds and concepts of human–non-human kinship and respect were not abandoned.[135] As we have seen, they were reworked, and some found defiant expression in celebrations of human–non-human intimacy. The modern political identification with hornbills and mithuns, the continuing performance of propitiating rituals, the revival of harvest festivals and the emergence of religious revitalisation movements such as Donyipolo[136] – all these can be read as contemporary assertions of multispecies belonging.

In other words, today the Triangle is characterised by multiple cosmological subjectivities – multiple ways of understanding the place of humans in the world. These are directly related to the multiple ways of understanding time that we discussed in the Introduction, but also to human understandings of the environment. Vertical conservation practices are powered by a conceptual separation between humans and the environment. This perspective is challenged by Triangle environmental subjectivities that do not frame 'the environment' as a separate realm to the same extent but instead insist on human–non-human mutuality and non-human agency.[137]

---

[135] Ramirez ('Enemy Spirits', 25) characterises these lifeworlds as 'eminently egalitarian'. See also Woodward, 'Gifts for the Sky People'; Aisher, 'Through "Spirits"'; Blackburn, *Himalayan Tribal Tales*; Blackburn, *The Sun Rises*; Allison, 'Enspirited Places'; Mukul, Manzoor and Manzoor, 'The Role of Spiritual Beliefs'; Varah, 'Situating the Humans Relationship'; Aiyadurai, '"Tigers Are Our Brothers"', PhD thesis; Longkumer, 'Spirits in a Material World'; Lainé, *Living and Working with Giants*; Nijhawan and Mihu, 'Relations of Blood'; Huber, *Source of Life*; Janaki, Pandit and Sharma, 'The Role of Traditional Belief Systems'; Claquin Chambugong, 'Sociocultural Conceptions'; Tashi, 'Contested Past'; Previato, 'Indigenous Beliefs'; Liu et al., 'The Lisu'.

[136] The prayer houses of the Donyipolo movement feature images of the goddess of food grains and prosperity and the god of domestic animals. Chaudhuri, 'Guardian Spirits, Omens', 269.

[137] Gros, 'Nature De-naturalised'; Montes et al., 'Cosmological Subjectivities'; Nijhawan and Mihu, 'Relations of Blood'; Wouters, 'Relatedness'.

These contesting world views were not static, and they influenced each other, leading to complex local adjustments.[138] In many cases, however, environmental subjectivities led to tensions and clashes over who actually owns the local habitat and has the right to fashion it. But this struggle between humans is far from the full story. As we shall see in the next chapter, there are other – non-human – actors in this drama, and their presence results in a range of human–non-human tensions and confrontations.

---

[138] Montes et al., 'Cosmological Subjectivities'; Nijhawan and Mihu, 'Relations of Blood'; De Maaker, 'Aloof but Not Abandoned'. Current conservation practices are increasingly subject to critical comment. For example, Büscher and Fletcher ('Towards Convivial Conservation') call for 'convivial conservation' – a global vision that links up with what Lorimer ('Elephants as Companion Species') termed 'multispecies conviviality.'

11

The Elephant Strikes Back

The long history of humans in the Triangle is essentially a rural tale. As late as the 1970s, nine out of ten people lived rural lives. People, plants and animals lived in proximity, and therefore human encounters with plants and animals were intimately woven into daily life.

As we have seen, these encounters took many intricate forms. They could be mutually beneficial. For example, over the centuries, rice plants allowed humans to fill their bellies and in turn humans helped rice plants to spread in countless numbers across the Triangle. Microbes helped people to preserve food by fermenting it and thereby gave rise to distinct food cultures that cherished an astonishing diversity of fermented foods: bamboo shoots, soybeans, yak cheese, fish paste, rice beer and many more (Chapter 8).[1] Encounters were also complex. Take cannabis, a native plant.[2] Humans fed it to their household cattle, chickens or dogs to treat diarrhoea and weakness; applied it to themselves to cure bone fractures; or smoked it as a form of religious worship.[3]

But human–non-human encounters could also be the opposite of beneficial. In Chapter 8 we saw that parasites and microbes wreaked havoc in human populations. Epidemics of measles, influenza, smallpox, cholera, malaria, and rinderpest occurred regularly. Besides, humans could also fall victim to combined plant–animal dynamics. Agricultural crops were attacked, and sometimes

---

[1] Singh, Singh and Sureja, 'Cultural Significance and Diversities'; Tamang and Tamang, 'Traditional Knowledge of Biopreservation'; Bhuyan et al., 'Biochemical and Nutritional'; Uchoi et al., 'Diversified Traditional Cured Food Products'; Kikon, 'Fermenting Modernity'; Hossain et al., 'Production Procedure'.

[2] Cannabis is likely to have been present in the region before humans arrived. It may have developed into a 'camp follower' of foraging groups that ultimately domesticated it. Small, 'Evolution and Classification', 195–7; McPartland, Hegman and Long, '*Cannabis* in Asia'.

[3] Sharma et al., 'Medico-religious Plants'; Nath and Dutta Choudhury, 'Ethno-medico-botanical Aspects'; Lokho, 'The Folk Medicinal Plants'.

decimated, by insects and mites.[4] Or wild pigs, elephants or monkeys would destroy them. And, occasionally, flowering bamboo plants and bamboo rats would cause 'bamboo famines' among humans (Plate 8.3).

As an invasive species in the Triangle, humans naturally depended for their survival on exploiting the wildlife that they found there. Foraging and hunting were forms of daily violent interference with their environment. The domestication of certain plants and animals may have started out as cross-species interaction and collaboration (Chapter 3), but it later developed into a form of purposeful genomic manipulation: selective breeding created organisms that suited humans better and made these dependent on human care. Routine ritualised killing of domestic animals – chicken, dog, pig, goat, water buffalo, mithun and more[5] – underlined the utter vulnerability of these largely human-designed non-humans at the hands of their masters (Plate 11.1).

For a long time, however, the power of humans over their ecological rivals remained limited, simply because humans were few in numbers and their fear of the environment was intense, as this passage from the 1840s explains:

> The country is infested with wild animals, and the footpaths are dangerous at all times. Some slight idea may be formed of the danger to human life from the denizens of the jungle, when I state that in the western quarter of the district of Kamroop alone, in the short period of six months, the police reports included twenty men killed by wild elephants and buffaloes. The damage done to the rice crops yearly by wild elephants and buffaloes is very considerable.[6]

The battleground began to shift, however, when humans fashioned the technology to accelerate their habitat expansion at the expense of forests and wildlife. Much of this destruction took place in recent decades.[7] By the twentieth century they were

---

[4] Das lists no less than 175 different insect and mite pests for vegetable crops in the lowlands. Das, *Insect and Mite Pests*.

[5] A regional pattern of sacrifices is presented in Urban, 'The Womb of Tantra'.

[6] [Butler], *Sketch of Assam*, 20. See also Hodgson, *Essay the First*, 163. For elephants and wild boars ravaging crops in the southern Triangle around this period, see also Tickell, 'Extracts from a Journal', 93, 96, 101.

[7] In 2016 a village headman in the Sajek Valley (Chittagong Hill Tracts, Bangladesh) described the process as follows:

> He said that in the past there had been dense forest all around, and animals like tigers, elephants, deer, wild pigs, and snakes were common. The headman said that these wild animals had roamed the area as late as the 1970s, when people would not dare to venture out alone at night. However, over the past forty years, the dense forests have declined rapidly and except for a few hens, pigs, and deer, most of the wild animals and birds are now lost from the area. (Rasel, 'Experiencing the Border', 87)

Plate 11.1 Sacrificing a mithun in Mizoram (India)

Source: Mizo Zirlai Pawl (MZP) collection. Probably early twentieth century; photographer unidentified.

thinking of themselves as rightly having the upper hand. Even so, they found out that not all non-human organisms were able or willing to be pushed aside. As these stood their ground, habitat conflicts multiplied, and hostile encounters ensued. We will look at five types of human–non-human conflict in some detail: zoonotic threats to human health; uncontrollable invasive species; wild animals attacking humans; wild animals attacking human property (livestock, crops, dwellings); and human resentment against protected species.

Zoonotic diseases

Disorders that animals pass on to humans are known as zoonotic.[8] In the Triangle, such unfriendly encounters between humans and other living organisms have long damaged human health and threatened human lives. A bacterium (hosted by rodent fleas) afflicted them with the plague, while others spread cholera and typhus; a parasite (hosted by mosquitoes) made people deadly ill with malaria; and

---

[8] Childs, Mackenzie and Richt (eds.), *Wildlife and Emerging Zoonotic Diseases*.

various viruses caused smallpox, measles and leprosy. Conversely, humans passed diseases such as tuberculosis on to animals.

Wildlife can be a direct source of pathogens to humans, but it is important to realise that emerging infections from wildlife today are driven mostly by human behaviour that brings people (and their livestock) in unusual contact with wildlife. Among the most unpredictable outcomes are diseases resulting from humans encountering new animal viruses that then spread epidemically from human to human. Many of these viruses will cause mild diseases in humans (common colds and influenzas) but humans have no natural defence against some. In this way, HIV/AIDS and COVID-19 turned out to be lethal threats to the Triangle's human populations.

As a meeting point of three biodiversity hotspots and home to many still unexplored forms of wildlife, the Triangle is home to many yet unknown animal viruses and parasites. The Triangle's human population has historically been poorly served with medical facilities – partly because these were few and far between, and partly because most people were living precarious lives and could not avail themselves of such facilities. As a result, old infectious diseases (such as typhoid fever, cholera and the plague[9]) are still stalking the Triangle today, and emerging ones spread easily. Most of these are passed on by animal hosts. For example, humans get Nipah fever via fruit bats, avian influenza via birds and dengue and West Nile fever via mosquitoes.[10]

Uncontrollable invasive species

A second form of human–non-human conflict concerns competition for a single ecological niche. A good example is the water hyacinth, an aquatic plant from the Amazon region that arrived in the Triangle in the late nineteenth century.[11] Humans soon noticed that the plant was a champion at niche construction. It spread rapidly on waterways and lakes, where it formed dense mats of vegetation and began to hamper human utilisation of water, first in the lowlands but increasingly in the uplands as well.[12] River transport, fishing, crop irrigation and

---

[9] For example, Roy et al., 'Epidemiological Investigation'; Islam, Clemens and Qadri, 'Cholera Control and Prevention in Bangladesh'; Shi et al., 'Reemergence of Human Plague'.
[10] Clayton, 'Nipah Virus'; Gurley et al., 'Convergence of Humans'; Mon et al., 'Highly Pathogenic Avian Influenza'; Dutta et al., 'Incrimination of *Aedes aegypti*'; Chowdhury et al., 'Characterization of West Nile Virus'.
[11] Iqbal, 'Fighting with a Weed'; *The Bengal Delta*, 140–59; see also Hill et al., 'Water Hyacinth'.
[12] Sharma et al., *Climate Change Impacts*, 14; Singh, 'Hydrological and Hydraulic Modelling'; Dorjee, 'Assessing the Risk', 229.

human health were particularly affected, and it contributed to agricultural decline.[13] It did not take humans long to spring into action to take on the competition. At first, they hesitated between eradicating the plant, or domesticating it by finding some human use for it, but soon the overwhelming response was to destroy it. By 1936 the Bengal Water Hyacinth Act had put the plant officially beyond the ecological pale. State authorities declared it a 'common enemy' and mobilised large groups of people in an all-out physical attack on it.[14] It was the first of many attempts to rid the human niche of this 'noxious' plant. All failed, however, and today the conflict between humans and water hyacinth continues unabated.

Many other invasive species competed with humans in ways that underscored the entangled connections between plants, animals and humans. For example, plant viruses could wreak havoc on agricultural crops as well as wild plants that sustained humans. Some were transmitted by aphids, such as a virus (accidentally imported from the Pacific region in the 1940s) that devastated both domesticated and wild bananas, or another that killed black cardamom, a valuable spice plant that was endemic in the Triangle.[15]

Animal attacks

A third form of human–non-human conflict are wild animal attacks on humans. These have always happened, and Triangle cultures are full of references to them. Fear of tigers, elephants and bears was especially intense. As Dala, an inhabitant of Mizoram, wrote in 1905:

> For a long time, Mizos worshipped their *Sakhua* as their God. We thought of it as the one who does everything for us, we also thought of it as the one who brought about death, as well as the one who ruled over us … [and yet] sometimes we fear the tiger more than it.[16]

Tiger attacks were not very frequent, however.[17] In the Chin Hills (Myanmar), early colonial officers observed:

> The Himalayan bear is the animal most feared by the Chin as, although elephants trample and tigers maul them, the most difficult animal to avoid is the bear, and

---

[13] Iqbal, 'Fighting with a Weed'.
[14] Ibid., 50.
[15] See contributions in Mandal et al. (eds.), *A Century of Plant Virology*, 27–48, 52–5, 205–11, 308–13.
[16] Dala, 'Sakhua', 13. Translated from Mizo by Joy L. K. Pachuau.
[17] Lekshmi, 'This Fearless Mizo Woman Fought'.

large numbers of the natives carry terrible wounds and disfigurements received in encounters with this animal.[18]

The creation of protected areas, or 'conservation islands', all over the Triangle introduced a new dynamic. As states fashioned separate human and non-human domains, 'nature' became territorialised and local concepts of environmental guardianship were ignored.[19] Animals that strayed out of their protected area were considered to be trespassing. They lost their protected status and could be branded 'rogues', or 'man-eaters' – and state agents were authorised to sedate or kill them (Plates 11.2 and 11.3).

At the same time, state agents were also authorised to expel or kill humans ('poachers', 'encroachers') who were found to be 'trespassing' in protected areas (Plate 11.4).[20]

In this way, biodiversity conservation exposed people living near or in protected areas to greater risk of bodily harm and death. Those who depended on the forest were faced with new threats to their livelihoods and their very lives, not only because armed forestry staff have 'the right to shoot people on sight',[21] but also because successful conservation protected populations of dangerous animals:

> Honey collectors are ... exposed to numerous dangers to their life including attacks by resident Bengal tigers or saltwater crocodiles or moderate to highly poisonous indigenous snake species who thrive in the mangrove ecosystem.[22]

---

[18] Carey and Tuck, *The Chin Hills*, 1:216.

[19] Aiyadurai, 'The Multiple Meanings of Nature Conservation'.

[20] This development has been theorised as a form of biopolitics or necropolitics, involving both humans and animals. Margulies, 'Making the "Man-Eater"'. For Triangle examples of the acceptability of human and nonhuman death in and around a 'conservation biopolis', see Smadja, 'A Chronicle of Law Implementation'; and Barbora, 'Riding the Rhino'. On the concept of biopolis as 'an environmentally sustainable [space], in which human and natural populations can live in harmonious balance', see Vlavianos Arvanitis, '"BIOPOLIS"', 101.

[21] The right of forest staff to kill humans with impunity was encoded in law:

> In July 2010 the Government of Assam passed a law under the provisions of Section 197 (2) of the CrPC (Criminal Procedure Code) according to which all forest officers and staff, including members of the Assam Forest Protection Force, are vested with the authority to use fire arms to protect forests and wildlife and they have been granted immunity from prosecution with no Government sanction. And in 2014 forestry staff running the State wildlife sanctuaries were provided with self-loading rifles to replace their old 303 rifles. (Smadja, 'A Chronicle of Law Implementation', 18)

Examples of killings can be found in Barbora, 'Riding the Rhino'.

[22] Basu and Cetzal-Ix, 'Traditional Honey Collectors', 248.

Plate 11.2 Forest guard trying to tranquilise a wild leopard that had entered a village just outside a wildlife sanctuary, injuring several people, northern West Bengal (India), 2011

Source: Photo by Diptendu Dutta. Courtesy of Agence France-Presse.

In protected areas, biodiversity conservation was rarely across the board. It tended to focus on the habitat needs of specific 'flagship species' – rhino, tiger, elephant – not on biodiversity per se. An expanding population of such privileged species was seen as a success rather than as a hazard to locally balanced biodiversity. Thus, 'conservation islands' could turn into virtual breeding stations of favoured

Plate 11.3 A wild elephant causing panic in Siliguri city, West Bengal (India), 2016
Source: Photo by Diptendu Dutta. Courtesy of Agence France-Presse.

Plate 11.4 An evicted woman is trying to stop armed police and an excavator during an 'anti-encroachment drive' in Amchang Wildlife Sanctuary, Assam (India), 2017.

Source: Photo by Ritu Raj Konwar.

species, creating environments that were detrimental to less favoured ones.[23] In some cases these less favoured ones included local humans, especially if protected animals proliferated to the point that they needed habitats beyond the confines of their designated domain. In these cases, humans could face increasing attacks by conservation flagship species. This is especially well documented for elephants (which were difficult to control when they moved along 'elephant corridors'[24]) but also for leopards, gaurs and bears.[25]

Plate 11.5 Killed by a train, an elephant lies on railway tracks in Assam (India), 2014

Source: Photographer unidentified. See 'Five Elephants Killed by Train in India', AryNews, 11 December 2017, https://arynews.tv/five-elephants-killed-train-india/ (accessed 17 November 2021).

---

[23] For the dynamics involved, see Li et al., 'Retreat of Large Carnivores'.

[24] Hossen, *Human–Elephant Conflict in Bangladesh*; Jadhav and Barua, 'The Elephant Vanishes'; Choudhury, 'Human–Elephant Conflicts'; Kaul et al. (eds.), *Canopies and Corridors*. On elephant corridors, see Menon et al. (eds.), *Right of Passage*, 314–573; Choudhury, 'Impact of Border Fence'; Motaleb et al., *The Asian Elephants*; Motaleb and Ahmed, *Status of Asian Elephants*; Motaleb et al., *Atlas*; *Survey Report*; Rahman, 'Rohingya Refugee Crisis'.

[25] Bhattacharjee and Parthasarathy, 'Coexisting with Large Carnivores'; Chakraborty, 'Human–Animal Conflicts'; Jamtsho and Wangchuk, 'Assessing Patterns'; Letro, Wangchuk and Dhendup, 'Distribution of Asiatic Black Bear'; Liu et al., 'The Lisu People's Traditional Natural Philosophy'.

The idea of state responsibility for such animal attacks was given shape in the form of compensation for victims' families.[26] Lethal encounters between protected species and humans could also lead to unintended animal deaths because of animals colliding with cars or trains – or getting electrocuted when they touched powerlines (Plate 11.5).[27]

Animals destroying human property

This fourth type of human–animal conflict in the Triangle is well researched. People's livestock were easy prey for many different carnivores. These included leopards, tigers and snow leopards; bears; jackals, wild dogs (dhole) and feral domestic dogs; civets; martens; wild cats; mongooses; and bandicoot rats.[28] Often humans responded by retaliatory killing of these predators.[29] Livestock was especially vulnerable if they grazed inside, or just beyond, protected areas.

Another habitat conflict that played out all over the region was wild animals raiding agricultural crops. This has been documented extensively for areas around 'conservation islands', but it is not confined to them.[30] The list of wild species feasting on crops is long. Monkey, wild boar, elephant, bear and porcupine are frequently mentioned in the literature.[31]

---

[26] Karanth, Gupta and Vanamamalai, 'Compensation Payments'; Mukherjee, 'A Brief Appraisal'; Roy, 'A Spatial and Temporal Analysis'; Smadja, 'A Chronicle of Law Implementation'; Sarker and Røskaft, 'Human–Wildlife Conflicts'; Liu et al., 'The Lisu People's Traditional Natural Philosophy'.

[27] Al-Razi, Maria and Muzaffar, 'Mortality of Primates Due to Roads'; Dasgupta and Ghosh, 'Elephant–Railway Conflict'; Sarma, Easa and Menon, *Deadly Tracks*; Ahmed, 'Elephant Crop Raiding'.

[28] Chaudhry et al., 'Conflict Identification and Priorization'; Dutta et al., 'Human–Wildlife Conflict'; Borah et al., 'Livestock Depredation by Bengal Tigers'; Bareigts, *Les Lautu*, 47; Sangay and Vernes, 'Human–Wildlife Conflict'; Jamtsho and Katen, 'Livestock Depredation'; Allendorf and Yang, 'The Role of Ecosystem Services', 191; Liu et al., 'The Lisu People's Traditional Natural Philosophy'.

[29] For example, Chowdhury et al., 'Dietetic Use of Wild Animals', 27.

[30] For example, Dutta et al., 'Human–Wildlife Conflict'; Ahsan and Uddin, 'Human–Rhesus Monkey Conflict'.

[31] For example, Nath et al., 'An Assessment of Human–Elephant Conflict'; Di Fonzo, 'Determining Correlates of Human–Elephant'; Uddin, Ahsan and Lingfeng, 'Human–Primates Conflict in Bangladesh'; Datta-Roy et al., 'Participatory Elephant Monitoring'; Choudhury, 'Human–Elephant Conflicts'; Wang et al., 'Farmer Perceptions of Crop Damage'; Allison, 'Enspirited Places, Material Traces', 258–61, 336; Allison, 'Spirits and Nature'; Chaudhry et al., 'Conflict Identification and Prioritization'; Mukherjee, 'A Brief Appraisal'; Dutta et al., 'Human–Wildlife Conflict'; Sarker and Røskaft, 'Human–Wildlife Conflicts'; Roy, 'A Spatial and Temporal Analysis'; Menon et al. (eds.), *Right of Passage*.

Elephant–human encounters could also lead to the destruction of people's houses and other property.³² When elephants chose pathways across human settlements, lethal and destructive encounters could ensue. In one unusual confrontation, wild elephants turned the tables, not by leaving their protected areas to confront humans outside, but by invading newly created protected areas for humans. In 2017 hundreds of thousands of Rohingya refugees fled Myanmar. Bangladesh gave them shelter in makeshift refugee camps, one of which is said to be the world's largest. Carved out of hill forests and wildlife sanctuaries, these camps displaced elephants and other wildlife – and disturbed important elephant corridors. In multiple elephant incursions, a number of refugees were trampled to death.³³

Human resentment against protected animals

Hostile encounters could take other forms as well. Animals that became flagship species of state-sponsored conservation in the Triangle could turn into formidable rivals to humans for scarce resources. Not surprisingly, people who lived around 'conservation islands' resented this state–animal alliance if it excluded them. They often took action to defend their habitat and protect their livelihoods. A range of actions was open to them. They could guard their crops at night, try to scare animals by means of noise, lights or burning chili powder; poison the animals; construct fences; or lock up their livestock.³⁴ They could also try to claim (or reclaim) areas within 'conservation islands' to live, cultivate crops or for religious purposes. In these places their livestock would compete with wild grazers (Plate 11.6). In conservationists' parlance, they became 'encroachers'.³⁵

---

[32] Bhuyan and Kar, 'The Pachyderm Dread'; Sarker and Røskaft, 'Human–Wildlife Conflicts'; Mukherjee, 'A Brief Appraisal'; Di Fonzo, 'Determining Correlates of Human–Elephant Conflict'.

[33] *Survey Report*; Rahman, 'Rohingya Refugee Crisis'.

[34] Sangay and Vernes, 'Human–Wildlife Conflict'; Nath et al., 'An Assessment of Human–Elephant Conflict'; Hossen, *Human-Elephant Conflict in Bangladesh*; Sarker and Røskaft, 'Human–Wildlife Conflicts'; Jadhav and Barua, 'The Elephant Vanishes'; Barua, 'Between Gods and Demons', 78; Jamtsho and Wangchuk, 'Assessing Patterns'; Wahed, Ullah and Irfanullah, *Human-Elephant Conflict*.

[35] Bhuyan and Kar, 'The Pachyderm Dread'; Choudhury, 'Human–Elephant Conflicts'; Mukherjee, 'A Brief Appraisal'; Mahanta and Das, 'Attitudes towards Biodiversity'.

The Elephant Strikes Back 253

Plate 11.6 Grazing domestic cattle encounter a rhinoceros in the Pobitora Wildlife Sanctuary in Assam (India)

Source: Photo by Pralay Lahiry. Courtesy of Arnab Lahiry.

Another strategy was to continue hunting and trapping animals and birds, fishing, and foraging forest and river products – timber, fuelwood, bamboo, fruits, thatching grass, fish, honey and so on – within protected areas, thereby threatening the survival of wildlife protected by law (Plate 11.7). For example, people who foraged for herbs in the Keibul Lamjao National Park in Manipur were in competition with the highly endangered endemic Manipur brow-antlered deer.[36] Conservationists branded these foragers for local consumption 'poachers'.[37]

---

[36] Devi, Singh and Choudhury, 'Income Generating Plants'. See also Pan et al., 'Low Input Parks Strategy'.

[37] Choudhury, 'Human–Elephant Conflicts'.

254 Entangled Lives

Plate 11.7 Meat of a protected river dolphin for sale at a roadside market in upper Assam (India)

Source: Photo by Lekha Borah. See Borah, 'Gangetic Dolphin Killed'.

Note: On the hunting of Gangetic dolphins for their meat and oil, see Wakid, 'Status and Distribution'; Choudhury et al., 'The Endangered Ganges River Dolphin'; Sinha and Kannan, 'Ganges River Dolphin'. See also Carter et al., 'A Conceptual Framework'.

Finally, some people who lived near protected areas became involved in wider circles of trade.[38] They could turn into local agents for international networks involved in the illegal, lucrative but dangerous trade in protected species and their parts, such as rhino horns, tiger and leopard skins, pangolin scales, caterpillar

---

[38] The transition from local consumption to trading beyond the locality is described in Saif et al., 'Local Usage of Tiger Parts'.

fungus, bear bile, musk-deer scent glands, red-panda pelts, hornbill feathers, tokay geckos, timber and orchids.[39] Conservationists framed them as 'traffickers', 'poachers' and 'enemies of nature'.[40]

In response to these livelihood strategies, conservationists developed policies (sometimes dubbed 'community buy-in'[41]) to involve local people in conservation and provide them with alternative sources of income. Some policies were more successful than others. One approach focused on mitigating the 'diminished psychosocial wellbeing' and increasing the 'tolerance levels' of people confronted with conservation ventures in their backyard.[42] Other approaches looked at material rewards (compensation for wildlife-caused damage, or creation of employment), education and 'community-based conservation'.[43] Less well documented are the ways in which local communities themselves responded to animal attacks by reasserting their cross-species connectedness, adapting their conduct and entangling the marauding animals in their livelihoods. Such responses were human attempts to create a new 'liveable landscapes' that would accommodate all of them.[44]

---

[39] Weckerle et al., 'People, Money, and Protected Areas'; Margulies et al., 'Illegal Wildlife Trade'; Badola et al., *Assessment of Illegal*. For exotic pets being smuggled into the Triangle, see Parashar and Hussain, 'Assam Forest Officials Seize Kangaroo'; Guha, 'Illegal Trade of Exotic Animals'.

[40] Barbora, 'Riding the Rhino'; Smadja, 'A Chronicle of Law Implementation'; Saikia, 'Kaziranga National Park'. On trading pangolins, caterpillar fungus, leopards and bears from the Triangle to Chinese customers, for example, see Zhang et al., 'Illegal Pangolin Trade'; D'Cruze et al., 'A Socio-economic Survey'; Kumar, Rajpoot and Rasaily, 'Peril for Pangolins'; Cannon et al., 'Steps Towards Sustainable Harvest'; Weckerle et al., 'People, Money, and Protected Areas'; Bawa and Kadur, *Himalaya*, 130–1; D'Cruze and Macdonald, 'Clouded in Mystery'; Nijman, Zhang and Shepherd, 'Pangolin Trade'; Nijman, Oo and Shwe, 'Assessing the Illegal Bear Trade'; Aiyadurai, '"Tigers Are Our Brothers"', PhD thesis.

[41] Sanders et al., 'Conservation Conversations'.

[42] Gogoi, 'Emotional Coping'; Talukdar and Gupta, 'Attitudes towards Forest and Wildlife'; Sarker and Røskaft, 'Human–Wildlife Conflicts'; Allendorf et al., 'Community Attitudes'; Barua et al., 'The Hidden Dimensions'; Chartier et al., 'Habitat Loss'.

[43] Datta-Roy et al., 'Participatory Elephant Monitoring'; Aiyadurai, 'The Multiple Meanings'; Letro and Wangchuk, 'Monpa, the Early Settlers of Bhutan'; Smadja, 'Belonging, Protected Areas'; Chowdhury and Koike, 'An Overview on the Protected Area'; Barbora, 'Riding the Rhino'; Horwich et al., 'Community Protection'; Kikon and Barbora, 'The Rehabilitation Zone'.

[44] Kikon and Barbora, 'The Rehabilitation Zone'. On the capacity of wild animals to change their behaviour to live in 'nonantagonistic or at least in nonconfrontational ways' in the proximity of humans, see Rangarajan, 'Animals with Rich Histories'. See also Larson and Fuller, 'The Evolution of Animal Domestication'.

Multispecies encounters

These five hostile encounters between humans and non-humans – zoonotic diseases, uncontrollable invasive species, wild animal attacks on humans, animal attacks on property (livestock, crops, dwellings), and resentment against privileged non-human species – reminded humans that they were neither masters of the universe nor detached from nature. In the Triangle, as elsewhere in the world, there is a growing awareness that we need to rethink our place in the global environment.

Even though we humans have obsessively focused on the history of our own species, our encounters with non-humans have always been the very stuff of life. Bringing these into the stories we tell ourselves about ourselves is essential, not just as a reality check, but also to enable us to develop more positive and collaborative relations with non-humans at a time when environmental degradation is progressing faster than ever before. Destruction of 'wildlife' leads us into a blind alley, but so does state-initiated elevation of selected 'wildlife' (sometimes backed up by armed force) over disadvantaged humans.

All over the Triangle, dialogues on environmental justice and a sustainable future are on the rise.[45] It remains to be seen how these can connect most effectively with elements of local cultural history that stressed spiritual connections between humans and non-humans, the notion of human–non-human respect and guardianship, and shared ownership of resources.[46] Two dimensions are of particular interest. Historically the boundaries of human communities were often conceptually blurred, or at least permeable, as the example of tiger-people shows. In many places throughout the Triangle, there were human communities that imagined themselves to be able to include non-humans. They formed 'multispecies communities' together with animals, plants and supernatural beings.[47] Although they saw themselves as distinct from other living beings, they did not subscribe to the sharp distinction between mankind and nature that characterised Western thought and colonial practice.

---

[45] Ahmed and Low, 'Environmental Justice Dialogues'. See also Celermajer et al., 'Multispecies Justice'.

[46] Aisher, 'Voices of Uncertainty'; Jackson, 'Colonial Conquest and Religious Entanglement'; Aiyadurai, 'The Multiple Meanings'; Aiyadurai and Banerjee, 'Bird Conservation'; Aiyadurai, '"Tigers Are Our Brothers"', PhD thesis; Chaudhuri, 'Guardian Spirits'; Bernot, *Les paysans arakanais du Pakistan Oriental*; Kikon and Barbora, 'The Rehabilitation Zone'; Previato, 'Indigenous Beliefs for Sustainability'. See also Kimmerer, *Braiding Sweetgrass*.

[47] For example, Lyngdoh, 'Water Spirit Possession'; Aisher, 'Introduction'; Longkumer, 'Spirits in a Material World'.

Furthermore, Triangle cultural history included a wealth of insights about how animals and plants were distributed, moved across the land, connected with other animals and plants, and behaved as living agents in (and co-shapers of[48]) the human world. This was vital knowledge in the case of dangerous animals that might threaten human lives, but also in the case of useful plants. Perhaps we should think of such Triangle insights as currently 'critically endangered' – a fast-fading cultural heritage in urgent need of rescue in the service of environmental recovery.

For example, to what extent does local knowledge about animal cartographies survive? How can old understandings of the mental maps that elephants use to navigate the changing Triangle be combined with conservationists' and biologists' understandings today? Can Triangle people still salvage their fading medicinal and foraging wisdom? If such knowledge can be recovered, it may help us to mitigate environmental decay in the Triangle. Today's hostile encounters between humans and non-humans should alert us to the fact that, today, humans are a far greater problem for non-humans than the other way around.

---

[48] Overton and Hamilakis, 'A Manifesto for a Social Zooarchaeology'.

Conclusion

This book has taken you on a whirlwind tour of a large world region. The sights included the earth's crust, a range of flora and fauna, and glimpses of people's mindsets and livelihoods. You may well be left with a kaleidoscope of impressions and questions – but rest assured: this was intentional. The main purpose of this introductory tour was to reflect on how humans, animals and plants have found ways to live together over countless generations – and how these ways have been changing in recent times.

Along the way, we – your tour guides – have attempted to deflate us – human beings – in the stories we tell ourselves about the past. We suggested that human histories are always utterly intertwined with plant and animal histories. History is co-created: it is always interspecies history. We presented empirical examples to make that point, but we had to hurry so we were highly selective, zipped through time, touched very lightly on complex cases, passed over many nuances and refrained from dipping deeply into ongoing scholarly debates. We hope that our numerous references, and the extensive bibliography, make up for this shortfall and help you on your way into the vast empirical and theoretical literature.

What have we learned? First, that the conventions of academic history-writing are inadequate to deal with the complexities that we have encountered. We historians need to reconfigure our craft, recalibrate our knowledge production, reconsider our methodological choices and make our theoretical work more globally inclusive than is currently the case. More of us should question the spatial categories that we routinely use to structure our accounts of the past (for example, state territories) and, instead, experiment with non-conventional ones. We need to rethink time periods (for example, 'prehistoric' or 'colonial'), and we should feel our way beyond the dogma of chronometric time.

Above all, it is important to reconsider what makes an authoritative account of the past. The stories we tell have an impact on how we, and others, act in the world. Academic history may claim authority, but it is only convincing if it recognises two things. To start with, we must acknowledge and analyse the power relations that exist between academically trained scholars and 'non-professional' thinkers about the past. Next, we should recognise that a historical narrative is enriched to the extent that it strives to hold multiple perspectives together, showing how these are connected. One way of doing this is to incorporate into our historical accounts both the spatial imaginations of the humans we study and the spatial patterns resulting from the niches that plants and animals create. Another way is to engage seriously with the non-chronometric concepts of time that many people used – and still use – to structure narratives of their past and their present. And a third is to make our historical accounts more sensitive to the fact that there are diverging assessments of the place of humans in the world.

Key to developing more convincing historical accounts is to take a leaf out of the book of Triangle cosmologies: the lives of all living beings have always been linked. Humans have been co-designing the Triangle's rich ecosystems for at least 400 centuries, ever since we arrived in the region and started constructing niches for ourselves. Likewise, plants and animals continuously constructed ecological niches for themselves, and in the process co-designed the Triangle's human societies. It is the work of historians to scrutinise how exactly these processes operated – and tell us which mixes of interspecies connections were the most meaningful in discrete spaces and at specific moments in time.

Local ways of telling the past focused on plant–animal–spirit–human partnerships (which could be friendly or fraught), the nearness of deep history and the blurriness of human–non-human boundaries. These narratives diverged markedly from assumptions regarding human 'species supremacy' and Western concepts of 'nature' that have shaped much conventional history-writing. To improve the quality of our work, it can help to see history as a never-ending three-cornered conversation between human beings, plants and animals. We historians can only do so if we become far more inquisitive and knowledgeable about the histories of plants and animals as well as about forms of interspecies communication.

Thinking of the Triangle as a multispecies site brings to historical narratives an additional layer of understanding in which to embed human history. For example, the history of human settlement in the region is inseparable from the migration of plants (rice, maize, betel nut, chili pepper and tea, to name a few) and animals (cows, yaks), and it owes much to microbe-borne diseases. The history of human trade networks is closely bound up with mule labour and waterways choked with water hyacinth – both imported species. And culinary history is centred around plant–animal–microbe–human collaborations in the production of fermented food.

The co-created quality of the Triangle's cultural history is thrown into sharp relief by showing how an ancient relationship between sacrificial animals, alcohol and people translated into contemporary forms of sacrifice in religions that formally disapprove of them. Histories of human political life also show interspecies connections. Elephant capabilities shaped the political expansion of the Ahom state. Flowering bamboo triggered a decades-long war of independence in Mizoram. And visions of ancient human–hornbill–mithun intimacies drive contemporary identity politics.

In other words, a focus on historical connections between living beings enriches historical narratives and strengthens their explanatory impact. Such narratives require historians to pay very close attention to the specificity of local lifeworlds as well as to local understandings of human–non-human pasts. More-than-human histories are best served when practitioners acquire new skills: combining conventional and 'proxy' source material, collaborating with field researchers in other disciplines and developing close partnerships with local and hitherto marginalised interlocutors (see Introduction). The more co-produced historical narratives are, the more relevant they will be.

At the same time, studying the Triangle as a multispecies site reminds us that even though it is impossible to pin down many aspects of the past to specific dates, such 'undatable' aspects are not to be dismissed. History is not about dates but about processes and sequences. Some of the long-term – and presently hard-to-date – sequences we have foregrounded are domestication, foraging-to-agriculture and the four phases of human-aided species migration (Chapter 10).

There is a general point to be made here. It goes without saying that more-than-human histories are, by definition, complicated histories. And yet, they should not remain the domain of experts; they are absolutely necessary in wider conversations. More-than-human histories have a crucial role to play in helping us cope with the urgent planetary challenges posed by massive loss of biodiversity and climate change. These challenges are caused by how humans think and act, so we need to find solutions by scrutinising human reasoning and behaviour – in the past as well as in the present. It is for this reason that it is essential to integrate more-than-human histories into global discussions about the future.

Currently, discussions of climate change and biodiversity loss are dominated by explanations of the world that draw heavily on economics and natural science. These result in recipes for action that are based on a narrow conceptual base. They tend to be insensitive to – and dismissive of – local and temporal variation, non-human agency, human signification and environmental subjectivities. Because more-than-human histories focus exactly on these aspects, they offer an indispensable and critical correction to these dominant conceptual frameworks and the policies they inspire.

That correction also includes concepts of space. We believe that studying an 'experimental space' – the Eastern Himalayan Triangle – opens new perspectives. We found that by combining adjoining portions of five national territories, as well as adjoining portions of uplands and lowlands, our attention was drawn to human–non-human connections that cross borders as well as elevations (Chapter 1). As a result, we discovered new questions and new spatial imaginations, such as Cowry Country, riverscapes, sticky-rice and lactose boundaries, and elephant corridors. Such more-than-human geographies can help us reorient our historical enquiries. For example, they allow us to frame our studies by starting from spaces shaped by plant and animal niche construction – such as global biodiversity hotspots (Chapter 1), or the mithun habitat (Map 8.2).

In this way, we can develop new research questions to better understand the specificity of this major Asian region that connects India and China. Regional studies are fundamental to deciphering the world at large. Problems may be global in their reach, but we all experience them in locally diverse ways. Space and location matter. Even though knowledge production may claim to be universal, it never is – it always originates from specific places and is embedded in unequal power relations. The production of knowledge in and on the Triangle is a case in point. Largely marginalised and made invisible by 'mainstream' histories, the Triangle remains *terra incognita* for most historians. And yet, Triangle histories are not only important in their own right, but they may also resonate with scholars who work on other parts of the world.

This book has tried to cover the vast expanse of 40,000 years of more-than-human history in the Eastern Himalayan Triangle. This is obviously a foolhardy mission, but we believe that it is an exercise that can help in setting off a much-needed conversation across disciplines. The ancient South Asian parable of the blind men and the elephant contains a warning: we all have limited, subjective experiences.[1] Only if we pool our insights can we get closer to the truth. Because no single disciplinary perspective can grasp the many facets of more-than-human histories alone, we must try to create platforms for exchange and critical engagement.

It is clear that we are only just beginning to make inroads into our ignorance about the Triangle. New archaeological research is now pushing back against

---

[1] *The Udāna*, 81–4.

pervasive conjecture about the deep past. Environmental studies have arrived, overturning explanations in terms of single causes. New concepts of space make us look in different directions. And comparative studies are beginning to build a counterweight to the tendency to fragment Triangle human history by viewing it primarily through the lens of discrete ethnic groups. Even so, we still have only the sketchiest understanding of many historical patterns, for example, human, plant and animal migrations. With the current quickening of research in several fields, however, we may expect huge advances in our ability to map the region's complex past.

We have argued that historians should take the Triangle's multispecies cosmologies seriously because during many generations these steered human behaviour and self-understanding. For many Triangle inhabitants today, these cosmologies have largely faded from memory – but for many others, rural and urban, multispecies awareness continues to be a lived reality, as recent studies demonstrate (Chapters 9 and 10). These underline that it takes careful local study to tease out variations in environmental subjectivities and that we should be wary of the assumption that twenty-first-century lifeworlds across the world can best be understood by applying universalising concepts such as globalisation, modernity and development.

How people express their relationships with other living beings and landscapes, and how these ideas evolve over time, must be at the heart of exploring more-than-human histories. In this respect we are fortunate. The Triangle is a privileged space for analysing multispecies cosmologies and how these evolve over time. We can think of the present situation as the outcome of a three-layered history. For a very long time the region has been home to perceptions of plant–animal–human entanglements that some scholars refer to as 'community religions,' or 'animism' (Chapters 5, 6 and 7). Later other cosmological orders, described as 'world religions' (Buddhism, Hinduism, Islam, Christianity), came up, and these merged with local beliefs, resulting in distinctly local forms of these world religions (Chapter 6). More recently, further cosmological accretions occurred in the form of 'wildlife conservation' (Chapter 10) and predictions of a catastrophic planetary future. These required yet other ways of imagining plant–animal–human relations. As a result, today we observe a complex and spirited cosmological dialogue about plant–animal–human entanglements across the Triangle.

When proponents of wildlife conservation dismiss how local people relate to plants and animals and portray them as destroyers of nature – as they often do – their conservation policies are doomed from the word go. When they can connect with local multispecies cosmologies and livelihoods, however, conservation efforts may bear fruit. Historians have an important role to play here because history is always with us. Remembering the past as more than human is key to navigating the fraught present and preparing for a sustainable future. Historical studies alert us to values that previously underlay less destructive interspecies relationships and how, and to what extent, these values still circulate. They also help us remember the environmental and social misadventures that resulted from previous struggles over conservation. This poses one of the most urgent questions for historians today. How can we best learn to imagine the past differently – 'multispeciesly' – and so navigate our way towards a viable more-than-human future?

We are well aware that we have flagged the possibilities of this approach without being able to address details. We galloped through time and across a variegated landscape. We connected only some dots and suggested only some contexts. The result is an introductory and experimental survey of how the ever-increasing footprint of *Homo sapiens* transformed the Triangle and ultimately created the challenges that we are facing today. We hope that this book may act as a springboard for more contextual and detailed studies that can help us increase our grasp on the entangled lives of humans, animals and plants – in the Triangle and beyond.

Copyrights and Sources

Cover Recky Maibram.

Plate

1.1 Willem van Schendel.
1.2 Willem van Schendel.
1.3 Willem van Schendel.
3.1 Tiatoshi Jamir.
3.2 Ajai Shankar (ed.), *Indian Archaeology 1992–93: A Review*, (New Delhi: Archaeological Survey of India, 1997), plate XXIIIB; Manjil Hazarika, 'Cord-Impressed Pottery in Neolithic-Chalcolithic Context of Eastern India', in *Neolithic-Chalcolithic Cultures of Eastern India*, ed. K. N. Dikshit (New Delhi: Indian Archaeological Society, 2013), 94.
3.3 Willem van Schendel.
3.4 Willem van Schendel.
3.5 Willem van Schendel.
4.1 Willem van Schendel.
4.2 Willem van Schendel.
4.3 Willem van Schendel.
4.4 Willem van Schendel.
4.5 Willem van Schendel.
5.1 J. H. Hutton, 'Carved Monoliths at Dimapur and an Angami Naga Ceremony', *Journal of the Royal Anthropological Institute of Great Britain and Ireland* 52 (January–June 1922): 58.
5.2 N. E. Parry, *The Lakhers* (London: Macmillan and Co., 1932), 495.
5.3 Willem van Schendel.
5.4 J. H. Hutton, *The Angami Nagas with Some Notes on Neighbouring Tribes* (London: Macmillan and Co., 1921), 19.

Copyrights and Sources

6.1 Sukumar Barkaith, *Hastividyārnava*, c. 1740 CE.
6.2 Emil Riebeck, *Die Hügelstämme von Chittagong: Ergebnisse einer Reise im Jahre 1882* (Berlin: A. Asher & Co., 1885), Tafel 16.
6.3 Manipur State Museum.
6.4 School of Oriental and African Studies, London, UK.
6.5 Willem van Schendel, Wolfgang Mey and Aditya Kumar Dewan, *The Chittagong Hill Tracts: Living in a Borderland* (Bangkok: White Lotus Press, 2000).
6.6 Department of Archaeology, Dhaka.
6.7 Ashok Elwin.
6.8 Recky Maibram.
6.9 Pitt Rivers Museum, Oxford.
6.10 Radio Free Asia, 2025 M St. NW, Suite 300, Washington, DC 20036.
6.11 Willem van Schendel.
6.12 American Museum of Natural History Library, New York.
6.13 Pitt Rivers Museum, Oxford.
6.14 Willem van Schendel.
6.15 James Henry Green Charitable Trust, Royal Pavilion & Museums Trust, Brighton & Hove.
6.16 Willem van Schendel.
6.17 Willem van Schendel.
6.18 Willem van Schendel.
6.19 V. Thangzama collection.
7.1 Willem van Schendel.
7.2 Lorenz G. Löffler (Claus-Dieter Brauns and Lorenz G. Löffler, *Mru: Hill People on the Border of Bangladesh* [Basel; Boston; Berlin: Birkhäuser Verlag, 1990], 85).
7.3 Lorenz G. Löffler (Claus-Dieter Brauns and Lorenz G. Löffler, *Mru: Hill People on the Border of Bangladesh* [Basel; Boston; Berlin: Birkhäuser Verlag, 1990], 111).
7.4 Robert Laltinchhawna.
7.5 Lalhruaitluanga Ralte collection.
7.6 Willem van Schendel.
7.7 Michael Aram Tarr.
7.8 Claus-Dieter Brauns (Claus-Dieter Brauns and Lorenz G. Löffler, *Mru: Hill People on the Border of Bangladesh* [Basel; Boston; Berlin: Birkhäuser Verlag, 1990], 210).
8.1 Ethnologisches Museum der Staatlichen Museen zu Berlin.

8.2	Pitt Rivers Museum, Oxford.
8.3	Emil Riebeck, *Die Hügelstämme von Chittagong: Ergebnisse einer Reise im Jahre 1882* (Berlin: A. Asher & Co., 1885).
8.4	Amiya Kanti Chakma. Courtesy of Niaz Zaman.
8.5	Ashok Elwin.
8.6	Ashok Elwin.
8.7	Magnus Lidén and Tana Showren.
8.8	Willem van Schendel.
8.9	Pakke Page Hornbill Festival (@PakkePagaFestival), 'Home', https://www.facebook.com/PakkePagaFestival/ (accessed 28 August 2020).
8.10	Willem van Schendel, Wolfgang Mey and Aditya Kumar Dewan, *The Chittagong Hill Tracts: Living in a Borderland* (Bangkok: White Lotus Press, 2000).
8.11	Willem van Schendel.
8.12	Willem van Schendel.
8.13	'Basic Facts on Nagaland State Logo or Emblem', Nagaland GK, 12 November 2019, https://nagalandgk.com/nagaland-state-logo/ (accessed 4 January 2022).
8.14	Willem van Schendel.
8.15	Willem van Schendel.
8.16	Joy Ngaihte.
8.17	Willem van Schendel.
8.18	Joy L. K. Pachuau.
8.19	Willem van Schendel.
8.20	Willem van Schendel.
8.21	Willem van Schendel.
8.22	Ethnologisches Museum, Staatliche Museen zu Berlin.
9.1	D. M. Dawngkima.
9.2	Pitt Rivers Museum, Oxford.
9.3	Willem van Schendel, Wolfgang Mey and Aditya Kumar Dewan, *The Chittagong Hill Tracts: Living in a Borderland* (Bangkok: White Lotus Press, 2000).
9.4	Willem van Schendel.
9.5	Pitt Rivers Museum, Oxford.
9.6	British Library, London.
9.7	Mizo National Front (MNF) collection.
9.8	Angus Library and Archive, Regent's Park College, Oxford, UK.

Copyrights and Sources 267

9.9 Willem van Schendel.
9.10 Willem van Schendel, Wolfgang Mey and Aditya Kumar Dewan, *The Chittagong Hill Tracts: Living in a Borderland* (Bangkok: White Lotus Press, 2000).
9.11 Willem van Schendel.
9.12 Willem van Schendel.
9.13 'Amber Is Myanmar's New Gold', *Ancient Artifacts*, 1 July 2018, https://psjfactoids.blogspot.com/2018/07/amber-is-myanmars-new-gold.html (accessed 12 May 2021).
9.14 Willem van Schendel.
9.15 Willem van Schendel.
10.1 Willem van Schendel.
10.2 Willem van Schendel.
10.3 Willem van Schendel.
10.4 American Museum of Natural History Library, New York.
10.5 Leo Golan/Odd Animals.
10.6 Krushnamegh Kunte.
10.7 Yin Yang.
10.8 Kezang Tobgay (Gyeltshen et al., 'New Species Discoveries').
10.9 Beta Mahatvaraj/Praveen Raj.
10.10 Hassan Al-Razi, Marjan Maria and Sabir Bin Muzaffar, 'A New Species of Cryptic Bush Frog (Anura, Rhacophoridae, *Raorchestes*) from Northeastern Bangladesh', *ZooKeys* 927 (April 2020).
10.11 Smithsonian Institution, Washington, DC.
10.12 Fitz William Thomas Pollok and W. S. Thom, *Wild Sports of Burma and Assam* (London: Hurst and Blackett, 1900).
10.13 Fitz William Thomas Pollok and W. S. Thom, *Wild Sports of Burma and Assam* (London: Hurst and Blackett, 1900).
10.14 'Tourist in Kaziranga National Park', Assam Info, http://www.assaminfo.com/wallpapers/2/2/5-tourist-in-kaziranga-national-park.htm (accessed 12 January 2021).
10.15 Willem van Schendel.
11.1 Mizo Zirlai Pawl (MZP) collection.
11.2 Diptendu Dutta/Agence France-Presse (AFP).
11.3 Diptendu Dutta/Agence France-Presse (AFP).
11.4 Ritu Raj Konwar.

11.5 'Five Elephants Killed by Train in India', *AryNews*, 11 December 2017, https://arynews.tv/five-elephants-killed-train-india/ (accessed 17 November 2021).

11.6 Arnab Lahiry.

11.7 Lekha Borah, 'Gangetic Dolphin Killed by Villagers, Assam', *Conservation India*, 20 September 2013, https://www.conservationindia.org/gallery/gangetic-dolphin-killed-by-villagers-assam (accessed 7 January 2022).

Bibliography

Acharyya, S. K. 'Indo-Burma Range: A Belt of Accreted Microcontinents, Ophiolites and Mesozoic–Paleogene Flyschoid Sediments'. *International Journal of Earth Sciences (Geologische Rundschau)* 104, no. 5 (2015): 1235–51.

Adhikari, Dibyendu, Raghuvar Tiwary and Saroj Kanta Barik. 'Modelling Hotspots for Invasive Alien Plants in India'. *PLoS ONE* 10, no. 7 (2015): e0134665, 1–20.

Adit, Arjun, Monika Koul and Rajesh Tandon. 'Twelve New Additions in the Orchid Flora of Tripura, North-East India'. *Check List* 16, no. 1 (2020): 17–25.

Ahmed, Bulbul (ed.). *Buddhist Heritage of Bangladesh*. Dhaka: Nymphea Publications, 2015.

Ahmed, Farid, and Nicholas P. Low. 'Environmental Justice Dialogues and the Struggle for Human Dignity in the Deciduous Forest of Bangladesh'. *Journal of Political Ecology* 27, no. 1 (2020): 300–16.

Ahmed, Imdad Ali. 'Elephants in Medieval Assam'. *Proceedings of the Indian History Congress* 76 (2015): 264–70.

Ahmed, M. M., and P. K. Singh. 'Traditional Knowledge System of the Muslim Community in Manipur'. *Indian Journal of Traditional Knowledge* 6, no. 2 (2007): 383–9.

Ahmed, Rekib. 'Elephant Crop Raiding and Railways Traffic: Temporal Determinants of Elephant–Train Collisions in Eastern Karbi Anglong, India'. *Applied Ecology and Environmental Sciences* 8, no. 3 (2020): 81–6.

Ahmed, Zia, Rafiul Alam, Syeda Ayshia Akter and Abdul Kadir. 'Environmental Sustainability Assessment Due to Stone Quarrying and Crushing Activities in Jaflong, Sylhet'. *Environmental Monitoring and Assessment* 192, no. 778 (2020): 1–20.

Ahrestani, Farshid S. '*Bos frontalis* and *Bos gaurus* (Artiodactyla: Bovidae)'. *Mammalian Species* 50, no. 959 (2018): 1–17.

Ahrestani, Farshid S., and Mahesh Sankaran (eds.). *The Ecology of Large Herbivores in South and Southeast Asia*. Dordrecht: Springer, 2016.

Ahsan, Md. Farid, and M. Monirul H. Khan (eds.). *Red List of Bangladesh*. Vol. 4, *Reptiles and Amphibians*. Dhaka: IUCN, International Union for Conservation of Nature Bangladesh Country Office, 2015.

Ahsan, M. Farid, and M. Mazbah Uddin. 'Human–Rhesus Monkey Conflict at Rampur Village under Monohardi Upazila in Narsingdi District of Bangladesh'. *Journal of Threatened Taxa* 6, no. 6 (2014): 5905–8.

Aier, Anungla, and Tiatoshi Jamir. 'Re-interpreting the Myth of Longterok'. *Indian Folklife* 33 (July 2009): 5–9.

Aisher, Alex. 'Scarcity, Alterity and Value: Decline of the Pangolin, the World's Most Trafficked Mammal'. *Conservation and Society* 14, no. 4 (2016): 317–29.

Aisher, Alex, and Vinita Damodaran. 'Introduction: Human–Nature Interactions through a Multispecies Lens'. *Conservation and Society* 14, no. 4 (2016): 293–304.

Aisher, Alexander. 'Through "Spirits": Cosmology and Landscape Ecology among the Nyishi Tribe of Upland Arunachal Pradesh, Northeast India'. PhD thesis, University College London, 2006.

———. 'Voices of Uncertainty: Spirits, Humans and Forests in Upland Arunachal Pradesh, India'. *South Asia: Journal of South Asian Studies* 30, no. 3 (2007): 479–98.

Aiyadurai, Ambika. 'Human–Animal Relations: A View from the Mishmi Hills'. *Seminar* 702 (2018): 26–30.

———. *Hunting in a Biodiversity Hotspot: A Survey on Hunting Practices by Indigenous Communities in Arunachal Pradesh, North-East India*. London: The Rufford Small Grants Foundation, 2007.

———. 'The Multiple Meanings of Nature Conservation: Insights from Dibang Valley, Arunachal Pradesh'. *Economic and Political Weekly* 53, no. 29 (2018): 37–44.

———. '"Tigers Are Our Brothers": Understanding Human–Nature Relations in the Mishmi Hills, Northeast India'. *Conservation and Society* 14, no. 4 (2016): 305–16.

———. '"Tigers Are Our Brothers": Understanding Human–Nature Relations in the Mishmi Hills, Northeast India'. PhD thesis, National University of Singapore, 2016.

———. 'Wildlife Hunting and Conservation in Northeast India: A Need for an Interdisciplinary Understanding'. *International Journal of Galliformes Conservation* 2 (2011): 61–73.

Aiyadurai, Ambika, and Sayan Banerjee. 'Bird Conservation from Obscurity to Popularity: A Case Study of Two Bird Species from Northeast India'. *GeoJournal* 85, no. 4 (2020): 901–12.

Aiyadurai, Ambika, Navinder J. Singh and E. J. Milner-Gulland. 'Wildlife Hunting by Indigenous Tribes: A Case Study from Arunachal Pradesh, North-East India'. *Oryx* 44, no. 4 (2010): 564–72.

Akhtar, Namia. 'The Wrong Kind of Sacrifice: Eid-ul-Azha Has Become More about the Price of Our Cattle than the Extent of Our Sacrifice'. *Dhaka Tribune,* 28 September 2015, 1.

Albert, Sandra. 'Medical Pluralism among the Indigenous Peoples of Meghalaya, Northeast India: Implications for Health Policy'. PhD thesis, University of London, 2014.

Ali, A. N. M. Irshad. 'Islam in the Hill Areas of Northeast India'. *NEHU Journal* 10, no. 1 (2012): 1–8.

Allen, B. C. *Assam District Gazetteers Volume VIII Lakhimpur.* Calcutta: City Press, 1905.

Allen, D. J., S. Molur and B. A. Daniel (comp.). *The Status and Distribution of Freshwater Biodiversity in the Eastern Himalaya.* Cambridge; Gland: IUCN; Coimbatore: Zoo Outreach Organisation, 2010.

Allendorf, Teri, Khaing Khaing Swe, Thida Oo, Ye Thut, Myint Aung, Myint Aung, Keera Allendorf, Lee-Ann Hayek, Peter Leimgruber and Chris Wemmer. 'Community Attitudes toward Three Protected Areas in Upper Myanmar (Burma)'. *Environmental Conservation* 33, no. 4 (2006): 344–52.

Allendorf, T. D., and J. Yang, 'The Role of Ecosystem Services in Park-People Relationships: The Case of Gaoligongshan Nature Reserve in Southwest China'. *Biological Conservation* 167 (August 2013): 187–93.

Allison, Elizabeth. 'Deity Citadels: Sacred Sites of Bio-cultural Resistance and Resilience in Bhutan'. *Religions* 10, no. 268 (2019): 1–17.

———. 'Spirits and Nature: The Intertwining of Sacred Cosmologies and Environmental Conservation in Bhutan'. *Journal for the Study of Religion, Nature and Culture* 11, no. 2 (2017): 197–226.

Allison, Elizabeth Aileen. 'Enspirited Places, Material Traces: The Sanctified and the Sacrificed in Modernizing Bhutan'. PhD thesis, University of California, Berkeley, 2009.

Al-Razi, Hassan, Marjan Maria and Sabit Hasan. 'First Record of the Recently Described *Cyrtodactylus tripuraensis* Agarwal, Mahony, Giri, Chaitanya and Bauer, 2018 (Squamata, Gekkonidae) in Bangladesh'. *Check List* 14, no. 6 (2018): 1105–8.

Al-Razi, Hassan, Marjan Maria and Sabir Bin Muzaffar. 'A New Species of Cryptic Bush Frog (Anura, Rhacophoridae, *Raorchestes*) from Northeastern Bangladesh'. *ZooKeys* 927 (April 2020): 127–51.

———. 'Mortality of Primates Due to Roads and Power Lines in Two Forest Patches in Bangladesh'. *Zoologica* 36 (October 2019): e33540, 1–6.

Amato, George, Mary G. Egan and Alan Rabinowitz. 'A New Species of Muntjac, *Muntiacus putaoensis* (Artiodactyla: Cervidae) from Northern Myanmar'. *Animal Conservation* 2, no. 1 (1999): 1–7.

Amin, Neel. 'Hunting for Meaning: British Hunters, Banjara Hunters, and Overcoming Threats to Colonial Order in Nineteenth-Century India'. *Environmental History* 25 (May 2020): 515–35.

Angami, A., P. R. Gajurel, P. Rethy, B. Singh and S. K. Kalita. 'Status and Potential of Wild Edible Plants of Arunachal Pradesh'. *Indian Journal of Traditional Knowledge* 5, no. 4 (2006): 541–50.

Ao, Temsula. *The Ao-Naga Oral Tradition*. Baroda, Bhasha Publications, 2012.

Ara, Dilshad Rahat, and Mamun Rashid. 'Between the Built and the Unbuilt in Vernacular Studies: The Architecture of the Mru of the Chittagong Hills'. *Journal of Architecture* 21, no. 1 (2016): 1–23.

———. 'Tracking Local Dwelling Changes in the Chittagong Hills: Perspectives on Vernacular Architecture'. *Journal of Cultural Geography* 33, no. 2 (2016): 229–46.

Arciero, Elena, Thirsa Kraaijenbrink, Asan, Marc Haber, Massimo Mezzavilla, Qasim Ayub et al. 'Demographic History and Genetic Adaptation in the Himalayan Region Inferred from Genome-Wide SNP Genotypes of 49 Populations'. *Molecular Biology and Evolution* 35, no. 8 (2018): 1916–33.

Ardussi, John A. 'Bhutan before the British: A Historical Study'. PhD thesis, Australian National University, 1977.

Arora, R. K. 'Plant Genetic Resources of Northeastern Region: Diversity, Domestication Trends, Conservation and Uses'. *Proceedings of Indian National Science Academy* B63, no. 3 (2015): 175–86.

Arroyo-Kalin, Manuel, David Wengrow, Dorian Q. Fuller, Chris J. Stevens and Michèle Wollstonecroft. 'Civilisation and Human Niche Construction'. *Archaeology International* 20 (2017): 106–9.

Arunachalam, A., R. Sarmah, D. Adhikari, M. Majumder and M. L. Khan. 'Anthropogenic Threats and Biodiversity Conservation in Namdapha Nature Reserve in the Indian Eastern Himalayas'. *Current Science* 87, no. 4 (2004): 447–54.

Asada, Haruhisa. 'Cultivation of Glutinous Rice in Northeast India, and Its Food Products'. In *Nature, Culture*, edited by Yokoyama, Matsumoto and Araki, 25–50. Singapore: Springer Nature, 2020.

Aung, Myint, Khaing Khaing Swe, Thida Oo, Kyaw Kyaw Moe, Peter Leimgruber, Teri Allendorf, Chris Duncan, Chris Wemmer. 'The Environmental History of Chatthin Wildlife Sanctuary, a Protected Area in Myanmar (Burma)'. *Journal of Environmental Management* 72 (April 2004): 205–16.

Aung, Pyi Soe. 'Social-Ecological Coevolution and Its Implications for Protected Area Management: Case Study in Natma Taung National Park, Myanmar'. PhD thesis, Technische Universität Dresden, 2020.

Aung, Tin Htut. 'Raw Material Utilization, Technology, and Typology of Palaeolithic Tools in Myanmar: Were There Lithic Technological Links in the Regional

Context?' *Journal of Humanities and Social Sciences Okayama University* 44 (November 2017): 189–204.

Ayam, Victor Singh. 'Ethnomedicine of Wild Plants of Ziro, Arunachal Pradesh'. *International Journal of Research Studies in Biosciences* 5, no. 7 (2017): 1–12.

Badola, Saket, Merwyn Fernandes, Saljagringrang R. Marak and Chiging Pilia. *Assessment of Illegal Trade-Related Threats to Red Panda in India and Selected Neighbouring Range Countries*. New Delhi: TRAFFIC, India Office, 2020.

Bae, Christopher J., Katerina Douka and Michael D. Petraglia. 'On the Origin of Modern Humans: Asian Perspectives'. *Science* 358, no. eaai9067 (2017): 1–7.

———. 'Human Colonization of Asia in the Late Pleistocene: An Introduction to Supplement 17'. *Current Anthropology* 58, supplement 17 (2017): S373–82.

Baig, Mumtaz, Bikas Mitra, Kaixing Qu, Min-sheng Peng, Irshad Ahmed, Yong-Wang Mia, Lin-sen Zan and Ya-ping Zhang. 'Mitochondrial DNA Diversity and Origin of *Bos frontalis*'. *Current Science* 104, no. 1 (2013): 115–20.

Bailey, F. M. *China–Tibet–Assam: A Journey, 1911*. London: Jonathan Cape, 1945.

Baldizzone, Tiziana, and Gianni Baldizzone. *Caravanes de bambous*. Paris: Editions du Seuil, 2004.

Balkenohl, Michael. '*Trilophidius gemmatus* sp. n., a New Species from Bhutan, with an Updated Identification Key to the Asian Species (Coleoptera, Carabidae, Scaritinae)'. *Alpine Entomology* 1 (November 2017): 51–6.

Banerjee, Ajit, Soumitra Ghosh and Oliver Springate-Baginski. *The Creation of West Bengal's Forest Underclass an Historical Institutional Analysis of Forest Rights Deprivations*. IPPG Discussion Paper 51. Manchester: School of Environment & Development, University of Manchester, 2010.

Banik, Ratan Lal. *Silviculture of South Asian Priority Bamboos*. Singapore: Springer Science+Business Media, 2016.

Bankoff, Greg, and Peter Boomgaard (eds.). *A History of Natural Resources in Asia: The Wealth of Nature*. New York; Houndsmills: Palgrave Macmillan, 2007.

Banks, E. Pendleton. 'Innovation in a Zanniat Chin Village'. *Southeast Asian Journal of Sociology* 3 (1970): 39–42.

Bar-Yosef, Ofer, Metin I. Eren, Jiarong Yuan, David J. Cohen and Yiyuan Li. 'Were Bamboo Tools Made in Prehistoric Southeast Asia? An Experimental View from South China'. *Quaternary International* 269 (2012): 9–21.

Barbe, M. 'Some Account of the Hill Tribes in the Interior of the District of Chittagong, in a Letter to the Secretary of the Asiatic Society'. *Journal of the Asiatic Society of Bengal* 14, no. 161 (1845): 380–91.

Barbora, Sanjay. 'Riding the Rhino: Conservation, Conflicts, and Militarisation of Kaziranga National Park in Assam'. *Antipode* 49, no. 5 (2017): 1145–63.

Barden, Angela, Noorainie Awang Anak, Teresa Mulliken and Michael Song. *Heart of the Matter: Agarwood Use and Trade and CITES Implementation for Aquilaria malaccensis*. Cambridge: TRAFFIC International, 2000.

Bareigts, André. *Les Lautu: Contribution à l'étude de l'organisation sociale d'une ethnie chin de Haute-Birmanie*. Paris : SELAF, 1981.

Barkataki-Ruscheweyh, Meenaxi. 'Best of All Worlds: Rangfraism; The New Institutionalized Religion of the Tangsa Community in Northeast India'. *Internationales Asienforum* 46, nos. 1/2 (2015): 149–67.

Barman, Bratatee. 'Early Medieval Archaeological Landscape of Assam (AD 600–AD 1200): Preliminary Survey in Western Assam, District Goalpara'. *Ancient Asia* 8, no. 4 (2017): 1–11.

Barman, Purnima Devi, D. K. Sharma, John F. Cockrem, Mamani Malakar, Bibekananda Kakati and Tracy Melvin. 'Saving the Greater Adjutant Stork by Changing Perceptions and Linking to Assamese Traditions in India'. *Ethnobiology Letters* 11, no. 2 (2020): 20–9.

Barua, Golap Chandra (ed.). *Ahom-Buranji: From the Earliest Times to the End of Ahom Rule*. Calcutta: Baptist Mission Press, 1930.

Barua, Maan, 'Affective Economies, Pandas, and the Atmospheric Politics of Lively Capital'. *Transactions of the Institute of British Geographers* 45, no. 3 (2020): 678–92.

———. 'Animating Capital: Work, Commodities, Circulation'. *Progress in Human Geography* 43, no. 4 (2019): 650–69.

———. 'Between Gods and Demons'. *Seminar* 651 (2013): 75–9.

Barua, Maan, Shonil A. Bhagwat and Sushrut Jadhav. 'The Hidden Dimensions of Human–Wildlife Conflict: Health Impacts, Opportunity and Transaction Costs'. *Biological Conservation* 157 (2013): 309–16.

Barua, Shuvashish P., M. Monirul H. Khan and A. H. M. Ali Reza. 'The Status of Alien Invasive Species in Bangladesh and Their Impact on the Ecosystems'. In *Report of the Workshop on Alien Invasive Species*, edited by P. Balakrishna, 1–8. Colombo: IUCN Biodiversity Programme, 2001.

Baruah, Sanjib. 'Whose River Is It Anyway? Political Economy of Hydropower in the Eastern Himalayas'. *Economic and Political Weekly* 47, no. 29 (2012): 41–52.

Basak, Bishnupriya, and Pradeep Srivastava. 'Earliest Dates of Microlithic Industries (42–25 ka) from West Bengal, Eastern India: New Light on Modern Human Occupation in the Indian Subcontinent'. *Asian Perspectives* 56, no. 2 (2017): 237–59.

Basnet, Deepa, Pratikshya Kandel, Nakul Chettri, Yongping Yang, Mahendra Singh Lodhi, Naing Zaw Htun, Kabir Uddin and Eklabya Sharma. 'Biodiversity Research Trends and Gaps from the Confluence of Three Global Biodiversity

Hotspots in the Far-Eastern Himalaya'. *International Journal of Ecology* 1323419 (January 2019): 1–14.

Basu, Saikat Kumar, and William Cetzal-Ix. 'Traditional Honey Collectors in the Sunderbans Region and Their Impact on the Local Mangrove Ecosystem and Biodiversity: A Case Study with Particular Reference to Human–Animal Conflict'. *Biodiversity* 19, nos. 3/4 (2018): 248–54.

Basumatary, Sadhan K., Swati Tripathi, Samir K. Bera, Chandra Mohan Nautiyal, Nilakshee Devi et al. 'Late Pleistocene Palaeoclimate Based on Vegetation of the Eastern Himalayan Foothills in the Indo-Burma Range, India'. *Palynology* 39, no. 2 (2015): 220–33.

Bawa, Kamal, and Sandesh Kadur. *Himalaya: Mountains of Life*. Bangalore: Ashoka Trust for Research in Education and the Environment, 2013.

Beal, Samuel (ed.). *Si-Yu-Ki: Buddhist Records of the Western World, Translated from the Chinese of Hiuen Tsang (AD 627)*. 2 vols. London: Trübner & Co., 1884.

Beames, John. *Memoirs of a Bengal Civilian: The Lively Narrative of a Victorian District Officer*. London: Chatto & Windus, 1961.

Beattie, James. 'Plants, Animals and Environmental Transformation: Indian–New Zealand Biological and Landscape Connections, 1830s–1890s'. In *The East India Company and the Natural World*, edited by Vinita Damodaran, Anna Winterbottom and Alan Lester, 219–48. Houndsmills: Palgrave Macmillan, 2015.

Beemer, Bryce. 'The Creole City in Mainland Southeast Asia: Slave Gathering Warfare and Cultural Exchange in Burma, Thailand and Manipur, 18th–19th C.' PhD thesis, University of Hawai'i at Mānoa, 2013.

Behera, Maguni Charan (ed.). *Tribal Studies in India: Perspectives of History, Archaeology and Culture*. Singapore: Springer Nature, 2020.

Bernot, Lucien. *Les paysans arakanais du Pakistan Oriental: L'histoire, le monde végétal et l'organisation des réfugiés Marma (Mog)*. 2 vols. Paris; The Hague: Mouton, 1967.

Bertocci, Peter J. 'A Sufi Movement in Bangladesh: The Maijbhandari *Tariqa* and Its Followers'. *Contributions to Indian Sociology*, n.s., 40, no. 1 (2006): 1–28.

Betlu, Sajem. 'Indigenous Knowledge of Zootherapeutic Use among the Biate Tribe of Dima Hasao District, Assam, Northeastern India'. *Journal of Ethnobiology and Ethnomedicine* 9, no. 56 (2013): 1–15.

Bezbaruah, Dwipen. 'Ethnography to Archaeology: Tracing the Past of the Tribes of Assam and Adjoining Areas'. In *Tribal Studies in India*, edited by Behera, 171–85. Singapore: Springer Nature, 2020.

Bezbaruah, Ranju. 'Kami-Sabong Affairs, 1906–1916: Question of British Intervention in the "Unadministered" Tract Between Burma and Assam'. *Proceedings of the Indian History Congress* 52 (1991): 643–9.

Bhatt, K. C., Pavan Kumar Malav and S. P. Ahlawat. '"Jumin", a Traditional Beverage of Nocte Tribe in Arunachal Pradesh: An Ethnobotanical Survey'. *Genetic Resources and Crop Evolution* 65 (2018): 671–7.

Bhatt, K. V., K. P. S. Chandel, T. M. Shivakumar and J. K. S. Sachan. 'Isozyme Diversity in Indian Primitive Maize Landraces'. *Journal of Plant Biochemistry and Biotechnology* 7 (January 1998): 23–7.

Bhattacharjee, Anushree, and N. Parthasarathy. 'Coexisting with Large Carnivores: A Case Study from Western Duars, India'. *Human Dimensions of Wildlife* 18, no. 1 (2013): 20–31.

Bhattacharjee, Pradip Nath. *Jamatia Folklore: A Sociological Study*. Agartala: Tripura State Tribal Cultural Research Institute and Museum, 1995.

Bhattacharya, Jayati. 'Old Routes, New Dreams: Reminiscences of the Southern Silk Road and Bengal–China Connectivities'. *Journal of the Economic and Social History of the Orient* 64 (2021): 302–41.

Bhattacharya, Neeladri, and Joy L. K. Pachuau (eds.). *Landscape, Culture, and Belonging: Writing the History of Northeast India*. Cambridge: Cambridge University Press, 2019.

Bhuyan, Bhaskarjyoti, and Bimal Kumar Kar. 'The Pachyderm Dread: A Case Study of Human–Elephant Conflict in the Fringe Areas of Sonai-Rupai Wildlife Sanctuary, Assam'. *Space and Culture, India* 6, no. 3 (2018): 142–55.

Bhuyan, Deep Jyoti, Mridula Sakia Barooah, Sudipta Sankar Bora and K. Singaravadivel. 'Biochemical and Nutritional Analysis of Rice Beer of North East India'. *Indian Journal of Traditional Knowledge* 13, no. 1 (2014): 142–8.

Biju, S. D., Gayani Senevirathne, Sonali Garg, Stephen Mahony, Rachunliu G. Kamei, Ashish Thomas, Yogesh Shouche, Christopher J. Raxworthy, Madhava Meegaskumbura, Ines Van Bocxlaer. 'Frankixalus, a New Rhacophorid Genus of Tree Hole Breeding Frogs with Oophagous Tadpoles'. *PLoS ONE* 11, no. 1 (2016): 1–17.

Birney, Charles F. *The Story of the Assam Railways and Training Company Limited, 1881–1951*. London: Harley Publishing, 1951.

Bisset, N. G., and G. Mazars. 'Arrow Poisons in South Asia, Part 1: Arrow Poisons in Ancient India'. *Journal of Ethnopharmacology* 12 (1984): 1–24.

Biswas, Animesh, M. A. Bari, Mohashweta Roy and S. K. Bhadra. 'Inherited Folk Pharmaceutical Knowledge of Tribal People in the Chittagong Hill Tracts, Bangladesh'. *Indian Journal of Traditional Knowledge* 9, no. 1 (2010): 77–89.

Biswas, Debashish, Emily S. Gurley, Shannon Rutherford and Stephen P. Luby. 'The Drivers and Impacts of Selling Soil for Brick Making in Bangladesh'. *Environmental Management* 62 (June 2018): 792–802.

Blackburn, Stuart. *Himalayan Tribal Tales: Oral Tradition and Culture in the Apatani Valley*. Leiden; Boston: Brill, 2008.

———. 'Memories of Migration: Notes on Legends and Beads in Arunachal Pradesh, India'. *European Bulletin of Himalayan Research* 25/26 (Autumn 2003–Spring 2004): 15–60.

———. 'Oral Stories and Culture Areas: From Northeast India to Southwest China'. *South Asia: Journal of South Asian Studies* 30, no. 3 (2007): 419–37.

———. 'Die Reise der Seele: Bemerkungen zu Bestattungsritualen und oralen Texten in Arunachal Pradesh, Indien'. In *Der Abschied von den Toten. Trauerrituale im Kulturvergleich*, edited by Jan Assmann, Franz Maciejewski and Axel Michaels, 82–109. Göttingen: Wallstein, 2005.

———. *The Sun Rises: A Shaman's Chant, Ritual Exchange and Fertility in the Apatani Valley*. Leiden; Boston: Brill, 2010.

Blench, Roger. 'Ethnographic and Archaeological Correlates for a Mainland Southeast Asia Linguistic Area'. In *Spirits and Ships: Cultural Transfers in Early Monsoon Asia*, edited by Andrea Acri, Roger Blench and Alexandra Landmann, 207–38. Singapore: ISEAS Publishing, 2017.

———. 'The Contribution of Linguistics to Understanding the Foraging/Farming Transition in Northeast India'. In *50 Years after Daojali-Hading*, edited by Jamir and Hazarika, 99–109. New Delhi: Research India Press, 2014.

Blench, Roger, and Mark W. Post. 'Rethinking Sino-Tibetan Phylogeny from the Perspective of North East Indian Languages'. In *Trans-Himalayan Linguistics*, edited by Owen-Smith and Hill, 71–104. Berlin; Boston: Walter De Gruyter, 2014.

Blinkhorn, James, and Michael D. Petraglia. 'Environments and Cultural Change in the Indian Subcontinent: Implications for the Dispersal of Homo sapiens in the Late Pleistocene'. *Current Anthropology* 58, supplement 17 (2017): S463–79.

Blood Amber: Military Resource Grab Clears ut Indigenous Peoples in Kachin State's Hugawng Valley. Kachin State: Kachin Development Networking Group, 2019.

Boddice, Rob (ed.). *Anthropocentrism: Humans, Animals, Environments*. Leiden; Boston: Brill, 2011.

Boko, Nung, and D. Narsinham. 'Rapid Survey of Plants Used by Adi Tribe of Bosing-Banggo, East Siang District, Arunachal Pradesh, India'. *Pleione* 8, no. 2 (2014): 271–82.

Bonavia, Duccio. *Maize: Origin, Domestication, and its Role in the Development of Culture*. Cambridge: Cambridge University Press, 2013.

Bora, Leema, Joken Bam, Vijay Paul and Sanjit Maiti. 'Traditional Milk, Meat Processing and Preservation Techniques of the Yak Pastoralists of Arunachal Pradesh'. *Indian Journal of Traditional Knowledge* 13, no. 1 (2014): 216–21.

Borah, Jimmy, Pranab Jyoti Bora, Amit Sharma, Soumen Dey, Anupam Sarmah, Niranjan Kumar Vasu and Nadisha Sidhu. 'Livestock Depredation by Bengal Tigers in Fringe Areas of Kaziranga Tiger Reserve, Assam, India: Implications for Large Carnivore Conservation'. *Human–Wildlife Interactions* 12, no. 2 (2018): 186–97.

Borah, Lekha. 'Gangetic Dolphin Killed by Villagers, Assam'. *Conservation India*, 20 September 2013. https://www.conservationindia.org/gallery/gangetic-dolphin-killed-by-villagers-assam. Accessed 7 January 2022.

Borkar, Minal, Fahim Ahmad, Faisal Khan and Suraksha Agrawal. 'Paleolithic Spread of Y-chromosomal Lineage of Tribes in Eastern and Northeastern India'. *Annals of Human Biology* 38, no. 6 (2011): 736–46.

Borkataky-Varma, Sravana. 'Red: An Ethnographic Study of Cross-Pollination between the Vedic and the Tantric'. *International Journal of Hindu Studies* 23 (June 2019): 179–94.

Borthakur, S. K. 'Ethnobiological Wisdom behind the Traditional Muga Silk Industry in Assam'. *Indian Journal of Traditional Knowledge* 2, no. 3 (2003): 230–5.

Bose, Shibani. 'From Eminence to near Extinction: The Journey of the Greater One-Horned Rhino'. In *Shifting Ground*, edited by Rangarajan and Sivaramakrishnan, 65–87. Oxford: Oxford University Press, 2014.

Boutry, Maxine, Saw Eh Htoo and Ye Wunna. *Social Anthropological Study, Chin State, Paletwa Township: Final Report*. n.p.: Action Contre la Faim, 2013.

Bower, Ursula Graham. *Naga Path*. London: John Murray, 1950.

———. *The Hidden Land*. London: John Murray, 1913.

Brahma, Jwngsar, Anirbid Sircar and G. P. Karmakar. 'Hydrocarbon Prospectivity in Central Part of Tripura, India, Using an Integrated Approach'. *Journal of Geography and Geology* 5, no. 3 (2013): 116–34.

Brauns, Claus-Dieter, and Lorenz G. Löffler. *Mru: Hill People on the Border of Bangladesh*. Basel; Boston; Berlin: Birkhäuser Verlag, 1990.

Brighenti, Francesco. 'Traditional Beliefs about Weretigers among the Garos of Meghalaya (India)'. *eTropic* 16, no. 1 (2017): 96–111.

Brinckmann, Ludwig M. 'The Táng Era "Annals of Yúnnán"'. 2021. https://yunnanexplorer.com/download/nanzhao/manshu.pdf. Accessed 7 January 2022.

Brown, G. E. R. Grant. *Burma Gazetteer: Upper Chindwin District*. Vol. A. Rangoon: Government Printing, 1913.

Brown, R. Grant. 'The Tamans of the Upper Chindwin, Burma'. *Journal of the Royal Anthropological Institute of Great Britain and Ireland* 41 (July–December 1911): 305–17.

Bruce, C. A. *An Account of the Manufacture of the Black Tea, as Now Practised at Suddeya in Upper Assam, by the Chinamen Sent Thither for That Purpose*. Calcutta: G. H. Huttmann, Bengal Military Orphan Press, 1838.

Brunnschweiler, R. O. 'On the Geology of the Indoburman Ranges (Arakan Coast and Yoma, Chin Hills, Naga Hills)'. *Journal of the Geological Society of Australia* 13, no. 1 (1966): 137–94.
Bryant, Raymond L. *The Political Ecology of Forestry in Burma 1824–1994*. London: Hurst & Company, 1997.
Bryant, Raymond. 'Burma and the Politics of Teak: Dissecting a Resource Curse'. In *A History of Natural Resources in Asia*, edited by Bankoff and Boomgaard, 143–61. New York; Houndsmills: Palgrave Macmillan, 2007.
Burke, W. S. *The Indian Field Shikar Book*. Calcutta: 'The Indian Field' Office, 1908.
Burling, Robbins. 'Language, Ethnicity and Migration in North-Eastern India'. *South Asia: Journal of South Asian Studies* 30, no. 3 (2007): 391–404.
———. *The Language of the Modhupur Mandi (Garo), Volume III: Glossary*. Morganville, NJ: Promilla and Co. Publishers, 2003.
Burma Frontier Areas Committee of Enquiry 1947. *Report Submitted to His Majesty's Government in the United Kingdom and to the Government of Burma*. London: His Majesty's Stationery Office, 1947.
Büscher, Bram, and Robert Fletcher. 'Towards Convivial Conservation'. *Conservation and Society* 17, no. 3 (2019): 283–96.
[Butler, John]. *Sketch of Assam with Some Account of the Hill Tribes*. London: Smith, Elder & Co., 1847.
Butler, John. *Travels and Adventures in the Province of Assam, during a Residence of Fourteen Years*. London: Smith, Elder and Co., 1854.
C., W. [William Cracroft]. 'Smelting of Iron in the Kasya Hills'. *Journal of the Asiatic Society of Bengal* 1, no. 4 (1832): 150–1.
Cairns, Malcolm. 'The Alder Managers: The Cultural Ecology of a Village in Nagaland, N. E. India'. PhD thesis, Australian National University, 2007.
Cannon, Paul F., Nigel L. Hywel-Jones, Norbert Maczey, Lungten Norbu, Tshitila, Tashi Samdup and Phurba Lhendup. 'Steps Towards Sustainable Harvest of *Ophiocordyceps sinensis* in Bhutan'. *Biodiversity Conservation* 18 (February 2009): 2263–81.
Cao, Huiming, Mingfang Tang, Hongbing Deng and Rencai Dong. 'Analysis of Management Effectiveness of Natural Reserves in Yunnan Province, China'. *International Journal of Sustainable Development and World Ecology* 21, no. 1 (2014): 77–84.
Carey, Bertram S., and H. N. Tuck. *The Chin Hills: A History of the People, Our Dealings with Them, Their Customs and Manners, and a Gazetteer of Their Country*. 2 vols. Rangoon: Government Printing, 1896.
Carey, William, and others. *A Garo Jungle Book, or The Mission to the Garos of Assam*. Philadelphia: The Judson Press, 1919.

Carter, Alison Kyra, Barbie Campbell Cole, Quentin Lemasson and Willemijn van Noord. 'Tracing the Trade of Heirloom Beads across Zomia: A Preliminary Analysis of Beads from the Upland Regions of Northeast India and Mainland Southeast Asia'. In *The Archaeology of Portable Art: Southeast Asian, Pacific, and Australian Perspectives*, edited by Michelle C. Langley, Mirani Litster, Duncan Wright and Sally K. May, 49–67. New York; London: Routledge, 2018.

Carter, Neil H., José Vicente López-Bao, Jeremy T. Bruskotter, Meredith Gore, Guillaume Chapron, Arlyne Johnson et al. 'A Conceptual Framework for Understanding Illegal Killing of Large Carnivores'. *Ambio* 46, no. 3 (2017): 251–64.

Carter, T. Donald. 'The Mammals of the Vernay-Hopwood Chindwin Expedition, Northern Burma'. *Bulletin of the American Museum of Natural History* 82, no. 4 (1943): 95–114.

Cederlöf, Gunnel. 'Fixed Boundaries, Fluid Landscapes: British Expansion into Northern East Bengal in the 1820s'. *Indian Economic and Social History Review* 46, no. 4 (2009): 513–40.

———. 'Tracking Routes: Imperial Competition in the Late 19th Century Burma–China Borderlands'. In *Flows and Frictions in Trans-Himalayan Spaces*, edited by Gunnel Cederlöf and Willem van Schendel, 77–103. Amsterdam: Amsterdam University Press, 2022.

Celermajer, Danielle, David Schlosberg, Lauren Rickards, Makere Stewart-Harawira, Mathias Thaler, Petra Tschakert, Blanche Verlie and Christine Winter. 'Multispecies Justice: Theories, Challenges, and a Research Agenda for Environmental Politics'. *Environmental Politics* 30, no. 1 (2021): 119–40.

Chakma, Kabita. 'The Androgynous House: The Symbolism of Chakma Domestic Architecture'. *Architectural Theory Review* 6, no. 2 (2001): 12–27.

Chakma, Manjulika, and Niaz Zaman. *Strong Backs Magic Fingers: Traditions of Backstrap Weaving in Bangladesh*. Dhaka: Nymphea Publication, 2010.

Chakma, Shyamal Bikash. 'Conservation Refugees: A Methodology of Tribal Marginalization'. In *The Problematics of Tribal Integration: Voices from India's Alternative Centers*, edited by Bodhi S. R. and Bipin Jojo, 162–75. Hyderabad: The Shared Mirror, 2019.

Chakrabarty, Dipesh. 'The Climate of History: Four Theses'. *Critical Enquiry* 35, no. 2 (2009): 197–222.

Chakraborty, Anup Shekhar. 'Identity and Virtual Spaces among the Zo hnahthlak: Emergent Zo Cyberpolitics'. In *The Virtual Transformation of the Public Sphere: Knowledge, Politics, Identity*, edited by Gaurav Desai, 169–93. New Delhi; London: Routledge, 2013.

Chakraborty, Debarati, and Avik Ray. 'Population Genetics Analyses of North-East Indian Indigenous Rice Landraces Revealed Divergent History and Alternate

Origin of Aroma in *Aus* Group'. *Plant Genetic Resources: Characterization and Utilization* 17, no. 5 (2019): 437–47.

Chakraborty, Kasturi, S. Sudhakar, K. K. Sarma, P. L. N. Raju and Ashesh K. Das. 'Recognizing the Rapid Expansion of Rubber Plantation: A Threat to Native Forest in Parts of Northeast India'. *Current Science* 114, no. 1 (2018): 207–13.

Chakraborty, Raja, Biplab De, N. Devanna and Saikat Sen. 'North-East India an Ethnic Storehouse of Unexplored Medicinal Plants'. *Journal of Natural Product and Plant Resources* 2, no. 1 (2012): 143–52.

Chakraborty, Souraditya. 'Human–Animal Conflicts in Northern West Bengal: Losses on Both Sides'. *International Journal of Pure and Applied Bioscience* 3, no. 3 (2015): 35–44.

Chakravarti, Ranabir. 'Early Medieval Bengal and the Trade in Horses: A Note'. *Journal of the Economic and Social History of the Orient* 42, no. 2 (1999): 194–211.

Champion, Matthew S. 'A Fuller History of Temporalities'. *Past and Present* 243, no. 1 (2019): 255–66.

———. 'The History of Temporalities: Introduction'. *Past and Present* 243, no. 1 (2019): 247–54.

Chandrasekar, Adimoolam, Satish Kumar, Jwalapuram Sreenath, Bishwa Nath Sarkar, Bhaskar Pralhad Urade, Sujit Mallick et al. 'Updating Phylogeny of Mitochondrial DNA Macrohaplogroup M in India: Dispersal of Modern Human in South Asian Corridor'. *PLoS ONE* 4, no. 10 (2009): e7447, 1–13.

Chang, Te-Tzu. 'Rice'. In *The Cambridge World History of Food*, edited by Kenneth F. Kiple and Kriemhild C. Ornelas, 2:132–49. Cambridge: Cambridge University Press, 2000.

Chang, Wen-Chin. 'Guanxi and Regulation in Networks: The Yunnanese Jade Trade between Burma and Thailand, 1962–88'. *Journal of Southeast Asian Studies* 35, no. 3 (2004): 479–501.

Chapman, Hazel, Mike Bickle, San Hla Thaw and Hrin Nei Thiam. 'Chemical Fluxes from Time Series Sampling of the Irrawaddy and Salween Rivers, Myanmar'. *Chemical Geology* 401 (February 2015): 15–27.

Chapman, Tyler. 'Chin Hope for Emigrees' Return'. *Radio Free Asia*, 14 June 2013. https://www.rfa.org/english/commentaries/return-06142013110751.html. Accessed 7 January 2022.

Charney, Michael. 'Demographic Growth, Agricultural Expansion, and Livestock in the Lower Chindwin in the Eighteenth and Nineteenth Centuries'. In *A History of Natural Resources in Asia*, edited by Bankoff and Boomgaard, 227–44. New York; Houndsmills: Palgrave Macmillan, 2007.

———. 'Literary Culture on the Burma–Manipur Frontier in the Eighteenth and Nineteenth Centuries'. *Medieval History Journal* 14, no. 2 (2011): 159–81.

Chartier, Laura, Alexandra Zimmermann and Richard J. Ladle. 'Habitat Loss and Human–Elephant Conflict in Assam, India: Does a Critical Threshold Exist?' *Oryx* 45, no. 4 (2011): 528–33.

Chatterji, Suniti Kumar. *Kirāta-Jana-Kṛti: The Indo-Mongoloids; Their Contribution to the History and Culture of India*. Calcutta: The Asiatic Society, 1951.

Chaudhry, Shivaji, Gopi Govindhan Veeraswahumami, Kripaljyoti Mazumdar and Prasanna Kumar Samal. 'Conflict Identification and Prioritization in Proposed Tsangyang Gyatso Biosphere Reserve, Eastern Himalaya, India'. *Journal of the Bombay Natural History Society* 107, no. 3 (2010): 189–97.

Chaudhuri, Sarit K. 'Guardian Spirits, Omens and Meat for the Clans: The Place of Animals among the Apatanis of Arunachal Pradesh'. *Religions of South Asia* 7 (2013): 126–40.

———. 'The Institutionalization of Tribal Religion: Recasting the Donyi-Polo Movement in Arunachal Pradesh'. *Asian Ethnology* 72, no. 2 (2013): 259–77.

Chauhan, Parth R. 'General Observations on the Northeast Indian Zone and Its Implications for Paleolithic Studies'. In *50 Years after Daojali-Hading*, edited by Jamir and Hazarika, 29–36. New Delhi: Research India Press, 2014.

Chen, Wen-Hong, Xiao-Hua Jin and Yu-Min Shui. 'Rediscovery and Amended Descriptions of *Begonia kingdon-wardii* (Begoniaceae) from North Myanmar'. *PhytoKeys* 94 (January 2018): 59–64.

Chen, Xiao-Yong, Tao Qin and Zhi-Ying Chen. '*Oreoglanis hponkanensis*, a New Sisorid Catfish from North Myanmar (Actinopterygii, Sisoridae)'. *ZooKeys* 646 (January 2017): 95–108.

Chhibber, H. L. *The Mineral Resources of Burma*. London: Macmillan & Co., 1934.

Childs, James E., John S. Mackenzie and Jürgen A. Richt (eds.). *Wildlife and Emerging Zoonotic Diseases: The Biology, Circumstances and Consequences of Cross-Species Transmission*. Berlin; Heidelberg; New York: Springer, 2007.

Chinlampianga, M., Ranjay K. Singh and Amritesh C. Shukla. 'Ethnozoological Diversity of Northeast India: Empirical Learning with Traditional Knowledge Holders of Mizoram and Arunachal Pradesh'. *Indian Journal of Traditional Knowledge* 12, no. 1 (2013): 18–30.

Choi, Jae Young, Adrian E. Platts, Dorian Q. Fuller, Yue-Ie Hsing, Rod A. Wing and Michael D. Purugganan. 'The Rice Paradox: Multiple Origins but Single Domestication in Asian Rice'. *Molecular Biology and Evolution* 34, no. 4 (2017): 969–79.

Chomicki, Guillaume, Gudrun Kadereit, Susanne S. Renner and E. Toby Kiers. 'Tradeoffs in the Evolution of Plant Farming by Ants'. *PNAS* 117, no. 5 (2020): 2535–43.

Choudhury, Anwaruddin. 'Human–Elephant Conflicts in Northeast India'. *Human Dimensions of Wildlife* 9, no. 4 (2004): 261–70.

———. 'Impact of Border Fence along India–Bangladesh Border on Elephant Movement'. *Gajah* 26 (2007): 27–30.

———. 'The Distribution, Status and Conservation of Hoolock Gibbon, *Hoolock hoolock*, in Karbi Anglong District, Assam, Northeast India'. *Primate Conservation* 24, no. 1 (2009): 117–26.

———. 'The Status of Endangered Species in Northeast India'. *Journal of the Bombay Natural History Society* 103, nos. 2/3 (2006): 157–67.

Choudhury, Baharul, Mohamed Latif Khan and Selvadurai Dayanandan. 'Genetic Structure and Diversity of Indigenous Rice (*Oryza sativa*) Varieties in the Eastern Himalayan Region of Northeast India'. *SpringerPlus* 2, no. 228 (2013): 1–10.

Choudhury, K. 'Rediscovery of Two Rare Butterflies *Papilio elephenor* Doubleday, 1845 and *Shijimia moorei* Leech, 1889 from Proposed Ripu-Chirang Wildlife Sanctuary, Assam, India'. *Journal of Threatened Taxa* 2, no. 4 (2010): 831–4.

Choudhury, Nazrana Begam, Muhammed Khairujjaman Mazumder, Himabrata Chakravarty, Amir Sohail Choudhury, Freeman Boro and Imrana Begam Choudhury. 'The Endangered Ganges River Dolphin Heads towards Local Extinction in the Barak River System of Assam, India: A Plea for Conservation'. *Mammalian Biology* 95 (March 2019): 102–11.

Chouvy, Pierre-Arnaud. 'Illegal Opium Production in the Mishmi Hills of Arunachal Pradesh, India'. *European Bulletin of Himalayan Research* 45 (Autumn–Winter 2014): 9–32.

Chowdhury, Mohammad Shaheed Hossain (ed.). *Forest Conservation in Protected Areas of Bangladesh Policy and Community Development Perspectives*. Cham; Heidelberg; New York; Dordrecht; London: Springer International Publishing Switzerland, 2014.

Chowdhury, Mohammad Shaheed Hossain, Shigeyuki Izumiyama, Nahid Nazia, Nur Muhammed and Masao Koike. 'Dietetic Use of Wild Animals and Traditional Cultural Beliefs in the Mro Community of Bangladesh: An Insight into Biodiversity Conservation'. *Biodiversity* 15, no. 1 (2014): 23–38.

Chowdhury, Pritom, Siraj Ahmed Khan, Prafulla Dutta, Rashmee Topno and Jagadish Mahanta. 'Characterization of West Nile Virus (WNV) Isolates from Assam, India: Insights into the Circulating WNV in Northeastern India'. *Comparative Immunology, Microbiology and Infectious Diseases* 37 (2014): 39–47.

Chowdhury, Shaheed, and Masao Koike. 'An Overview on the Protected Area System for Forest Conservation in Bangladesh'. *Journal of Forestry Research* 21, no. 1 (2010): 111–18.

Ciin, Ma Zam San. 'A Study of Anthropological Perspectives on Kinship Systems Practised by Chinpong (*Uppu*) National Living in Kanpetlet Township, Chin State'. Master's thesis, University of Yangon, 2012.

Civáň, Peter, Sajid Ali, Riza Batista-Navarro, Konstantina Drosou, Chioma Ihejieto, Debarati Chakraborty, Avik Ra, Pierre Gladieux and Terence A. Brown. 'Origin of the Aromatic Group of Cultivated Rice (*Oryza sativa* L.) Traced to the Indian Subcontinent'. *Genome Biology and Evolution* 11, no. 3 (2019): 832–43.

Claquin Chambugong, Timour. 'Sociocultural Conceptions: Representations and Practices among the Garos'. *Arts and Cultures*, no. 21 (2020), 194–205.

Clarence-Smith, William G. 'Breeding and Power in Southeast Asia: Horses, Mules and Donkeys in the Longue Durée'. In *Environment, Trade and Society in Southeast Asia: A Longue Durée Perspective*, edited by David Henley and Henk Schulte Nordholt, 32–45. Leiden; Boston: Brill, 2015.

Clayton, Bronwyn Anne. 'Nipah Virus: Transmission of a Zoonotic Paramyxovirus'. *Current Opinion in Virology* 22 (January 2017): 97–104.

Cobo, José M., Joaquim Fort and Neus Isern. 'The Spread of Domesticated Rice in Eastern and Southeastern Asia Was Mainly Demic'. *Journal of Archaeological Science* 101 (2019): 123–30 and supplementary information.

Coderey, Céline. 'Myanmar Traditional Medicine: The Making of a National Heritage'. *Modern Asian Studies* 55, no. 2 (2021): 514–51.

Cohen, Mark N. 'History, Diet, and Hunter-Gatherers'. In *The Cambridge World History of Food*, edited by K. Kiple and K. Ornelas, 63–71. Cambridge: Cambridge University Press, 2000.

Cole, Barbie Campbell. 'Heirloom Beads of the Kachin and Naga'. *Beads* 20 (2008): 3–25.

Colebrooke, H. T. 'Description of a Species of Ox, Named Gayál'. *Asiatick Researches* 8 (1808): 511–27.

Coleman, James M. 'Brahmaputra River: Channel Processes and Sedimentation'. *Sedimentary Geology* 3, nos. 2/3 (1969): 129–239.

Cons, Jason. 'Seepage'. Theorizing the Contemporary, *Fieldsights*, October 2017. https://culanth.org/fieldsights/seepage. Accessed 8 January 2022.

Cooch Behar, Maharajah of. *Thirty-Seven Years of Big Game Shooting in Cooch Behar, the Duars, and Assam: A Rough Diary*. London: Rowland Ward; Bombay: Bennett, Coleman & Co., 1908.

Cordaux, Richard, Gunter Weiss, Nilmani Saha and Mark Stoneking. 'The Northeast Indian Passageway: A Barrier or Corridor for Human Migrations?' *Molecular Biology and Evolution* 21, no. 8 (2004): 1525–33.

Cremin, Aedeen. 'Seeing Dian through Barbarian Eyes'. *Bulletin of the Indo-Pacific Prehistory Association* 30 (2010): 114–21.

Crémin, Émilie. 'Between Land Erosion and Land Eviction: Emerging Social Movements in the Mishing Fringe Villages of the Kaziranga National Park (Assam, North East India)'. *Environment and Development: Emerging Issues and Debates* (2011): 168–84.

Crosby, Alfred W. *The Columbian Exchange: Biological and Cultural Consequences of 1492*. Westport, CN: Greenwood Press, 1972.

Cruickshank, R. D., and Ko Ko. 'Geology of an Amber Locality in the Hukawng Valley, Northern Myanmar'. *Journal of Asian Earth Sciences* 21 (2003): 441–55.

Curray, Joseph R. 'The Bengal Depositional System: From Rift to Orogeny'. *Marine Geology* 352 (February 2014): 59–69.

Cusack, Jeremy J., Tom Bradfer-Lawrence, Zachary Baynham-Herd, Sofia Castelló y Tickell, Isla Duporge, Håvard Hegre et al. 'Measuring the Intensity of Conflicts in Conservation'. *Conservation Letters* 14, no. e12783 (2021): 1–11.

d'Alpoim Guedes, Jade, and Ethan E. Butler. 'Modeling Constraints on the Spread of Agriculture to Southwest China with Thermal Niche Models'. *Quaternary International* 349 (August 2014): 29–41.

Dal Martello, Rita, Rui Min, Chris Stevens, Charles Higham, Thomas Higham, Ling Qin and Dorian Q. Fuller. 'Early Agriculture at the Crossroads of China and Southeast Asia: Archaeobotanical Evidence and Radiocarbon Dates from Baiyangcun, Yunnan'. *Journal of Archaeological Science: Reports* 20 (June 2018): 711–21.

Dala. 'Sakhua'. *Mizo leh Vai*, February 1905, 13–14.

Dale, Stephen F. 'Silk Road, Cotton Road or … Indo-Chinese Trade in Pre-European Times'. *Modern Asian Studies* 43, no. 1 (2009): 79–88.

Dalton, Edward Tuite. *Descriptive Ethnology of Bengal*. Calcutta: Superintendent of Government Printing, 1872.

Daniels, Christian. 'Blocking the Path of Feral Pigs with Rotten Bamboo: The Role of Upland Peoples in the Crisis of a Tay Polity in Southwest Yunnan, 1792 to 1836'. *Southeast Asian Studies* 2, no. 1 (2013): 133–40.

———. 'Environmental Degradation, Forest Protection and Ethno-History in Yunnan (III): Nature Reserves and Swidden Cultivators'. *Chinese Environmental History Newsletter* 2, no. 2 (1995): 11–13.

———. 'Introduction: Upland Peoples in the Making of History in Northern Continental Southeast Asia'. *Southeast Asian Studies* 2, no. 1 (2013): 5–27.

———. 'Nanzhao as a Southeast Asian Kingdom, c. 738–902'. *Journal of Southeast Asian Studies* 52, no. 2 (2021): 188–213.

Daniels, Christian, and Jianxiong Ma (eds.). *The Transformation of Yunnan in Ming China: From the Dali Kingdom to Imperial Province*. London; New York: Routledge, 2020.

Das, Debojyoti. 'From Millet to Rice: The Politics of the New Faith and Time Discipline among Borderland Communities in Eastern Nagaland'. *Asian Ethnology* 79, no. 2 (2020): 377–94.

Das, Gitishree, Jayanta Kumar Patra, Sameer K. Singdevsachan, Sushanto Gouda and Han-Seung Shin. 'Diversity of Traditional and Fermented Foods of the Seven Sister States of India and Their Nutritional and Nutraceutical Potential: A Review'. *Frontiers in Life Science* 9, no. 4 (2016): 292–312.

Das, G. P. *Insect and Mite Pests Diversity in the Important Vegetable Crops Ecosystems in Bangladesh*. Dhaka: IUCN Bangladesh Country Office, 2004.

Das, Khirod Sankar, Sudipta Choudhury and K. Chanreila L. Nonglait. 'Zootherapy among the Ethnic Groups of North Eastern Region of India: A Critical Review'. *Journal of Critical Reviews* 7, no. 4 (2017): 1–9.

Das, Paromita. 'Terracotta Sculptures of Ambari in Guwahati, Assam'. In *50 Years after Daojali-Hading*, edited by Jamir and Hazarika, 422–7. New Delhi: Research India Press, 2014.

Das, Sudipta K. 'Dietary Use of Algae among Tribal of North-East India: Special Reference to the Monpa Tribe of Arunachal Pradesh'. *Indian Journal of Traditional Knowledge* 15, no. 3 (2016): 509–13.

Dasgupta, Shreya, and Asish K. Ghosh. 'Elephant–Railway Conflict in a Biodiversity Hotspot: Determinants and Perceptions of the Conflict in Northern West Bengal, India'. *Human Dimensions of Wildlife* 20, no. 1 (2015): 81–94.

Datta, Aparajita, Japang Pansa, M. D. Madhusudan and Charudutt Mishra. 'Discovery of the Leaf Deer *Muntiacus putaoensis* in Arunachal Pradesh: An Addition to the Large Mammals of India'. *Current Science* 84, no. 3 (2003): 454–8.

Datta, Chandan. 'Selling of Tokay Gecko (*Gecko gecko*): A Money Making Business in Forest-Fringe Area of Jalpaiguri District, West Bengal, India'. *Research Journal of Humanities and Social Sciences* 9, no. 4 (2018): 979–83.

Datta-Roy, Anirban, Nimesh Ved and A. Christy Williams. 'Participatory Elephant Monitoring in South Garo Hills: Efficacy and Utility in a Human–Animal Conflict Scenario'. *Tropical Ecology* 50, no. 1 (2009): 163–71.

D'Cruze, Neil, and David W. Macdonald. 'Clouded in Mystery: The Global Trade in Clouded Leopards'. *Biodiversity Conservation* 24 (October 2015): 3505–26.

D'Cruze, Neil, Bhagat Singh, Aniruddha Mookerjee, Lauren A. Harrington and David W. Macdonald. 'A Socio-economic Survey of Pangolin Hunting in Assam, Northeast India'. *Nature Conservation* 30 (December 2018): 83–105.

De, Biplab, Trijash Debbarma, Saikat Sen and Raja Chakraborty. 'Tribal Life in the Environment and Biodiversity of Tripura, India'. *Current World Environment* 5, no. 1 (2010): 59–66.

De, Lakshman Chandra, Promila Pathak, A. N. Rao and P. K. Rajeevan. *Commercial Orchids*. Warsaw; Berlin: De Gruyter Open, 2014.

De Maaker, Erik. 'Aloof but Not Abandoned: Relationality and the Exploitation of the Environment in the Garo hills of India'. In *Environmental Humanities in the New Himalayas*, edited by Smyer Yü and De Maaker, 135–51. London; New York: Routledge, 2021.

———. 'Have the Mitdes Gone Silent? Conversion, Rhetoric, and the Continuing Importance of the Lower Deities in Northeast India'. In *Asia in the Making of Christianity: Conversion, Agency, and Indigeneity, 1600s to the Present*, edited by Richard Fox Young and Jonathan A. Seitz, 135–59. Leiden: Brill, 2013.

———. 'Negotiating Life: Garo Death Rituals and the Transformation of Society'. PhD thesis, University of Leiden, 2006.

———. 'On the Nature of Indigenous Land: Ownership, Access, and Farming in Upland Northeast India'. In *Indigeneity on the Move*, edited by Gerharz, Uddin and Chakkarath, 29–48. New York; Oxford: Berghahn, 2018.

———. 'Performing the Garo Nation? Garo Wangala Dancing between Faith and Folklore'. *Asian Ethnology* 72, no. 2 (2013): 221–39.

———. 'Who Owns the Hills? Ownership, Inequality, and Communal Sharing in the Borderlands of India'. *Asian Ethnology* 79, no. 2 (2020): 357–75.

De Wet, J. M. J. 'Millets'. In *The Cambridge World History of Food*, edited by K. F. Kiple and K. C. Ornelas, 111–21. Cambridge: Cambridge University Press, 2008.

Debbarma, R. K. 'Celebrating a New "New Year" in Tripura: Space, Place and Identity Politics'. In *Northeast India*, edited by Saikia and Baishya, 201–22. Cambridge: Cambridge University Press, 2017.

DeFilipps, Robert A., and Gary A. Krupnick. 'The Medicinal Plants of Myanmar'. *PhytoKeys* 102 (June 2018): 1–341.

Delang, Claudio O., and Wing Man Li. *Ecological Succession on Fallowed Shifting Cultivation Fields: A Review of the Literature*. Dordrecht; Heidelberg; New York; London: Springer, 2013.

Dennell, Robin, and Michael D. Petraglia. 'The Dispersal of *Homo sapiens* across Southern Asia: How Early, How Often, How Complex?' *Quaternary Science Reviews* 47 (July 2012): 15–22.

Devi, M. H., P. K. Singh and M. Dutta Choudhury. 'Income Generating Plants of Keibul Lamjao National Park, Loktak Lake, Manipur and Man–Animal Conflicts'. *Pleione* 8, no. 1 (2014): 30–6.

Devi, Oinam S., Puspa Komor and Dhritiman Das. 'A Checklist of Traditional Edible Bio-resources from Ima Markets of Imphal Valley, Manipur, India'. *Journal of Threatened Taxa* 2, no. 11 (2010): 1291–6.

Devi, Potshangbam Binodini. 'Manipur Megaliths: From Menhirs of Social Status to Commemoratives'. *Journal of Neolithic Archaeology*, special issue no. 5 (2019): 107–24.

Dey, Lal Behari. *Bengal Peasant Life*. London: Macmillan and Co., 1878.

Di Fonzo, Martina M. I. 'Determining Correlates of Human–Elephant Conflict Reports within Fringe Villages of Kaziranga National Park, Assam'. Master's thesis, University of London, 2007.

Dikshit, K. N., and Manjil Hazarika. 'The Neolithic Cultures of Northeast India and Adjoining Regions: A Comparative Study'. *Journal of Indian Ocean Archaeology*, nos. 7/8 (2011–12): 98–148.

Dikshit, K. R., and Jutta K. Dikshit. *North-East India: Land, People and Economy*. Dordrecht; Heidelberg; New York; London: Springer, 2014.

Dipti, S. S., M. N. Bari and K. A. Kabir. 'Grain Quality Characteristics of Some *Beruin* Rice Varieties of Bangladesh'. *Pakistan Journal of Nutrition* 2, no. 4 (2003): 242–5.

Dokhuma, James. *Hmanlai Mizo Kalphung* [Past Mizo Traditions]. Aizawl: JD Press Publication, 1992.

Domon, Eiji, Min San Thein, Emiko Takei, Toshiki Osada and Makoto Kawase. 'A Field Study Collecting Cultivated Crops and Useful Plants in Sagaing Region of Myanmar in 2014'. *Annual Report on Exploration and Introduction of Plant Genetic Resources*, 31:343–65. Tsukuba: National Institute of Agrobiological Sciences, 2015.

Doniger, Wendy. *The Hindus: An Alternative History*. New York: Penguin Press, 2009.

Dorjee. 'Assessing the Risk of Alien Plant Invasions to the Developing World: Bhutan a Case Study', PhD thesis, University of Canberra, 2018.

Dorji, Tashi Y., Asta M. Tamang and Ronnie Vernoy. *The History of the Introduction and Adoption of Important Food Crops in Bhutan: Rice, Maize, Potato and Chili*. Thimphu: National Biodiversity Centre, Ministry of Agriculture and Forests, 2015.

Dowie, Mark. *Conservation Refugees: The Hundred-Year Conflict between Global Conservation and Native Peoples*. Cambridge, MA; London: MIT Press, 2011.

Duff-Sutherland-Dunbar, George. 'Abors and Galongs: Notes on Certain Hill Tribes of the Indo-Tibetan Border'. *Memoirs of the Asiatic Society of Bengal* 5 (August 1915): 1–113.

Dumbacher, John P., Jeremy Miller, Maureen E. Flannery and Xiaojun Yang. 'Avifauna of the Gaoligong Shan Mountains of Western China: A Hotspot of Avian Species Diversity'. In *Avifauna of the Eastern Himalayas and Southeastern Sub-Himalayan Mountains*, edited by Renner and Rappole, 30–63. Washington, DC: American Ornithologists' Union, 2011.

Dunbar, George. *Frontiers*. London: Ivor Nicholson & Watson Ltd, 1932.

Durkee, E. F., and M. J. Gerrard. 'An Integrated Oil Industry Runs in Chindwin Basin, Myanmar'. *Oil and Gas Journal* 95, no. 42 (1997): 63–6.

Dussubieux, Laure, and Thomas Oliver Pryce. 'Myanmar's Role in Iron Age Interaction Networks Linking Southeast Asia and India: Recent Glass and Copper-Base Metal Exchange Research from the *Mission Archéologique Française au Myanmar*'. *Journal of Archaeological Science: Reports* 5 (January 2016): 598–614.

Dutt, Som, Anil K. Gupta, Hai Cheng, Steven C. Clemens, Raj K. Singh and Vinod C. Tewari. 'Indian Summer Monsoon Variability in Northeastern India during the Last Two Millennia'. *Quaternary International* 571 (2021): 73–80.

Dutta, Anwesha, and Bert Suykens. 'Constellations of Power and Authority in the Political Economy of Illegal Timber Extraction in BTAD, Assam'. *Alternatives: Global, Local, Political* 42, no. 3 (2017): 146–65.

Dutta, H., H. Singha, B. K. Dutta, P. Debi and A. Das. 'Human–Wildlife Conflict in the Forest Villages of Barak Valley, Assam, India'. *Current World* Environment 10, no. 1 (2015): 245–52.

Dutta, Hemendra Nath. 'V-Shaped Columns at Kachari Monolithic Rajbari Site in Dimapur, Nagaland: Their Architectural and Social Reflections'. *Journal of Neolithic Archaeology*, special issue no. 5 (2019): 145–50.

Dutta, Prafulla, Siraj A. Khan, Sumi Chetry and Abdul M. 'Incrimination of *Aedes aegypti* for Dengue Virus Serotype–1 in Assam, Northeast India'. *Journal of Vector Borne Diseases* 55 (December 2018): 330–3.

Dwivedi, K. K. 'Possibility of New Uranium Discoveries in the Environment of Domiasiat, Meghalaya, India'. In International Atomic Energy Agency, *Recent Developments in Uranium Resources and Supply: Proceedings of a Technical Committee Meeting Held in Vienna, 24–28 May 1993*, 144–61. Vienna: IAEA, 1995.

Dzüvichü, Lipokmar, and Manjeet Baruah (eds.). *Modern Practices in North East India: History, Culture, Representation*. London; New York: Routledge, 2018.

Eaton, Richard M. *The Rise of Islam and the Bengal Frontier, 1204–1760*. Berkeley; Los Angeles; London: University of California Press, 1993.

Einzenberger, Rainer. 'Contested Frontiers: Land Enclosures and Indigenous Politics in Myanmar's Chin State'. PhD thesis, University of Vienna, 2019.

———. 'Frontier Capitalism and Politics of Dispossession in Myanmar: The Case of the Mwetaung (Gullu Mual) Nickel Mine in Chin State'. *Austrian Journal of South-East Asian Studies* 11, no. 1 (2018): 13–34.

Elwin, Verrier. *Myths of the North-East Frontier of India*. Shillong: North-East Frontier Agency, 1958.

———. *The Art of the North-East Frontier of India*. Shillong: North-East Frontier Agency, 1959.

——— (ed.). *India's North-East Frontier in the Nineteenth Century*. London: Oxford University Press, 1959.

Emmett, Robert S., and David E. Nye. *The Environmental Humanities: A Critical Introduction*. Cambridge, MA; London: MIT Press, 2017.

Endle, Sidney. *The Kacháris*. London: Macmillan and Company, 1911.

Ete, Mibi. 'Hydro-dollar Dreams: Emergent Local Politics of Large Dams and Small Communities'. In *Geographies of Difference*, edited by Vanderhelsken, Barkataki-Ruscheweyh and Karlsson, 109–27. London; New York: Routledge, 2018.

Evans, G. P. *Big-Game Shooting in Upper Burma*. London: Longmans, Green & Co., 1911.

Evans, Percy. 'The Oilfields of India and Burma'. *Journal of the Royal Society of Arts* 94, no. 4717 (1946): 369–79.

Fairhead, James, Melissa Leach and Ian Scoones. 'Green Grabbing: A New Appropriation of Nature?' *Journal of Peasant Studies* 39, no. 2 (2012): 237–61.

Faith, J. Tyler, John Rowan, Andrew Du and Paul L. Koch. 'Plio-Pleistocene Decline of African Megaherbivores: No Evidence for Ancient Hominin Impacts'. *Science* 362 (November 2018): 938–41.

Farías, Ignacio, Anders Blok and Celia Roberts. 'Actor–Network Theory as a Companion: An Inquiry into Intellectual Practices'. In *The Routledge Companion to Actor–Network Theory*, edited by Anders Blok, Ignacio Farías and Celia Roberts, xx–xxxv. London; New York: Routledge, 2020.

Faruque, Mohammad Omar, Gang Feng, Md Nurul Amin Khan, James W. Barlow, Umme Ruman Ankhi, Sheng Hu, M. Kamaruzzaman, Shaikh Bokhtear Uddin and Xuebo Hu. 'Qualitative and Quantitative Ethnobotanical Study of the Pangkhua Community in Bilaichari Upazilla, Rangamati District, Bangladesh'. *Journal of Ethnobiology and Ethnomedicine* 15, no. 8 (2019): 1–29.

Fava, Francesco, and Roberto Colombo. 'Remote Sensing-Based Assessment of the 2005–2011 Bamboo Reproductive Event in the Arakan Mountain Range and Its Relation with Wildfires'. *Remote Sensing* 9, no. 85 (2017): 1–14.

Faxon, Hilary Oliva. 'After the Rice Frontier: Producing State and Ethnic Territory in Northwest Myanmar'. *Geopolitics* (February 2021): 1–25.

Felder, Daniel, Daniel Burns and David Chang. 'Defining Microbial Terroir: The Use of Native Fungi for the Study of Traditional Fermentative Processes'. *International Journal of Gastronomy and Food Science* 1, no. 1 (2002): 64–9.

Ferrari, Fabrizio M. 'Devotion and Affliction in the Time of Cholera: Ritual Healing, Identity and Resistance among Bengali Muslims'. In *Disease, Religion and Healing in Asia: Collaborations and Collisions*, edited by Ivette Vargas-O'Bryan and Zhou Xun, 37–53. London; New York: Routledge, 2015.

Fisher, Michael H. *An Environmental History of India: From Earliest Times to the Twenty-First Century*. Cambridge: Cambridge University Press, 2018.

Fiskesjö, Magnus. 'China's Animal Neighbours'. In *The Art of Neighbouring: Making Relations Across China's Borders*, edited by Martin Saxer and Juan Zhang, 223–36. Amsterdam: Amsterdam University Press, 2017.

Fraser, David W., and Barbara G. Fraser. *Mantles of Merit: Chin Textiles from Myanmar, India and Bangladesh*. Bangkok: River Books, 2005.

Frischmann, Brett M., Alain Marciano and Giovanni Battista Ramello. 'Tragedy of the Commons after 50 Years'. *Journal of Economic Perspectives* 33, no. 4 (2019): 211–28.

Fuller, Dorian Q., Nicole Boivin, Tom Hoogervorst and Robin Allaby. 'Across the Indian Ocean: The Prehistoric Movement of Plants and Animals'. *Antiquity* 85, no. 328 (2011): 544–58.

Fuller, Dorian Q., Cristina Cobo Castillo and Charlene Murphy. 'How Rice Failed to Unify Asia: Globalization and Regionalism of Early Farming Traditions in the Monsoon World'. In *The Routledge Handbook of Globalization and Archaeology*, edited by Hodos et al., 711–29. Abingdon; New York: Routledge, 2017.

Fuller, Dorian Q., Jacob van Etten, Katie Manning, Cristina Castillo, Eleanor Kingwell-Banham, Alison Weisskopf, Ling Qin, Yo-Ichiro Sato and Robert J. Hijmans. 'The Contribution of Rice Agriculture and Livestock Pastoralism to Prehistoric Methane Levels: An Archaeological Assessment'. *The Holocene* 21, no. 5 (2011): 743–59.

Fuller, Dorian Q., and Emma L. Harvey. 'The Archaeobotany of Indian Pulses: Identification, Processing and Evidence for Cultivation'. *Environmental Archaeology* 11, no. 2 (2006): 219–46.

Fuller, Dorian Q., and Chris J. Stevens. 'Open for Competition: Domesticates, Parasitic Domesticoids and the Agricultural Niche'. *Archaeology International* 20 (2017): 110–21.

Fürer-Haimendorf, Christoph von. *The Apa Tanis and Their Neighbours: A Primitive Civilization of the Eastern Himalayas*. London: Routledge and Kegan Paul, 1962.

———. *The Konyak Nagas: An Indian Frontier Tribe*. New York; London: Holt, Rinehart and Winston, 1969.

———. 'The Morung System of the Konyak Nagas, Assam'. *Journal of the Royal Anthropological Institute of Great Britain and Ireland* 68 (July–December 1938): 349–78.

———. *The Naked Nagas: Head-Hunters of Assam in Peace and War*. London: Thacker, Spink and Co., 1946.

Gachui, Rangya. 'An Oinam Poumai Potter at Work: Some Implications for Ceramic Ethnoarchaeology'. In *50 Years after Daojali-Hading*, edited by Jamir and Hazarika, 218–26. New Delhi: Research India Press, 2014.

Gagliano, Monica, John C. Ryan and Patrícia Vieira (eds.). *The Language of Plants: Science, Philosophy, Literature*. Minneapolis; London: University of Minnesota Press, 2017.

Gale, Stephan W., Pankaj Kumar, Amy Hinsley, Mang Lung Cheuk, Jiangyun Gao, Hong Liu, Zhi-Long Liu and Sophie J. Williams. 'Quantifying the Trade in Wild-Collected Ornamental Orchids in South China: Diversity, Volume and Value Gradients Underscore the Primacy of Supply'. *Biological Conservation* 238, no. 108204 (2019): 1–14.

Gardner, Katy, Zahir Ahmed, Mohammad Masud Rana and Fatema Bashar. 'Field of Dreams: Imagining Development and Un-development at a Gas Field in Sylhet'. *South Asia Multidisciplinary Academic Journal* 9 (July 2014): 1–16.

Garigliano, Irene Majo. '"A Very Naughty Place!" The Attraction to the Frightening Other Reflected in Narratives about Assam'. *International Quarterly of Asian Studies* 49, nos. 3/4 (2018): 63–80.

Gee, E. P. 'The Wild Life Reserves in India: Assam'. *Journal of the Bombay Natural History Society* 49 (1950): 81–5.

Geissmann, Thomas, Ngwe Lwin, Saw Soe Aung, Thet Naing Aung, Zin Myo Aung, Tony Htin Hla, Mark Grindley and Frank Momberg. 'A New Species of Snub-Nosed Monkey, Genus *Rhinopithecus* Milne-Edwards, 1872 (Primates, Colobinae), from Northern Kachin State, Northeastern Myanmar'. *American Journal of Primatology* 73 (2011): 96–107.

Georjon, Cloé, U Aung Aung Kyaw, Daw Tin Tin Win, Daw Thu Thu Win, Baptiste Pradier, Anna Willis et al. 'Late Neolithic to Early-Mid Bronze Age Semi-Precious Stone Bead Production and Consumption at Oakaie and Nyaung'gan in Central-Northern Myanmar'. *Archaeological Research in Asia* 25, no. 100240, (2021): 1–21.

Gerharz, Eva, Nasir Uddin and Pradeep Chakkarath (eds.). *Indigeneity on the Move: Varying Manifestations of a Contested Concept*. New York; Oxford: Berghahn, 2018).

Ghosh, Manoranjan, and Somnath Ghosal. 'Historical Geography of Forestry and Forest Culture in Sub-Himalayan West Bengal, 1757–2015'. *Space and Culture, India* 6, no. 5 (2019): 215–27.

Gnecchi Ruscone, Guido Alberto. 'Unraveling the Combined Effects of Demography and Natural Selection in Shaping the Genomic Background of Southern Himalayan Populations'. PhD thesis, University of Bologna, 2018.

Gogoi, Mayuri. 'Emotional Coping among Communities Affected by Wildlife-Caused Damage in North-East India: Opportunities for Building Tolerance and Improving Conservation Outcomes'. *Oryx* 52, no. 2 (2018): 214–19.

Gohain, Swargajyoti. 'Robes, Rivers and Ruptured Spaces: Hydropower Projects in West Arunachal Pradesh'. In *Northeast India*, edited by Saikia and Baishya, 262–76. Cambridge: Cambridge University Press, 2017.

Gopinathan, Maheswaran. 'Ecology and Conservation of Endangered Hispid Hare *Caprolagus hispidus* in India'. In *Rare Animals of India*, edited by Natarajan Singaravelan, 179–203. Sharjah, UAE, Oak Park, IL, and Bussum: Bentham Science Publishers, 2013.

Goswami, Rajkamal. 'Forest Cover, Hunting and Animal Abundances across State and Community Forests of Meghalaya, India'. PhD thesis, Manipal University, 2015.

Govindrajan, Radhika. *Animal Intimacies: Interspecies Relatedness in India's Central Himalayas*. Chicago; London: University of Chicago Press. 2018.

Grange, David. 'Time, Space and Islands: Why Geographers Drive the Temporal Agenda'. *Past and Present* 243, no. 1 (2019): 299–312.

Grant, Capt. 'Mode of Extracting the Gold Dust from the Sand of the Ningthee River, on the Frontier of Manipur'. *Journal of the Asiatic Society of Bengal* 1, no. 4 (1832): 148–9.

Green, Monica H., and Lori Jones. 'The Evolution and Spread of Major Human Diseases in the Indian Ocean World'. In *Disease Dispersion and Impact in the Indian Ocean World*, edited by Gwyn Campbell and Eva-Maria Knoll, 25–57. London: Palgrave Macmillan, 2020.

Griffith, W. *Journals of Travels in Assam, Burma, Bootan, Afghanistan and the Neighbouring Countries*. 2 vols. Calcutta: Bishop's College Press, 1847.

Gros, Stéphane. 'Cultes de fertilité chez les Drung du Yunnan (Chine)'. *Moussons* 19, no. 1 (2012) : 111–36.

———. 'Nature De-naturalised: Modes of Relation with the Environment among the Drung of Northwest Yunnan (China)'. *Anthropological Forum* 27, no. 4 (2017): 321–39.

Grothmann, Kerstin. 'Migration Narratives, Official Classifications, and Local Identities: The Memba of the Hidden Land of Pachakshiri'. In *Origins and Migrations*, edited by Huber and Blackburn, 125–51. Leiden; Boston: Brill, 2012.

Guha, Nabarun. 'Illegal Trade of Exotic Animals Puts India at Risk of a Zoonotic Disease Outbreak'. *Scroll.in*, 25 April 2021. https://scroll.in/article/992890/illegal-trade-of-exotic-animals-puts-india-at-risk-of-a-zoonotic-disease-outbreak. Accessed 8 January 2022.

Guha, Ramachandra. 'The Prehistory of Community Forestry in India'. *Environmental History* 6, no. 2 (2001): 213–38.

Guite, Jangkhomang. 'Colonialism and Its Unruly? The Colonial State and Kuki Raids in Nineteenth Century Northeast India'. *Modern Asian Studies* 48, no. 5 (2014): 1188–232.

———. 'Representing Local Participation in INA–Japanese Imphal Campaign: The Case of the Kukis in Manipur, 1943–45'. *Indian Historical Review* 37, no. 2 (2010): 291–309.

Gupta, Vishal. 'Jhum Cultivation Practices of the Bangnis (Nishis) of Arunachal Pradesh'. *Indian Journal of Traditional Knowledge* 4, no. 1 (2005): 47–56.

Gurdon, P. R. T. *The Khasis*. London: Macmillan and Co., 1914.

Gurley, Emily S., Sonia T. Hegde, Kamal Hossain, Hossain M. S. Sazzad, M. Jahangir Hossain, Mahmudur Rahman et al. 'Convergence of Humans, Bats, Trees, and Culture in Nipah Virus Transmission, Bangladesh'. *Emerging Infectious* 23, no. 9 (2017): 1446–53.

Guyot-Réchard, Bérénice. *Shadow States: India, China and the Himalayas, 1910–1962*. Cambridge: Cambridge University Press, 2017.

———. 'Tangled Lands: Burma and India's Unfinished Separation, 1937–1948'. *Journal of Asian Studies*, 79 (2020): 1–23.

———. 'Tour Diaries and Itinerant Government in the Eastern Himalayas, 1909–1962'. *Historical Journal* 60, no. 4 (2017): 1023–46.

Gyeltshen, Choki, Kezang Tobgay, Nima Gyeltshen, Tshering Dorji and Sangay Dema. 'New Species Discoveries and Records in Bhutan Himalaya'. In *Biodiversität und Naturausstattung im Himalaya VI*, edited by Matthias Hartmann, Maxwell Barclay and Jörg Weipert, 59–82. Erfurt: Verein der Freunde und Förderer des Naturkundemuseums Erfurt e.V., 2018.

Hamilton, Francis. *An Account of Assam with Some Notices Concerning the Neighbouring Territories (1807–14)*. Edited by S. K. Bhuyan. Gauhati: Government of Assam, 1940.

Hamlin, Christopher. *Cholera: The Biography*. Oxford: Oxford University Press, 2009.

Hanson, O. *The Kachins, Their Customs and Traditions*. Rangoon: American Baptist Mission Press, 1913.

Hanss, Stefan. 'The Fetish of Accuracy: Perspectives on Early Modern Time(s)'. *Past and Present* 243, no. 1 (2019): 267–84.

Haokip, D. L. 'The Petroglyphs of Indo-Myanmar Frontier'. *Ancient Asia* 12, no. 6 (2021): 1–18.

Haokip, Lalsanglen. 'Salt Land and State Monopoly in Manipur, Circa 1890–1990'. *Indian Historical Review* 46, no. 2 (2020): 247–62.

Haokip, Thongkholal. 'Escape Agriculture, Foraging Culture: The Subsistence Economy of the Kukis during the Anglo-Kuki War'. In *Against the Empire*, edited by Kipgen and Haokip, 118–36. Abingdon; New York: Routledge, 2021.

Haokip, Seilen. 'Identity, Conflict and Nationalism: The Naga and Kuki Peoples of Northeast India and Northwest Burma (Myanmar)'. PhD thesis, University of Liverpool, 2001.

Haraway, Donna Jeanne. *When Species Meet*. Minneapolis: University of Minnesota Press, 2008.

Harder, Hans. *Sufism and Saint Veneration in Contemporary Bangladesh: The Maijbhandaris of Chittagong*. London; New York: Routledge, 2011.

Hardiman, David, and Projit Bihari Mukharji (eds.). *Medical Marginality in South Asia: Situating Subaltern Therapeutics*. London; New York: Routledge, 2012.

Harris, Oliver J. T., and Craig Cipolla. 'Multispecies Archaeology: People, Plants and Animals'. In *Archaeological Theory in the New Millennium: Introducing Current Perspectives*, 152–70. Abingdon; New York: Routledge, 2017.

Harriss-White, Barbara, Deepak K. Mishra and Vandana Upadhyay. 'Institutional Diversity and Capitalist Transition: The Political Economy of Agrarian Change in Arunachal Pradesh, India'. *Journal of Agrarian Change* 9, no. 4 (2009): 512–47.

Hasinoff, Erin L. *Confluences: An American Expedition to Northern Burma, 1935*. New York, NY: Bard Graduate Center, 2013.

Hays, Warren. 'Small Indian Mongoose'. In *Encyclopedia of Biological Invasions*, edited by Simberloff and Rejmánek, 631–4. Berkeley; Los Angeles; London: University of California Press, 2011.

Hazarika, Arup Kumar, and Unmilan Kalita. 'Conservation and Livelihood Conflict of Kaziranga National Park: A World Heritage Site of Assam, India'. *Space and Culture, India* 7, no. 3 (2019): 224–32.

Hazarika, Manjil. 'Archaeological Research in North-East India: A Critical Review'. *Journal of Historical Research* 16 (2008): 1–14.

———. 'Cord-Impressed Pottery in Neolithic-Chalcolithic Context of Eastern India'. In *Neolithic-Chalcolithic Cultures of Eastern India*, edited by K. N. Dikshit, 78–110. New Delhi: Indian Archaeological Society, 2013.

———. 'Lithic Industries with Palaeolithic Elements in Northeast India'. *Quaternary International* 269 (August 2012): 48–58.

———. *Prehistory and Archaeology of Northeast India: Multidisciplinary Investigation in an Archaeological Terra Incognita*. New Delhi: Oxford University Press, 2017.

———. 'Understanding the Process of Plant and Animal Domestication in Northeast India: A Hypothetical Approach'. *Asian Agri-History* 10, no. 3 (2006): 203–12.

———. 'Neolithic Pottery of Eastern Himalaya and Northeast India'. In *Development of Neolithic Cultures and Diversity of Pottery*, 3:79–107. Seoul: Amsadong Site Research Series, 2019.

Hazarika, Manjil, Raktim Patar, Y. S. Sanathana, Jayanta Roy and Jutimala Misra. 'The *Raj Sabha* at Silchang: Dolmens as Administrative Seats of the Ancient Khola Kingdom in Assam, India'. *Journal of Indo-Pacific Archaeology* 44 (2020): 351–75.

Hazarika, Manjil, N. R. Ramesh, B. C. Poddar, Salim Javed, Y. S. Sanathana and Hemant Dalavi. 'Geo-archaeological Explorations in Tripura (2018–2019): A Report'. *Man and Environment* 45, no. 1 (2020): 18–38.

He, Keyang, Houyuan Lu, Jianping Zhang, Can Wang and Xiujia Huan. 'Prehistoric Evolution of the Dualistic Structure Mixed Rice and Millet Farming in China'. *The Holocene* 27, no. 12 (2017): 1885–98.

Head, W. R. *Hand Book on the Haka Chin Customs*. Rangoon: Government Printing, 1917.

Heesterman, J. C. *The Inner Conflict of Tradition: Essays in Indian Ritual, Kinship, and Society*. Chicago: University of Chicago Press, 1985.

Heise, Ursula K., Jon Christensen and Michelle Niemann. (eds.). *The Routledge Companion to the Environmental Humanities*. London; New York: Routledge, 2017.

Heneise, Michael. 'The Naga Tiger-Man and the Modern Assemblage of a Myth'. In *Anthropology and Cryptozoology*, edited by Samatha Hurn, 91–106. Abingdon; New York: Routledge, 2016.

Hill, Martin, Julie Coetzee, Mic Julien and Ted Center. 'Water Hyacinth'. In *Encyclopedia of Biological Invasions*, edited by Simberloff and Rejmánek, 689–92. Berkeley; Los Angeles; London: University of California Press, 2011.

Hiremath, Ankila J., and Bharath Sundaram. 'Invasive Plant Species in Indian Protected Areas: Conserving Biodiversity in Cultural Landscapes'. In *Plant Invasions in Protected Areas: Patterns, Problems and Challenges*, edited by Llewellyn C. Foxcroft, Petr Pyšek, David M. Richardson and Piero Genovesi, 241–66. Dordrecht: Springer Science and Business Media, 2013.

Hlawndo, Zaichhawna. 'A Study of the Cultural Factors in the Foreign Missions Thinking of the Mizoram Presbyterian Church'. PhD thesis, University of Birmingham, 2011.

Hmingthanzuali, and Rekha Pande. 'Women's Indigenous Knowledge and Relationship with Forests in Mizoram'. *Asian Agri-History* 13, no. 2 (2009): 129–46.

Hodgson, B. H. *Essay the First; On the Kocch, Bódo and Dhimál Tribes, in Three Parts*. Calcutta: Baptist Mission Press, 1847.

Hodos, Tamar, Alexander Geurds, Paul Lane, Ian Lilley, Martin Pitts, Gideon Shelach, Miriam Stark and Miguel John Versluys (eds.). *The Routledge Handbook of Globalization and Archaeology*. Abingdon; New York: Routledge, 2017.

Hodson, T. C. *The Meitheis*. London: David Nutt, 1908.

———. *The Nāga Tribes of Manipur*. London: Macmillan and Company, 1911.

Holmes, Katie, Andrea Gaynor and Ruth Morgan. 'Doing Environmental History in Urgent Times'. *History Australia* 17, no. 2 (2020): 230–51.

Hoogervorst, Tom. 'Tracing Maritime Connections between Island Southeast Asia and the Indian Ocean World'. In *The Routledge Handbook of Globalization and Archaeology*, edited by Hodos et al., 751–67. Abingdon; New York: Routledge, 2017.

Hooker, Joseph Dalton. *Himalayan Journals, or Notes of a Naturalist....* 2 vols. London: John Murray, 1854.

Hopster, Jeroen. 'The Speciesism Debate: Intuition, Method, and Empirical Advances'. *Animals* 9, no. 1054 (December 2019): 1–15.

Hoque, Seema Pawankar. 'Faunal Remains from the Peats at Baghia-Chanda Beels of Gopalganj and Khulna Districts of Bangladesh'. *Man and Environment* 44, no. 2 (2019): 58–66.

Horam, Thingminao. 'Weaving Resistance and Identity: Politics of Contemporary Textile Practice of the Tangkhuls'. In *Materiality and Visuality in North East India*, edited by Nongbri and Bhargava, 201–13. Singapore: Springer Nature, 2021.

Horwich, Robert H., Rajen Islari, Arnab Bose, Bablu Dey, Mahesh Moshahary, Nirmal Kanti Dey, Raju Das and Jonathan Lyon. 'Community Protection of the Manas Biosphere Reserve in Assam, India, and the Endangered Golden Langur *Trachypithecus geei*'. *Oryx* 44, no. 2 (2010): 252–60.

Hosen, Md. Iqbal, and Tai-Hui Li. '*Phylloporus gajari*, a New Species of the Family Boletaceae from Bangladesh'. *Mycoscience* 56, no. 6 (2015): 584–9.

Hoskins, Janet. *The Play of Time: Kodi Perspectives on Calendars, History, and Exchange*. Berkeley: University of California Press, 1993.

Hossain, Md. Ismail, Fatema Hoque Shikha, Qamruzzaman Howlader and Bijoy Kumar Das. 'Production Procedure and Marketing of Ethnic Fermented Product *Nga-pi* in South-Eastern Region of Bangladesh'. *Bangladesh Journal of Fisheries* 32, no. 1 (2020): 115–24.

Hossen, Amir. *Human–Elephant Conflict in Bangladesh: Causes and Intensity of Fatalities*. Trondheim: Department of Biology, Norwegian University of Science and Technology, 2013.

Howlader, Mohammad Sajid Ali, Abhilash Nair, Sujith V. Gopalan and Juha Merilä. 'A New Species of Microhyla (Anura: Microhylidae) from Nilphamari, Bangladesh'. *PLoS ONE* 10, no. 3 (2015): e0119825.

Htin, Kyaw Minn. 'Where Maṇḍalas Overlap: Histories, Identities and Fates of the People from Arakan and South-Eastern Bangladesh'. PhD thesis, National University of Singapore, 2017.

Htwe, Ma Thant Sin. 'The Social Organization of the "Thet" Nationals of Tamangthar Village, Maungtaw Township, Rakhine State, Union of Myanmar'. Master's thesis, Yangon University, 1998–2000.

Huang, H. T. 'Hypolactasia and the Chinese Diet'. *Current Anthropology* 43, no. 5 (2002): 809–19.

Huang, Ji, and Chunlin Long. '*Coptis teeta*–based Agroforestry System and Its Conservation Potential: A Case Study from Northwest Yunnan'. *AMBIO: A Journal of the Human Environment* 36, no. 4 (2007): 343–9.

Huber, Toni. *The Cult of Pure Crystal Mountain: Popular Pilgrimage and Visionary Landscape in Southeast Tibet*. New York; Oxford: Oxford University Press, 1999.

———. *Source of Life: Revitalisation Rites and Bon Shamans in Bhutan and the Eastern Himalayas*. 2 vols. Vienna: Austrian Academy of Sciences Press, 2020.

Huber, Toni, and Stuart Blackburn (eds.). *Origins and Migrations in the Extended Eastern Himalayas*. Leiden; Boston: Brill, 2012.

Huda, Mohammed Kamrul, and Ishrath Jahan. 'Assessment of Conservation Status of the Family *Orchidaceae*: Possibly Extinct Species of Bangladesh'. *International Journal of Ecology and Environmental Sciences* 45, no. 4 (2019): 357–67.

Hudson, Bob, and Nyein Lwin. 'Earthenware from a Firing Site in Myanmar (Burma) Dates to More than 4,500 Years Ago'. *Bulletin of the Indo-Pacific Prehistory Association* 32 (2012): 19–22.

Huerta-Sánchez, Emilia, and Fergal P. Casey. 'Archaic Inheritance: Supporting High-Altitude Life in Tibet'. *Journal of Applied Physiology* 119 (August 2015): 1129–34.

Hughes, Diane Owen. 'Introduction'. In *Time: Histories and Ethnologies*, edited by Diane Owen Hughes and Thomas R. Trautmann, 1–18. Ann Arbor: University of Michigan Press, 1995.

Hughes, J. Donald. *What Is Environmental History?* Cambridge; Malden, MA: Polity Press, 2016.

Hughes, W. Gwynne. *The Hill Tracts of Arakan*. Rangoon: Government Press, 1881.

Hume, Julian P. 'A High Price to Pay: New Light on the Extinction of the Pink-Headed Duck *Rhodonessa caryophyllacea*'. *Forktail* 33 (2017): 56–63.

Hung, Hsiao-chun. 'Prosperity and Complexity without Farming: The South China Coast, c. 5000–3000 BC'. *Antiquity* 93, no. 368 (2019): 325–41.

Huntingford, G. W. B. (ed.). *The Periplus of the Erythraean Sea, by an Unknown Author*. London: Hakluyt Society, 1980.

Hutchinson, R. H. Sneyd. *An Account of the Chittagong Hill Tracts*. Calcutta: Bengal Secretariat Book Depôt, 1906.

———. *Chittagong Hill Tracts*. Allahabad: Eastern Bengal and Assam District Gazetteers, Pioneer Press, 1909.

Hutton, J. H. 'Carved Monoliths at Dimapur and an Angami Naga Ceremony'. *Journal of the Royal Anthropological Institute of Great Britain and Ireland* 52 (January–June 1922): 55–70.

———. 'Leopard Men in the Naga Hills'. *Journal of the Anthropological Institute of Great Britain and Ireland* 50 (January–June 1920): 41–51.

———. 'Some Astronomical Beliefs in Assam'. *Folklore* 36, no. 2 (1925): 113–31.

———. *The Angami Nagas with Some Notes on Neighbouring Tribes*. London: Macmillan and Co., 1921.

———. *The Ao Nagas, with Some Notes on Neighbouring Tribes*. London: Macmillan and Company, 1922.

———. *The Sema Nagas*. London: Macmillan and Company, 1921.

Imchen, Akiyala, and P. P. Joglekar. 'Traditional Fishing Practices among the Ao Nagas: A Case Study of Mangmetong Village, Nagaland'. *Heritage: Journal of Multidisciplinary Studies in Archaeology* 5 (October 2017): 380–90.

Imperial Institute. *Petroleum*. London: John Murray, 1921.

Ingold, Tim (ed.). *What Is an Animal?* London: Unwin Hyman, 1988.

IPCC. *Climate Change 2021: The Physical Science Basis. Contribution of Working Group I to the Sixth Assessment Report of the Intergovernmental Panel on Climate Change*. Cambridge: Cambridge University Press, 2021.

Iqbal, Iftekhar. 'Fighting with a Weed: Water Hyacinth and the State in Colonial Bengal, c. 1910–1947'. *Environment and History* 15, no. 1 (2009): 35–59.

———. 'From Zomia to Holon: Rivers and Transregional Flows in Mainland Southeastern Asia, 1840–1950'. *Suvannabhumi* 12, no. 2 (2020): 141–55.

———. *The Bengal Delta: Ecology, State and Social Change, 1840–1943*. London: Palgrave Macmillan, 2010.

Islam, Md. Saidul, and Md. Nazrul Islam. '"Environmentalism of the Poor": The Tipaimukh Dam, Ecological Disasters and Environmental Resistance beyond Borders'. *Bandung: Journal of the Global South* 3, no. 27 (2016): 1–16.

Islam, Md. Taufiqul, John D. Clemens and Firdausi Qadri. 'Cholera Control and Prevention in Bangladesh: An Evaluation of the Situation and Solutions'. *Journal of Infectious Diseases* 218, no. 3 (2018): S171–2.

Itan, Yuval, Bryony L. Jones, Catherine J. E. Ingram, Dallas M. Swallow and Mark G. Thomas. 'A Worldwide Correlation of Lactase Persistence Phenotype and Genotypes'. *BMC Evolutionary Biology* 36, no. 10 (2010): 1–11.

IUCN Bangladesh. *Red List of Bangladesh*. Vol. 1, *Summary*. Dhaka: International Union for Conservation of Nature, Bangladesh Country Office, 2015.

———. *Red List of Bangladesh*. Vol. 5, *Freshwater Fishes*. Dhaka: International Union for Conservation of Nature, Bangladesh Country Office, 2015.

Jack, H. S. Maclean. 'The Development of the Petroleum Industry in Assam'. *Journal of the Royal Society of Arts* 65, no. 3373 (1917): 589–96.

Jackson, Kyle C. 'Colonial Conquest and Religious Entanglement: A Mizo History from Northeast India (c. 1890–1920)'. PhD thesis, University of Warwick, 2016.

Jacobs, Julian, Alan Macfarlane, Sarah Harrison and Anita Herle. *The Nagas: Society, Culture and the Colonial Encounter*. London; New York: Thames and Hudson, 1990.

Jacquesson, François. 'The Linguistic Reconstruction of the Past: The Case of the Boro-Garo Languages'. [Translated by Seino van Breugel]. *Linguistics of the Tibeto-Burman Area* 40, no. 1 (2017): 90–122.

Jadhav, Sushrut, and Maan Barua. 'The Elephant Vanishes: Impact of Human–Elephant Conflict on People's Wellbeing'. *Health and Place* 18 (July 2012): 1356–65.

Jahan, Shahnaj Husne. 'Archaeology of Wari-Bateshwar'. *Ancient Asia* 2 (2010): 135–46.

———. 'Bhitargarh: A Ruined City of Pṛthu Rājā in Ancient Kāmrūpa'. In *50 Years after Daojali-Hading*, edited by Jamir and Hazarika, 394–409. New Delhi: Research India Press, 2014.

Jalais, Annu. *Forest of Tigers: People, Politics and Environment in the Sundarbans*. London; New York, 2010.

———. 'People and Tigers: An Anthropological Study of the Sundarbans of West Bengal, India'. PhD thesis, London School of Economics and Political Science, 2004.

Jamir, Tiatoshi. 'Piecing Together from Fragments: Re-evaluating the "Neolithic" Situation in Northeast India'. In *Neolithic-Chalcolithic Cultures of Eastern India*, edited by K. N. Dikshit, 45–68. New Delhi: Indian Archaeological Society, 2012.

Jamir, Tiatoshi, and Manjil Hazarika (eds.). *50 Years after Daojali-Hading: Emerging Perspectives in the Archaeology of Northeast India; Essays in Honour of Tarun Chandra Sharma*. New Delhi: Research India Press, 2014.

Jamir, Tiatoshi, David Tetso and Zokho Venuh. 'Recent Archaeological Investigation around the Naga Metamorphics and Ophiolite Belt of the Indo-Myanmar Border'. In *Prehistoric Research in the Subcontinent: A Reappraisal and New Directions*, edited by K. Paddayya and Bishnupriya Basak, 259–82. New Delhi: Primus Books, 2017.

Jamir, Tiatoshi, and Ditamulü Vasa. 'Archaeological Evidence of Beads from Naga Ancestral Sites: Implication for Regional Exchange Networks'. In *Trade and Values of Carnelian Ornaments in South Asia: Study on Change in 'Tradition' and Social System*, edited by Manabu Koiso and Hitoshi Endo, 3–12. Kobe: Kobe Yamate University, 2018.

Jamir, Watijungshi. 'Affinities of Naga Megaliths: An Ethnoarchaeological Study'. In *50 Years after Daojali-Hading*, edited by Jamir and Hazarika, 333–9. New Delhi: Research India Press, 2014.

Jamtsho, Yonten, and Om Katen. 'Livestock Depredation by Snow Leopard and Tibetan Wolf: Implications for Herders' Livelihoods in Wangchuck Centennial

National Park, Bhutan'. *Pastoralism: Research, Policy and Practice* 9, no. 1 (2019): 1–10.

Jamtsho, Yonten, and Sangay Wangchuk. 'Assessing Patterns of Human–Asiatic Black Bear Interaction in and around Wangchuck Centennial National Park, Bhutan'. *Global Ecology and Conservation* 8 (2016): 183–9.

Janaki, M., Rohan Pandit and Rishi K. Sharma. 'The Role of Traditional Belief Systems in Conserving Biological Diversity in the Eastern Himalaya Eco-Region of India'. *Human Dimensions of Wildlife* (June 2020): 1–18.

Janowski, Monica. 'Stones Alive!' *Bijdragen tot de Taal-, Land- en Volkenkunde* 176, no. 1 (2020): 105–46.

Janzen, Daniel H. 'Why Bamboos Wait So Long to Flower'. *Annual Review of Ecology and Systematics* 7, no. 1 (1976): 347–91.

Jayasimhan, Praveenraj, Uma Arumugam, Moulitharan Nallathambi and Heiko Bleher. '*Channa bipuli*, a New Species of Snakehead (Teleostei: Channidae) from Assam, Northeast India'. *Aqua-International Journal of Ichthyology* 24, no. 4 (2018): 153–66.

Jhala, Angma Dey. *An Endangered History: Indigeneity, Religion and Politics on the Borders of India, Burma and Bangladesh*. Delhi: Oxford University Press, 2019.

Jilangamba, Yengkhom. 'Beyond the Ethno-territorial Binary: Evidencing the Hill and Valley Peoples in Manipur'. *South Asia: Journal of South Asian Studies* 38, no. 2 (2015): 276–89.

Jiménez-Meijias, P., and H. J. Noltie. 'Carex drukyulensis (Cyperaceae), A "New" Species from the Himalayas (Bhutan)'. *Edinburgh Journal of Botany* 74, no. 1 (2017): 95–101.

Jimo, Lovitoli. 'Text, Knowledge and Representation: Reading Gender in Sumi Marriage Practices'. In *Modern Practices in North East India*, edited by Dzüvichü and Baruah, 144–71. London; New York: Routledge, 2018.

Johannessen, Carl L., and Anne Z. Parker. 'Maize Ears Sculptured in 12th and 13th Century A.D. India as Indicators of Pre-Columbian Diffusion'. *EconomicBotany* 43, no. 2 (1989): 164–80.

Jones, Clive G., John H. Lawton and Moshe Shachak. 'Positive and Negative Effects of Organisms as Physical Ecosystem Engineers'. *Ecology* 78, no. 7 (1997): 1946–57.

Jones, O. 'Nature–Culture'. In *International Encyclopedia of Human Geography*, edited by Rob Kitchin and Nigel Thrift, 309–23. Amsterdam: Elsevier Science, 2009.

Joy, K. J., Partha J. Das, Gorky Chakraborty, Chandan Mahanta, Suhas Paranjape and Shruti Vispute. (eds.). *Water Conflicts in Northeast India*. Abingdon; New York: Routledge, 2018.

Jugli, Salomi, Jharna Chakravorty and Victor Benno Meyer-Rochow. 'Tangsa and Wancho of North-East India Use Animals Not Only as Food and Medicine but Also as Additional Cultural Attributes'. *Foods* 9, no. 528 (2020): 1–29.

Kabir, Mohammad Humayun, Nur Hasan, Md Mahfuzur Rahman, Md Ashikur Rahman, Jakia Alam Khan, Nazia Tasnim Hoque, Md Ruhul Quddus Bhuiyan, Sadia Moin Mo, Rownak Jahan and Mohammed Rahmatullah. 'A Survey of Medicinal Plants Used by the Debbarma Clan of the Tripura Tribe of Moulvibazar District, Bangladesh'. *Journal of Ethnobiology and Ethnomedicine* 10, no. 19 (2014): 1–28.

Kakati, Banikanta. *The Mother Goddess Kāmākhyā: A Study of Mother Cult of Assam*. Guwahati: Publication Board Assam, 1989.

Kalita, Bipul C., Hui Tag, B. J. Gogoi and Pallabi K. Hui. 'Diversity and Traditional Uses of Some Poisonous Plants of Arunachal Pradesh'. *International Journal of Advance Research and Innovative Ideas in Education* 3, no. 1 (2017): 755–63.

Kamkhenthang, H. *Folk Songs of the Thadou*. Imphal, Manipur: Directorate for Development of Tribals and Backward Classes, 1989.

Kano, Yuichi, David Dudgeon, So Nam, Hiromitsu Samejima, Katsutoshi Watanabe, Chaiwut Grudpan et al. 'Impacts of Dams and Global Warming on Fish Biodiversity in the Indo-Burma Hotspot'. *PLoS ONE* 11, no. 8 (2016): e0160151, 1–21.

Kanungo, Alok Kumar. 'Naga Ornaments and the Indian Ocean'. *Bulletin of the Indo-Pacific Prehistory Association* 26 (2006): 154–62.

———. 'Ornaments of the Dead among the Nagas'. *Journal of the Borneo International Beads Conference* (2011): 75–104.

Kar, A., D. Bora, S. K. Borthakur, N. K. Goswami and D. Saharia. 'Wild Edible Plant Resources Used by the Mizos of Mizoram'. *Kathmandu University Journal of Science, Engineering and Technology* 9, no. 1 (2013): 106–26.

Kar, Bodhisattva. 'Heads in the Naga Hills'. In *New Cultural Histories of India: Materiality and Practices*, edited by Partha Chatterjee, Tapati Guha-Thakurta and Bodhisattva Kar, 335–69. New Delhi: Oxford University Press, 2014.

———. 'Historia Elastica: A Note on the Rubber Hunt in the North-Eastern Frontier of British India'. *Indian Historical Review* 36, no. 1 (2009): 131–50.

Karanth, Krithi K., Shriyam Gupta and Anubhav Vanamamalai. 'Compensation Payments, Procedures and Policies towards Human–Wildlife Conflict Management: Insights from India'. *Biological Conservation* 227 (September 2018): 383–9.

Karlsson, B. G. *Contested Belonging: An Indigenous People's Struggle for Forest and Identity in Sub-Himalayan Bengal*. London; New York: Routledge, 2000.

———. 'Introduction: Northeastern Research Entanglements'. In *Geographies of Difference*, edited by Vanderhelsken, Barkataki-Ruscheweyh and Karlsson, 1–13. London; New York: Routledge, 2018.

———. *Unruly Hills: A Political Ecology of India's Northeast*. (New York; Oxford: Berghahn Books, 2011.

Karst, Heidi. 'Protected Areas and Ecotourism: Charting a Path toward Social-Ecological Wellbeing'. PhD thesis, University of Waterloo, 2017.

Kauffmann, H. E. 'Die Fallen der Thadou-Kuki in Assam'. *Zeitschrift für Ethnologie* 70, nos. 1/2 (1938): 1–18.

Kaul, Rahul, Sandeep Kumar Tiwari, Sunil Kyarong, Ritwick Dutta and Vivek Menon (eds.). *Canopies and Corridors: Conserving the Forests of Garo Hills with Elephants and Gibbons as Flagships*. New Delhi: Wildlife Trust of India, 2010.

Khan, M. L., Ashalata Devi Khumbongmayum and R. S. Tripathi. 'The Sacred Groves and Their Significance in Conserving Biodiversity: An Overview'. *International Journal of Ecology and Environmental Sciences* 34, no. 3 (2008): 277–91.

Khan, M. Monirul H. *Protected Areas of Bangladesh: A Guide to Wildlife*. Dhaka: Nishorgo Program, Bangladesh Forest Department, 2008.

Khan, Mohammad Tanzimuddin. 'The Nishorgo Support Project, the Lawachara National Park, and the Chevron Seismic Survey: Forest Conservation or Energy Procurement in Bangladesh?' *Journal of Political Ecology* 17 (2010): 68–78.

Kharkongor, Peacefully. 'Khasi Myths and Matriliny'. *Artha – Journal of Social Sciences* 4, no. 2 (2004): 56–67.

Kharsyntiew, Teiborlang T. 'Youth Fashion and the Identity of Resistance in Northeast India'. In *Geographies of Difference*, edited by Vanderhelsken, Barkataki-Ruscheweyh and Karlsson, 159–73. London; New York: Routledge, 2018.

Khatoon, Nasima. 'Natural Resources and Biodiversity Conservation Practices in Tawang'. In *Tawang, Monpas and Tibetan Buddhism in Transition*, edited by Mayilvaganan, Khatoon and Bej, 89–102. Singapore: Springer Nature, 2020.

Khatun, Ummay Habiba, Md. Farid Ahsan and Eivin Røskaft. 'Attitudes of the Local Community towards the Conservation of the Common Langur (*Semnopithecus entellus*) in Keshabpur, Bangladesh'. *International Journal of Biodiversity and Conservation* 4, no. 11 (2012): 385–99.

Khomdram, S. D., L. Fanai and S. D. Yumkham. 'Local Knowledge of Edible Flowers Used in Mizoram'. *Indian Journal of Traditional Knowledge* 18, no. 4 (2019): 714–23.

Khumbongmayum, Ashalata Devi, M. L. Khan and R. S. Tripathi. 'Sacred Groves of Manipur, Northeast India: Biodiversity Value, Status and Strategies for their Conservation'. *Biodiversity and Conservation* 14 (2005): 1541–82.

Kikon, Dolly. 'Bamboo Shoot in our Blood: Fermenting Flavors and Identities in Northeast India'. *Current Anthropology* 62, suppl. 24 (2021): S376–S387.

———. 'Fermenting Modernity: Putting *Akhuni* on the Nation's Table in India'. *South Asia: Journal of South Asian Studies* 38, no. 2 (2015): 320–35.

———. *Living with Oil and Coal: Resource Politics and Militarization in Northeast India*. Seattle: University of Washington Press, 2019.

———. 'Operation Hornbill Festival 2004'. *Seminar* 550 (2005): 36–9.

Kikon, Dolly, and Sanjay Barbora. 'The Rehabilitation Zone: Living with Lemons and Elephants in Assam'. *Environment and Planning E: Nature and Space* 3 (August 2020): 1121–38.

Kikon, Dolly, and Duncan McDuie-Ra. *Ceasefire City: Militarism, Capitalism, and Urbanism in Dimapur*. Delhi: Oxford University Press, 2021.

Kikon, Dolly, P. Menangnichet and Mhademo Kikon. 'Taste So Good! Celebrating Bambooshoot (Fresh, Fermented, Dried)'. *Raiot*, 18 September 2020. https://raiot.in/taste-so-good-celebrating-bambooshoot-fresh-fermented-dried/. Accessed 4 January 2022.

Kimmerer, Robin Wall. *Braiding Sweetgrass: Indigenous Wisdom, Scientific Knowledge and the Teachings of Plants*. Minneapolis, MN: Milkweed Editions, 2013.

Kine, Phyo Kay, Stuart Lindsay and Jürgen Kluge. '*Selliguea kachinensis* (*Polypodiaceae*), a New Fern Species of Uncertain Affinity from Northern Myanmar'. *PhytoKeys* 62 (March 2016): 73–81.

King, Ben, and Julian P. Sonahue. 'The Rediscovery and Song of the Rusty-Throated Wren Babbler *Spelaeornis badeigularis*'. *Forktail* 22 (2006): 113–15.

Kingdon-Ward, F. *In Farthest Burma*. Philadelphia: J. B. Lippincott Company, 1921.

———. 'Report on the Forests of the North Triangle, Kachin State, North Burma'. *Journal of the Bombay Natural History Society* 52 (1954): 304–20.

Kingwell-Banham, Eleanor. 'Early Rice Agriculture in South Asia: Identifying Cultivation Systems Using Archaeobotany'. PhD thesis, University College London, 2015.

Kipgen, Ngamjahao. 'Forests, Ecology and Traditional Knowledge: A Kuki Woman's Perspective in the Northeast'. In *Regional Environmental History: Issues and Concepts in the Indian Subcontinent*, edited by Vulli Dhanaraju, 209–25. Delhi: Aakar Books, 2016.

———. 'Significance of LAWM in the Contemporary Kuki Society'. *Kukiforum.com*, November 2008. http://kukiforum.com/2008/11/significance-of-lawm-in-the-contemporary-kuki-society/. Accessed 5 May 2020.

———. 'The Enclosures of Colonization: Indigeneity, Development, and the Case of Mapithel Dam in Northeast India'. *Asian Ethnicity* 18, no. 4 (2017): 505–21.

Kipgen, Ngamjahao, and Doungul Letkhojam Haokip (eds.). *Against the Empire: Polity, Economy and Culture during the Anglo-Kuki War 1917–1919*. Abingdon; New York: Routledge, 2021.

Kipgen, Sheikhohao. 'Resistance, War Council and Formation of Militia: The Role of Kuki Chiefs in the Anglo-Kuki War'. In *Against the Empire*, edited by Kipgen and Haokip, 15–33. Abingdon; New York: Routledge, 2021.

Kirchherr, Julian, Katrina J. Charles and Matthew J. Walton. 'The Interplay of Activists and Dam Developers: The Case of Myanmar's Mega-Dams'. *International Journal of Water Resources Development* 33, no. 1 (2017): 111–31.

Knight, John. 'The Anonymity of the Hunt: A Critique of Hunting as Sharing'. *Current Anthropology* 53, no. 3 (2012): 334–55.

Kohn, Eduardo. *How Forests Think: Toward an Anthropology beyond the Human*. Berkeley; Los Angeles: University of California Press, 2013.

Kolkman, René, and Stuart Blackburn. *Tribal Architecture in Northeast India*. Leiden; Boston: Brill, 2014.

Kopnina, Helen, Haydn Washington, Bron Taylor and John J Piccolo. 'Anthropocentrism: More than Just a Misunderstood Problem'. *Journal of Agricultural and Environmental Ethics* 31, no. 1 (2018): 109–27.

Kotar, S. L., and J. E. Gessler. *Cholera: A Worldwide History*. Jefferson, NC: McFarland and Company, 2014.

Kour, Kawal Deep. *A History of Intoxication: Opium in Assam, 1800–1959*. Abingdon; New York: Routledge, 2020.

Krutak, Lars. 'Neo-Naga'. *TätowierMagazin*, July 2015, 50–4.

———. 'Tattoos der Tigerjäger und Krieger'. *TätowierMagazin*, August 2016, 50–4.

Kuchling, Gerald, Wikn Ko Ko, Tint Lwin, Sein Aung Min, Khin Myo Myo, Thin Thin Khaing (II), Win Win Mar and Thin Thin Kaing (I). 'The Softshell Turtles and Their Exploitation at the Upper Chindwin River, Myanmar: Range Extensions for *Amyda cartilaginea*, *Chitra vandijki*, and *Nilssonia Formosa*'. *Salamandra – German Journal of Herpetology* 40, nos. 3/4 (2004): 281–96.

Kullander, Sven O., Md. Mizanur Rahman, Michael Norén and Abdur Rob Mollah. '*Laubuka tenella*, a New Species of Cyprinid Fish from Southeastern Bangladesh and Southwestern Myanmar (Teleostei, Cyprinidae, Danioninae)'. *ZooKeys* 742 (March 2018): 105–26.

Kullander, Sven, and Ralf Britz. 'Description of *Danio absconditus*, New Species, and Redescription of *Danio feegradei* (Teleostei: Cyprinidae), from the Rakhine Yoma Hotspot in South-Western Myanmar'. *Zootaxa* 3948, no. 2 (2015): 233–47.

Kumar, Awadhesh, Ashalata Devi, Atul Kumar Gupta and Kuladip Sarma. 'Population, Behavioural Ecology and Conservation of Hoolock Gibbon in Northeast India'.

In *Rare Animals of India*, edited by Natarajan Singaravelan, 142–66. Sharjah, UAE, Oak Park, IL, and Bussum: Bentham Science Publishers, 2013.

Kumar, Ved P., Ankita Rajpoot and S. S. Rasaily. 'Peril for Pangolins: An Evaluation of the Status of the Last Decade in India'. *Forensic Science International: Reports* 2, no. 100058 (2020): 1–6.

Kurien, Amit John, Sharachchandra Lele and Harini Nagendra. 'Farms or Forests? Understanding and Mapping Shifting Cultivation Using the Case Study of West Garo Hills, India'. *Land* 8, no. 133 (2019): 1–26.

Laha, Ramachandra. 'Bamboo Uses for Housing by the Different Tribes of Northeast India'. *Bamboo Science and Culture* 14, no. 1 (2000): 10–14.

Lainé, Nicolas. 'Conduct and Collaboration in Human–Elephant Working Communities of Northeast India'. In *Rethinking Human–Elephant Relations in South Asia: Conflict, Negotiation, and Coexistence*, edited by Piers Locke and Jane Buckingham, 180–205. Delhi: Oxford University Press, 2016.

———. 'Effects of the 1996 Timber Ban in Northeast India: The Case of the Khamtis of Lohit District, Arunachal Pradesh'. In *Nature, Environment and Society: Conservation, Governance and Transformation in India*, edited by Nicolas Lainé and T. B. Subba, 73–93. Delhi: Orient Blackswan, 2012.

———. 'Les éléphants sous la cour ahom (XIIIe–XIXe s.)'. *Anthropozoologica* 45, no. 2 (2010) : 7–25.

———. *Living and Working with Giants: A Multispecies Ethnography of the Khamti and Elephants in Northeast India*. Paris: Muséum National d'Histoire Naturelle, 2020.

———. '*Phi Muangs*: Khamti Forces of Place in Arunachal Pradesh'. *Asian Ethnology* 79, no. 2 (2020): 239–58.

———. 'Travail Interespèces et conservation: Le cas des éléphants d'Asie'. *Écologie and Politique* 54, no. 1 (2017) : 45–64.

Laishramcha, Jinine. 'Hydrocarbon Extraction in Manipur and Its Impact on Barak Downstream'. In *Water Conflicts in Northeast India*, edited by Joy, Das, Chakraborty, Mahanta, Paranjape and Vispute, 203–17. Abingdon; New York: Routledge, 2018.

Laloo, Hakani Sae Paia. 'Re-reading Khasi Folktales: Interpreting Social and Political Expressions'. *IUN Journal of Social Sciences* 2, no. 4 (2018): 58–68.

Lambert, E. T. D. 'From the Brahmaputra to the Chindwin'. *Geographical Journal* 89, no. 4 (1937): 309–23.

Larson, Greger, and Dorian Q. Fuller. 'The Evolution of Animal Domestication'. *Annual Review of Ecology, Evolution, and Systematics* 45 (September 2014): 115–36.

Laskar, Boni Amin, Kenjum Bagra and D. N. Das. 'Invasion of Rainbow Trout in Arunachal Pradesh'. *Science and Culture* 76, nos. 1/2 (2010): 67–9.

Latt, Tint Swe, Than Than Aye, Ei Sandar U., Yin Yin Win, Khin Thawdar Wint and Ei Thinzar Khin. 'Traditional Medicine and Diabetes Care in Myanmar'. *Journal of Social Health and Diabetes* 7, no. 1 (2019): 1–21.

Lawler, Andrew. 'Dawn of the Chicken Revealed in Southeast Asia: Chicken Domestication—Debated since Charles Darwin—Tracked by Genomic Survey'. *Science* 368, no. 6498 (2020): 1411.

Lehman, F. K. *The Structure of Chin Society: A Tribal People of Burma Adapted to a Non-Western Civilization*. Urbana, IL: University of Illinois Press, 1963.

Lekshmi Priya S. 'This Fearless Mizo Woman Fought a Tiger with Her Bare Hands to Save Her Child!' *The Better India*, 25 July 2018. https://www.thebetterindia.com/152554/news-mizo-woman-tiger-pi-zadingi-legend/. Accessed 8 January 2022.

Leslie, David M., and George B. Schaller. '*Bos grunniens* and *Bos mutus* (Artiodactyla: Bovidae)'. *Mammalian Species* 836 (May 2009): 1–17.

Letro, Letro, and Sangay Wangchuk. 'Monpa, the Early Settlers of Bhutan in Jigme Singye Wangchuck National Park and Conservation Strategy'. *European Online Journal of Natural and Social Sciences* 5, no. 4 (2016): 988–95.

Letro, Letro, Sangay Wangchuk and Tashi Dhendup. 'Distribution of Asiatic Black Bear and Its Interaction with Humans in Jigme Singye Wangchuk National Park, Bhutan'. *Nature Conservation Research* 5, no. 1 (2020): 44–52.

Lewin, Thomas Herbert. *Progressive Colloquial Exercises in the Lushai Dialect of the "Dzo" Or Kúki Language, With Vocabularies and Popular Tales*. Annotated. Calcutta: Calcutta Central Press Company, Limited, 1874.

———. *The Hill Tracts of Chittagong and the Dwellers Therein; With Comparative Vocabularies of the Hill Dialects*. Calcutta: Bengal Printing Company, 1869.

Lewis, Jovan Scott. 'Releasing a Tradition: Diasporic Epistemology and the Decolonized Curriculum'. *Cambridge Journal of Anthropology* 36, no. 2 (2018): 21–33.

Li, Sheng, William J. McShea, Dajun Wang, Xiaodong Gu, Xiaofeng Zhang, Li Zhang and Xiaoli Shen. 'Retreat of Large Carnivores across the Giant Panda Distribution Range'. *Nature Ecology and Evolution* 4 (2020): 1327–31.

Li, Xueyou, William V. Bleisch, Xinwu Liu and Xuelong Jiang. 'Camera-Trap Surveys Reveal High Diversity of Mammals and Pheasants in Medog, Tibet'. *Oryx* 55, no. 2 (2021): 177–80.

Li, Xueyou, Cheng Huang and Xuelong Jiang. 'Spatiotemporal Occurrence of Mishmi Takin *Budorcas taxicolor* in Dulongjiang Region, Southwestern China'. *Mammalia* 84, no. 6 (2020): 513–19.

Liedigk, Rasmus, Mouyu Yang and C. Roos. 'Evolutionary History of the Odd-Nosed Monkeys and the Phylogenetic Position of the Newly Described Myanmar Snub-Nosed Monkey *Rhinopithecus strykeri*'. *PLoS ONE* 7, no. 5 (2012): e37418.

Lindsay, Alexander. *Lives of the Lindsays; or, A Memoir of the Houses of Crawford and Balcarres*. 3 vols. London: John Murray, 1849.

Lintner, Bertil. *The Kachin: Lords of Burma's Northern Frontier*. Chiang Mai: Asia Film House, 1997.

Lister, Diana L., Huw Jones, Hugo R. Oliveira, Cameron A. Petrie, Xinyi Liu, James Cockram, Catherine J. Kneale, Olga Kovaleva and Martin K. Jones. 'Barley Heads East: Genetic Analyses Reveal Routes of Spread through Diverse Eurasian Landscapes'. *PLoS ONE* 13, no. 7 (2018): e0196652, 1–29.

Liu, Jie, Dejing Li, Tetsuro Matsuzawa and Satoshi Hirata. 'The Lisu People's Traditional Natural Philosophy and Its Potential Impact on Conservation Planning in the Laojun Mountain Region, Yunnan Province, China'. *Primates* 62 (July 2021): 153–64.

Liu, Xinyi, Diane L. Lister, Zhijun Zhao, Cameron A. Petrie, Xiongsheng Zeng, Penelope J. Jones et al. 'Journey to the East: Diverse Routes and Variable Flowering Times for Wheat and Barley *en route* to Prehistoric China'. *PLoS ONE* 12, no. 11 (2017): e0187405, 1–16.

Locke, Harvey, and Karsten Heuer. 'Yellowstone to Yukon: Global Conservation Innovations through the Years'. In *Protecting the Wild*, edited by George Wuerthner, Crist and Butler, 120–30. Washington: Island Press, 2015.

Lokho, Adani. 'The Folk Medicinal Plants of the Mao Naga in Manipur, North East India'. *International Journal of Scientific and Research Publications* 2, no. 6 (2012): 1–8.

Lokho, Kapesa, Birendra P. Singh and Ansuya Bhandari. 'A Synoptic Review of Eocene-Miocene Faunal Records of the Indo-Burma Range (IBR), Northeast India and Coeval Northwestern Himalaya: Paleoenvironmental and Tectonic Inferences'. *Journal of the Palaeontological Society of India* 63, no. 2 (2018): 1–9.

Londo, Jason P., Yu-Chung Chiang, Kuo-Hsiang Hung, Tzen-Yuh Chiang and Barbara A. Schaal. 'Phylogeography of Asian Wild Rice, *Oryza rufipogon*, Reveals Multiple Independent Domestications of Cultivated Rice, *Oryza sativa*'. *PNAS* 103, no. 25 (2006): 9578–83.

Longkumer, Arkotong. '"As Our Ancestors Once Lived": Representation, Performance and Constructing a National Culture amongst the Nagas of India'. *Himalaya* 35, no. 1 (2015): 51–64.

———. *Reform, Identity and Narratives of Belonging: The Heraka Movement in Northeast India*. London; New York: Continuum International, 2010.

———. 'Representing the Nagas: Negotiating National Culture and Consumption'. In *Landscape, Culture, and Belonging*, edited by Bhattacharya and Pachuau, 151–75. Cambridge: Cambridge University Press, 2019.

———. 'Rice-Beer, Purification and Debates over Religion and Culture in Northeast India'. *South Asia: Journal of South Asian Studies* 39, no. 2 (2016): 444–61.

———. 'Spirits in a Material World: Mediation and Revitalization of Woodcarvings in a Naga Village'. *Numen* 65 (August 2018): 46–98.

———. 'Who Sings for the Hornbill? The Performance and Politics of Culture in Nagaland, Northeast India'. *South Asianist* 2, no. 2 (2013): 87–96.

Longvah, Shonreiphy. 'Christian Conversions: The Rise of Naga National Consciousness, and Naga Nationalist Politics'. *South Asianist* 5, no. 1 (2017): 121–39.

Loofs, H. H. E. *Elements of the Megalithic Complex in Southeast Asia: An Annotated Bibliography*. Canberra: Australian National University Press, 1967.

Lorimer, Jamie. 'Elephants as Companion Species: The Lively Biogeographies of Asian Elephant Conservation in Sri Lanka'. *Transactions of the Institute of British Geographers* 35, no. 4 (2010): 491–506.

Lorrain, J. Herbert. *Dictionary of the Lushai Language*. Calcutta: Asiatic Society, 1940.

Lorrain, Reginald A. *Fifty Years in Unknown Jungles for God and Empire*. London: Pioneer Mission, 1912.

Lotha, Abraham. *The Raging Mithun: Challenges of Naga Nationalism*. Kohima: Barkweaver Publications, 2013.

López-Sampsoni, Arlene, and Tony Page. 'History of Use and Trade of Agarwood'. *Economic Botany* 72, no. 1 (2018): 107–29.

Lubbock, John. 'The Stone Age'. *The Athenaeum*, no. 2069, 22 June 1867, 822.

Luce, G. H. *Phases of Pre-Pagán Burma: Languages and History*. Oxford: Oxford University Press, 1985.

Luce, Gordon H., and G. P. Oey. *Man Shu: Book of the Southern Barbarians*. Ithaca, NY: Cornell University, 1961.

Ludden, David. 'Cowry Country: Mobile Space and Imperial Territory'. In *Asia Inside Out: Itinerant People*, edited by Eric Tagliacozzo, Helen F. Siu and Peter C. Perdue, 75–100. Cambridge, MA; London: Harvard University Press, 2019.

———. 'History outside Civilization and the Mobility of South Asia'. *South Asia: Journal of South Asian Studies* 17, no. 1 (1994): 1–23.

———. 'India's Spatial History in the Brahmaputra–Meghna River Basin'. In *Landscape, Culture, and Belonging*, edited by Bhattacharya and Pachuau, 23–37. Cambridge: Cambridge University Press, 2019.

Ludwig, Ferdinand, Wilfrid Middleton, Friederike Gallenmüller, Patrick Rogers and Thomas Speck. 'Living Bridges Using Aerial Roots of *Ficus elastica*: An Interdisciplinary Perspective'. *Scientific Reports* 9, no. 12226 (2019): 1–11.

Lungphi, P., A. V. Singh and A. P. Das. '"Phalap-Khah": The Bitter Tea of Tangsa Community in the Changlang District of Arunachal Pradesh, India'. *Pleione* 13, no. 1 (2019): 33–40.

Luo, Lan, Darryl E. Granger, Hua Tu, Zhongping Lai, Guanjun Shen, Christopher J. Bae, Xueping Ji and Jianhui Liu. 'The First Radiometric Age by Isochron 26Al/10Be Burial Dating for the Early Pleistocene Yuanmou Hominin Site, Southern China'. *Quaternary Geochronology* 55 (February 2020): 1–7.

Luttikhuis, Bart, and Arnout H. C. van der Meer. 'New Turning Points in Southeast Asian History: Re-writing Southeast Asian Chronologies from Within'. *TRaNS: Trans-Regional and -National Studies of Southeast Asia* 8, no. 2 (2020): 81–3.

Lydecker, Richard. *The Game Animals of India, Burma, Malaya, and Tibet*. London: Rowland Ward, 1907.

Lyngdoh, J. P., D. Syiem and A. A. Mao. 'Pattern of Traditional Medicine Usage in East Khasi Hills of Meghalaya'. *Indian Journal of Traditional Knowledge* 1, no. 13 (2014): 164–70.

Lyngdoh, Margaret. 'An Interview with a Goddess: Possession Rites as Regulators of Justice Among the Pnar of Northeastern India'. *Religious Studies and Theology* 36, no. 1 (2017): 55–78.

———. 'On Wealth and Jealousy among the Khasis: Thlen, Demonization and the Other'. *Internationales Asienforum* 46, nos. 1/2 (2015): 169–86.

———. 'Tiger Transformation among the Khasis of Northeastern India: Belief Worlds and Shifting Realities'. *Anthropos* 111, no. 2 (2016): 649–58.

———. 'Water Spirit Possession among the Khasis: Representation of Fear through Narratives'. *International Quarterly of Asian Studies* 49, nos. 3/4 (2018): 81–102.

Ma, Jianxiong. 'Salt and Revenue in Frontier Formation: State Mobilized Ethnic Politics in the Yunnan–Burma Borderland since the 1720s'. *Modern Asian Studies* 48, no. 6 (2014): 1637–69.

Ma, Jianxiong, and Cunzhao Ma. 'The Mule Caravans of Western Yunnan: An Oral History of the Muleteers of Zhaozhou'. *Transfers* 4, no. 3 (2014): 24–42.

McColl, Hugh, Fernando Racimo, Lasse Vinner, Fabrice Demeter, Takashi Gakuhari, J. Víctor Moreno-Mayar et al. 'The Prehistoric Peopling of Southeast Asia'. *Science* 361 (July 2018): 88–92.

M'Cosh, John. *Topography of Assam*. Calcutta: Bengal Military Orphan Press, 1837.

McCulloch, W. *Account of the Valley of Munnipore and of the Hill Tribes; With a Comparative Vocabulary of the Munnipore and other Languages*. Calcutta: Bengal Printing Company, 1859.

McDuie-Ra, Duncan. 'Adjacent Identities in Northeast India'. *Asian Ethnicity* 17, no. 3 (2016): 400–13.

———. *Civil Society, Democratization and the Search for Human Security: The Politics of the Environment, Gender, and Identity in Northeast India*. New York: Nova Science Publishers, 2009.

McDuie-Ra, Duncan. *Debating Race in Contemporary India*. Houndsmills; New York: Palgrave Macmillan, 2015.

———. *Northeast Migrants in Delhi: Race, Refuge and Retail*. Amsterdam: Amsterdam University Press, 2012.

McDuie-Ra, Duncan, and Dolly Kikon. 'Tribal Communities and Coal in Northeast India: The Politics of Imposing and Resisting Mining Bans'. *Energy Policy* 99 (December 2016): 261–9.

MacNeill, J. R., and Peter Engelke. *The Great Acceleration: An Environmental History of the Anthropocene since 1945*. Cambridge, MA; London: Harvard University Press, 2014.

McPartland, John M., William Hegman and Tengwen Long. '*Cannabis* in Asia: Its Center of Origin and Early Cultivation, Based on a Synthesis of Subfossil Pollen and Archaeobotanical Studies'. *Vegetation History and Archaeobotany* 28 (May 2019): 691–702.

Mahanta, Ratul, and Daisy Das. 'Attitudes towards Biodiversity Conservation of Forests Dwellers and Encroachers: A Case Study of Assam in Northeast India'. *Small-Scale Forestry* 12 (2013): 307–19.

Mahmud. *Ang Ing Mru Rung: Life and Struggles of the Mro People in Bangladesh*. Dhaka: Matri Production, 2007.

Majumdar, Aparajita. 'The Colonial State and Resource Frontiers: Tracing the Politics of Appropriating Rubber in the Northeastern Frontier of British India, 1810–84'. *Indian Historical Review* 43, no. 1 (2016): 25–41.

Malla, Bansi Lal, and Dwipen Bezbaruah (eds.). *Cultural Ecology: Prehistory and Ethnoarchaeological Context of Indian Rock Art; With Emphasis on North-Eastern States*. Delhi: Aryan Books International, 2017.

Mallick, Jayanta Kumar. 'Past and Present Status of the Indian Tiger in Northern West Bengal, India: An Overview'. *Journal of Threatened Taxa* 2, no. 3 (2010): 739–52.

Malsawmliana. 'A Typological Classification of Megaliths of Mizoram'. *Journal of Neolithic Archaeology*, special issue no. 5 (2019): 125–34.

Mandal, Bikash, Govind Pratap Rao, Virendra Kumar Baranwal and Rakesh Kumar Jain(eds.). *A Century of Plant Virology in India*. Singapore: Springer Nature, 2017.

Mang, Kyin Lam. 'Ethnographic Textile Art Expressing Symbolic Culture of Asho-Chin Nationals'. Master's thesis, University of Yangon, 2008–2009.

Mani, Fiona. 'Guns and Shikaris: The Rise of the Sahib's Hunting Ethos and the Fall of the Subaltern Poacher in British India, 1750–1947'. PhD thesis, West Virginia University, 2011, 180–212.

Marak, Queenbala. 'Rice from *A·ba*: Stories, Rituals and Practices of the Garos'. *South Asian Anthropologist* 18, no. 2 (2018): 161–75.

———. 'Women and Clay: A Study of the Craft of Pot Making among the Garos'. In *The Cultural Heritage of Meghalaya*, edited by Marak and Chaudhuri, 443–56. New York; London: Routledge, 2020.

Marak, Queenbala, and Sarit K. Chaudhuri (eds.). *The Cultural Heritage of Meghalaya*. New York; London: Routledge, 2020.

Marchese, Christian. 'Biodiversity Hotspots: A Shortcut for a More Complicated Concept'. *Global Ecology and Conservation* 3 (January 2015): 297–309.

Margulies, Jared D. 'Making the "Man-Eater": Tiger Conservation as Necropolitics'. *Political Geography* 69 (2019): 150–61.

Margulies, Jared D., Leigh-Anne Bullough, Amy Hinsley, Daniel J. Ingram, Carly Cowell, Bárbara Goettsch, Bente B. Klitgård, Anita Lavorgna, Pablo Sinovas and Jacob Phelps. 'Illegal Wildlife Trade and the Persistence of "Plant Blindness"'. *Plants, People, Planet* 1 (2019): 173–82.

Mark, SiuSue. '"Fragmented Sovereignty" over Property Institutions: Developmental Impacts on the Chin Hills Communities'. *Independent Journal of Burmese Scholarship* 1, no. 1 (2016): 131–60.

Marrero, Patricia, Khaled K. Abu-Amero, Jose M. Larruga and Vicente M. Cabrera. 'Carriers of Human Mitochondrial DNA Macrohaplogroup M Colonized India from Southeastern Asia'. *BMC Evolutionary Biology* 16, no. 246 (2016): 1–13.

Mawlong, Cecile. 'History Etched in Stone: A Study of Khasi-Jaintia Megalithic Tradition'. In *The Cultural Heritage of Meghalaya*, edited by Marak and Chaudhuri, 47–68. New York; London: Routledge, 2020.

Mayilvaganan, M., Nasima Khatoon and Sourina Bej. (eds.). *Tawang, Monpas and Tibetan Buddhism in Transition: Life and Society along the India–China Borderland*. Singapore: Springer Nature, 2020.

Mayr, Ernst. 'The Birds of the Vernay-Hopwood Chindwin Expedition'. *Ibis* 80, no. 2 (1938): 197–390.

Means, Gordon P. 'Human Sacrifice and Slavery in the "Unadministered" Areas of Upper Burma during the Colonial Era'. *Sojourn: Journal of Social Issues in Southeast Asia* 15, no. 2 (2000): 184–221.

Medhi, Pramod, and Sachin Kumar Borthakur. 'Sacred Groves and Sacred Plants of the Dimasas of North Cachar Hills of Northeast India'. *African Journal of Plant Science* 7, no. 2 (2013): 67–77.

Medhi, R. P., and Syamali Chakrabarti. 'Traditional Knowledge of NE People on Conservation of Wild Orchids'. *Indian Journal of Traditional Knowledge* 8, no. 1 (2009): 11–16.

Medicinal Plants of Myanmar. Nyapyidaw: Department of Traditional Medicine, Ministry of Health, Government of the Union of Myanmar, n.d.

Meitei, Akoijam Milan, and Q. Marak. 'A Study on Megalithic Burial Stones from Jaintia Hills, Meghalaya'. *South Asian Anthropologist* 13, no. 2 (2013): 157–66.

Mellars, Paul, Kevin C. Gori, Martin Carr, Pedro A. Soares and Martin B. Richards. 'Genetic and Archaeological Perspectives on the Initial Modern Human Colonization of Southern Asia'. *PNAS* 110, no. 26 (2013): 10699–704.

Menon, Vivek, Sandeep K. Tiwari, K. Ramkumar, Sunil Kyarong, Upasana Ganguly and Raman Sukumar (eds.). *Right of Passage: Elephant Corridors of India*. New Delhi: Wildlife Trust of India, 2017.

Menzies, Rohan K., Megha Rao and Rohit Naniwadekar. 'Assessing the Status of the Critically Endangered White-bellied Heron *Ardea insignis* in North-East India'. *Bird Conservation International* 31, no. 2 (2021): 255–67.

Meyer, M. C., Ch.-Ch. Hofmann, A. M. D. Gemmell, E. Haslinger, H. Häusler and D. Wangda. 'Holocene Glacier Fluctuations and Migration of Neolithic Yak Pastoralists into the High Valleys of Northwest Bhutan'. *Quaternary Science Reviews* 28 (2009): 1217–37.

Michaud, Jean. 'Editorial – Zomia and Beyond'. *Journal of Global History* 5, no. 2 (2010): 187–214.

Millington, Powell. *On the Track of the Àbor*. London: Smith, Elder and Co., 1912.

Mills, J. P. *The Ao Nagas*. London: Macmillan and Company, 1926.

———. *The Lhota Nagas*. London: Macmillan and Co., 1922.

———. 'The Mishmis of the Lohit Valley, Assam'. *Journal of the Royal Anthropological Institute of Great Britain and Ireland* 82, no. 1 (1952): 1–12.

———. *The Rengma Nagas*. London: Macmillan and Company, 1937.

———. 'The Were-Tigers of the Assam Hills'. *Journal of the Society for Psychical Research* 20 (November 1922): 381–8.

Min, Sapai. 'Impacts of Wildlife Trade on Conservation in Kachin State, Myanmar'. *TRAFFIC Bulletin* 24, no. 2 (2012): 57–64.

Mir, Aabid Hussain, Dilip Kumar Roy and Krishna Upadhaya. 'Taxonomy, Recollection and Conservation Implications of *Aquilaria khasiana* (Thymelaeaceae): An Endemic and Threatened Species of India'. *Rheedea* 27, no. 2 (2017): 85–9.

Mir, Aabid Hussain, Krishna Upadhaya, Nripemo Odyuo and Brajesh Kumar Tiwari. 'Rediscovery of *Magnolia rabaniana* (Magnoliaceae): A Threatened Tree Species of Meghalaya, Northeast India'. *Journal of Asia-Pacific Biodiversity* 10, no. 1 (2017): 127–31.

Mir, Aabid Hussain, Krishna Upadhaya and Dilip Kumar Roy. 'Rediscovery, Distribution and Conservation Implications of *Cleyera grandiflora* Wall. ex Choisy (Pentaphylacaceae): An Endangered and Endemic Tree Species of Meghalaya, Northeast India'. *National Academy of Sciences and Letters* 40, no. 3 (2017): 205–9.

Mir, Aabid Hussain, Krishna Upadhaya, Dilip Kumar Roy, Chaya Deori and Bikarma Singh. 'A Comprehensive Checklist of Endemic Flora of Meghalaya, India'. *Journal of Threatened Taxa* 11, no. 12 (2019): 14527–61.

Mirza, Zeeshan A., Rajesh Sanap and Krushnamegh Kunte. 'A New Species of the Genus *Thaicharmus* Kovařík, 1995 (Scorpiones: Buthidae) from Northeast India'. *Euscorpius* 215 (January 2016): 1–11.

Mirza, Zeeshan A., Harshal Bhosale, Pushkar Phansalkar and Mandar Sawant. 'A New Species of Green Pit Vipers of the Genus *Trimeresurus Lacépède*, 1804 (Reptilia, Serpentes, Viperidae) from Western Arunachal Pradesh, India'. *Zoosystematics and Evolution* 96, no. 1 (2020): 123–38.

Mishra, B. P., O. P. Tripathi, R. S. Tripathi and H. N. Pandey. 'Effects of Anthropogenic Disturbance on Plant Diversity and Community Structure of a Sacred Grove in Meghalaya, Northeast India'. *Biodiversity and Conservation* 13 (February 2004): 421–36.

Mishra, U. K., and S. Sen. 'Dinosaur Bones from Meghalaya'. *Current Science* 80, no. 8 (2001): 1053–6.

Mitra, Abhijit. *Mangrove Forests in India: Exploring Ecosystem Services*. Cham, Switzerland: Springer Nature, 2020.

Mitri, Marco. 'Exploring the Monumentality of Khasi-Jaintia Hills Megaliths'. *Journal of Neolithic Archaeology*, special issue no. 5 (2019): 163–78.

Miyamoto, Mari. 'Contesting Values of Brewing "Chang" in a National Park of Bhutan'. In *Nature, Culture*, edited by Yokoyama, Matsumoto and Araki, 113–25. Singapore: Springer Nature, 2020.

Miyamoto, Mari, Jan Magnusson and Frank J. Korom. 'Animal Slaughter and Religious Nationalism in Bhutan'. *Asian Ethnology* 80, no. 1 (2021): 121–45.

Mizuno, Kazuharu. 'The Distribution and Management of Forests in Arunachal Pradesh, India'. In *Environmental Geography of South Asia: Contributions toward a Future Earth Initiative*, edited by R. B. Singh and Pawel Prokop, 189–207. Tokyo; Heidelberg; New York; Dordrecht; London: Springer, 2017.

Mizuno, Kazuharu, and Lobsang Tenpa. *Himalayan Nature and Tibetan Buddhist Culture in Arunachal Pradesh, India: A Study of Monpa*. Tokyo; Heidelberg; New York; Dordrecht; London: Springer, 2015.

Mohamed, Rozi (ed.). *Agarwood: Science Behind the Fragrance*. Singapore: Springer Nature, 2016.

Moktan, Mani Ram, Lungten Norbu, Harilal Nirola, Kencho Dukpa, Tek Bahadur Rai and Rinchen Dorji. 'Ecological and Social Aspects of Transhumant Herding in Bhutan'. *Mountain Research and Development* 28, no. 1 (2008): 41–8.

Mon, Pont Pont, Jiradej Lapkuntod, Min Thein Maw, Bundit Nuansrichay, Sujira Parchariyanon, Thanawat Tiensin et al. 'Highly Pathogenic Avian Influenza (H5N1) in Myanmar, 2006–2010'. *Archives of Virology* 157 (July 2012): 2113–23.

Montes, Jesse, Bhuwan Kafley and Thinley Dema. 'Territory, Relationality and the Labour of Deities: Importing Raffestin on the Bhutanese Spiritual Landscape'. *Rig Tshoel: Research Journal of the Royal Thimphu College* 3, no. 1 (2020): 27–45.

Montes, Jesse, Sonam Tshering, Tenzin Phuntsho, and Robert Fletcher. 'Cosmological Subjectivities: Exploring "Truth" Environmentalities in the Haa Highlands of Bhutan'. *Conservation and Society* 18, no. 4 (2020): 355–65.

Moore, Elizabeth. 'Archaeology of the Shan Plateau: The Bronze to Buddhist Transition'. *Contemporary Buddhism: An Interdisciplinary Journal* 10, no. 1 (2009): 91–110.

———. 'Carnelian in Myanmar: Prehistoric to Early Buddhist Beads; An Introductory Note on Archaeological and Ethnological Observations in Myanmar'. *Nagaland University Research Journal* 8 (January 2015): 138–43.

Moore, Elizabeth, and U Aung Myint. 'Beads of Myanmar (Burma): Line Decorated Beads amongst the Pyu and Chin'. *Journal of the Siam Society* 81, no. 1 (1993): 54–87.

Moore, Elizabeth, and Pauk Pauk. 'Nyaung-gan: A Preliminary Note on a Bronze Age Cemetery near Mandalay, Myanmar (Burma)'. *Asian Perspectives* 40, no. 1 (2001): 35–47.

Moore, Jason W. 'The Rise of Cheap Nature'. In *Anthropocene or Capitalocene? Nature, History, and the Crisis of Capitalism*, edited by Jason W. Moore, 78–115. Oakland, CA: PMPress, 2016.

Morey, Stephen. *Turung: A Variety of Singpho Language Spoken in Assam*. Canberra: Pacific Linguistics, 2010.

Morley, C. K., Tin Tin Naing, M. Searle and S. A. Robinson. 'Structural and Tectonic Development of the Indo-Burma Ranges'. *Earth-Science Reviews* 200, no. 102992 (2020): 1–43.

Morris, Brian. *Animals and Ancestors: An Ethnography*. London: Routledge, 2020.

Morris, R. C. 'The Vernay-Hopwood Upper Chindwin Expedition'. *Journal of the Bombay Natural History Society* 38, no. 4 (1936): 647–71.

Morrison, Kathleen D. 'Conceiving Ecology and Stopping the Clock: Narratives of Balance, Loss, and Degradation'. In *Shifting Ground*, edited by Rangarajan and Sivaramakrishnan, 39–60. Oxford: Oxford University Press, 2014.

Motaleb, Mohammad Abdul, and Mohammad Sultan Ahmed. *Status of Asian Elephants in Bangladesh*. Dhaka: IUCN, International Union for Conservation of Nature, 2016.

Motaleb, Mohammad Abdul, Mohammad Sultan Ahmed, Hasibul Islam and Md. Ashraful Haque. *Atlas: Elephant Routes and Corridors in Bangladesh*. Dhaka: International Union for Conservation of Nature, 2016.

Motaleb, Mohammad Abdul, Sayad Mahmudur Rahman, Shahriar Rahman and Marufa Sultana. *The Asian Elephants and Associated Human–Elephant Conflict in South-Eastern Bangladesh*. Dhaka: IUCN, International Union for Conservation of Nature, 2011.

Mountfort, Guy, and Eric Hosking. *The Vanishing Jungle: The Story of the World Wildlife Fund Expeditions to Pakistan*. London: Collins, 1969.

Møller, Henrik Kloppenborg. *Spectral Jade: Materiality, Conceptualisation, and Value in the Myanmar–China Jadeite Trade*. Lund: Lund University, 2019.

Mukharji, Projit. 'Lokman, Chholeman and Manik Pir: Multiple Frames of Institutionalising Islamic Medicine in Modern Bengal'. *Social History of Medicine* 24, no. 3 (2011): 720–38.

———. 'Dis-locating Subaltern Therapeutics: Totka Chikitsha, Nomad Sociality, and Anti-Consumerism in Colonial Bengal'. *Asian Medicine* 13 (September 2018): 134–69.

Mukherjee, Nabanita. 'A Brief Appraisal of Human Wildlife Conflict in Jalpaiguri and Alipurduar Districts of West Bengal'. *International Journal of Scientific and Research Publications* 6, no. 8 (2016): 131–6.

Mukul, Sharif Ahmed, 'Biodiversity Conservation and Ecosystem Functions of Traditional Agroforestry Systems: Case Study from Three Tribal Communities in and Around Lawachara National Park'. In *Forest Conservation*, edited by Chowdhury, 171–9. Cham; Heidelberg; New York; Dordrecht; London: Springer International Publishing Switzerland, 2014.

———. 'Biodiversity Conservation Strategies in Bangladesh: The State of Protected Areas'. *Tigerpaper* 34, no. 3 (2007): 28–34.

Mukul, Sharif Ahmed, J. Herbohn, A. Z. M. M. Rashid and M. B. Uddin. 'Comparing the Effectiveness of Forest Law Enforcement and Economic Incentives to Prevent Illegal Logging in Bangladesh'. *International Forestry Review* 16, no. 3 (2014): 363–75.

Mukul, Sharif Ahmed, A. Z. M. Manzoor and Mohammad Belal Manzoor. 'The Role of Spiritual Beliefs in Conserving Wildlife Species in Religious Shrines of Bangladesh'. *Biodiversity* 13, no. 2 (2012): 108–14.

Muzaddadi, A. U. 'Naturally Evolved Fermented Fish Products of Northeast India (*Seedal* and *Shidal*): A Comparative Study'. *Indian Journal of Natural Products and Resources* 4, no. 2 (2013): 170–7.

Myo, Maung Tet. *Customary Law of the Chin Tribe*. Rangoon: Government Press, 1884, 5–17.

Myochit, Salai. *A Threatened Identity: Social Structure and Traditional Leadership in Cho Chin Society before Christianity*. Chiang Mai: Regional Center for Social Science and Sustainable Development (RCSD), Chiang Mai University, 2016.

Nadasdy, Paul. 'The Gift in the Animal: The Ontology of Hunting and Human–Animal Sociality'. *American Ethnologist* 34, no. 1 (2007): 25–43.

Nag, Sajal. *Pied Pipers in North East India, Bamboo-Flowers, Rat Famine and the Politics of Philanthropy, 1881–2007*. Delhi: Manohar Publications, 2008.

Nahar, Nazmun, Mohammad Asaduzzaman, Utpal Kumar Mandal, Nadia Ali Rimi, Emily S. Gurley, Mahmudur Rahman, Fernando Garcia, Susan Zimicki, Rebeca Sultana and Stephen P. Luby. 'Hunting Bats for Human Consumption in Bangladesh'. *EcoHealth* 17, no. 1 (2020): 139–51.

Namgay, Kuenga, Joanne E. Millar, Rosemary S. Black and Tashi Samdup. 'Changes in Transhumant Agro-pastoralism in Bhutan: A Disappearing Livelihood?' *Human Ecology* 42, no. 5 (2014): 779–92.

———. 'Transhumant Agro-pastoralism in Bhutan: Exploring Contemporary Practices and Socio-cultural Traditions'. *Pastoralism: Research, Policy and Practice* 3, no. 13 (2013): 1–26.

Namsa, Nima D., Manabendra Mandal, Sumpam Tangjang and Subhash C. Mandal. 'Ethnobotany of the Monpa Ethnic Group at Arunachal Pradesh, India'. *Journal of Ethnobiology and Ethnomedicine* 7, no. 31 (2011): 1–14.

Nandy, Ashis. 'History's Forgotten Doubles'. *History and Theory* 34, no. 2 (1995): 44–66.

Nandy, Subrata, and Ashesh Kumar Das. 'Comparing Tree Diversity and Population Structure between a Traditional Agroforestry System and Natural Forests of Barak Valley, Northeast India'. *International Journal of Biodiversity Science, Ecosystem Services and Management* 9, no. 2 (2013): 104–13.

Nash, Linda. 'The Agency of Nature or the Nature of Agency?' *Environmental History* 10, no. 1 (2005): 67–9.

Nath, Mautushi, and M. Dutta Choudhury. 'Ethno-medico-botanical Aspects of Hmar Tribe of Cachar District, Assam (Part I)'. *Indian Journal of Traditional Knowledge* 9, no. 4 (2010): 760–4.

Nath, Naba K., Bibhuti P. Lahkar, Namita Brahma, Santanu Dey, Jyoti P. Das, Pranjit K. Sarma and Bibhab K Talukdar. 'An Assessment of Human–Elephant Conflict in Manas National Park, Assam, India'. *Journal of Threatened Taxata* 1, no. 6 (2009): 309–16.

Nath, Tapan Kumar, Mohammed Jashimuddin and Makoto Inoue. *Community-Based Forest Management (CBFM) in Bangladesh*. Cham: Springer International Switzerland, 2016.

Neckel, Sighard. 'Scholastic Fallacies? Questioning the Anthropocene'. *Thesis Eleven* 165 (August 2021): 1–9.

Nicholls, Frank. *Assam Shikari: A Tea Planter's Story of Hunting and High Adventure in the Jungles of North East India*. Auckland, NZ: Tonson Publishing House, 1970.

Nienu, V. 'The Prehistoric Archaeology and Human Ecology of Nagaland'. In *50 Years after Daojali-Hading*, edited by Jamir and Hazarika, 117–25. New Delhi: Research India Press, 2014.

Nijhawan, Sahil, and Achili Mihu. 'Relations of Blood: Hunting Taboos and Wildlife Conservation in the Idu Mishmi of Northeast India'. *Journal of Ethnobiology* 40, no. 2 (2020): 149–66.

Nijman, Vincent, Ming Xia Zhang and Chris R. Shepherd. 'Pangolin Trade in the Mong La Wildlife Market and the Role of Myanmar in the Smuggling of Pangolins into China'. *Global Ecology and Conservation* 5 (January 2016): 118–26.

Nijman, Vincent, Htun Oo and Nay Myo Shwe. 'Assessing the Illegal Bear Trade in Myanmar through Conversations with Poachers: Topology, Perceptions, and Trade Links to China'. *Human Dimensions of Wildlife* 22, no. 2 (2017): 172–82.

Nongbri, Natasha. 'Elephant Hunting in Late 19th Century North-East India: Mechanisms of Control, Contestation and Local Reactions'. *Economic and Political Weekly* 38, no. 30 (2003): 3189–99.

Nongbri, Tiplut. 'Culture and Biodiversity: Myths, Legends and the Conservation of Nature in the Hills of North-East India'. *Indian Anthropologist* 36, nos. 1/2 (2006): 1–21.

Nongbri, Tiplut, and Rashi Bhargava (eds.). *Materiality and Visuality in North East India: An Interdisciplinary Perspective*. Singapore: Springer Nature, 2021.

Nongkynrih, Kynpham Sing. 'U Thlen: The Man-Eating Serpent; MEGHALAYA'. *India International Centre Quarterly* 32, nos. 2/3 (2005): 33–8.

Norton, Christopher J., and David R. Braun (eds.). *Asian Paleoanthropology: From Africa to China and Beyond*. Dordrecht; Heidelberg; London; New York: Springer, 2010.

Nunthara, C. *Impact of the Introduction of Grouping of Villages in Mizoram*. Delhi: Omsons Publications, 1989.

———. *Mizoram: Society and Polity*. Delhi: Indus Publishing, 1996.

Núñez-Farfán, Juan, and Pedro Luis Valverde (eds.). *Evolutionary Ecology of Plant–Herbivore Interaction*. Cham: Springer Nature, 2020.

O'Brien, Michael J., and Kevin N. Laland. 'Genes, Culture, and Agriculture: An Example of Human Niche Construction'. *Current Anthropology* 53, no. 4 (2012): 434–70.

Odling-Smee, F. John, Kevin N. Laland and Marcus W. Feldman. *Niche Construction: The Neglected Process in Evolution*. Princeton; Oxford: Princeton University Press, 2003.

O'Gorman, Emily, and Andrea Gaynor. 'More-Than-Human Histories'. *Environmental History* 25 (August 2020): 711–35.

Okoshi, Masako, Tomotaro Nishikawa, Hiromori Akagi and Tatsuhito Fujimura. 'Genetic Diversity of Cultivated Rice (*Oryza sativa* L.) and Wild Rice (*Oryza rufipogon* Griff.) in Asia, Especially in Myanmar, as Revealed by Organelle Markers'. *Genetic Resources and Crop Evolution* 65 (October 2018): 713–26.

Oldham, Thomas. 'On the Geological Structure of a Portion of the Khasi Hills, Bengal'. In *Memoirs of the Geological Survey of India*, 1:99–210. Calcutta: Bengal Military Orphan Press, 1849.

Ong, Homervergel G., Shein Man Ling, Thet Thet Mar Win, Dae-Hyun Kang, Jung-Hoon Lee and Young-Dong Kim. 'Ethnobotany of Wild Medicinal Plants Used by the Müün Ethnic People: A Quantitative Survey in Southern Chin State, Myanmar'. *Journal of Herbal Medicine* 13 (September 2018): 91–6.

Ong, Homervergel G., and Young-Dong Kim. 'Medicinal Plants for Gastrointestinal Diseases among the Kuki-Chin Ethnolinguistic Groups across Bangladesh, India, and Myanmar: A Comparative and Network Analysis Study'. *Journal of Ethnopharmacology* 251, no. 112415 (2020): 1–14.

Oppitz, Michael. 'Die Geschichte der verlorenen Schrift. Frobenius-Vorlesung 2005'. *Paideuma: Mitteilungen zur Kulturkunde* 52 (2006): 27–50.

Ormsby, Alison. 'Analysis of Local Attitudes toward the Sacred Groves of Meghalaya and Karnataka, India'. *Conservation and Society* 11, no. 2 (2013): 187–97.

Out in the Cold: The Ongoing Threat of Snow Leopard Trade. London: Environmental Investigation Agency, 2018.

Overton, Nick J., and Yannis Hamilakis. 'A Manifesto for a Social Zooarchaeology: Swans and Other Beings in the Mesolithic'. *Archaeological Dialogues* 20, no. 2 (2013): 111–36.

Ovesen, Jan. 'Man or Beast? Lycanthropy in the Naga Hills'. *Ethnos* 48, nos. 1/2 (1983): 5–25.

Owen-Smith, Thomas, and Nathan Hill (eds.). *Trans-Himalayan Linguistics*. Berlin; Boston: Walter De Gruyter, 2014.

Owens, J. David (ed.). *Indigenous Fermented Foods of Southeast Asia*. Boca Raton, FL: CRC Press, 2015.

Pachuau, Joy L. K. *Being Mizo: Identity and Belonging in Northeast India*. Delhi: Oxford University Press, 2014.

———. 'Sartorial Matters: A Brief History of Attire in Mizoram'. In *Materiality and Visuality in North East India*, edited by Nongbri and Bhargava, 105–27. Singapore: Springer Nature, 2021.

Pachuau, Joy L. K., and Willem van Schendel. *The Camera as Witness: A Social History of Mizoram, Northeast India*. Delhi: Cambridge University Press, 2015.

Pachuau, Margaret L. 'Orality: Analysing Its Politics within the Domains of the Mizo Narrative'. In *Modern Practices in North East India*, edited by Dzüvichü and Baruah, 172–94. London; New York: Routledge, 2018.

Padmalal, D., and K. Maya. *Sand Mining: Environmental Impacts and Selected Case Studies*. Dordrecht; Heidelberg; New York; London: Springer, 2014.

Pan, Wen-bin, Wei Ding, Xiao-Dong He, Li-Xiang Zhang, Xiao-Fei Zhao, Chi Ma, Zhi-Pang Huang, Guo-Peng Ren and Wen Xiao. 'Low Input Parks Strategy Can Work: Dynamic Profile of Mishmi Takins under Constrained Conservation Management in Mt. Gaoligong, China'. *Global Ecology and Conservation* 19, no. e00659 (2019): 1–8.

Pandit, M. K., and C. R. Babu. 'Biology and Conservation of *Coptis teeta Wall.*: An Endemic and Endangered Medicinal Herb of Eastern Himalaya'. *Environmental Conservation* 25, no. 3 (1998): 262–72.

Pangging, Govinda, Chaman Lal Sharma and Madhubala Sharma. 'Ethnobotanical Study of Plants Used in Magico-religious Practices of *Deori* Tribe in Assam, India'. *Plant Archives* 19, no. 1 (2019): 387–99.

Pangging, Govinda, M. Sharma, C. L. Sharma, N. Rai, J. Gogoi and Nyishi Tribe. '*Byopa*: A Traditional Headgear of Nyishi Tribe from Arunachal Pradesh (India) and Its Relevance to Geographical Indication'. *Pleione* 13, no. 1 (2019): 12–18.

Papworth, Sarah, Madhu Rao, Myint Myint Oo, Kyaw Thinn Latt, Robert Tizard, Thomas Pienkowski and L. Roman Carrasco. 'The Impact of Gold Mining and Agricultural Concessions on the Tree Cover and Local Communities in Northern Myanmar'. *Scientific Reports* 7, no. 46594 (2017): 1–11.

Parashar, Utpal, and Sabir Hussain. 'Assam Forest Officials Seize Kangaroo, Exotic Wildlife from Smugglers near Mizoram Border'. *Hindustan Times*, 29 July 2020. https://www.hindustantimes.com/india-news/assam-forest-officials-seize-kangaroo-exotic-wildlife-from-smugglers-near-mizoram-border/story-RZKCMGOrMeDrpfRiEoot3K.html. Accessed 8 January 2022.

Pardharasadhi, A. 'Ecological Biogeography of Freshwater Fishes in the North-East Regions of India'. PhD thesis, North-Eastern Hill University, Shillong, 1986.

Parratt, Saroj Nalini. 'The Religion of Manipur: Beliefs, Rituals, and Historical Development'. PhD thesis, Australian National University, 1974.

———. *The Court Chronicle of the Kings of Manipur: The Cheitharon Kumpapa*. London; New York: Routledge, 2005.

Parry, N. E. *The Lakhers*. London: Macmillan and Co., 1932.

Pau, Pum Khan. *Indo-Burma Frontier and the Making of the Chin Hills: Empire and Resistance*. London; New York: Routledge, 2020.

———. 'Rethinking Religious Conversion: Missionary Endeavor and Indigenous Response among the Zo (Chin) of the India–Burma Borderland'. *Journal of Religion and Society* 14 (2012): 1–17.

———. 'Transborder People, Connected History: Border and Relationships in the Indo-Burma Borderlands'. *Journal of Borderlands Studies* 35, no. 4 (2020): 619–39.

Pau, Pum Khan, and Thang Sian Mung. 'Fragmented Tribes of the India–Burma–Bangladesh Borderlands: Representation of the Zo (Kuki-Chin) People in Colonial Ethnography'. *Asian Ethnicity* (February 2021): 1–22.

Peal, S. E. 'Notes on a Visit to the Tribes Inhabiting the Hills South of Sibságar, Ásám'. *Journal of the Asiatic Society of Bengal* 41, no. 1 (1872): 9–31.

Pelletier, Alexandre. 'Identity Formation, Christian Networks, and the Peripheries of Kachin Ethnonational Identity'. *Asian Politics and Policy* 13, no. 1 (2021): 72–89.

Pelliot, Paul. 'Deux itinéraires de Chine en Inde à la fin du VIIIe siècle'. *Bulletin de l'École française d'Extrême-Orient* 4 (1904): 131–413.

Pemberton, R. Boileau. 'Abstract of the Journal of a Route Travelled by Capt. S. F. Hannay, of the 40th Regiment Native Infantry, from the Capital of Ava to the Amber Mines of the Hukong Valley on the South-East Frontier of Assam'. *Journal of the Asiatic Society of Bengal* 6 (1837): 245–78.

———. *Report on Bootan*. Calcutta: Bengal Military Orphan Press, 1838.

———. *Report on the Eastern Frontier of British India*. Calcutta: Baptist Mission Press, 1835.

Penjore, Dorji. 'Digging the Past: The State of Archaeological Study of Bhutan'. *Journal of Bhutan Studies* 36 (Summer 2017): 40–57.

———. *On the Mule Track to Dagana*. Thimphu: The Centre for Bhutan Studies, 2003.

Phayre, A. P. 'Account of Arakan'. *Journal of the Asiatic Society of Bengal* 10, no. 117 (1841): 679–712.

Phukan, R., and S. N. Chowdhury. 'Traditional Knowledge and Practices Involved in *Muga* Culture of Assam'. *Indian Journal of Traditional Knowledge* 5, no. 4 (2006): 450–3.

Piang, L. Lam Khan. 'Contestation of Etic Categorizations and Emic Categories: Resurgence of Zo Ethno-national Identity in the Indo-Myanmar Borderland'. *South East Asia Research* 28, no. 3 (2020): 284–300.

Platt, Steven G., Win Ko Ko, Khin Myo Myo, Lay Lay Khaing, Kalyar Platt, Aung Maung and Thomas R. Rainwater. 'Notes on *Melocanna baccifera* and Bamboo Brakes in the Rakhine Hills of Western Myanmar'. *Bamboo Science and Culture: The Journal of the American Bamboo Society* 23, no. 1 (2010): 38–48.

Playfair, A. *The Garos*. London: David Nutt, 1909.

Pokharia, Anil K., Tiatoshi Jamir, David Tetso and Zokho Venuh. 'Late First Millennium BC to Second Millennium AD Agriculture in Nagaland: A Reconstruction Based on Archaeobotanical Evidence and Radiocarbon Dates'. *Current Science* 104, no. 10 (2013): 1341–53.

Pollok, Fitz William Thomas, and W. S. Thom. *Wild Sports of Burma and Assam*. London: Hurst and Blackett, 1900.

Pommaret, Françoise. 'The Community of Ngangla Trong'. In *Twilight Cultures: Tradition and Change in Four Rural Communities in Bhutan*, edited by Karma Phuntsho, 13–49. Thimphu: Shejun and Helvetas, 2015.

Post, Mark W. 'Morphosyntactic Reconstruction in an Areal-Historical Context: A Pre-Historical Relationship between North East India and Mainland Southeast Asia?' In *Languages of Mainland Southeast Asia: The State of the Art*, edited by N. J. Enfield and Bernard Comrie, 209–65. Berlin; Boston: De Gruyter Mouton, 2015.

Prabhu, Vandana R., Moolamkudy Suresh Arjun, Karippadakam Bhavana, Ranganathan Kamalakkannan and Muniyandi Nagarajan. 'Complete Mitochondrial Genome of Indian Mithun, *Bos frontalis* and Its Phylogenetic Implications'. *Molecular Biology Reports* 46 (February 2019): 2561–6.

Prasse-Freeman, Elliott. 'Necroeconomics: Dispossession, Extraction, and Indispensable/ Expendable Laborers in Contemporary Myanmar'. *Journal of Peasant Studies* (July 2021): 1–31.

Previato, Tommaso. 'Indigenous Beliefs for Sustainability: On the Significance of Ritual in the Gender Ecology of Tibetan and Mosuo Matricultures of Northwestern Yunnan'. *Matrix: A Journal for Matricultural Studies* 2, no. 1 (2021): 34–65.

Prokop, Pawel, and Ireneusz Suliga. 'Two Thousand Years of Iron Smelting in the Khasi Hills, Meghalaya, North East India'. *Current Science* 104, no. 6 (2013): 761–8.

Pryce, Thomas Oliver, Aung Aung Kyaw, Myo Min Kyaw, Tin Tin Win, Thu Thu Win, Khin Htwe Win et al. 'A First Absolute Chronology for Late Neolithic to Early Bronze Age Myanmar: New AMS 14C Dates from Nyaung'gan and Oakaie'. *Antiquity* 92, no. 363 (2018): 690–708.

Punyu, Khonyu. 'Oral History of the Angami Nagas'. PhD thesis, North Eastern Hill University, 1995.

Qadri, Fozail Ahmad. *Pre-Colonial Northeast India: A Portrait from Persian Accounts*. Guwahati: Centre for Northeast India, South and Southeast Asia Studies, OKD Institute, 2004.

Qiu, Ming Jiang and William V. Bleisch. 'Preliminary Assessment of Large Mammals in the Namcha Barwa Region of South-Eastern Tibet'. *Oryx* 30, no. 1 (1996): 37–44.

Qiu, Qiang, Lizhong Wang, Kun Wang, Yongzhi Yang, Tao Ma, Zefu Wang et al. 'Yak Whole-Genome Resequencing Reveals Domestication Signatures and Prehistoric Population Expansions'. *Nature Communications* 6, no. 10283 (2015): 1–7.

Qu, Yanhua, Xu Luo, Ruiying Zhang, Gang Song, Fasheng Zou and Fumin Lei. 'Lineage Diversification and Historical Demography of a Montane Bird *Garrulax elliotii*: Implications for the Pleistocene Evolutionary History of the Eastern Himalayas'. *BMC Evolutionary Biology* 11, no. 174 (2011): 1–17.

Rafy, Mrs. *Folk-Tales of the Khasis*. London: Macmillan and Company, 1920.

Rahman, M. Atiqur, Khudeja Begum, M. Enamur Rashid and M. Harun-ur-Rashid. 'Medicinal Plant Diversity in the Flora of Bangladesh and their Conservation: 2. A Report on Ten Angiosperm Families'. *Plant Archives* 12, no. 2 (2012): 1023–35.

Rahman, Md. Habibur. 'Rohingya Refugee Crisis and Human vs. Elephant (*Elephas maximus*) Conflicts in Cox's Bazar District of Bangladesh'. *Journal of Wildlife and Biodiversity* 3, no. 3 (2019): 10–21.

Rahman, Mizanur, Cristina Cobo Castillo, Charlene Murphy, Sufi Mostafizur Rahman and Dorian Q. Fuller. 'Agricultural Systems in Bangladesh: The First Archaeobotanical Results from Early Historic Wari-Bateshwar and Early Medieval Vikrampura'. *Archaeological and Anthropological Sciences* 12, no. 37 (2020): 1–17.

Rahman, Mizanur, Charlene Murphy, Alison Weisskopf, Louis Champion, Cristina Castillo and Dorian Q. Fuller. 'Wari-Bateshwar and Vikrampura: Successful Case Studies in Archaeobotany, Bangladesh'. *Man and Environment* 44, no. 1 (2019): 62–72.

Rahman, Mohammad Atiqul. 'Indigenous Knowledge of Herbal Medicines in Bangladesh. 3. Treatment of Skin Diseases by Tribal Communities of the Hill Tracts Districts'. *Bangladesh Journal of Botany* 39, no. 2 (2010): 169–77.

Rai, Prabhat Kumar, and M. Muni Singh. '*Lantana camara* Invasion in Urban Forests of an Indo-Burma Hotspot Region and Its Ecosustainable Management Implication through Biomonitoring of Particulate Matter'. *Journal of Asia-Pacific Biodiversity* 8 (December 2015): 375–81.

Raina, Vimala. *Khamba Thoibi and Poems on Manipur*. Imphal, Manipur: The Government Press, 1963.

Ramashankar, Sourabh Deb, and Bipin Kumar Sharma (eds.). *Traditional Healing Practices in North East India*. Pasighat, Arunachal Pradesh: North Eastern Institute of Folk Medicine, 2009.

Ramirez, Philippe. 'Conversions, Population Movements and Ethno-cultural Landscape in the Assam–Meghalaya Borderlands'. *Asian Ethnicity* 17, no. 3 (2016): 340–52.

———. 'Enemy Spirits, Allied Spirits: The Political Cosmology of Arunachal Pradesh Societies'. *NEHU Journal* 3, no. 1 (2005): 1–28.

———. 'Ethnic Conversions and Transethnic Descent Groups in the Assam–Meghalaya Borderlands'. *Asian Ethnology* 72, no. 2 (2013): 279–97.

———. *People of the Margins: Across Ethnic Boundaries in North-East India*. Guwahati: Spectrum, 2014.

Rangarajan, Mahesh. 'Animals with Rich Histories: The Case of the Lions of Gir Forest, Gujarat, India'. *History and Theory* 52 (December 2013): 109–27.

Rangarajan, Mahesh, and K. Sivaramakrishnan (eds.). *Shifting Ground: People, Animals, and Mobility in India's Environmental History*. Oxford: Oxford University Press, 2014.

Rao, Madhu, Than Zaw, Saw Htun and Than Myint. 'Hunting for a Living: Wildlife Trade, Rural Livelihoods and Declining Wildlife in the Hkakaborazi National Park, North Myanmar'. *Environmental Management* 48 (March 2011): 158–67.

Rasel, Azizul. 'Experiencing the Border: The Lushai People and Transnational Space'. In *Borders and Mobility in South Asia and Beyond*, edited by Reece Jones and Md. Azmeary Ferdoush, 81–97. Amsterdam: Amsterdam University Press, 2018.

Rashid, Mohammad Mamunur. 'The Exploration of Natural Gas and Its Export Potential in Bangladesh'. *Science, Technology and Society* 12, no. 2 (2007): 245–68.

Rasul, Golam. 'Political Ecology of the Degradation of Forest Commons in the Chittagong Hill Tracts of Bangladesh'. *Environmental Conservation* 34, no. 2 (2007): 153–63.

Rathod, Nenavath Krishna Kumar, Jyoti Kumari, Firoz Hossain, Rashmi Chhabra, Somnath Roy, Ganjalagatta Dasaiah Harish, Rakesh Bhardwaj, Raveendra N. Gadag and Anup Kumar Misra. 'Characterization of Mimban Maize Landrace from North-Eastern Himalayan Region Using Microsatellite Markers'. *Journal of Plant Biochemistry and Biotechnology* 29, no. 2 (2020): 323–35.

Ray, Avik, and Rajasri Ray. 'The Birth of Aus Agriculture in the South-Eastern Highlands of India: An Exploratory Synthesis'. *Ancient Asia* 9, no. 3 (2018): 1–7.

Ray, Sohini. 'Boundaries Blurred? Folklore, Mythology, History and the Quest for an Alternative Genealogy in North-East India'. *Journal of the Royal Asiatic Society*, series 3, 25, no. 2 (2015): 247–67.

Rayhan, Morshed. 'Prospects of Public Archaeology in Heritage Management in Bangladesh: Perspective of Wari-Bateshwar'. *Archaeologies: Journal of the World Archaeological Congress* (Octoberv2011): 1–19.

Reddy, B. Mohan, B. T. Langstieh, Vikrant Kumar, T. Nagaraja, A. N. S. Reddy, Aruna Meka, A. G. Reddy, K. Thangaraj and Lalji Singh. 'Austro-Asiatic Tribes of Northeast India Provide Hitherto Missing Genetic Link between South and Southeast Asia'. *PLoS ONE* 2, no. 11 (2007): e1141, 1–12.

Rees, Robert N., and Gordon H. Rodda. 'Burmese Python and Other Giant Constrictors'. In *Encyclopedia of Biological Invasions*, edited by Simberloff and Rejmánek, 85–91. Berkeley; Los Angeles; London: University of California Press, 2011.

Reghunathan, Sudhamahi. 'Sunshine on Faith: Life and Belief in Some Arunachal Communities'. *India International Centre Quarterly* 26, no. 2 (1999): 138–47.

Reich, David. *Who We Are and How We Got Here: Ancient DNA and the New Science of the Human Past*. Oxford: Oxford University Press, 2018.

Reid, A. S. *Chin-Lushai Land, Including a Description of the Various Expeditions into the Chin-Lushai Hills and the Final Annexation of the Country*. Calcutta: Thacker, Spink, 1893.

Renner, Swen C. 'Bird Species-Richness Pattern in the Greater Himalayan Mountains: A General Introduction'. In *Avifauna of the Eastern Himalayas and Southeastern Sub-Himalayan Mountains*, edited by Sven C. Renner and John H. Rappole, 1–9. Washington, DC: American Ornithologists' Union, 2011.

Renner, Sven C., and John H. Rappole (eds.). *Avifauna of the Eastern Himalayas and Southeastern Sub-Himalayan Mountains: Center of Endemism or Many Species in Marginal Habitats?* Ornithological Monographs 70. Washington, DC: American Ornithologists' Union, 2011.

Renner, Swen C., John H. Rappole, Christopher M. Milensky, Myint Aung, Nay Myo Shwe and Thein Aung. *Avifauna of the Southeastern Himalayan Mountains and Neighboring Myanmar Hill Country*. Bonn Zoological Bulletin Supplementum vol. 62. Bonn: Zoologisches Forschungsmuseum Alexander Koenig – Leibniz-Institut für Biodiversität der Tiere, 2015.

Rethy, P., B. Singh, R. Kagyung and P. R. Gajurel. 'Ethnobotanical Studies of Dehang-Debang Biosphere Reserve of Arunachal Pradesh with Special Reference to Memba Tribe'. *Indian Journal of Traditional Knowledge* 9, no. 1 (2010): 61–7.

Reyes-Centeno, Hugo, Hannes Rathmann, Tsunehiko Hanihara and Katerina Harvati. 'Testing Modern Human Out-of-Africa Dispersal Models Using Dental Nonmetric Data'. *Current Anthropology* 58, supplement 17 (2017): S406–17.

Riccio, Maria Eugenia, José Manuel Nunes, Melissa Rahal, Barbara Kervaire, Jean-Marie Tiercy and Alicia Sanchez-Mazas. 'The Austroasiatic Munda Population from India and Its Enigmatic Origin: A HLA Diversity Study'. *Human Biology* 83, no. 3 (2011): 405–35.

Richards, Keith, Hugh Brammer and Patricia L. Saunders. 'The Historical Avulsion of the Tista River, and Its Relationship to the Brahmaputra: Map and Archive Evidence from 1750 to 1835'. *Geographical Journal* 87, no. 3 (2021): 1–16.

Riebeck, Emil. *Die Hügelstämme von Chittagong: Ergebnisse einer Reise im Jahre 1882*. Berlin: A. Asher & Co., 1885.

Rinzin, Chhewang, Walter J. V. Vermeulen, Martin J. Wassen and Pieter Glasbergen. 'Nature Conservation and Human Well-Being in Bhutan: An Assessment of Local Community Perceptions'. *Journal of Environment and Development* 18, no. 2 (2009): 177–202.

Rippa, Alessandro, Galen Murton and Matthäus Rest. 'Building Highland Asia in the Twenty-First Century'. *Verge: Studies in Global Asias* 6, no. 2 (2020): 83–111.

Rippa, Alessandro, and Yi Yang. 'The Amber Road: Cross-Border Trade and the Regulation of the Burmite Market in Tengchong, Yunnan'. *TRaNS: Trans-Regional and -National Studies of Southeast Asia* 5, no. 2 (2017): 243–67.

Roberts, Patrick, Eric Delson, Preston Miracle, Peter Ditchfield, Richard G. Roberts, Zenobia Jacobs et al. 'Continuity of Mammalian Fauna over the Last 200,000 Y in the Indian Subcontinent'. *Proceedings of the National Academy of Sciences of the United States of America (PNAS)* 111, no. 16 (2014): 5848–53.

Robinne, François. 'Memorial Art as an Anthropological Object (Chin State of Burma)'. *Journal of Burma Studies* 19, no. 1 (2015): 199–241.

Rookmaker, Kees. 'Lady Curzon and the Establishment of Kaziranga National Park'. *Pachyderm* 60 (July 2018–June 2019): 110–11.

Rosati, Paolo Eugenio. 'The Goddess Kāmākhyā: Religio-political Implications in the Tribalisation Process'. *History and Sociology of South Asia* 11, no. 2 (2017): 137–55.

Ross, Andrew. 'The Remarkable Palaeodiversity in Burmese Amber'. In *AMBERIF 2018: International Fair of Amber, Jewellery and Gemstones. International Symposium Amber. Science and Art Abstracts*, 12–17. Gdańsk: International Fair Co, 2018.

Ross, Andrew J. *Burmese (Myanmar) amber taxa*. Online supplement, 2021. http://www.nms.ac.uk/explore/stories/natural-world/burmese-amber/. Accessed on 30 June 2021.

Ross, Denise. 'Development of Local Theology of the Chin (Zomi) of the Assemblies of God (AG) in Myanmar: A Case Study in Contextualisation'. PhD thesis, University of Birmingham, 2019.

Rowan, Andrew N. (ed.). *Animals and People Sharing the World*. Lebanon, NH: University Press of New England, 1988.

Rowlatt, E. A. 'Report of an Expedition into the Mishmee Hills to the North-East of Sudyah'. *Journal of the Asiatic Society of Bengal* 12, no. 2 (1845): 477–95.

Roy, Mukti. 'A Spatial and Temporal Analysis of Elephant–Human Conflict at Gorumara and Jalpaiguri Forest Divisions of Northern West Bengal'. *Journal of Wildlife Research* 5, no. 3 (2017): 41–9.

Roy (née Chowdhury), Ruma. 'The Donyi-Polo Cult of Arunachal Pradesh: A Study in Textualising Tribal Oral Religion'. PhD thesis, North-Eastern Hill University, Shillong, 1995.

Roy, Samaren. *The Roots of Bengali Culture and Other Essays*. Calcutta: Eureka Publishers, 1966.

Roy, Somnath, Mrita Banerjee, Nabaneeta Basak, Torit Baran Bagchi, Nimai Prasad Mandal, Bhaskar Chandra Patra, Anup Kumar Misra, Sanjeev Kumar Singh, Ranbir Singh Rathi and Arunava Pattanayak. 'Genetic Diversity Analysis of Specialty Glutinous and Low-Amylose Rice (*Oryza sativa* L.) Landraces of Assam Based on Wx Locus and Microsatellite Diversity'. *Journal of Biosciences* 45, no. 86 (2020): 1–16.

Roy, Tashbeer Singh, Lahari Saikia, Mithu Medhi and Dipak Tassa. 'Epidemiological Investigation of an Outbreak of Typhoid Fever in Jorhat town of Assam, India'. *Indian Journal of Medical Research* 144, no. 4 (2016): 592–6.

Ryley, J. Horton. *Ralph Fitch, England's Pioneer to India and Burma*. London: T. Fisher Unwin, 1899.

Sadan, Mandy. *Being and Becoming Kachin: Histories beyond the State in the Borderworlds of Burma*. Oxford: Oxford University Press, 2013.

Saha, Jonathan. 'Among the Beasts of Burma: Animals and the Politics of Colonial Sensibilities, c. 1840–1940'. *Journal of Social History* 48, no. 4 (2015): 910–32.

———. 'Colonizing Elephants: Animal Agency, Undead Capital and Imperial Science in British Burma'. *British Journal for the History of Science Themes* 2 (April 2017): 169–89.

———. 'Milk to Mandalay: Dairy Consumption, Animal History and the Political Geography of Colonial Burma'. *Journal of Historical Geography* 54 (October 2016): 1–12.

Saha, S. S. 'A New Genus and a New Species of Flying Squirrel (Mammalia: Rodentia: Sciuridae) from Northeastern India'. *Bulletin of the Zoological Survey of India* 4, no. 3 (1981): 331–6.

Sahlins, Marshall. 'In Anthropology, It's Emic All the Way Down: Response to Comments on Sahlins, Marshall, 2017, "The Original Political Society"'. *Hau: Journal of Ethnographic Theory* 7, no. 2 (2017): 91–128.

———. 'The Original Political Society'. In *On Kings*, edited by David Graeber and Marshall Sahlins, 23–64. Chicago: HAU Books, 2017.

Saif, Samia, Aal M. Russell, Sabiha I. Nodie, Chloe Inskip, Petra Lahann, Adam Barlow, Christina Greenwood Barlow, Md. A. Islam and Douglas C. MacMillan. 'Local Usage of Tiger Parts and Its Role in Tiger Killing in the Bangladesh Sundarbans'. *Human Dimensions of Wildlife* 21, no. 2 (2016): 95–110.

Saif, Samia, H. M. Tuihedur Rahman and Douglas Craig MacMillan. 'Who Is Killing the Tiger *Panthera tigris* and Why?' *Oryx* 52, no. 1 (2018): 46–54.

Saikia, Arupjyoti. *Forests and Ecological History of Assam, 1826–2000*. New Delhi: Oxford University Press, 2011.

———. 'Imperialism, Geology and Petroleum: History of Oil in Colonial Assam'. *Economic and Political Weekly* 46, no. 12 (2011): 48–55.

———. 'Kaziranga National Park: History, Landscape and Conservation Practices'. *Economic and Political Weekly* 46, no. 32 (2011): 12–13.

———. 'Making Room Inside Forests: Grazing and Agrarian Conflicts in Colonial Assam'. In *Shifting Ground*, edited by Rangarajan and Sivaramakrishnan, 155–79. Oxford: Oxford University Press, 2014.

———. *The Unquiet River: A Biography of the Brahmaputra*. New Delhi: Oxford University Press, 2019.

Saikia, P., and M. L. Khan. 'Homegardens of Upper Assam, Northeast India: A Typical Example of On-Farm Conservation of Agarwood (*Aquilaria malaccensis* Lam.)'. *International Journal of Biodiversity Science, Ecosystem Services and Management* 10, no. 4 (2014): 262–9.

Saikia, Prasanta K. 'Indian Gharial (Gavialis gangeticus): Status, Ecology and Conservation'. In *Rare Animals of India*, edited by Singaravelan, 76–100. Sharjah, UAE, Oak Park, IL, and Bussum: Bentham Science Publishers, 2013.

Saikia, Raktim Ranjan, and Nurul Amin. 'A Study on the Salt Production of Ancient Assam'. *Indian Journal of History of Science* 54, no. 4 (2019): 485–96.

Saikia, Yasmin. *Fragmented Memories: Struggling to be Tai-Ahom in India*. Durham; London: Duke University Press, 2004.

Saikia, Yasmin, and Amit R. Baishya (eds.). *Northeast India: A Place of Relations*. Cambridge: Cambridge University Press, 2017.

Sailo, Lalawmawia. 'Ecological Studies on Grey Peacock Pheasant *Polyplectron bicalcaratum* (Linn, 1758) in the Tropical Forest of Mizoram, India'. PhD thesis, Mizoram University, 2019.

Sailo, Sailiana. *The Bongchers*. Agartala, Tripura: Tribal Research Department, 1992.

Sakhong, Lian H. *In Search of Chin Identity: A Study in Religion, Politics and Ethnic Identity in Burma*. Copenhagen: NIAS Press, 2003.

San, Myint Myint, Nway Mon Mon Aung, Htike San Soe and Yunn Mi Mi Kyaw. *Study on Distribution and Medicinal Uses of Orchid Species in Matu pe Township, Southern Chin State*. Yangon: Forest Department, The Republic of the Union of Myanmar, 2015.

Sanders, Michele Jeanette, Laura Miller, Shonil A. Bhagwat and Alex Rogers. 'Conservation Conversations: A Typology of Barriers to Conservation Success'. *Oryx* 55, no. 2 (2021): 245–54.

Sangay, Tiger, and Karl Vernes. 'Human–Wildlife Conflict in the Kingdom of Bhutan: Patterns of Livestock Predation by Large Mammalian Carnivores'. *Biological Conservation* 141 (2008): 1272–82.

Sangma, Sanatombi K. 'Shape-Shifting or Transformation Myth in Garo Culture'. *The Criterion: An International Journal in English* 7, no. 3 (2016): 277–80.

Sangma, Semeri Alva B. 'Rites of Passage in the Garo Oral Literature'. PhD thesis, North Eastern Hill University, 2011.

Sanyal, Charu Chandra. *The Meches and the Ṭoṭos: Two Sub-Himalayan Tribes of North Bengal*. 2 vols. Darjeeling: The University of North Bengal, 1969.

Sarker, A. H. M. Raihan, and Eivin Røskaft. 'Human–Wildlife Conflicts and Management Options in Bangladesh, with Special Reference to Asian Elephants (*Elephas maximus*)'. *International Journal of Biodiversity Science, Ecosystem Services and Management* 6, nos. 3/4 (2010): 164–75.

Sarma, Dhritiman. 'Ethnoarchaeology of the Karbi Megaliths'. In *50 Years After Daojali-Hading*, edited by Jamir and Hazarika, 352–9. New Delhi: Research India Press, 2014.

Sarma, Pranab, and Manjil Hazarika. 'Situating Northeast Indian Archaeology in Chronological Perspective: Fresh Observations'. In *50 Years After Daojali-Hading*, edited by Jamir and Manjil Hazarika, 37–59. New Delhi: Research India Press, 2014.

Sarma, Ujjal Kumar, P. S. Easa and Vivek Menon. *Deadly Tracks: A Scientific Approach to Understanding and Mitigating Elephant Mortality Due to Train Hits in Assam*. New Delhi: Wildlife Trust of India, 2006.

Sarmah, R., D. Adhikari, M. Majumder and A. Arunachalam. 'Traditional Medicobotany of Chakma Community Residing in the Northwestern Periphery of Namdapha National Park in Arunachal Pradesh'. *Indian Journal of Traditional Knowledge* 7, no. 4 (2008): 587–93.

Sarmah, R., A. Arunachalam, D. Adhikari and M. Majumder. 'Indigenous Technical Knowledge and Resource Utilization of Lisus in the South Eastern Part of Namdapha National Park, Arunachal Pradesh'. *Indian Journal of Traditional Knowledge* 5, no. 1 (2006): 51–6.

Sastrawan, Wayan Jarrah. 'Temporalities in Southeast Asian Historiography'. *History and Theory* 59, no. 2 (2020): 210–26.
Sawian, Bijoya. *Khasi Myths, Legends and Folk Tales*. Shillong: Ri Khasi Press, 2006.
Scheid, Claire S. 'Talom Rukbo and the Donyipolo Yelam Kebang: Restructuring Adi Religious Practices in Arunachal'. *Internationales Asienforum* 46, nos. 1/2 (2015): 127–48.
Scott, James C. *Against the Grain: A Deep History of the Earliest States*. New Haven; London: Yale University Press, 2017.
———. *The Art of Not Being Governed: An Anarchist History of Upland Southeast Asia*. New Haven; London: Yale University Press, 2009.
Searle, Mike. *Colliding Continents: A Geological Exploration of the Himalaya, Karakoram, and Tibet*. Oxford: Oxford University Press, 2013.
Seddiky, M. Assraf. 'Poverty and Social Vulnerability of Stone Quarry Workers in Bangladesh: An Ethnographic Study'. *Journal of Emerging Trends in Educational Research and Policy Studies* 5, no. 6 (2014): 684–94.
Selections of Papers Regarding the Hill Tracts between Assam and Burmah and on the Upper Brahmaputra. Calcutta: Bengal Secretariat Press, 1873.
Sen, Dineshchandra (ed.). *Eastern Bengal Ballads*. 4 vols. Calcutta: University of Calcutta, 1923–32.
Sen, Sukumar. *Vipradāsa's Manasā-Vijaya: A Fifteenth Century Bengali Text....* Calcutta: Asiatic Society, 1953.
Serajuddin, A. M., and John Buller. 'The Chakma Tribe of the Chittagong Hill Tracts in the 18th Century'. *Journal of the Royal Asiatic Society of Great Britain and Ireland* 1 (1984): 90–8.
Shah, Alpa. *In the Shadows of the State: Indigenous Politics, Environmentalism, and Insurgency in Jharkhand, India*. Durham; London: Duke University Press, 2010.
Shaha, Chandra Shekhar, and Masrur Mamun Mithun. *Behind Products: A Study on Crafts from Bangladesh*. Dhaka: Design and Technology Centee, 2004.
Shakespear, J. *The Lushei Kuki Clans*. London: Macmillan and Co., 1912.
———. 'Tangkhul Folk Tales and Notes on Some Festivals of the Hill Tribes South of Assam'. *Folklore* 33, no. 3 (1922): 265–81.
———. 'The Pleasing of the God Thangjing'. *Man* 13, no. 50 (1913): 81–6.
Shakespear, J., and T. C. Hodson. 'Folk-Tales of the Lushais and Their Neighbours'. *Folklore* 20, no. 4 (1909): 388–420.
Shakya, Bandana, Kabir Uddin, Yi Shaoliang, Laxmi Dutt Bhatta, Mahendra Singh Lodhi, Naing Zaw Htun and Yang Yongping. 'Mapping of the Ecosystem Services Flow from Three Protected Areas in the Far-Eastern Himalayan Landscape: An Impetus to Regional Cooperation'. *Ecosystem Services* 47, no. 101222 (2021): 1–18.

Shankar, Ajai (ed.). *Indian Archaeology 1992–93: A Review*. New Delhi: Archaeological Survey of India, 1997.

Sharma, Chandan Kumar. 'Dam, "Development" and Popular Resistance in Northeast India'. *Sociological Bulletin* 67, no. 3 (2018): 317–33.

Sharma, Eklabya, Nakul Chettri, Karma Tse-ring, Arun B. Shrestha, Fang Jing, Pradeep Mool and Mats Eriksson. *Climate Change Impacts and Vulnerability in the Eastern Himalayas*. Kathmandu: International Centre for Integrated Mountain Development, 2009.

Sharma, Jayeeta. 'British Science, Chinese Skill and Assam Tea: Making Empire's Garden'. *Indian Economic and Social History Review* 43 (2006): 429–55.

———. *Empire's Garden: Assam and the Making of India*. Durham, NC: Duke University Press, 2011.

Sharma, M., C. L. Sharma and J. Debbarma. 'Ethnobotanical Studies of Some Plants Used by Tripuri Tribe of Tripura, N. E. India, with Special Reference to Magico-religious Beliefs'. *International Journal of Plant, Animal and Environmental Sciences* 4, no. 3 (2014): 518–28.

Sharma, Saba. 'Territories of Belonging: Citizenship and Everyday Practices of the State in Bodoland'. PhD thesis, University of Cambridge, 2019.

Sharma, Sukanya, and Pankaj Singh. 'Luminescence Dating of Neolithic Pottery in North East India'. *Current Science* 113, no. 3 (2017): 492–6.

Sharma, U. K., Shyamanta Pegu, Diganta Hazarika and Arpana Das. 'Medico-religious Plants Used by the Hajong Community of Assam, India'. *Journal of Ethnopharmacology* 143 (August 2012): 787–800.

Sharma, Uma Kanta, and Shyamanta Pegu. 'Ethnobotany of Religious and Supernatural Beliefs of the Mising Tribes of Assam with Special Reference to the "Dobur Uie"'. *Journal of Ethnobiology and Ethnomedicine* 7, no. 16 (2011): 1–13.

Shaw, William. *Notes on the Thadou Kukis*. Calcutta: Published on behalf of the Government of Assam, 1929.

Shell, Jacob. 'Elephant Convoys beyond the State: Animal-Based Transport as Subversive Logistics'. *Environment and Planning D: Society and Space* 37, no. 5 (2019): 905–23.

Shetol, M. Hassan, M. Moklesur Rahman, Ratneshwar Sarder, M. Ismail Hossain and F. Kabir Riday. 'Present Status of Bangladesh Gas Fields and Future Development: A Review'. *Journal of Natural Gas Geoscience* 4 (2019): 347–54.

Shi, Liyuan, Guirong Yang, Zhikai Zhang, Lianxu Xia, Ying Liang, Hongli Tan et al. 'Reemergence of Human Plague in Yunnan, China in 2016'. *PLoS ONE* 13, no. 6 (2018): e0198067.

Shin, Jae-Eun. 'Descending from Demons, Ascending to Kshatriyas: Genealogical Claims and Political Process in Pre-modern Northeast India: The Chutiyas and the Dimasas'. *Indian Economic and Social History Review* 57, no. 1 (2020): 49–75.

———. 'Yoni, Yoginīs and Mahāvidyās: Feminine Divinities from Early Medieval Kāmarupa to Medieval Koch Behar'. *Studies in History* 26, no. 1 (2010): 1–29.

Showren, Tana. 'Exploring Ethnohistory of Arunachal Pradesh'. In *Tribal Studies in India*, edited by Behera, 51–66. Singapore: Springer Nature, 2020.

Silva, Fabio, Alison Weisskopf, Cristina Castillo, Charlene Murphy, Eleanor Kingwell-Banham, Ling Qin and Dorian Q Fuller. 'A Tale of Two Rice Varieties: Modelling the Prehistoric Dispersals of Japonica and Proto-Indica Rices'. *The Holocene* 28, no. 11 (2018): 1745–58.

Simberloff, Daniel, and Marcel Rejmánek (eds.). *Encyclopedia of Biological Invasions*. Berkeley; Los Angeles; London: University of California Press, 2011.

Simoons, Frederick J. 'Dairying, Milk Use, and Lactose Malabsorption in Eurasia: A Problem in Culture History'. *Anthropos* 74, nos. 1/2 (1979): 61–80.

———. 'The Geographic Hypothesis and Lactose Malabsorption: A Weighing of the Evidence'. *Digestive Diseases* 23, no. 11 (1978): 963–80.

———. 'The Traditional Limits of Milking and Milk Use in Southern Asia'. *Anthropos* 65, nos. 3/4 (1970): 547–93.

Simoons, Frederick J., and C. F. W. Higham. 'More on Higham's Study of Bovine Bones'. *Current Anthropology* 12, no. 3 (1971): 405.

Simoons, Frederick J., and Elizabeth S. Simoons. *A Ceremonial Ox of India: The Mithun in Nature, Culture and History*. Berkeley; Los Angeles; London: University of Wisconsin Press, 1968.

Singaravelan, Natarajan (ed.). *Rare Animals of India*. Sharjah, UAE, Oak Park, IL, and Bussum: Bentham Science Publishers, 2013.

Singh, Anamika, Ranjay K. Singh and Amish K. Sureja. 'Cultural Significance and Diversities of Ethnic Foods of Northeast India'. *Indian Journal of Traditional Knowledge* 6, no. 1 (2007): 79–94.

Singh, Bikarma, Sandhaya Jyoti Phukan, Bipin Kumar Sinha, Vivek Narayan Singh and Sashin Kumar Borthakur. 'Conservation Strategies for *Nepenthes Khasiana* in the *Nokrek* Biosphere Reserve of Garo Hills, Northeast, India'. *International Journal of Conservation Science* 2, no. 1 (2011): 55–64.

Singh, Chabungbam Rajagopal. 'Hydrological and Hydraulic Modelling for the Restoration and Management of Loktak Lake, Northeast India'. PhD thesis, University College London, 2010.

Singh, Daman. *The Last Frontier: People and Forests in Mizoram*. New Delhi: Tata Energy Research Institute, 1996.

Singh, H. Birkumar. 'Plants Associated in Forecasting and Beliefs within the Meitei Community of Manipur, Northeast India'. *Indian Journal of Traditional Knowledge* 10, no. 1 (2011): 190–3.

Singh, H. Birkumar, and R. K. Arora. 'Raishan (*Digitaria sp.*): A Minor Millet of the Khasi Hills, India'. *Economic Botany* 26, no. 4 (1972): 376–80.

Singh, Khuraijam Bijoykumar. 'Religious Revivalism and Colonial Rule: Origins of the Sanamahi Movement'. In *Colonialism and Resistance: Society and State in Manipur*, edited by Arambam Noni and Kangujam Sanatomba, 75–90. Abingdon; New York: Routledge, 2016.

Singh, M. Rameshwor, and Dhanamanjuri L. 'The Legendary Ballad of Khamba-Thoibi: A Cultural Text of Manipur'. *Spectrum: An International Journal of Humanities and Social Sciences* 6, no. 1 (2018): 98–101.

Singh, Ranjay K., Orik Rallen and Egul Padung. 'Elderly Adi Women of Arunachal Pradesh: "Living Encyclopedias" and Cultural Refugia in Biodiversity Conservation of the Eastern Himalaya, India'. *Environmental Management* 52 (July 2013): 712–35.

Singh, Ranjay K., Anshuman Singh, Stephen T. Garnett, Kerstin K. Zander, Lobsang and Darge Tsering. 'Paisang (*Quercus griffithii*): A Keystone Tree Species in Sustainable Agroecosystem Management and Livelihoods in Arunachal Pradesh, India'. *Environmental Management* 55 (2015): 187–204.

Singh, S. Khonachand, R. K. Birjit Singh and H. Manoranjan Sharma. 'Ethnobotanical Studies in Relation to Certain Traditional Culture of Chothe Tribe in Bishnupur District of Manipur, India'. *Pleione* 9, no. 1 (2015): 144–59.

Singh, Salam Shyam. 'New Discoveries of Petroglyphs in Vangchhia: A Preliminary Study'. *Journal of Neolithic Archaeology*, special issue no. 5 (2019): 135–44.

Singh Roy, Jayanta, and Syed M. Kamrul Ahsan. 'Raw Material and Technology of Stone Age Artifacts from Lalmai Hills and Chaklapunji Area'. *Pratnatattva* 13 (2007): 49–56.

Singha, Sukla. 'Wari Leeba: The Declining Storytelling Tradition of the Meiteis of Manipur and Tripura'. *Journal of North East India Studies* 7, no. 1 (2017): 33–46.

Singleton, Grant, Steve Belmain, Peter Brown and Bill Hardy (eds.). *Rodent Outbreaks: Ecology and Impacts*. Manila: International Rice Research Institute, 2010.

Sinha, Anindya, Aparajita Datta, M. D. Madhusudan and Charudutt Mishra. '*Macaca munzala*: A New Species from Western Arunachal Pradesh, Northeastern India'. *International Journal of Primatology* 26, no. 4 (2005): 977–89.

Sinha, Ravindra K., and Kurunthachalam Kannan. 'Ganges River Dolphin: An Overview of Biology, Ecology, and Conservation Status in India'. *Ambio* 43, no. 8 (2012): 1029–46.

Sirnate, Vasundhara. 'Students versus the State: The Politics of Uranium Mining in Meghalaya'. *Economic and Political Weekly*. 44, no. 47 (2009): 18–23.
Sitlhou, Hoineilhing. 'Food Culture and Identity in Northeast India: Prospects for Social Science Research'. *Explorations, ISS E-Journal* 4, no. 2 (2020): 49–66.
———. 'Land and Identity: A Sociological Study of the Thadou-Kuki Tribes of Manipur'. PhD thesis, Jawaharlal Nehru University, 2011.
———. 'Sacred Ecology and Ritual Practices of the Thadou Kukis of Manipur'. *Eastern Anthropologist* 73, nos. 3/4 (2020): 445–62.
———. 'The Shifting "Stages" of Performance: A Study of "Chavang Kut" Festival in Manipur'. *Asian Ethnicity* 19, no. 4 (2018): 468–88.
Sivaramakrishnan, K. 'Ethics of Nature in Indian Environmental History'. *Modern Asian Studies* 49, no. 4 (2015): 1261–310.
———. 'The Politics of Fire and Forest Regeneration in Colonial Bengal'. *Environment and History* 2, no. 2 (1996): 145–94.
Smadja, Joëlle. 'A Chronicle of Law Implementation in Environmental Conflicts: The Case of Kaziranga National Park in Assam (North-East India)'. *South Asia Multidisciplinary Academic Journal* 17 (2018): 1–37.
———. 'Belonging, Protected Areas, and Participatory Management: The Case of Kaziranga National Park (Assam) and of the Misings' Shifting Territory'. In *The Politics of Belonging in the Himalayas: Local Attachments and Boundary Dynamics*, edited by Joanna Pfaff-Czarnecka and Gérard Toffin, 246–7. New Delhi; Thousand Oaks CA; London; Singapore: Sage, 2011.
Small, Ernest. 'Evolution and Classification of *Cannabis sativa* (Marijuana, Hemp) in Relation to Human Utilization'. *Botanical Review* 81 (August 2015): 189–294.
Smith, W. L. *The One-Eyed Goddess: A Study of the Manasā Maṅgal*. Stockholm: Almqvist & Wicksell International, 1980.
Smith, William C. *The Ao Naga Tribe of Assam: A Study in Ethnology and Sociology*. London: Macmillan and Company, 1925.
Smyer Yü, Dan. 'Introduction: Trans-Himalayas as Multistate Margins'. In *Trans-Himalayan Borderlands: Livelihoods, Territorialities, Modernities*, edited by Dan Smyer Yü and Jean Michaud, 11–40. Amsterdam: Amsterdam University Press, 2017.
Smyer Yü, Dan. 'Perpendicular Geospatiality of Corridors and Borderlands: An Introduction'. In *Yunnan–Burma–Bengal Corridor Geographies*, edited by Dan Smyer Yü and Karin Dean, 1–26. London; New York: Routledge, 2021.
———. 'Situating Environmental Humanities in the New Himalayas: An Introduction'. In *Environmental Humanities in the New Himalayas*, edited by Dan Smyer Yü and Eric De Maaker, 1–24. London; New York: Routledge, 2021.

Smyer Yü, Dan, and Karin Dean (eds.). *Yunnan–Burma–Bengal Corridor Geographies: Protean Edging of Habitats and Empires*. London; New York: Routledge, 2021.

Smyer Yü, Dan, and Erik de Maaker (eds.). *Environmental Humanities in the New Himalayas: Symbiotic Indigeneity, Commoning, Sustainability*. London; New York: Routledge, 2021.

Spate, O. H. K. *India and Pakistan: A General and Regional Geography*. London: Methuen; New York: E. P. Dutton, 1954.

Spicer, Robert A. 'Tibet, the Himalaya, Asian Monsoons and Biodiversity: In What Ways Are They Related?' *Plant Diversity* 39, no. 5 (2017): 233–44.

Spielmann, Hans-Jürgen. 'Die Bawm-Zo: Eine Chin-Gruppe in den Chittagon Hill Tracts (Ostpakistan)'. PhD thesis, University of Heidelberg, 1969.

Sridhara, Shakunthala, and T. P. Rajendran. 'Gregarious Bamboo Flowering and Rodent Outbreaks: An Overview'. *Proceedings of the Vertebrate Pest Conference* 24, no. 24 (2010): 228–34.

Srinivasan, Umesh. 'Oil Palm Expansion: Ecological Threat to North-East India'. *Economic and Political Weekly* 49, no. 36 (2014): 1–6.

Srivastava, L. R. N. *The Gallongs*. Shillong: Research Department, Adviser's Secretariat, 1962.

Stack, Edward, and Charles Lyall. *The Mikirs*. London: David Nutt, 1908.

Stadler, Bernhard, and Anthony F. G. Dixon. 'Ecology and Evolution of Aphid–Ant Interactions'. *Annual Review of Ecology, Evolution, and Systematics* 36 (2005): 345–72.

State of Corruption: The Top-Level Conspiracy behind the Global Trade in Myanmar's Stolen Teak. London: Environmental Investigation Agency, 2019.

Stebbing, E. P. *The Diary of a Sportsman Naturalist in India*. London: John Lane, 1920.

Steel, E. H. 'Report on Jade Celts'. *Proceedings of the Asiatic Society of Bengal* (September 1870): 266–8.

Steen, Charlie R. 'Material Culture of the Langsing Nagas, Northern Burma'. *Southwestern Journal of Anthropology* 4, no. 3 (1948): 263–98.

Stevenson, H. N. C. *The Economics of the Central Chin Tribes*. Bombay: The Times of India Press, 1943.

Stewart, R. 'Notes on Northern Cachar'. *Journal of the Asiatic Society of Bengal* 24 (1855): 582–701.

Stirn, Aglaja, and Peter Van Ham. *The Seven Sisters of India: Tribal Worlds between India and Burma*. Munich; London; New York: Prestel Verlag, 2000.

Stonor, C. R. 'Notes on Religion and Ritual among the Dafla Tribes of the Assam Himalayas'. *Anthropos* 52, nos. 1/2 (1957): 1–23.

Stonor, C. R., and Edgar Anderson. 'Maize among the Hill Peoples of Assam'. *Annals of the Missouri Botanical Garden* 36, no. 3 (1949): 355–404.

Stop Damming the Chindwin. n.p.: Burma Rivers Network, 2011.

Suarez-Rubio, Marcela, Grant Connette, Thein Aung, Myint Kyaw and Swen C. Renner. 'Hkakabo Razi Landscape as One of the Last Exemplar of Large Contiguous Forests'. *Scientific Reports* 10, no. 14005 (2020): 1–13.

Sur, Malini. *Jungle Passports: Fences, Mobility, and Citizenship at the Northeast India–Bangladesh Border*. Philadelphia: University of Pennsylvania Press, 2021.

Survey Report on Elephant Movement, Human–Elephant Conflict Situation, and Possible Intervention Sites in and around Kutupalong Camp, Cox's Bazar. Dhaka: IUCN Bangladesh Country Office, 2018.

Sutradhar, Biswajit, Dipankar Deb, Koushik Majumdar and B. K. Datta. 'Short Communication: Traditional Dye Yielding Plants of Tripura, Northeast India'. *Biodiversitas* 16, no. 2 (2015): 121–7.

Swart, Sandra. 'Animals in African History'. *Oxford Research Encyclopedia of African History*, April 2020. https://doi.org/10.1093/acrefore/9780190277734.013.443.

Tag, Hui, and A. K. Das. 'Ethnobotanical Notes on the Hill Miri Tribe of Arunachal Pradesh'. *Indian Journal of Traditional Knowledge* 3, no. 1 (2004): 80–5.

Talon, Manuel, Marco Caruso and Fred G. Gmitter Jr. *The Genus Citrus*. Duxford; Cambridge MA; Kidlington: Elsevier – Woodhead Publishing, 2018.

Talukdar, Simi, and Abhik Gupta. 'Attitudes towards Forest and Wildlife, and Conservation-Oriented Traditions, around Chakrashila Wildlife Sanctuary, Assam, India'. *Oryx* 52, no. 3 (2018): 508–18.

Talukdar, Nazimur Rahman, Parthankar Choudhury, Rofik Ahmed Barbhuiya, Firoz Ahmad, Deborah Daolagupu and Jyoti Bikash Baishya. 'Mammals of Northeastern India: An Updated Checklist'. *Journal of Threatened Taxa* 13, no. 4 (2021): 18059–98.

Tamang, Buddhiman, and Jyoti Prakash Tamang. 'Traditional Knowledge of Biopreservation of Perishable Vegetable and Bamboo Shoots in Northeast India as Food Resources'. *Indian Journal of Traditional Knowledge* 8, no. 1 (2009): 89–95.

Tamang, Jyoti Prakash. *Himalayan Fermented Foods: Microbiology, Nutrition, and Ethnic Values*. Boca Raton, FL: CRC Press, 2009.

——— (ed.). *Ethnic Fermented Foods and Alcoholic Beverages of Asia*. Delhi: Springer India, 2016.

——— (ed.). *Ethnic Fermented Foods and Beverages of India: Science History and Culture*. Singapore: Springer Nature, 2020.

Tamm, Marek. 'Introduction: A Framework for Debating New Approaches to History'. In *Debating New Approaches to History*, edited by Marek Tamm and Peter Burke, 1–19 (London; New York: Bloomsbury Academic, 2019).

Tamm, Marek, and Zoltán Boldizsár Simon. 'More-than-Human History: Philosophy of History at the Time of the Anthropocene'. In *Philosophy of History: Twenty-First-Century Perspectives*, edited by Jouni-Matti Kuukkanen, 198–215. London: Bloomsbury, 2021.

Tarr, Michael Aram, and Stuart Blackburn. *Through the Eye of Time: Photographs of Arunachal Pradesh 1859–2006; Tribal Cultures in the Eastern Himalayas*. Leiden; Boston: Brill, 2008.

Tashi, Kelzang (Tingdzin). 'Contested Past, Challenging Future: An Ethnography of Pre-Buddhist Bon Religious Practices in Central Bhutan'. PhD thesis, Australian National University, 2020.

Taylor, Gordon D. 'Crop Distributions by Tribes in Upland Southeast Asia'. *Southwestern Journal of Anthropology* 9, no. 3 (1953): 296–308.

Taylor, Sean, Sayantani Neogi, Tiatoshi Jamir and David Tetso. 'Soil Micromorphological Analysis of Sediments from Cave and Rock Shelter Sites, Kiphire District, Nagaland'. *Man and Environment* 45, no. 2 (2020): 7–14.

Tālish, Ahmad Shihāb al-Dīn. *Tarikh-i Asham: Récit de l'expédition de Mir-Djumlah au pays d'Assam*, translated by Théodore Pavié. Paris: Benjamin Duprat, 1845.

Terangpi, Reena, Urmika Engtipi and Robindra Teron. 'Utilization of Less Known Plants, *Gnetum gnemon* L. and *Rhynchotechum ellipticum* (Dietr.)A. DC. among the Karbis, Northeast India'. *Journal of Scientific and Innovative Research* 2, no. 5 (2013): 943–9.

Teron, Robindra. 'Ethnic Food Plants and Ethnic Food Preparation of North-East India'. In *North-East India and Andaman and Nicobar Islands*, edited by T. Pullaiah, Kulithalai V. Krishnamurthy and Bir Bahadur, 55–92. Vol. 3 of *Ethnobotany of India*. Oakville, ON; Waretown, NJ: Apple Academic Press, 2018.

———. 'Hor, the Traditional Alcoholic Beverage of Karbi Tribe in Assam'. *Natural Product Radiance* 5, no. 5 (2006): 377–81.

Terra, Hellmut de, Hallam L. Movius, Jr., Edwin H. Colbert and J. Bequaert. 'Research on Early Man in Burma, with Supplementary Reports upon the Pleistocene Vertebrates and Mollusks of the Region, and Pleistocene Geology and Early Man in Java'. *Transactions of the American Philosophical Society* 32, no. 3 (1943): 263–464.

Terrell, John Edward, John P. Hart, Sibel Barut, Nicoletta Cellinese, Antonio Curet, Tim Denham et al. 'Domesticated Landscapes: The Subsistence Ecology of Plant and Animal Domestication'. *Journal of Archaeological Method and Theory* 10, no. 4 (2003): 323–68.

Terwiel, B. J. 'Myths Associated with Belief of the Tai Ahom'. *Indian Journal of Tai Studies* 16 (2016): 24–32.

———. *The Tai of Assam and Ancient Tai Ritual*. Vol. 1, *Life-cycle Ceremonies*. Vol. 2, *Sacrifices and Time-reckoning*. Gaya: Centre for South East Asian Studies, 1980–1981.

Thakur, Amrendra Kumar. 'Iron in the History of Northeast India: Awaiting Researches'. In *50 Years after Daojali-Hading*, edited by Jamir and Hazarika, 442–53. New Delhi: Research India Press, 2014.

Thakuria, Tilok. 'Hollowed Monoliths of North Cachar, Assam: Prospects for Archaeology and Ethno-history'. In *50 Years after Daojali Hading*, edited by Jamir and Hazarika, 243–9. New Delhi: Research India Press, 2014.

Tham, Soso. 'U Rngiew–The Dark One'. In *Tales of Darkness and Light: Soso Tham's The Old Days of the Khasis*, translated by Janet Hujon, 43–50. Cambridge: Open Book Publishers, 2018.

Thang, Rual Lian. 'The Dynamics of Natural Resources Government Systems in Chin State'. Master's thesis, Central European University, 2018.

The Assam Code in Two Volumes. Calcutta: Superintendent Government Printing, India, 1915.

The Burma Code. Calcutta: Superintendent Government Printing, India, 1910.

The Croatian Connection Exposed: Importing Illicit Myanmar Teak through Europe's Back Door. London: Environmental Investigation Agency, 2020.

The Imperial Gazetteer of India: Vol. 26, Atlas. Oxford: Oxford University Press, 1909.

The Udāna and the Itivuttaka: Two Classics from the Pali Canon, translated from the Pali by John D. Ireland. Kandy: Buddhist Translation Society, 2007.

Thompson, Christian. *The Eastern Himalayas: Where Worlds Collide*. Thimphu; New Delhi; Kathmandu: Living Himalayas Initiative, WWF – World Wide Fund For Nature, 2009.

Thompson, Christian, Sami Tornikoski, Phuntsho Choden and Sonam Choden. *Hidden Himalayas: Asia's Wonderland; New Species Discoveries in the Eastern Himalayas, Volume 2 2009–2014*. Thimphu; New Delhi; Kathmandu: Living Himalayas Initiative, WWF – World Wide Fund for Nature, 2015.

Thong, Tezenlo. *Colonization, Proselytization, and Identity: The Nagas and Westernization in Northeast India*. London: Palgrave Macmillan, 2016.

Thu, Zaw Min, Mya Mu Aye, Hnin Thanda Aung, Myint Myint Sein and Giovanni Vidari. 'A Review of Common Medicinal Plants in Chin State, Myanmar'. *Natural Product Communications* 13, no. 11 (2018): 1557–67.

Thwin, Hazel Khin Ma Ma, Kyi Soe Lwin, Swen C. Renner, and John P. Dumbacher. 'Ornithology of Northern Myanmar'. In *Avifauna of the Eastern Himalayas and Southeastern Sub-Himalayan Mountains*, edited by Renner and Rappole, 109–41. Ornithological Monographs 70. Washington, DC: American Ornithologists' Union, 2011.

Tickell, S. R. 'Extracts from a Journal up the Koladyn River, Aracan, in 1851'. *Journal of the Royal Geographical Society of London* 24 (1854): 86–114.

Tiwari, B. K., H. Tynsong, M. M. Lynrah, E. Lapasam, S. Deb and D. Sharma. 'Institutional Arrangement and Typology of Community Forests of Meghalaya, Mizoram and Nagaland of North-East India'. *Journal of Forestry Research* 24, no. 1 (2013): 179–86.

Tiwari, Umeshkumar L., Krishna Chowlu and Souravjyoti Borah. '*Impatiens cyclosepala* Hook. f. ex W.W. Sm.: A New Species Record for the Flora of India from Arunachal Pradesh'. *Biodiversity: Research and Conservation* 49, no. 1 (2018): 1–6.

Tomalin, Emma. *Biodivinity and Biodiversity: The Limits to Religious Environmentalism*. London: Ashgate, 2009.

Tordoff, Andrew W., Tim Appleton, Jonathan C. Eames, Karin Eberhardt, Htin Hla, Khin Ma Ma Thwin, Sao Myo Saw, Saw Moses and Sein Myo Aung. 'The Historical and Current Status of Pink-Headed Duck *Rhodonessa caryophyllacea* in Myanmar'. *Bird Conservation International* 18, no. 1 (2008): 38–52.

Torri, Davide. 'In the Shadow of the Devil: Traditional Patterns of Lepcha Culture Reinterpreted'. In *Health and Religious Rituals in South Asia: Disease, Possession, and Healing*, edited by Fabrizio M. Ferrari, 149–65. London; New York: Routledge, 2011.

Trant, T. A. 'Notice of the Khyén Tribe, Inhabiting the Yúma Mountains, between Ava and Aracan'. *Asiatic Researches* 16 (1828): 261–9.

———. 'Report on a Route from Pakung Yeh in Ava, to Aeng in Arracan. By Lieut. Trant, of the Q. M. G. Dept.'. *Journal of the Asiatic Society of Bengal* 11, no. 2 (1842): 1136–57.

Trautmann, Thomas R. *Elephants and Kings: An Environmental History*. Chicago: University of Chicago Press, 2015.

Travis, Anthony J., Gareth J. Norton, Sutapa Datta, Ramendra Sarma, Tapash Dasgupta, Filipe L. Savio et al. 'Assessing the Genetic Diversity of Rice Originating from Bangladesh, Assam and West Bengal'. *Rice* 8, no. 1 (2015): 1–9.

Troup, R. S. *The Work of the Forest Department in India*. Calcutta: Superintendent Government Printing, 1917.

Tsering, Jambey, Ngilyang Tam, Hui Tag, Baikuntha Jyoti Gogoi and Ona Apang. 'Medicinal Orchids of Arunachal Pradesh'. *Bulletin of Arunachal Forest Research* 32, nos. 1/2 (2017): 1–16.

Tshewang, Ugyen, Jane Gray Morrison and Michael Charles Tobias. *Bionomics in the Dragon Kingdom: Ecology, Economics and Ethics in Bhutan*. Singapore: Springer, 2018.

Tun, Aung Zaw, Pokkate Wongsasuluk and Wattasit Siriwong. 'Heavy Metals in the Soils of Placer Small-Scale Gold Mining Sites in Myanmar'. *Journal of Health and Pollution* 10, no. 27 (2020): 1–12.

Turner, Terence S. 'The Social Skin [1980]'. *HAU: Journal of Ethnographic Theory* 2, no. 2 (2012): 486–504.

Tzüdir, Lanusangla. 'Appropriating the Ao Past in a Christian Present'. In *Landscape, Culture, and Belonging*, edited by Bhattacharya and Pachuau, 266–93. Cambridge: Cambridge University Press, 2019.

Uchoi, Devananda, Deepayan Roy, Ranendra K. Majumdar and Prabir Debbarma. 'Diversified Traditional Cured Food Products of Certain Indigenous Tribes of Tripura, India'. *Indian Journal of Traditional Knowledge* 14, no. 3 (2015): 440–6.

Uddin, Ashraf, and Neil Lundberg. 'A Paleo-Brahmaputra? Subsurface Lithofacies Analysis of Miocene Deltaic Sediments in the Himalayan–Bengal System, Bangladesh'. *Sedimentary Geology* 123 (February 1999): 239–54.

Uddin, Kabir, Nakul Chettri, Yongping Yang, Mahendra Singh Lodhi, Naing Zaw Htun and Eklabya Sharma. 'Integrating Geospatial Tools and Species for Conservation Planning in a Data-Poor Region of the Far Eastern Himalayas'. *Geology, Ecology, and Landscapes* 4, no. 3 (2020): 1–16.

Uddin, M., M. F. Ahsan and H. Lingfeng. 'Human–Primates Conflict in Bangladesh: A Review'. *Journal of Animal and Plant Sciences* 30, no. 2 (2020): 1–7.

Uddin, Nasir. 'In Search of Self: Identity, Indigeneity, and Cultural Politics in Bangladesh'. In *Indigeneity on the Move*, edited by Gerharz, Uddin and Chakkarath, 119–39. New York; Oxford: Berghahn, 2018.

Uddin, Nasir. 'Living on the Margin: The Positioning of the "Khumi" within the Sociopolitical and Ethnic History of the Chittagong Hill Tracts'. *Asian Ethnicity* 9, no. 1 (2008): 33–53.

Uddin, Sufia. 'In the Company of *Pirs*: Making Vows, Receiving Favors at Bangladeshi Sufi Shrines'. In *Dealing with Deities: The Ritual Vow in South Asia*, edited by Selva J. Raj and William P. Harman, 87–105. New York: SUNY Press, 2006.

Urban, Hugh B. *The Power of Tantra: Religion, Sexuality and the Politics of South Asian Studies*. London; New York: I. B. Tauris, 2010.

———. 'The Womb of Tantra: Goddesses, Tribals, and Kings in Assam'. *Journal of Hindu Studies* 4, no. 2 (October 2011): 231–47.

Vadarajan, Lotika. 'Silk in Northeastern and Eastern India: The Indigenous Tradition'. *Modern Asian Studies* 22, no. 3 (1988): 561–70.

Vakkayil, Jacob, and Anna Canato. 'Muddling Through: Searching for the Ideal in the Coal Mining Fields of Meghalaya'. *Extractive Industries and Society* 2, no. 4 (2015): 419–25.

Van Dooren, Thom, Eben Kirksey and Ursula Münster. 'Multispecies Studies: Cultivating Arts of Attentiveness'. *Environmental Humanities* 8, no. 1 (2016): 5–21.

Van Driem, George. 'From the Dhaulagiri to Lappland, the Americas and Oceania'. In *Himalayan Bridge*, edited by Niraj Kumar, George van Driem and Phunchok Stobdam, 45–71. Abingdon; New York: Routledge, 2021.

———. 'The Domestications and the Domesticators of Asian Rice'. In *Language Dispersal Beyond Farming*, edited by Martine Robbeets and Alexander Savelyev, 183–214. Amsterdam: John Benjamins, 2017.

———. 'The Eastern Himalaya and the Mongoloid Myth'. In *Gender, Poverty and Livelihood in the Eastern Himalayas*, edited by Sanjoy Hazarika and Reshmi Banerjee, 12–41. Abingdon; New York: Routledge, 2018.

———. 'The Eastern Himalayan Corridor in Prehistory'. In Проблемы китайского и общего языкознания [Problems in Chinese and General Linguistics], edited by Elena Nikolaevna Kolpačkova, 2:467–524. St. Petersburg: Izdatel'stvo Studija NP-Print, 2016.

———. 'Trans-Himalayan'. In *Trans-Himalayan Linguistics*, edited by Thomas Owen-Smith and Nathan W. Hill, 11–40. Berlin; Boston: Walter de Gruyter, 2014.

Van Schendel, Willem. *A History of Bangladesh*. Cambridge: Cambridge University Press, 2020.

———. 'A Politics of Nudity: Photographs of the "Naked Mru" of Bangladesh'. *Modern Asian Studies* 36, no. 2 (2002): 341–74.

———. 'Fragmented Sovereignty and Unregulated Flows: The Bangladesh–China–India–Myanmar Corridor'. In *Shadow Exchanges along the New Silk Roads*, edited by Eva P. W. Hung and Tak-Wing Ngo, 37–73. Amsterdam: Amsterdam University Press, 2020.

——— (ed.). *Francis Buchanan in Southeast Bengal (1798): His Journey to Chittagong, the Chittagong Hill Tracts, Noakhali and Comilla*. Dhaka: University Press Limited, 1992.

———. 'Modern Times in Bangladesh'. In *Time Matters: Global and Local Time in Asian Societies*, edited by Willem van Schendel and Henk Schulte Nordholt, 37–55. Amsterdam: VU University Press, 2001.

Van Schendel, Willem, Wolfgang Mey and Aditya Kumar Dewan. *The Chittagong Hill Tracts: Living in a Borderland*. Bangkok: White Lotus Press, 2000.

VanBik, Kenneth. *Proto-Kuki-Chin: A Reconstructed Ancestor of the Kuki-Chin Languages*. Berkeley: University of California, 2009.

Vanderhelsken, Mélanie, and Bengt G. Karlsson. 'Fluid Attachments in Northeast India: Introduction'. *Asian Ethnicity* 17, no. 3 (2015): 330–9.

Vanderhelsken, Mélanie, Meenaxi Barkataki-Ruscheweyh and Bengt G. Karlsson (eds.). *Geographies of Difference: Explorations in Northeast Indian Studies*. London; New York: Routledge, 2018.

Varah, Franky. 'Situating the Humans Relationship with Nature in the Tangkhul Naga's Lifeworld'. *Journal of Human Ecology* 41, no. 3 (2013): 247–54.

Varsangzuali, Rosaline. 'Evolution of Mizo Dress: A Historical Study'. PhD thesis, Mizoram University, 2018.

Vasa, Ditamulü. 'Experimenting with the Non-material Aspect of Pottery of Nagaland: Some Theoretical and Historical Considerations'. In *50 Years after Daojali-Hading*, edited by Jamir and Hazarika, 206–17. New Delhi: Research India Press, 2014.

Velho, Nandini, and William F. Laurance. 'Hunting Practices of an Indo-Tibetan Buddhist Tribe in Arunachal Pradesh, North-East India'. *Oryx* 47, no. 3 (2013): 389–92.

'Viewpoints: Temporalities'. Special issue, *Past and Present* 243, no. 1 (2019).

Vishwanath, W. 'Diversity and Conservation Status of Freshwater Fishes of the Major Rivers of Northeast India'. *Aquatic Ecosystem Health and Management* 20, nos. 1/2 (2017): 86–101.

Viveiros de Castro, Eduardo. *Cosmological Perspectivism in Amazonia and Elsewhere*. Masterclass Series 1. Manchester: HAU Network of Ethnographic Theory, 2012.

Vlavianos Arvanitis, Agni. '"BIOPOLIS": Biopolicy for Greener and More Livable Cities'. *Cadmus* 2, no. 1 (2013): 100–13.

Von Stockhausen, Alban. *Imag(in)ing the Nagas: The Pictorial Ethnography of Hans-Eberhard Kauffmann and Christoph von Fürer-Haimendorf*. Stuttgart: Arnoldsche Art Publishers, 2014.

Waddell, L. A. 'Note on the Poisoned Arrows of the Akas'. *Journal of the Anthropological Institute of Great Britain and Ireland* 24 (1895): 57.

Wade, John P. *An Account of Assam, 1800*. Modhupur Tea Estate, North Lakhimpur, Assam: R. Sarmah, n.d.

Wahed, Md. Ahsanul, Mohammad Rahmat Ullah and Haseeb Md. Irfanullah. *Human–Elephant Conflict Mitigation Measures: Lessons from Bangladesh*. Dhaka: IUCN, International Union for Conservation of Nature, 2016.

Wakid, Abdul. 'Status and Distribution of the Endangered Gangetic Dolphin (*Platanista gangetica gangetica*) in the Brahmaputra River within India in 2005'. *Current Science* 97, no. 8 (2009): 1143–51.

Walker, Brett L. 'Animals and the Intimacy of History'. *History and Theory* 52 (December 2013): 45–67.

Walker, Mike, Martin J. Head, John Lowe, Max Berkelhammer, Svante Björk, Hai Cheng et al. 'Subdividing the Holocene Series/Epoch: Formalization of

Stages/Ages and Subseries/Subepochs, and Designation of GSSPs and Auxiliary Stratotypes'. *Journal of Quaternary Science* 34, no. 3 (2019): 173–86.

Wandersee, James H., and Elisabeth E. Schussler. 'Preventing Plant Blindness'. *American Biology Teacher* 61, no. 2 (1999): 82, 84, 86.

Wang, Hua-Wei, Bikash Mitra, Tapas Kumar Chaudhuri, Malliya Gounder Palanichamy, Qing-Peng Kong and Ya-Ping Zhang. 'Mitochondrial DNA Evidence Supports Northeast Indian Origin of the Aboriginal Andamanese in the Late Paleolithic'. *Journal of Genetics and Genomics* 38, no. 3 (2011): 117–22.

Wang, Ling-Xiang, Yan Lu, Chao Zhang, Lan-Hai Wei, Shi Yan, Yun-Zhi Huang et al. 'Reconstruction of Y-Chromosome Phylogeny Reveals Two Neolithic Expansions of Tibeto-Burman Populations'. *Molecular Biology and Evolution* 293 (June 2018): 1293–300.

Wang, Sonam W., Paul D. Curtis and James P. Lassoie. 'Farmer Perceptions of Crop Damage by Wildlife in Jigme Singye Wangchuck National Park, Bhutan'. *Wildlife Society Bulletin* 34, no. 2 (2006): 359–65.

Wangchuk, Kesang, and Jigme Wangdi. 'Mountain Pastoralism in Transition: Consequences of Legalizing *Cordyceps* Collection on Yak Farming Practices in Bhutan'. *Pastoralism: Research, Policy and Practice* 5, no. 4 (2015): 1–10.

Wangchuk, Phurpa, and Tashi Tobgay. 'Contributions of Medicinal Plants to the Gross National Happiness and Biodiscovery in Bhutan'. *Journal of Ethnobiology and Ethnomedicine* 11, no. 48 (2015): 1–12.

Wangchuk, Phurpa, Karma Yeshi and Kinga Jamphel. 'Pharmacological, Ethnopharmacological, and Botanical Evaluation of Subtropical Medicinal Plants of Lower Kheng Region in Bhutan'. *Integrative Medicine Research* 6 (September 2017): 372–87.

Wary, Jaysagar, and Oinam Ranjit Singh. 'Sal Timber Trade in Goalpara District During Colonial Period'. *NEHU Journal* 14, no. 2 (2016): 87–99.

Webb, Thomas, Chris Pearson, Penny Summerfield and Mark Riley. 'More-Than-Human Emotional Communities: British Soldiers and Mules in Second World War Burma'. *Cultural and Social History* 17, no. 2 (2020): 245–62.

Weckerle, Caroline S., Yongping Yang, Franz K. Huber and Qiaohong Li. 'People, Money, and Protected Areas: The Collection of the Caterpillar Mushroom *Ophiocordyceps sinensis* in the Baima Xueshan Nature Reserve, Southwest China'. *Biodiversity and Conservation* 19, no. 9 (2010): 2685–98.

Weil, Benjamin. 'Conservation, Exploitation, and Cultural Change in the Indian Forest Service, 1875–1927'. *Environmental History* 11 (April 2006): 319–43.

Wellens, Koen. 'Migrating Brothers and Party-State Discourses on Ethnic Origin in Southwest China'. In *Origins and Migrations in the Extended Eastern Himalayas*, edited by Huber and Blackburn, 299–319. Leiden; Boston: Brill, 2012.

West-Pavlov, Russell. *Temporalities*. London; New York: Routledge, 2013.

Westerweel, Jan, Pierrick Roperch, Alexis Licht, Guillaume Dupont-Nivet, Zaw Win, Fernando Poblete, Gilles Ruffet, Hnin Hnin Swe, Myat Kai Thi and Day Wa Aung. 'Burma Terrane Part of the Trans-Tethyan Arc during Collision with India According to Palaeomagnetic Data'. *Nature Geoscience* 12 (September 2019): 863–8.

Wettstein, Marion. *Naga Textiles: Design, Technique, Meaning and Effect of a Local Craft Tradition in Northeast India*. Stuttgart: Arnoldsche Art Publishers, 2014.

Weyrich, Laura S. 'The History of the Human Microbiome: Insights from Archaeology and Ancient DNA'. In *Multispecies Archaeology*, edited by Suzanne E. Pilaar Birch, 230–50. London; New York; Routledge, 2018.

Wiart, Christophe. *Medicinal Plants of Bangladesh and West Bengal: Botany, Natural Products, and Ethnopharmacology*. Boca Raton, FL: CRC Press, 2019.

Willson, John D., Michael E. Dorcas and Raymond W. Snow. 'Identifying Plausible Scenarios for the Establishment of Invasive Burmese Pythons (*Python molurus*) in Southern Florida'. *Biological Invasions* 13 (2011): 1493–504.

Wilcox, R. 'Memoir of a Survey of Asam and the Neighbouring Countries, Executed in 1825–6–7–8'. *Asiatic Researches* 17 (1832): 314–469.

Winston, W. R. *Four Years in Upper Burma*. London: C. H. Kelly, 1892.

Wong, Shan, and Hong Liu. 'Wild-Orchid Trade in a Chinese E-Commerce Market'. *Economic Botany* 20, no. 10 (2019): 1–18.

Wood, H. S. *Shikar Memories: A Record of Sport and Observation in India and Burma*. London: H. F. & G. Witherby, 1934.

Woodthorpe, R. G. 'Explorations on the Chindwin River, Upper Burma'. *Proceedings of the Royal Geographical Society and Monthly Record of Geography* 11, no. 4 (1889): 197–216.

Woodward, Mark R. 'Gifts for the Sky People: Animal Sacrifice, Headhunting and Power among the Naga of Burma and Assam'. In *Indigenous Religions: A Companion*, edited by Graham Harvey, 219–29. London; New York: Cassell, 2000.

Wouters, Jelle J. P. *In the Shadows of Naga Insurgency: Tribes, State, and Violence in Northeast India*. Delhi: Oxford University Press, 2018.

———. 'Reconfiguring Colonial Ethnography: The British Gaze over India's North East'. In *North-East India: A Handbook of Anthropology*, edited by T. B. Subba, 99–121. Hyderabad: Orient Blackswan, 2012.

———. 'Relatedness, Trans-species Knots and Yak Personhood in the Bhutan Highlands'. In *Environmental Humanities in the New Himalayas*, edited by Smyer Yü and De Maaker, 27–43. London; New York: Routledge, 2021.

Wouters, Jelle J. P., and Michael Heneise. 'Introduction to Highland Asia'. In *The Routledge Handbook to Contemporary Highland Asia*, edited by Jelle J. P. Wouters and Michael Heneise. London; New York: Routledge, forthcoming.

Wouters, Jelle J. P., and Tanka B. Subba. 'The "Indian Face", India's Northeast, and "The Idea of India"'. *Asian Anthropology* 12, no. 2 (2013): 126–40.

Wuerthner, George. 'Yellowstone as Model for the World'. In *Protecting the Wild*, edited by Wuerthner, Crist and Butler, 131–43. Washington: Island Press, 2015.

Wuerthner, George, Eileen Crist and Tom Butler (eds.). *Protecting the Wild: Parks and Wilderness, the Foundation of Conservation*. Washington: Island Press, 2015.

Wunderlich, Maria, Tiatoshi Jamir and Johannes Müller. 'Hierarchy and Balance: The Role of Monumentality in European and Indian Landscapes'. *Journal of Neolithic Archaeology*, special issue no. 5 (2019): 13–26.

Wunderlich, Maria, Tiatoshi Jamir, Johannes Müller, Knut Rassman and Ditamulü Vasa. 'Societies in Balance: Monumentality and Feasting Activities among Southern Naga Communities, Northeast India'. *PLoS ONE* 16, no. 3 (2021): e0246966, 1–36.

Wunna, Kazuo N. Watanabe, Ryo Ohsawa, Mitsuhiro Obara, Seiji Yanagihara, Pa Pa Aung and Yoshimichi Fukuta. 'Genetic Variation of Rice (*Oryza sativa* L.) Germplasm in Myanmar Based on Genomic Compositions of DNA Markers'. *Breeding Science* 66, no. 5 (2016): 762–7.

Yadav, Sandeep. 'Illegal Wildlife Trade Victim – Million Dollar Gecko'. *Science Reporter* 56, no. 3 (2019): 24–5.

Yang, Bin. *Cowrie Shells and Cowrie Money: A Global History*. Abingdon; New York: Routledge, 2019.

———. 'Horses, Silver, and Cowries: Yunnan in Global Perspective'. *Journal of World History* 15, no. 3 (2004): 281–322.

Yang, Yin, Guopeng Ren, Wenjuan Li, Zhipang Huang, Aung Ko Lin, Paul A. Garber et al. 'Identifying Transboundary Conservation Priorities in a Biodiversity Hotspot of China and Myanmar: Implications for Data Poor Mountainous Regions'. *Global Ecology and Conservation* 20, no. e00732 (2019): 1–13.

Yeshi, Karma, Yangbum Gyal, Katharina Sabernig, Jigme Phuntsho, Tawni Tidwell, Tenzin Jamtsho, Rinchen Dhondup, Eliot Tokar and Phurpa Wangchuk. 'An Integrated Medicine of Bhutan: *Sowa Rigpa* Concepts, Botanical Identification, and the Recorded Phytochemical and Pharmacological Properties of the Eastern Himalayan Medicinal Plants'. *European Journal of Integrative Medicine* 8, no. 29 (2019): 100927, 1–15.

Yhoshü, Alice. 'Nagaland Conservationist Nuklu Phom Gets Prestigious Whitley Awards 2021'. *Hindustan Times*, 14 May 2021. https://www.hindustantimes.com/environment/nagaland-conservationist-nuklu-phom-gets-prestigious-whitley-awards-2021-101620967137243.html. Accessed 8 January 2022.

Yin, U Tun. 'Wild Life Preservation and Sanctuaries in the Union of Burma'. *Journal of the Bombay Natural History Society* 52, nos. 2/3 (1954): 264–84.

Yin, Jiandong, and Weiwei Liu. 'Traditional Continuation and Modern Transformation: A Study on the Changes of Structures and Functions of Border Markets in Yunnan Province'. *International Journal of Business Anthropology* 8, no. 2 (2019): 90–104.

Yokoyama, Satoshi, Jun Matsumoto and Hitoshi Araki (eds.). *Nature, Culture and Food in Monsoon Asia*. Singapore: Springer Nature, 2020.

Young, E. C. 'A Journey from Yün-Nan to Assam'. *Geographical Journal* 30, no. 2 (1907): 152–80.

Yu, Xiaogang, Chen Xiangxue and Carl Middleton. 'From Hydropower Construction to National Park Creation: Changing Pathways of the Nu River'. In *Knowing the Salween River: Resource Politics of a Contested Transboundary River*, edited by Carl Middleton and Vanessa Lamb, 49–69. Cham: Springer Open, 2019.

Yule, Henry. 'Notes on the Iron of the Kasia Hills, for the Museum of Economic Geology'. *Journal of the Asiatic Society of Bengal* 11, no. 2 (1842): 853–7.

Yumnam, J. Y., and O. P. Tripathi. 'Ethnobotany: Plants Use in Fishing and Hunting by Adi Tribe of Arunachal Pradesh'. *Indian Journal of Traditional Knowledge* 12, no. 1 (2013): 157–61.

Zahulha. 'Thihna Chhuana'. *Mizo leh Vai*, July 1922, 82–4.

Zakaria, Muhammad. 'A Grammar of Hyow'. PhD thesis, Nanyang Technological University, Singapore, 2018.

Zakaria, Saymon. *Pronomohi Bongomata: Indigenous Cultural Forms of Bangladesh*. Dhaka: Nymphea Publication, 2011.

Zama, Margaret Ch. 'Origin Myths of the Mizo: MIZORAM'. *India International Centre Quarterly* 32, nos. 2/3 (2005): 7–11.

Zeder, Melinda A. 'The Domestication of Animals'. *Journal of Anthropological Research* 68, no. 2 (2012): 161–90.

Zeng, Xingquan, Yu Guo, Qijun Xu, Martin Mascher, Ganggang Guo, Shuaicheng Li et al. 'Origin and Evolution of Qingke Barley in Tibet'. *Nature Communications* 9, no. 5433 (2018): 1–11.

Zethner, Ole, Rie Koustrup and Dilip Barooah. *South Asian Ways of Silk: A Patchwork of Biology, Manufacture, Culture and History*. Guwahati: Bookbell, 2015.

Zhang, Ling. 'The Matter of Time'. *Verge: Studies in Global Asias* 7, no. 1 (2021): 80–90.

Zhang, Mingxia, Ana Gouveia, Tao Qin, Ruichang Quan and Vincent Nijman. 'Illegal Pangolin Trade in Northernmost Myanmar and Its Links to India and China'. *Global Ecology and Conservation* 10 (April 2017): 23–31.

Zhang, Xiaoming, Shiyu Liao, Xuebin Qi, Jiewei Liu, Jatupol Kampuansai, Hui Zhang et al. 'Y-Chromosome Diversity Suggests Southern Origin and Paleolithic Backwave Migration of Austro-Asiatic Speakers from Eastern Asia to the Indian Subcontinent'. *Scientific Reports* 5, no. 15486 (2015): 1–8.

Zhao, Min. 'Chapter 1: Salt, Grain and the Change of Deities in Early Ming Western Yunnan'. In *The Transformation of Yunnan in Ming China*, edited by Daniels and Ma, 19–42. London; New York: Routledge, 2020.

Zheng, Xi, Li-Xiang Zhang, Zheng-Hua Yang and Bosco Pui Lok Chan. 'Flocking of Hornbills Observed in Tongbiguan Nature Reserve, Yunnan, China'. *Hornbill Natural History and Conservation* 1, no. 1 (2020): 42–4.

Zherikhin, V. V., and A. J. Ross. 'A Review of the History, Geology and Age of Burmese Amber (Burmite)'. *Bulletin of the Natural History Museum (Geology)* 56, no. 1 (2000): 3–10.

Zhimomi, Salome. 'Christianity and Politics in Nagaland: An Ethnographic Study in Lazami Village'. PhD thesis, Australian National University, 2001.

Zhou, Shi-Shun. '*Coelogyne victoria-reginae* (Orchidaceae, Epidendroideae, Arethuseae), a New Species from Chin State, Myanmar'. *PhytoKeys* 98 (May 2018): 123–33.

Zomi, Ginzamang T. 'Marriage Practices of the Zou Tribe in Manipur: Continuity and Change'. *International Journal of Humanities and Social Science Invention* 3, no. 10 (2014): 31–7.

Zou, David Vumlallian. 'A Historical Study of the "Zo" Struggle'. *Economic and Political Weekly* 45, no. 14 (2010): 56–63.

———. 'Production of Place: Folk Geographies and Religious Desire in Colonial Mizoram'. In *Orality and Folk Literature in the Age of Print Culture: India's Northeast Experience*, edited by Malsawmdawngliana, Lalmareng K. Gangte and Rohmingwawii, 110–21. Dispur: Scientific Book Centre, 2015.

———. 'Raiding the Dreaded Past: Representations of Headhunting and Human Sacrifice in North-East India'. *Contributions to Indian Sociology* 39, no. 1 (2005): 75–105.

———. 'The Past of a Fringe Community: Ethno-history and Fluid Identity of the Zou in Manipur'. *Indian Historical Review* 36, no. 2 (2009): 209–35.

Zou, S. Thangboi. 'Riverine Bazaars, Trade and Chiefs in the Colonial Lushai Hills'. *Asian Ethnicity* 22, no. 1 (2021): 563–82.

Zumbroich, Thomas J. 'The Origin and Diffusion of Betel Chewing: A Synthesis of Evidence from South Asia, Southeast Asia and Beyond'. *eJournal of Indian Medicine* 1, no. 3 (2007–2008): 87–140.

Index

Aabhu Thanyi, 73
Abo Tani, 73, 97, 102
Abor, 14, 66
aconite, 136
actor–network theory, 3
Adi, 14, 66–7, 75
adlay. *See* Job's tears
Africa, 28, 32, 161, 166, 213–15, 234
afterlife. *See* afterworld
afterworld, 80–2, 87, 106–7, 109, 112, 126, 130
agarwood, 28, 135, 218, 237
agency, 3, 65, 130, 141, 240, 261
agential entanglements, 3
agricultural crops, 137–8. *See also* agriculture
agriculture, 4, 42–5, 51, 52, 54–6, 59–60, 137–8, 142, 148, 188–9, 201, 213, 216–17, 235
Ahom, 14, 67, 72, 93, 117, 119, 122, 194, 260
ahu. See *aus*
ai ceremony, 81, 107–9
Aka, 66–7, 79
Akyab. *See* Sittwe
alcohol, 12, 130, 159–60, 175, 260
almanac, 11
almond, 169
altar, 119, 144
amaranth, 138

amber, 28, 205–7
amber species, 28, 30, 207
Amchang, 249
Americas, 32, 146, 213, 220
American Museum of Natural History, 113, 220, 265
Andaman Islands, 33
Angami, 67, 73–4, 76, 83–4, 94–5, 128
animal
   attacks, 246–52, 255
   cartographies, 257
   destroying human property, 251–2
   exchange and trade, 115–17
   exploiting, 47–51
   geographies, 166–78
   gold rush, 196
   history, 4, 91–126
   hunted, 103–6
   husbandry, 42, 52, 55, 116, 175, 188–9, 192
   as kin, 94–7
   power of, 97–102
   sacrifice, 117–19
   sacrifice and religious traditions, 119–26
   symbols of self-identification, 179–83
   wild and domestic, 102–3, 114–15
animism, 262
ant, 78
antelope, 231

Index

Anthropocene, 2, 37
anthropocentrism, 2, 127, 197
anthropology, 5, 8–10, 65
Anyathian, 31
Ao, 67, 71, 73, 75, 79, 94
Apatani, 13, 67–8, 72, 77, 83, 97, 102, 116, 128, 144, 148
Arabia, 135
Arakan. *See* Rakhine
archaeological, archaeology, 5, 7–8, 31, 38–41, 48, 64, 104, 167, 202, 204–5, 261
areca (*Areca catechu*), 81, 129–31
Armenian, 204
arrow, 10, 46, 94, 105, 136, 169, 195
Arunachal macaque, 223
Arunachal Pradesh, Arunachali, 45, 54, 57, 59, 68–9, 72, 76–7, 95–6, 105, 116, 144, 145, 168, 170–2, 180, 184, 223, 233, 237–8
Asian black bear, 29. *See also* bear
Assam, Assamese, 14–15, 24, 26, 44–5, 51, 63, 71, 88, 92–3, 99, 117, 119–23, 130, 148, 154, 156, 170, 185, 192, 194, 200, 208–9, 211, 214, 216, 218–19, 224, 227–8, 232, 234–5, 249–50, 253–4
Assam Sadri, 15
aus (*ahu*), 44–5
Australia, 32, 227
Austroasiatic languages, 34
Ayeyarwadi, 26, 31
aynshu, 94
Ayurveda, 133

bachelors' dormitory, 141, 182
bamboo, 4, 16, 78, 96–7, 119, 128, 135, 163, 206, 210, 227, 252, 260
  art, 149–50
  culture, 162
  famines, 12, 162, 243

  fermented products from, 47, 159, 190, 242
  foraging, 189–90
  meanings of, 143–6
  rat, 162, 243
  as raw material, 192–3
  rice, 162
  and scientific forestry, 226
  uses, 46–7
  varieties of, 46
  water-filled, 198–9
banana, 42, 131, 189, 246
Bangladesh, 1, 11, 14–15, 23, 26, 44, 58–9, 69, 77, 80, 96, 101, 104, 139–40, 145, 148, 164, 171, 186, 193, 196, 200, 214, 216
Barail, 33
Barak–Surma–Meghna, 26
barbarian, 154
Barkaith, Sukumar, 94
barley, 45, 52–4, 59, 146, 159, 213
basil, 131
basketry, 41, 143, 150, 192
bat, 48, 190, 193, 245
Bawm-Zo, 67, 88, 112, 164
Bay of Bengal, 26, 31–2, 34, 165, 167, 198. *See also* Indian Ocean
bead, 51, 80, 135, 168, 205–6
bear, 29–30, 101, 106, 112, 166, 232, 235, 246, 251, 255
bel (*Aegle marmelos*), 131
Bengal, Bengali, 26, 51, 59, 63, 67, 69, 88, 119–20, 133, 154, 156–7, 167, 169
Bengal Water Hyacinth Act, 246
Benglama, 97
betel (*Piper betle*), 12, 129–31, 259
betel nut. *See* areca
Bethitzza, 133
Bhasu Vihara, 104
Bhattacharya, Jayati, 6

Bhutan, Bhutanese, 1, 11, 16, 23–4, 54, 67–9, 88, 92, 96, 117, 122, 135, 174, 177, 219, 223–4, 233, 238
Bible, 8, 9, 189
biodiversity, 2, 27, 37, 43, 127–8, 169, 174, 187, 221, 238
biodiversity hotspot, 6, 27–8, 127, 169, 174, 187, 221, 245, 261
bio-piracy, 129
biopolis, 247
biopolitics, 247
Bishnudol, 194
bitter vine (*Mikania micrantha*), 213
Black Mountains, 15, 23
black (or Myanmar) snub-nosed monkey (*Rhinopithecus strykeri*), 223
Blackburn, Stuart, 68–9
boar, 48, 102, 106, 112–14, 120, 139, 193, 243, 251
Bodo, Boro, 66–7, 74, 95, 97, 119, 120, 131, 148, 177
Bogra, 33, 104
Bonbibi, 120
bone tools, 38, 41
Bongcher, 67, 73
borderlands, 31, 43, 69, 123, 183
Bos frontalis. See *mithun*
Bos gaurus. See gaur
bow, 46, 78, 81, 105, 136, 195, 215
Brahmaputra, 15, 24, 26, 33, 44, 83, 157, 165, 198, 203
Brazil, 214–15
brick, 202
bridge, 33, 99, 135, 143
Brokpa, 67, 83, 88
Buddhism, 63, 88, 119, 122, 126, 262
buffalo, 30, 48, 58, 76, 103, 113, 119–23, 177, 184, 219, 232, 243
bullock, ox, 58, 123, 227
Burhi-Dihing, 204
Burma, Burmese. See Myanmar
butterfly, 221

calendrical system, 11
Cambodia, 218
camel, 123–4
camp follower, 242
cane. See rattan
cannabis, 242
caravan, 184–5
cardamom, 246
Caribbean, 146, 214
carnelian, 205–6
cassia (*Cinnamomum tamala*), 189
catch crop, 146
caterpillar fungus (*Cordyceps sinensis*), 54
cave, 13, 25, 38, 78–9, 147, 193
Cederlöf, Gunnel, 6, 27
Central Asia, 32
ceremonial plants, 129–32
Chainpango, 85
Chakma, 67, 85, 133, 145
chameleon, 80
Champanugger, 85
Chandraghona, 193
chang ai, 109
Chang, 67, 94
Chawngchili, 98
Chawngtinleri, 141
Cherrapunji, 129
chicken, 48, 72, 99, 103, 114, 117, 119–20, 122–5, 138, 171, 177, 182, 213, 242–3
chili pepper, 56, 146, 213, 252, 259
Chin, 16, 59, 67, 78, 106, 108, 115, 168, 246. See also Zo
Chin Hills, 15, 69, 99, 101, 103, 109, 111, 155, 160, 168, 246
Chin State, 59, 85, 107, 110, 114, 171, 176, 195, 229, 238
China, Chinese, 1, 23, 31, 33–4, 44, 67–9, 104, 154, 165, 206, 235, 238, 261. See also Yunnan
Chindwin, 24, 26, 85, 192, 206, 220, 225

Index   351

Chindwin expedition. *See* Vernay-
    Hopwood Chindwin Expedition
Chittagong, 57, 80, 123, 198
Chittagong Hill Tracts, 45, 77, 85, 96,
    101, 119, 123, 139–40, 164, 168–9,
    176, 196, 201, 214, 228
cholera, 123, 161, 214, 242, 244–5
Christianity, 63, 76, 92, 124, 126, 159
chronology, 8–9, 82
    regional, 41
    religious, 8
chronometric time, 9–11, 14, 64, 69, 90,
    258–9
chronopolitics, 10
circumcision, 131
citron, citrus, 47, 213
'civilisation', 153–6, 211
climate change, 25, 33, 37, 260
clouded leopard, 30, 118, 219, 235
coal, 208–10
cobra, 231
cockroach, 71
code name, 108
co-evolution, 157
coins, 166
Colney, Hrangthanga, 196
colonial period, 69, 228–9
Columbian exchange, 213, 216, 246–7
commons, 212, 235–9
community buy-in, 255
community religion, 262
companion plants, 135–6
conch shell, 169
conservation
    biopolis, 247
    community-based, 255
    conflict, 17, 229
    refugees, 227
    convivial, 241
    vertical, 228–9

wildlife, 14, 17, 153, 200, 212, 218,
    225–9, 232–40, 247–8, 250–2, 255,
    262–3
Cooch Behar, 121, 169, 229
corded pottery, 40. *See also* pottery
corridor, 1, 32, 35
cosmic polity, 89
cosmology/cosmological, 12, 16, 63–5,
    76, 86–90, 119, 123–7, 144, 150,
    153, 156, 159, 175, 240, 259, 262
    centres, 87–8
    commonalities, 86–7, 153
cotton, 4, 47, 56, 140, 148, 150, 163–6
COVID-19, 245
cow, 54, 86, 123, 259
cowrie, cowry (*kauri*), 166–9, 186, 261
Cox's Bazar, 15
crab, 48, 80
creation of the world, 70–3
creole languages, 15
creolisation, 15
Criminal Procedure Code, 247
crocodile, 30, 49, 120, 123, 218, 247
crop cultivation. *See* agriculture
crops of vice, 130
cultivation, fixed-field, 56–60
cultivation, shifting 54–6
cultural geographies, 153–87
cultural groups, 67
cultural variety, 66–8
culture area, 69, 87
currency, 116, 166–8
cyclone, 12, 80

Dafla, 66
dairy, 157–8
Dala, 246
dams, 188, 200–1, 217
darkness, 78, 80
Darthlalang, 195

death, 4, 12, 80–2
deep history, 68, 70–1, 86, 89–90
deer, 30, 48–9, 106, 110, 113, 119, 139, 182, 194, 222, 231
deforestation, 59, 217
deity landlords, 89
delta, 26, 45, 201
Desana, 133
deshification, 88
development, 211, 215
Dhimal, 67
dhole. *See* wild dog
Dian kingdom, 167
dibble, 139–40
Dimapur, 191
dinosaur, 28, 207
discovery of species, 207, 221–5
disease, 161, 245
divination, 100
DNA, 32, 35
dog, 48, 72, 76–7, 99, 114, 116, 183, 194, 242–3. *See also* wild dog
Dokkhin Rai, 120
dolphin, 30, 254
domestic animals, 114–15
domesticated landscape, 43, 197
domestication, 41–4, 46, 48–9, 52, 60, 103, 114, 173, 188, 190, 243, 260
three pathways of, 48
Doniger, Wendy, 88, 126
Donyipolo, 76–7, 240
draught animal, 53, 56, 58
drongo, 118
duck, 119–21, 123, 171, 220
dyes, 47, 163, 166, 189

earthquake, 12, 22, 26, 71, 79, 98
earthworm, 71
East Asia, 32–3, 157
Eastern Himalayan Triangle. *See* Triangle
ecological engineer. *See* ecosystem engineer

ecological identity, 239
ecologies, 27–30
ecosystem, 23, 28, 36, 169, 230, 247, 259
ecosystem engineer, 35–6, 41, 47, 188, 211, 213, 215
egg, 36, 48, 100, 115, 119, 122, 148
Egypt, 189
electricity, 198
elephant, 4, 12, 30, 36, 48, 58, 80, 92–3, 97, 103–4, 106, 108, 112, 114, 119, 136, 182–3, 200, 218–19, 227, 231, 234, 243, 246, 248–52, 260–1
elephant corridor, 250
Elephant Preservation Act, 231
Elwin, Verrier, 68, 70, 80, 144
embodied infrastructure, 184
encroachers, 247, 252
endemic, 28
endonym/exonym, 14
entanglement, 3, 12, 65–6, 89, 92, 166, 173, 183, 240, 262
environmental awareness, 216–20
environmental decay, 211–41
environmental history, 3, 5, 206
environmental humanities, 3, 5
environmental movement, 222
environmental subjectivities, 239–41
enzymes, 156
epidemic, pandemic, 161, 214, 242
epistemic incuriosity, 13
eri. *See* silk
erotic play. *See* sex
Ethiopian eggplant, 56
ethnic border crossing, 15
ethnic conversion, 15
ethnic label, 15
Europe, 8–9
eviction, 232, 249
evolution, 2, 7–8, 13, 35, 37, 72, 80, 157
experimental space, 23, 25, 261
extinction, 8, 28, 30, 32, 49, 161, 217–19, 221. *See also* amber species

falcon, 28
fallow, 12, 56, 201
Far-Eastern Himalayas, 28
feast of merit, 118, 124, 138, 150, 159, 175–7, 179
feather, 104, 111–13, 118–19, 148, 168–71, 179, 217, 255
fermentation, 143, 156, 159–60, 186, 242, 260
fertility, 56, 106, 118, 122, 145, 182
fetish of accuracy, 13
field maize, 146
Fiji, 214
fire, 36, 47, 53, 71–2, 80, 84, 143, 202
firearm, 136–7, 195
fishing, 4, 12, 44–6, 51, 54–5, 137, 183, 191–2, 245, 253
fixed-field cultivation, 56–0
flagship species, 248, 250, 252
floating ethnonym, 15
flood, 12, 26–7, 85
Florida, 216
fluid attachment, 15
Fo Lyan Sôn, 111
folk medicine, 132, 134
folklore, 70, 86
folklorist. *See* folklore
foraging, 44–5, 54–6, 60, 189–97, 242–3, 253, 257, 260
forest, 128, 226–8
forest bitter-berry (*Solanum anguivi*), 56
Forest Department, 172, 226, 228–9, 232
fossil, 28, 30, 32, 207
fossil fuels, 197, 205, 208–10
fossil wood, 41
fox, 166, 191
frog, 58, 73, 76, 198, 207, 221, 225
fungus, 54, 135, 255

Galo, 67, 170
Ganges, 26

Gaoligongshan, 233
garbage dump, 191
Garo, 12, 16, 66–7, 73–4, 76, 83, 87, 94, 108, 117, 120, 124, 133–4, 154, 156, 174, 236
gas, 205, 208–10
gaur (*Bos gaurus*), 30, 48–50, 58, 106–7, 113, 196, 231, 250
gayal. *See* mithun
gecko, 101, 218, 221, 255
gender, 72–3, 80, 108–10, 137, 148–50, 170
gendering plants, 148–50
genetics, 5, 32–3, 35–6, 43, 49, 51–2, 65, 135, 147, 157, 188
genna, 94, 103
geological *terra incognita*, 23
geology, 2, 5–8, 16, 23, 25–7, 36–7, 63, 79, 188
Ghazi Khan, 120
giant sensitive plant (*Mimosa diplotricha*), 213
gibbon, 30, 81, 96–7, 102, 112, 183, 193, 218
ginger, 56, 131, 134, 139, 189
global biodiversity hotspot. *See* biodiversity hotspot
gold, 154, 204, 207, 210
golden cat, 218
goose, 28
Great Acceleration, 211
Great Bear, 74
greater adjutant (*Leptoptilos dubius*), 218–19
Greek, 204
green grabbing, 238
Greenwich Mean Time (GMT), 11
grey peacock pheasant, 220
guava, 213
Guwahati, 121–2, 185
Guyot-Réchard, Bérénice, 6

Haimenkou, 43
Hangrum, 192
Hastividyārnava, 93
Hawaii, 214
hawk, 106
Hazarika, Manjil, 38
headhunting, 111, 117
healthcare, 132–5
Heavenly Louse Man, 78
hemp, 163
Heraka, 76
Herakandingpeu, 134
Highland Asia, 23
hill, 22
'Himalaya', 27
Himalayan spikenard, 189
Himalayan tahrs, 214
Himalayas, 1, 22–8, 32–4, 44, 52–4, 69, 116, 136, 157, 162, 174–5, 213
Hinduism, 63, 76, 88, 106, 119, 122, 126, 262
hispid hare, 221
history-writing, 8–14, 258–63
HIV/AIDS, 245
Homo erectus, 31, 217
Homo sapiens, 17, 31–2, 212, 235, 263
honey, 48, 137, 247, 253
hornbill festival, 172–3
hornbill, 92, 111–12, 118–19, 168–73, 179, 181, 255, 260
horse, 93, 119, 167, 183–4, 186
hotspot. *See* biodiversity hotspot
Hrusso, 66
Htin, Kyaw Minn, 6
Hukawng valley, 33, 233
human–elephant companionship, 4
human exceptionalism, 2, 4
human–non-human
 conflict, 244–6 (*see also* animal attacks)
 hierarchy, 92
 history, 3, 8, 66, 91–126
 interaction, 11, 13, 16, 43, 126, 153, 178, 186, 233, 239
 kinship, 94–7, 240
human origins, 17, 63–4, 77–80, 89, 91, 98
human resentment against protected animals, 252–5
human–tiger kinship, 94–6
hunter-hero, 106–8
hunting, 105–6, 108–10, 112, 190–1, 193
 and gender, 48, 108–10
 ground, 228–9
 tools, 195
Hutton, John H., 12, 69, 73–4, 94
hydropower, 198, 201–2
hyena, 30, 49, 217

Ibudhou Thangjing, 107
Ice Age, 30, 33
iguana, 216
illiteracy. *See* literacy
ill-omened animal, 101
incest, 97
India, 1, 5, 12, 14, 21, 23, 44, 68, 85, 106, 123, 135–6, 164–7, 171, 204–5, 209, 213, 229, 233, 235, 239, 261
Indian Ocean, 22, 25, 166
indica, 44–5
indigenous, 8–12, 33, 156
indigo, 56, 163, 166
'Indo-Burma', 27
Indo-Burma Arc, 1, 22–3, 26, 32–3, 38, 199, 205
 eastern Himalayas and, 22
 shifting cultivation in, 55
industrialisation, 166, 236
Inpui, 67
intentionality, 66

Index

interspecies. *See also* multispecies
  communication, 3, 77–8, 87, 126, 129, 138, 150, 259
  history, 258–9
  labour relationships, 183–6
  love, 98
  relationships, 16, 127, 186, 259–60, 263
  sexuality, 98
'intra-species practice', 112
invasive species, 30–1, 51, 161, 243–6, 256
Iqbal, Iftekhar, 6
iron, 79, 204
Irrawaddy. *See* Ayeyarwadi
irrigation, 57, 188, 198, 201, 245
Islam, Muslim, 63, 119–20, 123–4, 126, 131, 149
ivory, 112, 218, 231

jackal, 49, 120, 251
Jackson, Kyle, 95
jade, 41, 205–6, 210
Jagannath Dighi, 200
Jaintia, 14, 66, 87–8, 174, 176, 235
Jamuna. *See* Brahmaputra
Japan, 135, 162
japonica, 44–5
Jessore, 214
Jinghpaw, 66
Job's tears (*Coix lacryma-jobi*), 146, 160, 212
Jumma, 14
jungle fowl, 47–8, 103, 114, 213
jute, 97, 148, 163, 165–6

Kabui, 66–7, 73
Kacha Naga, 66, 147
Kacha, 66
Kachari, 66, 95, 97, 120. *See also* Bodo
Kachin, 14, 23, 80, 83, 204, 223, 232–3

Kamakhya, 120–2, 126
Kamarupa, Kamroop, 93, 244
kangaroo, 216
Kaptai, 200–1
Karnaphuli, 198
Kassalong, 200
kauri. *See* cowrie
Kaziranga, 232, 234
Keibul Lamjao, 253
Khamba and Thoibi, 106–7
Khamti, 67, 123
Khasi Hills, 25, 204, 221
Khasi, 11, 71
Khezhakheno, 84
Khiamniungan, 106
Khumi, 67, 77, 128
Kigwema, 84
kinship, 94, 96–7
kirāta, 154
kite, 101
Koch, 67, 120
Kohima, 84
Konyak, 67, 100, 112, 119, 182
Koyu, 170
Krama, 76
Kuki, 67–8, 109, 148, 175, 228–9, 236
Kuki-Anglo War, 175

labour, 56, 109, 183–6
  interspecies, 183–6
Lachaba, 71
lactose, 157–8, 261
ladder, 79, 195
Laisong, 194
Lakher, 66, 179
landscape architect, 35
landslide, 57
language, 14, 33–6, 65–6, 70, 154, 188, 211
langur, 30, 117, 216
Laos, 44

Lautu, Lutuv, 67, 103, 108, 141
leaf muntjac (*Muntiacus putaoensis*), 222
lemon, 216
lemur, 106
leopard, 4, 94–6, 106, 112, 195, 200, 231–2, 248, 250, 254
Lepcha, 67, 122
Liangmei, 66–7
life-substance, 118
lifeworld, 14, 63, 65–6, 70, 91–2, 102, 105–6, 117–18, 126–7, 150, 240, 260, 262
limestone, 204
Lindsay, Robert, 204
linguistics, 5, 33
lion, 78, 96, 120, 182
literacy, 7, 63–4, 86, 92, 134
lively capital, 218
loris, 30, 101
Lorrainville, 15
lost script. *See* literacy
Lotha, 67, 94, 97, 103, 110–11
louse, lice, 47, 114
Ludden, David, 6, 167
Lungterok, 79
Lushai, 66, 195, 200
lycanthropy, 94–6, 154, 256
Lyngam, 67

Ma, Jianxiong, 6
macaw, 216
Magh, 14
Mahasthangarh, 33
maize, 81, 139, 141, 146–7, 159–60, 260
Maize Festival, 12
Makhel, 83–5
Makum, 209
malabathrum. *See* cassia
Malacca, 85
malaria, 161, 198, 242, 244
Maldives, 166–7

Mali Hka, 23
Manas, 121, 233
Manasa, 121, 131
Mandi, 66
Mang Hnin, 107
mango, 42, 47, 131, 197, 213
mangrove, 28, 247
Manik Pir, 124
Manipur, 16, 45, 83, 85, 88, 98–9, 109, 131, 138, 148, 181, 187, 225, 230, 253
Mara, 67, 74–5, 179
Margherita, 15
Marma, 11, 14
Mars, 75
Maru, 67
masculinity, 193, 230. *See also* gender
Matabari, 122
matrilineal descent, 88
Mawmluh Cave, 25
Mech, 67, 85, 119
medicinal plants, 132–5
Mediterranean, 165, 189, 213
megalith, 175–8
Meghalaya, 14, 25, 28, 87, 129, 133, 135, 154, 167, 174, 176–7, 204–5, 208, 215, 232
Meghalayan, 25
meilam (fire way), 228
Meitei, 67, 73, 88, 92, 98, 106, 133
Meitei-Pangal, 67, 131
memorial stone. *See* megalith
Mesopotamia, 157
Mexico, 146
microbes, 156–1
microbial terroir, 160
microbiome, 28, 157
micro-organism, 35, 153, 156–61, 211–12
migration
  human, 82–6
  plant, 212–16, 259, 262

Index 357

species, 212–16
Miji, 67
militarisation, 234
milk. *See* dairy
Milky Way, 75
millets, 45, 55, 141, 146, 147, 159, 160, 212
mining, 204–7
Mishmi teeta (*Coptis teeta*), 28
Mishmi, 28, 67, 73–4, 95, 108, 110, 112, 119, 236, 239
Mising, 67, 73, 75, 105
missionaries, 15, 63, 70, 124
Mithun Country, 174
mithun (*Bos frontalis*), 16, 49–50, 81, 102–3, 106, 109, 116–18, 125, 139, 158, 161, 168, 173–83, 231, 240, 243–4, 260–1
Mizo, 13, 57, 67–8, 71, 73, 75, 77–8, 102, 106–7, 128, 133, 138, 206
Mizoram, 14, 21
  agriculture, 138
  bamboo and rattan bridge in, 143
  famine refugees, 163
  mule caravan, 185
  were-tigers, 96
modernity, 11–14, 92
Moirang, 107
mole, 101
mollusc, 30, 130
Mongolia, 28
mongoose, 120, 191, 214, 251
monkey, 30, 48–9, 120, 123, 139, 148, 182, 222, 243, 251
monsoon climate, 11, 25–6, 28, 57
moon, 71, 73–4
more-than-human geography, 106
more-than-human history, 2–7, 11, 16–17, 65–6, 103, 151, 153, 216, 260–1
mosquito, 47, 58, 161, 244–5

mountain agriculture, 138–43
mountain knot, 23
'Mountains of Southwest China', 27
mouth organ, 149
Mru, Mro, 66–7, 101, 103, 149, 169
mud, 66, 71, 74, 197, 201–4
muga. *See* silk
mule, 184–6, 259
multispecies. *See also* interspecies
  conviviality, 4, 241
  encounters, 256–7
  history, 2, 5
mushroom, 189, 222
musk, 235
musk deer, 108, 235, 255
Muslim deities, 120, 123–4. *See also* Islam, Muslim
Myanmar, Burmese, 1, 5, 11, 15, 23–4, 26, 31, 33, 43–5, 51, 63, 69, 83, 85, 88, 110, 113–14, 116–17, 123, 155–6, 158, 160, 171, 176–7, 181, 183–4, 192, 195–6, 207–8, 210, 220, 222–3, 226, 229, 233, 235, 239, 246, 252
Myanmar Farmland Law, 229
Myitsone, 23

Naga Heritage Village, 182
Naga, 14
Naga, Mo, 179
Nagaland, 14, 39, 43, 45, 69, 71, 83–4, 97, 100, 167–8, 172, 179–80, 182, 191, 193, 208
Nagamese, 15
Namcha Barwa, 24, 26, 219
Namdapha, 233
national park, 216, 229–36, 253. *See also* conservation, wildlife
nationalised periods, 7
nationalised time, 11
nationally territorialised narratives, 5–8

natural phenomena, 73–7
natural resources, 17, 35, 46–7, 56, 128, 153, 188–210, 236–8, 252, 257
nature, 2, 4, 183, 233, 237–40, 247, 255–6, 259, 262
Nawab Badshah, 120
Neanderthals, 32
necropolitics, 247
Nefamese, 15
Neolithic, 41, 157
Nepal, 53, 167, 233
New Zealand, 214
niche, 35–6, 41–3, 47–9, 54–8, 141, 197–8, 201, 211, 217, 225–6, 229–30, 235, 237, 245–6, 261
nickel, 205
Ningthoujas, 98
Nmai Hka, 23
Nocte, 67
non-human personhood, 103
Northeast India, 1, 6, 26, 28, 38, 219, 233
Nyishi, 66–7, 74, 102–3, 108, 116–19, 128, 133, 147

Odisha, 44
oil, 189, 205, 208–10, 215, 254
oil palm, 215
Oinam, 85
okra, 213
Ola Bibi, 123–4, 126
onceness, 9
ontology, 65
opium, 56
oral narratives, oral tradition, 13, 63–6, 68–70, 73, 76, 82–3, 132
orchid, 28, 189, 218, 224, 255
origin stories, 63–90
Orion, 74
Oryza sativa. *See* rice
otter, 112, 183, 191, 218, 235

Ovesen, Jan, 94
owl, 75–6

Pacific, 146, 246
Pakhangba, 98–9
Pakistan, 14, 193, 196, 218
Pakke Paga, 173
Palaeolithic (or Old Stone Age), 41
palm, 28, 78, 129, 159, 215
pangasius, 215
Pangkhua, 67, 78, 88
pangolin, 218, 235, 254–5
panji, 47
papaya, 146, 213
parasite, 43, 161, 242, 245. *See also* pathogens
Pasighat, 134
pastoralism, 45, 54, 91
patent, 129, 135, 221
pathogens, 4, 161, 245–6
Patkai, 117
Pau Chin Hau, 76
Pau, Pum Khan, 6
periodisation, 7–9, 69, 258
Persia, 135
Peru, 146
Pial Ral. *See* afterworld
Pidaung, 232
pig, 12, 48, 72, 74, 76, 98, 103, 106, 114–16, 119, 121–4, 177, 197, 243
pig kitchen, 115
pigeon, 119–21, 123
pine, 28
pineapple, 146, 213
pink-headed duck, 220
plague, 244–5
plant
    blindness, 127
    ceremonial, 127, 129–32, 135
    clothing human bodies, 147–8
    companion, 135–6

Index

crops (*see* agriculture)
exploiting, 43–7
gendering, 148–50
geographies, 161–6
medicinal, 28, 132–5, 190, 218
poisonous (*see* poison)
textile, 148, 162, 163–6
plantation, 135, 166, 214–15, 217, 228, 236
Pleiades, 73–4
Pnar, 14, 66–7
Pobitora, 253
poison, 136–7, 191, 195, 252
pollution, 117, 207, 210, 217
polo, 187
pond, 74, 191–2, 198, 200, 225
porcupine, 48, 71, 78, 193, 235, 251
post, sacrificial, 118–19, 175–6
potato, 146, 213
pottery, 40–1, 85, 203
Poumai, 67, 84
predator satiation hypothesis, 162
'primitive' maize, 146
'primitive' societies, 91, 183
provisions spreadsheet, 197
proxy records, 5, 8, 13, 64, 260
Pundravardhana. *See* Mahasthangarh
Punyu, Khonyu, 83
pygmy hog, 218
python, 100, 216

quarrying, 201, 204–7, 237
rabbit, 120, 191
racialisation, 16, 156
railways, 188, 209, 217, 226, 236, 250
rainbow, 73, 76
rainbow trout, 215
raishan (*Digitaria cruciata*), 212
Rakhine, Arakan, 15, 24, 67, 88, 99, 156, 158, 169, 205
ram sa (wild flesh), 102
Rangfraa, 76

Ranyak Khen, 39
rat, 49, 75–6, 80, 94, 102, 111, 146, 148, 162, 213–14, 243, 251
rattan, 47, 135, 143, 192
reciprocity, 48, 91–2, 96, 107, 116, 141, 240
red goral, 218
red panda, 112, 255
rediscovery of species, 28, 221
refugium, 30
regional studies, 167, 261
Rengma, 67, 168
retting, 165
revitalisation movement, 76, 240
rhinoceros, 30, 35, 92–3, 104, 120, 196, 218–19, 231–2, 234, 248, 253–4
rhododendron, 28, 53, 137, 214
rice (*Oryza sativa*), 43–5, 162. See also *aus, indica, japonica*
cultivar, 44–5
domestication, 43–4
sticky, 55, 162–3, 186, 213, 261
varieties, 44–5, 162
wild, 28, 43
Rih Dil, 106
rock art, 178
rodent, 4, 47–8, 114, 163, 193, 244
Rohingya, 67, 252
rubber, 135, 146, 166, 215, 227
Rûlpui, 98

sa (flesh), 102
sacred grove, 92, 128–9, 133, 225–6
sacrifice, animal, 12, 92, 107–8, 116–26, 134, 160, 178
Sadan, Mandy, 6
sago, 45, 78, 146
Saikia, Arupjyoti, 6
Saittwe. *See* Sittwe
Sajek valley, 243
Saka Haphong/Mowdok Taung/Tlang Moy, 15

sal, 28, 218, 226
salt, 135, 175, 204
Sanamahi, 76
sand, 202–4, 210, 237
Sandoway, 24
Sanskrit, 154
Santali, 34
saphun, 15
Schlich, Dr, 228
scientific forestry, 226–9
Sclater's monal, 119
scorpion, 207, 221
Scotland, 166
script. *See* literacy
sea snail. *See* cowrie
selective breeding, 42, 44, 48–9, 52, 114, 243
semi-precious stones, 51, 197, 205–7
Seng Khasi, 76
serow, 30, 48, 193
serpent being. *See* snake
sex, sexuality, 98, 110, 130, 145, 182–3
Shakespear, John, 92, 98
sheep, 53–4, 120, 122–3, 148, 166
shield, 104–5, 168
Shifodong, 43
shifting cultivation, 45, 54–7, 59, 116, 138, 216–17, 227–9, 238
Shillong, 79
Shiva, 121–2
Showren, Tana, 171
shrub verbena (*Lantana camara*), 213
Siberia, 28, 34
Sibsagar, 194
sijou (*Euphorbia spp.*), 131
Sikkim, 26, 122
Siliguri, 249
silk, 148, 165–6
Silk Road, 167, 184
Singpho, 66–7, 73

Sino-Tibetan. *See* Trans-Himalayan languages
Sittwe, 15
skull, 111–13, 118, 121–2, 175, 182, 197, 230
skull rack, 111–12
slow loris, 101
Smit, 128
Smyer Yü, Dan, 67
'Snake Feeding Hole' (Rûlchawm Kua), 98
snakehead fish, 224
snake, 58, 77–8, 80, 85, 92, 97–9, 100–1, 108, 221, 247
snow leopard, 29–30, 218–19, 251
snub-nosed monkey, 223
Sohpet Byneng Hill, 79
solar eclipse, 73, 76
Sonowal Kachari, 67, 204
soul, 76, 81–2, 94, 103, 141, 147, 150
South Africa, 214
South Asia, 25, 32–3, 49, 52, 133, 157, 163, 229, 261
Southeast Asia, 32–4, 41, 44–5, 49, 69, 83, 130, 162, 165, 175
Southeast Asian Megalithic Complex, 175
Sowa-Rigpa, 133–4
soybean, 56, 159, 242
spatial construct, 6
spatial imaginations, 186–7
species migration. *See* migration, species
speciesism, 2
spider, 72, 80, 207
spirit, 48, 72–3, 80, 82, 87–9, 94, 97, 102–3, 107–8, 111, 118–19, 123, 128–9, 138–9, 144, 147, 191, 225, 239
Spring Festival, 12
squirrel, 97, 108–9, 117, 148, 191, 193, 195, 221

Index   361

staple crop, 146–7. *See also* agriculture
state territory, 6
stone, 41, 51, 71, 79, 142, 175, 201, 205–7
stone tool, 3, 38, 41, 46
stone worship, 178
Subansiri, 170, 204
sub-Himalayan route, 32–3, 53
Sufi, 123
Sümi, 16, 67, 73, 76, 94–5, 102, 111
sun, 71–4, 76, 80, 147
surface processes, 27
Sylhet, 167, 225
synthetic beak, 171

tagashi (wild/jungle flesh), 102
takin, 30, 218, 235, 239
Taman, 67
Tangsa, 67, 102
Taraon, 66
taro, 34, 45, 55–6, 146, 189
tassar. *See* silk
tattoo, 74, 179
tea, 92, 135–6, 159, 166–7, 213–14, 226–7, 259
teak, 28, 166, 192, 200, 213–14, 218, 226–7
tectonic plates, 22, 205
tejpata. *See* cassia
temporalities, 10–13, 64, 143, 187
tentative patterns, 86
terminology, 14–16
terracotta, 104, 203–4
textile plants. *See* plants, textile
Thadou, 67, 78–80, 85, 97, 131, 133, 230
Thailand, 44
Thangal, 67
thangchhuah, 106, 109
Thapar, Romila, xiii
thianglo, 96

Thimphu, 24
Tibet, Tibetan, 6, 15, 24–6, 32, 34, 53, 67, 83, 85, 116, 154, 157, 167, 184, 233, 238
Tibeto-Burman. *See* Trans-Himalayan languages
tiger, 4, 16, 30, 49, 58, 73, 75–6, 81, 94–7, 103, 106–7, 111–12, 118, 120, 182, 195, 218–19, 231–2, 246–8, 254
  club, 106
  dance, 95
tiger-people. *See* lycanthropy
tikishi (house flesh), 102
tilapia, 215
time regime, 11
timescape, 10, 13, 16
Tipong, 208
Tista, 26
toad, 73, 76
tobacco, 130, 159, 213
tomato, 56, 146, 213
toungtha, 161
tourism, 129, 155, 172, 174, 182–3, 218, 234
trade, 115–17, 254
trade and travel route, 33, 51, 164, 183–6
'tragedy of the commons', 235–9
Trans-Himalayan languages, 34, 173
Trans-Himalayan studies, 187
transhumance, 52–4
transhumant agro-pastoralism, 54
trespassing, 247
Triangle, 1–2, 6, 23–6
  arrival of modern humans, 5, 16, 33, 36, 212
  global biodiversity hotspots, 27
  in Kachin State, 23
  location of, 1–2, 6, 23–6
'tribal', 9, 14, 156, 229

Tripura, 16, 122, 173, 200
Tripura Sundari, 122
trophy species, 196, 230
Tuisen Chhantlang, 196
Turkey, 135
turmeric, 163
turtle, 123, 191, 218, 225

U Thlen, 97–8, 121
Udaipur, 122, 200
Ugrotara, 122
ujok (preserved trees), 228
umbilical cord, 79
Unani, 133–4
Uralo-Siberian, 34
uranium, 205
Uyu, 204

Vaishnavism, 88
Vangchhia, 177
Vedic, 88, 120–1
Venus, 73
Vernay-Hopwood Chindwin Expedition, 220–1
vertical conservation, 228–9, 238–40
Vezzadara, 133
viper, 106
virus. *See* pathogens
Viswema, 84
vulture, 101

Wade, John, 99
Wakching, 183
Wanching, 182
Wancho, 67
Wangala festival, 12
war, 69, 83, 93, 108, 115, 136–7, 162, 175, 184, 186, 228–9, 260
Waste Land Grant Rule, 236

water, 4, 26, 47, 57, 66, 71–2, 76, 85–6, 154, 165, 167, 191–2, 197–201, 204, 210, 215, 226–7
water beetle, 71
water buffalo, 30, 48, 58, 103, 112, 120, 177, 184, 243
water hyacinth, 214, 245–6, 259
watershed, 184
weaving, 150, 164, 218
wedding, 12, 102, 125, 178
weeding, 12, 42, 138, 141–2
weed, 43, 72, 140–1, 213
were-tiger. *See* lycanthropy
white-bellied heron (*Ardea insignis*), 28, 219
wild animals
  displaying, 111–12
  eating, 110–11
  and human inequality, 112–13
wild dog, 30, 48, 231, 251
wildlife conservation. *See* conservation, wildlife
wildlife explorations, 220–5
wildlife sanctuary. *See* national park
wildlife smuggling, 216, 254
wolf, 4, 30
woodpecker, 80
world religions, 88, 126, 262
world views, 63, 65, 88, 90, 147. *See also* cosmology
World War II, 186
World Wildlife Fund, 200
writing. *See* literacy

Xuanzang, 93

yak, 30, 52–4, 69, 115, 121, 166, 183, 242
yam, 42, 45, 56, 135, 146
Yang, Bin, 167

Yarlung Tsangpo. *See* Brahmaputra
Yellowstone model, 236
Yuanmou, 31
Yunnan, 33–4, 43–4, 51, 69, 166–8, 184, 205–6, 233

Zeme, 67, 134
Ziro, 83, 237

Zo, 14, 115, 171
Zomi National Day, 179, 181
Zomi Re-unification Organisation, 171
Zomi, 67
zoonotic diseases, 244–5, 256
Zophei, 67, 85
Zou, David Vumlallian, xiii, 6